ONLY CONNECT

READINGS ON CHILDREN'S LITERATURE

THIRD EDITION

Edited by
Sheila Egoff, Gordon Stubbs,
Ralph Ashley, and Wendy Sutton

D0024146

OXFORD UNIVERSITY PRESS
Toronto   New York   Oxford
1996

Oxford University Press
70 Wynford Drive, Don Mills, Ontario M3C 1J9

Oxford New York
Athens Auckland Bangkok Bombay
Calcutta Cape Town Dar es Salaam Delhi
Florence Hong Kong Istanbul Karachi
Kuala Lumpur Madras Madrid Melbourne
Mexico City Nairobi Paris Singapore
Taipei Tokyo Toronto

and associated companies in
Berlin Ibadan

Oxford is a trade mark of Oxford University Press.

This book is printed on permanent (acid-free) paper. ∞

Canadian Cataloguing in Publication Data

Main entry under title:

Only connect : readings on children's literature
3rd ed.
Includes bibliographical references and index.
ISBN 0-19-541024-6

1. Children's literature – History and criticism.
I. Egoff, Sheila.

PN1009.A1065 1996   809'.89282   C95-932213-2

Design: Brett Miller
Compositor: Indelible Ink

1 2 3 4 5 99 98 97 96

CONTENTS

POETRY

PICTURE BOOKS AND ILLUSTRATION

GENDER RELATIONS

YOUNG ADULT LITERATURE

Recent Trends and Overview   Part IX

ILLUSTRATIONS

ACKNOWLEDGEMENTS

JOAN AIKEN. 'Interpreting the Past: Reflections of an Historical Novelist' from *Encounter*, Vol. 64, May 1985, pp. 37–43. © Joan Aiken Enterprises Ltd 1985. Reprinted by permission of the author.

MARILYN FAIN APSELOFF. 'Abandonment: The new realism of the eighties' from *Children's Literature in Education*, Vol. 23, no. 2, 1992, pp. 101–6. Reprinted by permission.

BRIAN ATTEBERY. 'Women's Coming of Age in Fantasy' from *Strategies of Fantasy*, Indiana University Press, 1992, pp. 87–104. Reprinted by permission of Indiana University Press.

MARGARET ATWOOD. 'There Was Once', from *Good Bones*, © 1992 O.W. Toad Ltd. Published by Coach House Press and reprinted by permission.

NATALIE BABBITT. 'Protecting Children's Literature' from *The Horn Book Magazine*, November/December 1990. Reprinted by permission of The Horn Book, Inc.

JULIA BRIGGS. 'Reading Children's Books' from *Essays in Criticism*, Vol. XXXVIX, No. 1, January 1989. Reprinted by permission of the author and the Editors of *Essays in Criticism*.

ELEANOR CAMERON. 'Of Style and the Stylist' from *The Green and Burning Tree* by Eleanor Cameron. Copyright © 1962, 1964, 1966, 1969 by Eleanor Cameron, renewed. Reprinted by permission of Little, Brown and Company.

TESSA ROSE CHESTER. 'Black and White Set the Tone' from *Country Life*, 22 December 1988. © Tessa Rose Chester. Reprinted by permission of the author.

ROSALIND COWARD. 'Greening the Child' from *New Statesman & Society*, 28 March 1995. Copyright © *New Statesman & Society*. Reprinted by permission.

SARAH ELLIS, 'Innocence and Experience in the Young Adult Romance' from *Lands of Pleasure: Essays on Lillian H. Smith and the Development of Children's Libraries*, A.M. Fasick, M. Johnston, and R. Osler eds, Scarecrow Press, 1990. Reprinted by permission of the publisher.

JAMES CROSS GIBLIN. 'Trends in Children's Books Today' © 1992. Reprinted by permission of the author.

PETER HOLLINDALE. 'The Adolescent Novel of Ideas' from *Children's Literature in Education*, Vol. 26, No. 1, 1995, pages 83–94. Reprinted by permission of Human Sciences Press.

MONICA HUGHES. 'Science Fiction as Myth and Metaphor' from *The ALAN Review*, Spring 1992. © Monica Hughes. Reprinted by permission of the author.

PETER HUNT. 'Defining Children's Literature' from *Criticism, Theory and Children's Literature*. Reprinted by permission of Blackwell Publishers Ltd.

X.J. KENNEDY. 'Strict and loose: two worlds of children's verse'. © copyright 1991 by X.J. Kennedy. First published in *School Library Journal*. Reprinted by permission of the author.

DAVID LEWIS. 'The Constructedness of Texts: Picture Books and the Metafictive' from *Signal Approaches to Children's Books*, May 1990, pages 131–46, published by Thimble Press, Lockwood, Station Road, Woodchester, Stroud, Glos. GL5 5EQ, UK.

MYRA COHN LIVINGSTON. 'The Poem on Page 81' from *Climb Into the Bell Tower* by Myra Cohn Livingston. Copyright © 1990 by Myra Cohn Livingston. Reprinted by permission of HarperCollins Publishers, Inc. and Marian Reiner for the author.

JOANNE L. LYNN. 'Runes to ward off sorrow: rhetoric of the English nursery rhyme' from *Children's Literature in Education*, Vol. 16, 1985, pp. 3–13. Reprinted by permission of Human Sciences Press, Inc.

MARGARET MAHY. 'A Dissolving Ghost' © Margaret Mahy 1993. Reprinted by permission of Vanessa Hamilton Books Ltd.

PERRY NODELMAN. 'How Picture Books Work' from *Children's Literature Association Quarterly*. Reprinted with permission of The Children's Literature Association.

KATHERINE PATERSON. 'Cultural Politics from a Writer's Point of View' is reprinted from *The New Advocate*, Vol. 7, No. 2, Spring 1994, by permission of the author.

TAMORA PIERCE. 'Fantasy: Why Kids Read It, Why Kids Need It'. Reprinted by permission of Harold Ober Associates Incorporated. Copyright © 1993 by Tamora Pierce. First published in *School Library Journal*.

TERRY PRATCHETT, 'Let there be dragons' from *The Bookseller*, 11 June 1993. Reprinted by permission of Colin Smythe on behalf of Terry Pratchett. This article was originally a speech given by Terry Pratchett as Guest of Honour at the Booksellers Association of Great Britain and Ireland Conference dinner, April 1993.

CHET RAYMO. 'Dr Seuss and Dr Einstein: Children's Books and Scientific Imagination' from *The Horn Book Magazine*, September 1992. Reprinted by permission of the Horn Book, Inc.

M.L. ROSENTHAL. 'Alice, Huck, Pinocchio, and the Blue Fairy: Bodies Real and Imagined' from *The Southern Review*, Vol. 29, Summer 1993. Copyright © M.L. Rosenthal, 1993. Reprinted by permission of the author.

URI SHULEVITZ. 'What is a Picture Book? from *Writing With Pictures*, copyright © 1980 by Uri Shulevitz. *Wilson Library Bulletin* October 1980. Reprinted by permission of the author. Copryright © 1985 Uri Shulevitz. Reprinted by permission of Watson-Guptill Publications.

WILLIAM SLEATOR. 'What Is It About Science Fiction?' Copyright © 1988 by William Sleator. All rights reserved. Used with permission.

SUSAN SMITH. 'The Lion, the Witch and the Drug Addict' from *The Globe and Mail*, 26 November 1993. Reprinted by permission of The Globe and Mail.

JOHN STAHL. 'The Imaginative Uses of Secrecy in Children's Literature' by John Stahl from *Triumphs of the Spirit in Children's Literature* © 1986 edited by Francelia Butler and Richard Rotert. Reprinted by permission of Library Profession Publications, North Haven.

ROY STOKES. Review, 'Fin de Siècle' is reprinted from *The Children's Reader*, Winter 1995.

JOYCE THOMAS. 'Woods and Castles, Towers and Huts: Aspects of Setting in the Fairy Tale' from *Children's Literature in Education*, Vol. 17, No. 2, pages 126–33. Reprinted by permission of Human Sciences Press.

JOHN ROWE TOWNSEND. 'The Turbulent Years' from *Written for Children* by John Rowe Townsend, The Bodley Head, 1995. Reprinted by permission of Random House UK Ltd and the author.

P.L. TRAVERS. 'Unknown Childhood' is reprinted from *Parabola, The Magazine of Myth and Tradition*, Vol. xv, No. 3, by permission of the author.

MICHAEL VALPY. 'Fathers fare poorly in children's books' from *The Globe and Mail*, 11 October 1989. Reprinted by permission of The Globe and Mail.

MARINA WARNER. 'Old Wives Tales' from *History Today*, 41 (April 1991).

PATRICIA WRIGHTSON. 'Deeper Than You Think' from *The Horn Book Magazine*, March/April 1991, reprinted by permission of The Horn Book, Inc.

TIM WYNNE-JONES. 'An Eye for Thresholds' from *Canadian Children's Literature*, No. 48, 1987. Copyright © Tim Wynne-Jones. Reprinted by permission of the author.

JANE YOLEN. 'Turtles All the Way Down'. Reprinted by permission of Curtis Brown Ltd. Copyright © 1991 Jane Yolen. First published in *Writing Science Fiction and Fantasy* by Davis Publications.

JACK ZIPES. 'Taking Political Stock: New Theoretical and Critical Approaches to Anglo-American Children's Literature in the 1980s' from *The Lion and the Unicorn*, The Johns Hopkins University Press, Baltimore/London, Vol. 14, No. 1, June 1990, pp. 7–20. Reprinted by permission of The Johns Hopkins University Press.

ILLUSTRATIONS

JOHN BURNINGHAM. Illustration from *Courtney* (1994) used by permission of Jonathan Cape.

JOHN BURNINGHAM. Illustration from *The Baby* (1975) used by permission of Jonathan Cape.

CINDERELLA: 16th century German woodcut. Used by permission of The British Library.

ERROL LE CAIN. Cover Illustration from *Thorn Rose* by The Brothers Grimm illustrated by Errol Le Cain. Reprinted by permission of the publisher, Faber and Faber Ltd.

ERNEST SHEPARD. Line illustration, by E.H. Shepard is the frontispiece from *The House at Pooh Corner* by A.A. Milne, illustrations by E.H. Shepard. Copyright 1928 by E.P. Dutton, renewed © 1956 by A.A. Milne. Used by permission of Dutton Children's Books, a division of Penguin

PREFACE
TO THE THIRD EDITION

The Second Edition of *Only Connect* (1980) was a partial revision of the original 1969 compilation. This time we, the editors, have selected articles which were not in either of the two previous editions. The decision to provide a completely new book was not undertaken lightly, as many of our readers assured us that some of the older articles are classics of their kind.

Our reasons for a selection of new articles were few, but to us, compelling. First, there are the rapid social changes of our time: writing for children is no more static than that for adults. Indeed, in its realistic vein it frequently interprets social change more quickly than its adult counterpart. Certain issues apparently attract many writers simultaneously. This aspect of recent children's literature can be seen in Marilyn Apseloff's essay, 'Abandonment: the New Realism of the Eighties' as well as in the 'Epilogue' by Sheila Egoff and Wendy Sutton. New issues such as feminism, political correctness, cultural appropriation, and concern for the environment have brought a new type of criticism, a criticism which embodies different vocabulary and approaches. Of course, the more traditional aspects of children's literature still have validity, as can be deduced from Joan Aiken's view of historical fiction, 'Interpreting the Past'. Second, we felt that many buyers of this new edition, especially institutions, would already possess copies of the earlier editions. Together the three volumes form a valuable resource for the study of children's literature. Finally, the work involved in developing an entirely new anthology provided us with a great deal of pleasurable reading. After a very thorough search of recent critical writing, we discovered sufficient material of quality and interest to make a stimulating, sometimes provocative, collection.

Perhaps the greatest change in children's literature since the previous two editions is found in its *quantity*. It is obvious that the multiplicity of new titles militates against the commonality once characteristic of children's reading. With so many publications, even the best make less of an impact; they are continually being pushed aside by a new crop or all too quickly are out of print. This makes comparative criticism difficult because often within a year individual titles have been forgotten. Even a recent critical article can suddenly be dated. This trend has one beneficial consequence, however, in that critical interest in the older children's classics continues as shown in M.L. Rosenthal's combining of 'Alice, Huck, Pinocchio, and the

Blue Fairy', and Perry Nodelman's 'Progressive Utopia'. The profusion of new titles also has changed the nature of criticism. It has become obvious to us that overview articles are almost passé. Two examples: the picture-book and the novel for young adults are so profuse and multifaceted that they preclude any generalization.

These are certainly aspects of children's books, and important ones, that have not been covered in this collection. Books in translation need to become an important part of the reading of children, if only to broaden their experiences. As Emily Dickinson so wisely and so poetically stated many years ago: 'There is no frigate like a book/To take us lands away.' But it is equally important for children to understand that important ideas and great literature have never been the exclusive property of any one culture. It is to be hoped that books in translation will increase, in spite of the difficulties involved, and that critical articles will follow. Another omission, and for much the same reason, is a consideration of books written in English that highlight the lives of children from other cultures, many of whom have become part of an English-language society. Such books, real-istically matching society itself, are on the increase and one may well expect critical articles to be forthcoming. There are also some other aspects of modern writing, illustrating, and publishing for children that are exten-sions of the traditional book that have not been addressed here: for example, computer books, talking books, games, clothing, films, videos and CD-ROMs. Will such extensions bring children to the original books? The debate on this question is unresolved and may well last into the next century.

We stated in the preface to the First Edition: 'Our primary aim has been to find selections that deal with children's literature as an essential part of the whole realm of literary activity, to be discussed in the same terms and judged by the same standards that would apply to any other branch of writing. We do not subscribe to the view that criticism of chil-dren's books calls for the adoption of a special scale of values. We looked for insight and informed contemporary thinking, and rejected any material that was too concerned with recapturing childhood or with presenting coy and sentimental attitudes. With these criteria in mind we also sought writers who had a distinctive message to offer: one that is fresh, original, and illuminating and not necessarily unorthodox or provocative.' We have adhered to the same purpose in assembling this collection.

As in the first two editions, byways of periodical literature have been explored as well as more familiar ground. We could well have chosen more articles from such stalwarts of children's literature as the *Horn Book* and *Children's Literature in Education*, but since these journals are so well-known we made space for contributions from sources not so easily obtainable. Our decision not to include anything published before the Second Edition of *Only Connect* was relaxed only for Eleanor Cameron's 'Of Style and the Stylist', since a discussion of the craft of writing can never be out of date. A new feature of this edition is the inclusion of some short items, often from newspapers. These are juxtaposed with longer ones on the same subject in the hope that they will provide a counterpoint to a longer analysis or at least spark interest in debatable issues.

We have kept the same title in spite of the totally new content and some urgings to choose a different one. We believe in the spirit of the title, and again quote from the Preface to the First Edition: 'For the title *Only Connect* we are indebted both to E.M. Forster who made the phrase memorable in *Howard's End* and to Pamela Travers who borrowed it to form the title and motif of her address at the Library of Congress.[1] . . . Our interpretation of the Forster epigraph, like Miss Travers's, implies a need to gain understanding through the linking of one world with another.' In the Third Edition many perspectives are brought into focus, which we hope will assist teachers, librarians, authors, critics, students, and parents to 'connect' with literature for the young and so with the young themselves.

S.A.E.

G.T.S.

L.F.A.

W.K.S.

[1]Which appeared in the First and Second Editions of *Only Connect*.

PART I

BOOKS AND CHILDREN

DEFINING CHILDREN'S LITERATURE

Peter Hunt

Though there are no intrinsic norms and constraints that determine how we must read literary texts, as soon as we begin to read the text norms and constraints of some sort will come into operation since the very activity of reading cannot take place without them. . . .

It would be bad faith to conceal the fact, even from young students, that no norms or constraints are integral to literary discourse and therefore privileged. Certain norms will, of course be dominant and there may be justification for stressing their advantage and the dangers of discarding them but there can be no justification for claiming that these norms are intrinsic to the very existence of literary discourse.

K.M. Newton, *Twentieth Century Literary Theory*

I come more and more to the view that there *are* no children's books. They are a concept invented for commercial reasons, and kept alive by the human instinct for classification and categorization. The honest writer . . . writes what is inside him and must out. Sometimes what he writes will chime with the instincts and interests of young people, sometimes it will not. . . . If you must have a classification it is into books good and bad.

Marcus Crouch, *The Nesbit Tradition*

Aspects of Definition

Just as most questions imply their answers, so definitions are controlled by their purpose. There can be, therefore, no single definition of 'Children's Literature'. What is regarded as a 'good' book might be 'good' in the sense which the currently dominant literary/academic establishment prescribes; 'good' in terms of effectiveness for education, language acquisition, or socialization/acculturization or for entertainment for a specific child or group of children in general or specific circumstances; or 'good' in some moral or religious or political sense; or 'good' in a therapeutic sense. 'Good' as an abstract and 'good for' as a practical application are constantly in conflict in judgements about children's literature.

There is also tension between the way in which people accept plurality of meaning of the word 'literature' intellectually, yet assume a deeply ingrained concept of absolute values. Thus Eeyore and Hamlet are not, in the current system of critical values, comparable figures: not because one is actually, cosmically, any greater than the other, but because the system says so. Hence, the system (although it is crumbling) places Shakespeare as a number-one writer, Blyton, Blume, Dahl, and even Mayne a long way down the scale.

But, if we are going to unravel the tangle of judgements, we should consider ways of defining. As we have seen, although there are some characteristics that seem to make it obvious when we are reading a 'children's book', textual features are unreliable.

There is also a wide disagreement as to whether children's literature can be treated in the same way as adult literature. We might contrast Rebecca Lukens's view that 'Literature for children differs from literature for adults in degree, not in kind . . . and writing for children should be judged by the same standard as writing for adults. . . . To fail to apply the same critical standard to children's literature is to say in effect that children's literature is inferior to adult literature'[1] with James Steele Smith's, that 'we can still get involved in the mistaken view that children's literature involves the same criteria of literary excellence as adult literature does'.[2]

There has equally been a certain confusion as to whether children's literature is actually a different creature, as well as to how it should be treated. Egoff, Stubbs, and Ashley, in the introduction to *Only Connect*, 'do not subscribe to the view that the criticism of children's literature calls for the adoption of a special scale of values'.

In a sense, we have stepped backwards; as Lance Salway points out, 'a great deal of critical attention was paid to children's literature during the nineteenth century. . . . In many respects critical discussion . . . was less restricted than it is now; books for the young were considered to be part of the general body of literature and writing about them was not confined to specialised journals.'[3]

Jill Paton Walsh's comment on the problems of writing children's books (admirably level-headed among much that is not), suggests that

> The children's book presents a technically more difficult, technically more interesting problem—that of making a fully serious adult statement, as a good novel of any kind does, and making it utterly simple

and transparent. . . . The need for comprehensibility imposes an emotional obliqueness, an indirection of approach, which like elision and partial statement in poetry is often a source of aesthetic power.[4]

This positive approach leads on to one thing that is fundamental not only to the argument about status and children's books, but also to the way in which we define the field—that is, to the argument that reading children's literature is, for the adult, a more complex process than reading an adult book.

Ways of Reading Children's Literature

We are dealing with texts designed for a non-peer audience, texts that are created in a complex social environment by adults. In terms of what this means to a sub- or anti-culture, it is tantamount to reading a translation.

Three situations need to be distinguished here: the adult reading a book intended for adults, the adult reading a book intended for children, and the child reading a book intended for children. The differences between these situations are fundamental to our discussion. Criticism tends to talk of them as though they were the same—but they are not, except in a rather dangerously illusory way.

The closest of the two are in the first and the last, because they share a basic factor of reading. In other words, our background and purpose are vital. It is clear that adult readers can never share the same background (in terms of reading life experience) as children; what is less obvious is that they only rarely share the same purpose in reading (just as reviewers are quite untypical as readers). When adults are reading books for adults, they normally read either purely for their own entertainment or edification, taking the book on its own terms and playing the part of, or reacting against, the reader-role implied in the text; or they are reading for an extrinsic purpose—to criticize, comment, or discuss.

When adults find themselves reading children's books, they usually have to read in four different ways, simultaneously. First, despite occasional protestations to the contrary, adults commonly read children's books *as if they were peer-texts*. If we read for anything except pleasure, then we will register the presence of, but 'read against', the implied readership.

Thus a text must 'imply' a reader; that is, the subject-matter, language, allusion levels, and so on clearly 'write' the level of readership. (It is no accident that the Pooh books, or several of Roald Dahl's books, have proved popular with adults as well as children: the audience implied in the books is as much an adult one as a child one.) This is easiest to see where a high level is implied; without certain knowledge or experience, the text will not be—cannot be—'understood' to a reasonable level. But, equally, very often a limited range of experience is implied; items may be explained to an extent that the experienced reader does not require. This can happen at very elementary levels, and takes us into a consideration of the relationship of the child to the text as text—consider, for example, the levels of experience required to understand Pat Hutchins's *Rosie's Walk*.

But we are under no obligation to accept the implied reader's role. In a peer-text, we generally do so; we select a text according to the level it implies (is this a 'hard' or an 'easy' read?). But with children's books, it is easy to read against the implication. This is why the context of reading— the attitude to the text, and the things surrounding the text, the 'peritext'— is so important. In many circumstances, this first way of reading will probably dominate; it may be a more profound and perceptive reading than a child will make, but is it an appropriate reading?

Secondly, and normally for most adult-readings of children's texts, the adult will very often be reading *on behalf of a child*, to recommend or censor for some personal or professional reason. The criteria used here may certainly register the implied readership, and lead to an intellectual judgement as to whether the book in question is appropriate to that readership. The criteria to the fore would then be personal preference (political, sexual, topical), suitability of content (as the adult perceives it) for the use to which the text is going to be put (skills education, social education, enjoyment), and, perhaps easiest, linguistic complexity. (As we shall see, it is this ideological area that most commonly reveals the blindnesses of readers and publishers.)

More rarely, but increasingly, the adult may be reading the text *with an eye to discussing it with other adults*. The analytic eye may then be dominant, and we may not become engaged with the book, as in the first way of reading. This is, as it were, the super-ego reading, modifying both the first and second types of reading into acceptable communications.

Anyone who has read much in children's books as an adult will probably agree that the most rewarding type of reading—and again, the most unacknowledged by those uncertain of the status of the activity—is that involving acceptance of the implied role; for then the reader will *surrender to the book on its own terms*. This is as close as we can get to *reading as a child*; but this is a very long way from reading as an actual child does.

There are other complicating subtleties here. Do you read as the child you were, or as the child you are? on your self-image as a child or the memory of the 'feel' of youthful reading? How far can experienced readers forget their adult experience?

Research has shown that children are far more competent text-handlers than is generally assumed; but even so, it is difficult to replicate their encounters with texts. We cannot rely on, as Stanley Fish put it, 'the authority of interpretive communities'—that most readers will understand broadly the same thing from a text. After all, most reception and response theory is based upon peer investigations.

If we wish to define our field of study, then, we must acknowledge that the very perception of the texts within it is problematic. There is a confusion between quality and audience, which has so often bracketed children's books with 'popular culture' and low-level books in general.

Defining 'Literature'

The positive aspect of this is that the concept of 'literature' as it is defined by the cultural establishment—and thus subconsciously accepted—must be seen for what it is, whether or not it is to be challenged. One of the characteristics of the literary establishment has been a reluctance to define.

The question of what 'literature' is, has, until fairly recently, seemed scarcely worth discussing to those most intimately concerned with it. As Jeremy Tambling puts it:

> [T]he category of 'literature' cannot be held to have any essential meaning; there is no body of writing that 'ought' to be studied as such, as the repository of 'cultural values' or of important traditions
> . . .
> To say, 'we know what literature is', and then to mention some famous names—Shakespeare, Milton, Wordsworth—means that we work in a circle: we know what literature is because we have these writers, and the writers set up an imaginary standard where literature is defined in relationship to them.[5]

This may seem either a radical or an obvious statement—or, I suspect, both. In my experience, students of literature in higher education carry both a residual resistance to establishment values, together with a shrewd appreciation of what they are expected to say (which is, in its own way, comforting). This is not merely an educational truism; it is important for children's books, where orality and the sub-culture, or anti-culture, or parallel culture of childhood are significant factors in the interpretation of texts.

'Literature', then, is a very persuasive term. Let us summarize its meanings. The first distinction is between what literature is generally thought to be and what it logically or conjecturally might be. Literature, as compared to other texts, is thought to be 'higher', 'denser', 'more highly charged', 'special', 'apart', and so on; it is also thought to be the 'best' that a culture can offer. These may seem to be two ways of saying the same thing, but they commonly give rise to a sort of schizophrenia in 'children's book people', as we have seen; for 'literature' is seen as not being 'suitable' for children—not that they are not yet ready for it, but that it does not relate to the normal child.

The complexity of the situation might be illustrated by Elaine Moss's broadside against a new, prose edition of *The Pied Piper of Hamelin* in which there is a 'happy' ending (the mayor and the corporation are drowned, and the children return), and there is no place in the story for the lame boy. Moss's argument is convincing emotionally, but her judgement that 'young people should come across a great deal of literature that, at some point in their lives, they will return to and understand better, even return to for an enlightenment they had recognised as being there but had not been ready fully to absorb'[6] has overtones of a superiority of certain texts, rather than certain *kinds* of texts.

But she provides an important clue. On her definition, literature (as opposed to non-literature) is something to which you can return, something that gives more each time—although there is a residual impression that the classical work is inherently superior, even if I am sure that is not the intention. *Any* work to which you can return has this quality—and, of course, if a text is 'returnable-to' by virtue of its private associations, then, is it not 'literature'? Or is there something more? It is this kind of distinction that we need to explore.

Definitions of literature can be conveniently divided into definitions by features, definition by cultural norms, and definitions according to the uses of text by individuals.

It is not at all obvious to many readers that you cannot tell from simply looking at a text whether it is 'literature' or not. It is not the type of feature, but the value you place upon it which is significant. Certainly the literary text has a tendency to certain linguistic features. These are generally a function of the fact that the message is linguistically 'self-sufficient' and does not need a context of immediate human interaction to be understood. There are certain characteristic 'markers' in the text, such as the fact that whereas in normal discourse the sender and receiver, addresser and addressee, are marked as first and third person, in literature, this is not necessarily so. But that does not make the text 'literature' in its generally accepted sense. It is the cultural context that dominates the categorization.

This is important for children's literature because it is generally assumed that there is an appropriate 'register' of children's books—characteristic words and structures—that identifies the type just as readily as does the 'content'. It is also often assumed that this register is restrictive to the point at which it excludes 'literariness'. Hence, if what constitutes the surface characteristics of literature is a cultural decision, then, whatever image of childhood is current, positive or negative, children's books will inevitably be excluded from the value-system. Cultural norms do not usually apply to a disregarded type.

But if literature cannot usefully be defined by its surface features, can it be defined by use? We read literature in a different way from non-literature; we extract from the text certain feelings or responses. Yet with children's books, we cannot escape the fact that they are written by adults; that there is going to be control, and that it is going to involve moral decisions. Equally, the book is going to be used not to entertain or modify *our* views, but to form the views of the child. Thus the kind of readings that texts for children are given by adults involves acquiring both culture and language. This means that the 'non-functional' definition of 'literature' either excludes all children's literature or does not apply.

Here again, because the single thing that distinguishes children's literature is its audience, it is commonly assumed that aesthetic appreciation is not something available to the child, and therefore not something likely to be inherent in its literature. We have seen that narrative is a poor relation of literary studies; but consider this comment by C.S. Lewis, a writer commonly assumed to be on the side of the child. Writing 'Of stories', he notes:

> In talking of books which are 'mere stories' . . . nearly everyone makes the assumption that 'excitement' is the only pleasure they ever give or are intended to give. *Excitement*, in this sense, may be defined as the alternate tension and appeasement of imagined anxiety. This is what I think is untrue. In some such books, and for some readers, another factor comes in. . . . Something which the educated receive from poetry can reach the masses through stories of adventure, and almost no other way. . . . The re-reader is looking not for actual surprises (which can only come once) but for a certain ideal surprisingness. . . . It must be understood that . . . the plot . . . is only really a net whereby to catch something else. The real theme may be, and

usually is, something that has no sequence in it, something other than a process and much more like a state or quality.[7]

Lewis's sub-text is worth considering, for his choice of words betrays a basic disrespect for his audience. The child is equated with 'the masses'; narrative is 'a net', and nets catch the unworldly and incapable, and imprison them. We are approaching the idea that children must necessarily have something not only different, but lesser.

The fact that narrative is the dominant mode of children's books has not helped. The study of narrative has, of course, burgeoned since 1949, when Wellek and Warren (in *Theory of Literature*) could say that 'Literary theory and criticism concerned with the novel are much inferior in both quantity and quality to theory and criticism of poetry', and with it the possibility of accepting other texts as being amenable to criticism. But, as Lewis's sub-text shows, narrative of itself is not considered to be the highest of modes, as Lewis demonstrated in his own fiction for children, where the narrative, skilled though it is, is merely the carrier.

This may seem like a quagmire, so let us approach the definition from the point of view of logic, language, and culture, and see what the implications are. John M. Ellis points out that the word 'literature' is like the word 'weed'; it organizes, rather than describes, our world.[8] It is not the characteristics of the plant that makes it a weed, but rather where it happens to be growing. Similarly, 'Literary texts are not defined as those of a certain shape or structure, but as those pieces of language used in a certain way by the community.' This use is that *the text is not taken as specifically relevant to the immediate context of its origin.* That is, the text is used aesthetically, not practically. Therefore, text may *become* literature, may be used in different ways. Diaries and letters, for example, become literature by virtue of being read by an audience for whom they were not intended and for a different purpose. This, of course, causes problems for children's books, which tend to be used for practical purposes such as education or socialization.

There is also a problem with 'popular' literature: that is, books used (and consumed) specifically for immediate gratification (thrillers, pornography and so on). When used as such, they are *not* (by logic) literature; but when used for something else, they are—and vice versa. Thus, for example, Defoe and Chandler have become 'literature'; whereas *Lady Chatterley's Lover* has sometimes been used as pornography.

Children's literature has this problem, with the added difficulty that we cannot tell how a child reads it—as a 'literary' experience or a functional one. Any text can be given a 'literary' reading—and we must beware of circularity in saying that some reward it more than others—because the values we apply are also part of the cultural system.

As we have seen, a linguistician might characterize 'literary' texts as constituting a small and deviant part of human communication which has become 'fossilized'. Such texts deviate from 'normal' language, and the deviations tend to be organized into patterns. This definition makes no reference to value-judgements, likes, or dislikes; it merely describes.

None of this satisfies the basic idea that some texts are 'better' than others—not therapeutically, but culturally. We need to take on board the obvious, relative idea that 'literature' is the writing authorized and prioritized by a powerful minority. The concept of a 'canon' or a 'mainstream' is class- and society-based. That 'canon' has been influenced by universities, and if children's literature is to accede to this privileged status, it must either become part of the power structure or that power structure must change.

There is no reason why children's books should not be included within the respectable canon (as one alternative) or studied with the same rigour (as the other). Equally, there is no reason why another, different, and parallel discourse should not be created to deal with children's literature. The only real question is one of status, and that is a matter of power.

The same is true of the idea of 'literary language' as something that defines literature. This is not the same as a linguistic definition: the fact of a certain verse-form does not produce poetry. 'Literary language' is different, in the sense that the discourse to which it belongs is exclusive.

This has led, and leads, to a confusion between generic characteristics of language and value-judgements; and again, children's literature is very prone to these. The most common argument against these definitions is that they lead into a quagmire of personal interpretation, where one judgement is as 'good' as another.

There are several problems with this approach. Sticking to a canon and a 'culture' in effect means prioritizing one group and one discourse, and thereby alienating the rest (in this case, children's literature). The established culture is thus weakened anyway. The second point is that we are, in effect, in such a quagmire now, except that the wild personal interpretations and preferences happen to be those agreed to by a single group.

What we need is agreement on the rigour of the method, not a pre-ordained conception of the answers we will find. For children's literature, that will mean a freedom to study it and a clear intellectual approach which will make its study relevant to its users—and a concomitant loss of exclusiveness which will make it acceptable to its users. Far from leading to chaos, such relativity would enable users of children's literature to see clearly whether what they think is admirable commits them to a certain sort of political or social teaching.

There is another dimension to the definition with regard to children's literature. Whereas we might agree that with literature in general the dominant culture decides what is or is not 'good' and that we are—or at least should be—free to agree or not, to join that particular club or not, with children's literature, the non-functionality of art does not apply. Children's books are defined as much by 'good for' as by 'good'; and, again by definition, that which is useless cannot be good for the child-reader. This problem has been well confronted by Peter Dickinson in an early and influential essay 'In defence of rubbish'. Dickinson defined 'rubbish' as 'all forms of reading matter which contain to the adult eye no visible value, either aesthetic or educational'.[9] After arguing for the social value of non-recognized texts, he concludes: 'It may not be rubbish after all. The adult eye is not necessarily a perfect instrument for discerning certain sorts of values.'

In a sense, then, literature is what we choose to make it, which radically suggests that children's *literature* is an inevitable concept, unrelated to other kinds of literature, although it may over-lap with them. That such a 'system', as Shavit calls it, should have a lower status is perhaps inevitable; but that depends a good deal upon how society sees children and childhood. (See Shavit, *Poetics of Children's Literature.*)

Literature is a value-term; and it seems that children's literature, in separating itself (for administrative convenience), defines itself in terms (uniquely) of its audience. Hence, when we are admitting to this club, we need to ask what the other half of the term entails. What is a child?

Defining the Child

The answer is culture-bound both synchronically and diachronically. Nicholas Tucker in his *What is a Child?* draws together features of childhood which are transcultural and diachronic. These include spontaneous play, receptivity to the prevailing culture, physiological constraints (children are generally smaller and weaker), and sexual immaturity (which implies that certain concepts are not immediately relevant to them). They have the tendencies to form emotional attachments to mature figures, to be incapable of abstract thought, to have less of a concentration-span than adults, and to be at the mercy of their immediate perceptions. As a result they tend to be more adaptable than the mature person (whose 'schemas' of the world tend to be set), which in turn has many implications for the writer. There is considerable evidence that their cognitive skills develop in a common sequence, although there is a good deal of dispute as to how far the 'stages' can be recognized.

Tucker himself, in *The Child and the Book*, has taken the developmental stages posited by the pioneering child psychiatrist Jean Piaget, and correlated them to likely texts. That book demonstrates the difficulty of generalization, in that the individual child will differ considerably from the norm. However, it might be useful here to consider the more general implications of these characteristics.

Broadly we can say that, at different stages, children will have different attitudes to death, fear, sex, perspectives, egocentricity, causality, and so on. They will be more open to genuinely radical thought and the ways of understanding texts; they will be more flexible in their perceptions of text; and, because play is a natural part of their outlook, they will regard language as another area for playful exploration. They are less bound by fixed schemas, and in this sense see more clearly.

On the negative side—at least as far as the adult is concerned—they have less knowledge about language and book structures; the distinctions they make between fact and fantasy and between the desirable and the actual are unstable; and they are capable of unconscious animism, since the attribution of human characteristics to inanimate objects is less controlled than it is in adults.

It can be argued that they belong, in effect, to a different culture— possibly an anti-culture or counter-culture. All this is very uncomfortable for the adult dealing with children and texts. Children in some sense belong to an 'oral' culture, which means, as we shall see, that they may well have different modes of thinking, different story-shapes.

Research on children's story telling and the acquisition of story-shapes makes similar claims.[10] Thus, in terms of 'appropriate' types of story, structures will be appreciated differently, even if they are not designed differently. Children may be more susceptible to matters based on folk-memory and not overlaid by schemas, hence the 'relegation', as Tolkien put it (in *Tree and Leaf*) of fairy tales to the nursery.

> Actually, the association of children and fairy-stories is an accident of our domestic history. Fairy-stories have in the modern lettered world been relegated to the 'nursery', as shabby or old-fashioned furniture is relegated to the play-room, primarily because the adults do not want

it, and do not mind if it is misused. It is not the choice of the children which decides this. Children as a class—except in common lack of experience they are not one—neither like fairy-stories more, nor understand them better than adults do. (p. 34)

For all these reasons, then, 'misreadings' or mismatchings of both form and content (against the 'adult' norm) are inevitable, and the literature *of* the child may not be the same as that *for* the child. In short, the relationship between the child—that is, a developing reader—and the text is a complex one, and has implications for the way in which we discuss, teach, and select material.

All this leads the adult community to create or allow different kinds of childhood—which, socially, might best be defined as a period of lack of responsibility, as well as one merely of incomplete development.

Diachronically, the concept of childhood is extremely complex, and not well documented. In the past, there have been extreme versions of childhood, from the Romantic noble-savage child who is nearest to God, to the child seen as having been born evil as a result of original sin. When the mortality rate was high, and in strata of society where poverty and subsistence were the norm (that is, until the eighteenth century), the view of childhood as a protected developmental stage was not possible. In medieval times, there was little concept of childhood; in Elizabethan times, little concept of different needs. The rise of the middle classes in the wake of the Industrial Revolution suggests that it is contrasts which define childhood.

In essence, childhood is defined in terms of seriousness—hence the concept of 'childishness'. Consequently, when considering the history of children's books, it may be that the type of childhood for which they were intended—that is, the kind of childhood that they *defined*—varied considerably. Children's books for the working-class child seem to be a good deal more authoritarian and harsh than those for the sheltered middle classes; indeed, they scarcely seem to be children's books at all. And, since the kind of life the young experienced was not childhood as we might know it, this is not surprising.

Hence the definition of childhood shifts, even within a small, apparently homogeneous culture, just as the understanding of past childhoods shifts. However, some generalizations have the virtue of alerting the reader to over-simplifications. For example, if one attempts to describe 'childhood' at any given moment, one is confronted by a series of paradoxes. What is childhood in Britain in the early 1990s? Generally, there is adult-child segregation; that is, children are regarded as, in principle, a different kind of person; they are protected from adult preoccupations, and work in different places. On the other hand, there has been a relaxation of the boundaries of formality. But then, the ubiquity of media input may mean that they are less protected from taboo subjects—or does TV give only the image and not the feeling? Then, children's clothing has become less distinct; fashions for children make them clones of adults. Popular music now caters for children as part of its market. Diet has become homogenized. Yet there is a clear marketing thrust to maintain certain aspects of childhood, even though in Britain it is still legal to sell toy weapons. Childhood is protected by law, and yet the period of 'irresponsibility' lengthens, on average, with increasing technological process.

In short, childhood is not now (if it ever has been) a stable concept. The literature defined by it, therefore, cannot be expected to be a stable entity. Consequently we must be very careful about the mismatch between readings of a book by a given child in a given period as compared with what it might have been at the time of production.

Thus Pierre Machery's opinion in his *A Theory of Literary Production* needs considerable modification, because concepts of childhood will radically alter the text, and are far more unstable than concepts of adulthood. He writes: 'In fact, the conditions of its communication are produced at the same time as the book, at least the more important conditions. . . . Readers are made by what makes the book . . . for otherwise, the book, written from some inscrutable impulse, would be the work of its readers, reduced to the function of an illustration' (p. 70).

With children's books, of course, this is particularly true. The adaptation of texts or the re-casting of fairy tales or the re-writing and/or re-illustration of Beatrix Potter's books are examples of the ways in which the book culture makes decisions about childhood, and in many ways creates or destroys it.

We thus have two very 'open' and variable definitions to cope with.

Defining 'Children's Literature'

How, then, do we define children's literature? As Paul Heins puts it, pragmatically, 'Perhaps we should distinguish in the long run between two different ways of approaching children's books: (1) the criticism of those books as they concern the different kinds of people who use and work with them, and (2) the literary criticism of children's literature.' I would extend this to the books themselves. There are 'live' books and 'dead' books, books which no longer concern their primary audience (and concern no one else except historians). Paradoxically, although many books 'sink' towards childhood, so many rise towards adulthood. The children's book is, by definition, then, something immediate; and the immediate is prone to be ephemeral, and to interact with the immediate culture. Not many books from such a background subsequently rise to become 'high culture'.

We define children's literature, then, according to our purposes—which, after all, is what all definitions do: they divide the world according to our needs. Children's literature, disturbingly enough, can quite reasonably be defined as books read by, especially suitable for, or especially satisfying for, members of the group currently defined as children. However, such an accommodating definition is not very practical, as it obviously includes every text ever read by a child, so defined.

Most of us, I think, would also be inclined to regard as legitimate children's books only those which are essentially contemporary; there is a limit to which children's books can be said to survive as 'live' books. The ephemeral books have, because of the insensitivity of children and the cupidity of adults, a remarkably long 'shelf-life'; thus, whereas, say, 'Bulldog Drummond' or, to a lesser extent, 'The Saint' survive as period pieces, there is little sense in which Blyton's 'Famous Five' (1942–63) with its marked class and period flavour, is seen by its primary readers as historical. However, with a few obvious exceptions (such as *Treasure Island*), anything else is dispensable. This is not, as might be assumed, because it has no merit in terms of 'old-fashioned' practical literary values. Rather, concepts of childhood change so rapidly that there is a sense in which books no longer applicable to childhood must fall into a limbo in which they are the preserve of the bibliographer, since they are of no interest to the current librarian or child.

We have to put historical children's books—and by that I mean books which can only be presented to a majority of literate modern children with some 'apparatus'—in a separate category. I have little doubt that a survey of what is taught in contemporary universities would show a massive trend towards the contemporary novel. In the case of children's literature, it happens to be true that historical constraints—social, educational, and moral, all manifestations of the Victorian 'protect and control' syndrome—have meant that it is only in the twentieth century that the most notable talents have directed themselves towards children's literature. But in looking at books from the past (in the sense of the inaccessible past) we have to take a modified view: that we are involved in an academic study, in the real sense.

On the whole, then, that a particular text was written expressly for children who are recognizably children, with a childhood recognizable today, must be part of the definition. Hence the fact that little literary distinction was made before the eighteenth century does not admit anything pre-1744 into the reckoning. Even the book usually cited as the first modern children's book, *A Little Pretty Pocket-Book* of 1744, published by John Newbery, can be dismissed.

The history of the children's book may be interesting to the adult, but not for the child, and it is this dichotomy which is central. The same applies, by and large, to books adopted by children. I say by and large, because the distinction between, say, *The Hobbit* and *The Lord of the Rings* may be more theoretical than actual.

Which brings us to pragmatics. One of the most clear-thinking of modern critics, John Rowe Townsend, has written:

> Yet children are part of mankind and children's books are part of liter-ature, and any line which is drawn to confine children of their books to their own special corner is an artificial one. . . . The only practical definition of a children's book today—absurd as it sounds—is 'a book which appears on the children's list of a publisher'. (*A Sense of Story*, p. 9)

Any attempt to define books by their characteristics may be accurate, but in fact describes the least deviant, and hence the least interesting, aspects of the text. Miles McDowell's definition has its merits at this level:

> Children's books are generally shorter; they tend to favour an active rather than a passive treatment, with dialogue and incident rather than description and introspection; child protagonists are the rule; conventions are much used; the story develops within a clear-cut moral schematism which much adult fiction ignores; children's books tend to be optimistic rather than depressive; language is child-oriented; plots are of a distinctive order, probability is often discarded; and one could go on endlessly talking of magic, and fantasy, and simplicity, and adventure.[11]

To define children's literature may seem to be marking out a territory. It is, but only in so far as the subject needs some delimitation if it is to be manageable. Yet, despite the flux of childhood, the children's book can be defined in terms of the implied reader. It will be clear, from a careful reading, who a book is designed for: whether the book is on the side of the child totally, whether it is for the developing child, or whether it is aiming somewhere over the child's head. Whether the text can then be given a value depends upon the circumstances of use.

Finally, we will have to take into account the attitudes of the majority, who remain convinced of the need, culturally, for a distinction in literature that is in some way referable to higher authority—and for the residual need for that in ourselves.

Notes

[1] Rebecca Lukens, *A Critical Handbook of Children's Literature* (Scott, Foresman, Glenview, Ill., 1976): v; see also Lillian H. Smith, *The Unreluctant Years, a critical approach to children's literature* (American Library Association, Chicago, 1953): 7.

[2] James Steele Smith, *A Critical Approach to Children's Literature* (McGraw Hill, New York, 1967): 13.

[3] Lance Salway (ed.), *A Peculiar Gift, nineteenth century writings on books for children* (Kestrel [Penguin], London, 1976): 11.

[4] Jill Paton Walsh, 'The Rainbow Surface', in *The Cool Web: the pattern of children's reading*, eds Margaret Meek et al. (Bodley Head, London, 1977): 192–3.

[5] Jeremy Tambling, *What is Literary Language?* (Open University Press, Milton Keynes, 1988): 8–9.

[6] Elaine Moss, 'Selling the children short', *Signal* 48 (September 1985): 138.

[7] C.S. Lewis, 'On stories', in *Essay Presented To Charles Williams* (Oxford University Press, London, 1947); repr. in Meek et al., *Cool Web*: 76–90, at 78–89.

[8] John M. Ellis, *The Theory of Literary Criticism, a logical analysis* (University of California Press, Berkeley, 1974): 41.

[9] Peter Dickinson, 'In defence of rubbish', repr. in *Writers, Critics, and Children*, eds Geoff Fox et al. (Agathon Press, New York; Heinemann Educational, London, 1976): 74–6.

[10] See Arthur N. Applebee, *The Child's Concept of Story: ages two to seventeen* (University of Chicago Press, Chicago, 1978).

[11] Myles McDowell, 'Fiction for children and adults: some essential differences', *Children's Literature in Education* 10 (March 1973); repr. in *Writers, Critics, and Children*, eds Fox et al.: 141–2.

CRITICAL OPINION: READING CHILDREN'S BOOKS

Julia Briggs

In October 1986 the Bodleian Library launched an appeal for half a million pounds with which to buy the collection of children's books made by Iona and Peter Opie. The Opies had assembled it to support their remarkable research into the language, songs and folklore of children, research otherwise pursued with notebook and tape-recorder, in draughty school rooms and playgrounds. Because Peter was a collector by nature, his library included rare presentation volumes and association copies of the great children's classics—*Alice, Peter Rabbit, The Wind in the Willows*—but the real value of the collection lay in the forgotten, the lost, the items once so readily available that nobody thought to keep them: unique copies of eighteenth-century chapbooks and schoolbooks, nineteenth-century school prizes, twentieth-century ephemera that never reached the great copyright libraries. These long-lost books, sometimes the sole surviving copies, had once been part of a child's inner life; yet the inner lives of those children only become accessible to us if they grow up to become writers who in turn re-work their imaginative experiences for others. Everyone has had the experience of opening a forgotten book or comic familiar from childhood, and finding within it a sense of a former self, a self to whom that text, those pictures held a particular and important meaning. We seldom know what given individuals thought about their childhood reading but we may be sure that it helped to determine their subsequent imaginative life.

The Opies' collection is not as large as either the Renier collection, now being deposited at the Bethnal Green Museum of Childhood or the two great transatlantic collections, the Osborne Library at Toronto and the Baldwin Library of the University of Florida at Gainesville, but it is far richer in rare eighteenth-century holdings than any of these. It seemed important that it should stay in the United Kingdom as an illustration of our incomparably rich tradition of writing for children, spreading over the last three centuries and providing a variety of forms and models that have been translated and enjoyed all over the world. The Bodleian Appeal flourished, and by April 1988 had reached its target, rather to the surprise of its instigators. Oxford University was drawn in and in May 1987 put on five public lectures on children and their books whose speakers included Humphrey Carpenter (co-editor of *The Oxford Companion to Children's Literature*), the children's author Gillian Avery and the historian Keith Thomas. With the addition of fifteen further contributions, these will be published later this year in a sort of *festschrift* for the Opies entitled *Children and their Books*. The University's involvement was the more striking because the study and criticism of children's books, well-established as a serious and even an academic subject in the United States, is largely neglected in British universities. Shorter, more inviting and less demanding than adult literature, children's books are commonly relegated to education departments, which regard their study as an aspect of teacher training rather than an end in itself.

The role of children's books within the wider process of education, and in particular self-education, is of such importance that it has tended to eclipse their study as works of imagination with a history and taxonomy worth exploration, displaying complex significances that different critical approaches might unpack. In some areas, notably in the eighteenth century, some of the basic groundwork of serious scholarship has scarcely begun, and part of the reason for this lies in the great rarity of what were once commonplace and popular books. Two volumes of *Bible Stories* (1802), attributed to one William Scolfield, survive in perhaps two or three copies, though evidently widely read in their day. Its preface, as Geoffrey Summerfield acknowledges (in *Fantasy and Reason: Children's Literature in the Eighteenth Century*, 1984) 'offers the most coherent and radical critique of "moral" literature' for children outside Wordsworth. What he does not add is that 'William Scolfield' was actually a nom-de-plume adopted by William Godwin because his own name had become popularly associated with atheism, free love and revolution, and would thus have repelled potential customers. His authorship was discovered by William St Clair, whose forthcoming biography will show how Godwin's writing for children shared many of the aims of his novels and philosophical works. We have recently learned to attend to the political implications of contemporary children's books, but our awareness focuses primarily upon the child as consumer. We have scarcely begun to think about how politics determined the writing of children's books in the past, though it is clear that they were influenced by the policy debates of their times in a number of ways. Current scholarship has scarcely progressed beyond antiquarianism in this field; its reluctance to engage with political determinants is only one aspect of a more general problem: there is no critical consensus as to whether children's books are appropriately examined by the same criteria

that are applied to adult literature, or whether they constitute a special—
and different—case.

The most rigorous investigation into the status of children's books is
that conducted by Jacqueline Rose in *The Case of Peter Pan or The Impossibility of Children's Fiction* (1984). She concentrates her discussion on a work
that exposes the inadequacies of current critical thinking about the whole
subject, as well as introducing some further exemplary problems, since
Peter Pan has no status as an authorized text produced by J.M. Barrie.
Peter, 'the Boy who Wouldn't Grow Up', first made his appearance in *The
Little White Bird* (1902), a queasy narrative about the writer's yearning to
possess a small boy called 'David'. At one point the narrator manages to
spend the night with David. Putting him to bed,

> I placed him on my knee and removed his blouse. This was a
> delightful experience, but I think I remained wonderfully calm until I
> came somewhat too suddenly to his little braces, which agitated me
> profoundly.
> I cannot proceed in public with the disrobing of David.

(Curiously, this passage seems to be parodied in another children's classic,
Winnie-the-Pooh, where Piglet is 'agog at the thought of seeing Christopher
Robin's blue braces again. He had only seen them once before, when he
was much younger, and being a little over-excited by them, had had to go
to bed half an hour earlier than usual . . .'.) Peter figured in an ongoing
story that Barrie was making up for his own 'David', George Llewelyn
Davies, the outcome of which was the stage play of *Peter Pan*, first
performed at the Duke of York's Theatre in December 1904. The text of
this version survives only in a series of incomplete and revised typescripts.
At this point the familiar story of Peter, Wendy and the Lost Boys moved
into the public domain and was written up in several versions by different
hands. At first Barrie himself refused to write a narrative of it, and when in
1912 he finally attempted to do so, it had to be rewritten (as a school
reading book) by someone else. The play script was finally published in
1928 in a collection of Barrie's plays for adults.

The text of *Peter Pan* thus exists in a series of unofficial states and
forms; each version blends adult fantasies about children and the avoidance of growing up with fantasies created for children, designed to seduce
the imagination of a specific small listener (the origin of many, perhaps
most, nursery classics). Jacqueline Rose demonstrates that the complexity
of the conditions under which children's fiction is produced guarantees

that the end product can never be unproblematic. One major complication is the legislative role of adults in the whole process, both as producers and consumers. Children's books are written for a special readership but not, normally, by members of that readership; both the writing and, quite often, the buying of them, is carried out by adult non-members on behalf of child members. Inevitably the production of children's books is governed by what adults want children to be and to do, and furthermore it offers an opportunity to induce them to share those adult goals. Adults have always determined children's reading, though quite early in the history of children's books, crude didacticism gave way to subtler methods of persuasion.

Lewis Carroll's *Alice in Wonderland* (1865) was one of the earliest books to make fun of the way instruction had dominated earlier writing for children. This was another book intended to grip the attention of one particular beautiful child. Among his efforts to amuse her, Dodgson burlesqued Alice Liddell's schoolroom lessons—the improving hymns of Isaac Watts ('How doth the little crocodile' and ''Tis the voice of the lobster'), the poems of Southey and Wordsworth ('You are old, Father William' and the White Knight's song, respectively), as well as Havilland Chepmell's *Short Course of History* (1862), so desiccated that the Mouse recites a paragraph from it to help dry the creatures soaked in the Pool of Tears. Carroll habitually and gratifyingly subverts the standard educational assumptions of his day, sometimes simply by appearing to advocate them:

> 'You're thinking about something my dear, and that makes you forget to talk. I can't tell you just now what the moral of that is, but I shall remember it in a bit.'
> 'Perhaps it hasn't one,' Alice ventured to remark.
> 'Tut, tut, child!' said the Duchess. 'Everything's got a moral, if only you can find it.' And she squeezed herself up closer to Alice's side as she spoke.

In *Alice* the events and location are consistently surreal and the viewpoint is that of the child, constrained and sometimes oppressed by the hegemonic world of adults; after a particularly severe identity crisis induced by her sudden changes in size, Alice decides that she may have to resort to resistance:

> If I'm Mabel, I'll stay down here! It'll be no use their putting their heads down and saying, 'Come up again, dear!' I shall only look up and say 'Who am I, then? Tell me that first, and then, if I like being

that person, I'll come up: if not, I'll stay down here till I'm somebody else'—

Her alienation from the adult world is registered not only in this temporary rejection but in her constant impatience with apparently meaningless rules and adult rituals—the etiquette of the tea-party and the banquet, the protocol of the law-court. In stylistic terms, the two *Alice* books endorse her alienation by mocking dominant literary models, either through parody or through subtly reductive changes of scale and reference.

The impact of Carroll's experiment can be seen on his successors: Christina Rossetti's stories for children in *Speaking Likenesses* (1874) were set in a Carrollian dream world that released their author into a private fantasy of persecution that recalls *Goblin Market*. The best of later nineteenth-century fiction for children was prepared to acknowledge its readers' autonomous life. The child's alienation from the normative world of adults had been imaginatively recognized by Wordsworth. It was to offer crucial perspectives within the fictions of Mark Twain and Charles Dickens. The latter gleefully inverted the whole power structure in his *Holiday Romance* (1868), most of which is supposedly written by children. The last story tells how Mrs Orange and Mrs Lemon struggle to discipline their naughty grown-ups who persistently gamble, flirt, eat and drink too much and whose games of Parliament and the City only too often end in tears. No one recalled more vividly than Dickens how children felt, their continuous fascination and bafflement with the incongruous and illogical world created by the adults around them. Other Victorian writers began to reconstruct childhood responses to the adult world from memory: Stevenson in his essay on 'Child's Play' (*Virginibus Puerisque*, 1881) wondered 'Were there ever such unthinkable deities as parents?', while Kenneth Grahame, in his prologue to *The Golden Age* (1895), represented adults as a species at once alien and peculiarly inert:

> On the whole the existence of these Olympians seemed to be entirely void of interests, even as their movements were confined and slow, and their habits stereotyped and senseless. To anything but appearances they were blind.

The tone here is ironic, and Grahame shares with Barrie something of that disturbed and disturbing desire to be 'boy eternal', but the identification of adults as 'Olympians' acknowledges a power structure that the Darlings, the charming but ineffectual parents in *Peter Pan*, seem to deny.

Children's fiction from 1880 up to the First World War, the so-called 'Golden Age', enters the child's world to an unprecedented degree and from a number of angles, yet the child presented and addressed remains firmly defined as middle class, and though the values invoked are translated into a language that might plausibly be spoken in the nursery or the school-room, they are still recognisable as part of the prevailing moral terminology of their day. E. Nesbit's Bastable family (in *The Story of the Treasure Seekers*, 1899 and its sequels), lively and anarchic as they sometimes are, regard themselves as 'gentlemen' and the children of a gentleman. They set great store by 'owning up', and on no account sneaking or snivelling. They are full of generous impulses and that desire to do good to those less privileged than themselves that had so often motivated evangelical children in earlier books, as well as Victorian charitable enterprise more generally. But such impulses now needed to be reconciled on the one hand with a sharper insight into children's own reactions, and on the other with the new spirit of initiative and adventure promoted by the public schools in response to the needs of Britain's expanding overseas empire. After the formation of 'The New Society for Being Good In' (in *The Wouldbegoods*, 1901), Oswald and Dickie review the situation:

> 'We must do something,' Dickie said; 'it's very hard, though. Still there must be *some* interesting things that are not wrong.'
>
> 'I suppose so,' Oswald said, 'but being good is so much like being a muff, generally. Anyhow, I'm not going to smooth the pillows of the sick, or read to the aged poor, or any rot out of *Ministering Children*.'
>
> 'No more am I,' Dickie said. He was chewing a straw . . ., 'but I suppose we must play the game fair. Let's begin by looking out for something useful to do—something like mending things or cleaning them, not just showing off.'
>
> 'The boys in books chop kindling wood and save their pennies to buy tea and tracts.'
>
> 'Little beasts!' said Dick. 'I say, let's talk about something else.' And Oswald was glad to, for he was beginning to feel jolly uncomfortable.

This curious blend of high-mindedness and masculine independence was inspired by Kipling's *Stalky and Co* (1899) where 'beastly Ericking' is roundly condemned: the reference is to *Eric, or Little by Little* (by F.W. Farrar, 1858), the heavily moralised tale of a child corrupted by his schoolfellows who nevertheless died an exemplary death.

Class and gender distinctions are deeply embedded in E. Nesbit's writing for children, where their often unapologetic appearance is the more striking since she herself was a founding Fabian and the main wage-earner in her household. Boys need to distinguish their activities from the 'do-gooding' of the girls, and neither the characters nor their author can quite believe that servants are people, though there are sudden pangs of conscience, as when Oswald has set a booby-trap for the housekeeper:

> Oswald was not willingly vicious . . . And he is sorry . . . because he knows it is ungentlemanly to play tricks on women.
>   I remember mother telling Dora and me when we were little that you ought to be very kind and polite to servants, because they have to work very hard, and do not have so many good times as we do.

Class distinctions pervade Edwardian fantasy writing quite as strongly as they do more naturalistic texts: several recent critics have interpreted *The Wind in the Willows* (1908) as a fable of class struggle between Toad as a playboy aristocrat or landed *rentier* who does not take his responsibilities seriously enough, and that envious and underprivileged proletariat, the Stoats and Weasels; or else (and the two are not incompatible) between the rural traditionalists protecting the receding greenery of the Thames Valley and the invading urban masses. Moral lessons about purposiveness, significant toil and fresh air also permeate Frances Hodgson Burnett's *The Secret Garden* (1911). As long as society attributes to education the power to determine its own future character, so long will children's fiction voice its authors' favourite solutions to contemporary social problems, even if, as in the case of Grahame, it seems to do so unconsciously. Grahame's solution, in Toad's words, is to 'Whack 'em and whack 'em and whack 'em', a sentiment at once heroic, embattled and reactionary; it could only have been expressed thus in a fable whose meaning he kept from himself.

Because of a general obligation to instruct, and in particular to teach the child about his place in society, children's fictions express with particular clarity their society's sense of itself and its structures, as well as its justification of those structures. Even in children's books where there is no evident didactic intention, the necessity to simplify is inclined to reveal the nature of social interaction. Many books written for earlier generations now look unsuitable for today's young readers because of the unsympathetic social assumptions they voice: in a society that pays lip service to egalitarian ideals, Edwardian attitudes to social and personal differences can be regarded as regressive: 'Are the classics of children's literature influencing children to see the world in racist and sexist terms?' asks Judith Stinton, editor of *Racism and Sexism in Children's Books* (1979). While her book does not advance any very strong evidence that they are, the best-loved children's books have already become key works for a middle-class clerisy whose values look increasingly parochial and defensive in a larger conspectus.

Censorship, usually so loathsome to liberals, looks as if it may be the only way to remove illiberal texts from the hands of young readers. In this morally troubling debate, the shelves of public libraries have become the main sites of battle, their custodians being rightly conscious of a wider accountability. Individual librarians have acquired overnight notoriety by banning Blyton, Billy Bunter or Helen Bannerman from their shelves. It would be difficult to argue that the removal of the latter's *Little Black Sambo* books (1899 onwards) involved serious deprivation of anyone other than sentimental adults, but censorship is seldom so uncomplicated. Should Hugh Lofting's Dr Doolittle books (1920 onwards) also go, with their condescending portrait of the stupid, ugly but well-meaning black Prince Bumpo? And how should we respond to a recent bowdlerised edition of *Huckleberry Finn*, when the book and its author so clearly set their face against racial injustice?

A little while ago a librarian wrote to me complaining that copies of Walter de la Mare's *Collected Stories for Children* (1947) were being removed on the grounds that one story, 'Sambo and the Snow Mountains', was racist. Invited to condemn what looked like an act of literary vandalism, I was uncertain how to reply, since the losses or gains seemed almost impossible to calculate. As an adult reader, I greatly admire de la Mare's fiction and value it more highly than his poetry; as a child reader I felt exactly the reverse: I loved the strong rhythms and nursery-rhyme dottiness of the verses, but entirely failed to enjoy or appreciate the *Collected Stories for Children*. They didn't seem to me then and don't seem to me now to be suitable for children in any respect other than their free use of fantasy elements. But how far should I judge by my own childhood response? Was it typical or exceptional? Would the extraordinary delicacy of imagination and subtlety of structure now apparent to me in stories such as 'Miss Jemima', 'Maria Fly' and 'Alice's Grandmother' communicate itself to children? And what, more importantly, about the question of racism itself, which occasioned this act of censorship?

'Sambo and the Snow Mountains' is the story of a little black boy who, longing to be white, goes to live in the snow and whitewashes his face. Both in terms of his name, his language (pidgin English) and his country of origin ('Poojooboo' in Africa), he is a stereotype, the thoughtless construct of white superiority. Yet the story sets out to explore the nature of self-hatred and self-division induced by racial intolerance: Sambo's longing for whiteness is instilled by his white tormentors, who themselves would have looked 'different' in his own country, though, the narrator carefully points out, Sambo's own people would have been too polite to jeer. Sambo's desire to be white precisely parallels that of black children brought up in predominantly white communities, who express their unease with their self-image by identifying with white dolls, or drawing themselves as white. The story is thus intensely relevant to the modern black child's plight and possibly even diagnostic of the feelings of self-loss that are a part of it; it is nevertheless couched in terms stained with their own dark history, and nowhere moves out of its fictive mode to offer an explicit condemnation of intolerance. In reinforcing the child's experience, this story might be either a source of comfort or of distress. And if it made a single child unhappy or ashamed, would anyone want it left on the library shelf? The process of reading, whether undertaken by children or adults, still remains as deeply mysterious as it is subjective.

Their ignorance and lack of preconceptions leave children peculiarly vulnerable to outside influences. The claim that they need protection can be extended to justify the exercise of censorship on a variety of grounds. Nicholas Tucker (in *The Child and the Book*, 1981) cites an Ipswich librarian who caused furore some years ago by suppressing Frank Richards's Billy Bunter stories on the grounds that 'Nowadays we . . . realise that excessive fatness is a physical disability like any other—not the result of gluttony'. Humourless or humane? Outstandingly popular children's authors sometimes seem to release a backlash of public opinion against themselves that is fuelled by their very success; the case example would be Enid Blyton who as a literary export far outsells Shakespeare but who arouses passionate debates as to her merits. It is difficult to make a serious case against her except on grounds of derivativeness, or of dated prejudices of the sort that also afflict considerably better writers, or else of style. She wrote rapidly, carelessly and without depth; her books instil an unexceptionable if old-fashioned boy-scout morality. Roald Dahl, a more recent target, is more energetic, original and inventive than Blyton, but also considerably less *bien-pensant*. Are their books any more undesirable for children to read than their equivalents among adult fiction—Barbara Cartland, say, or Ian Fleming? Children, it seems, consume fast fiction for much the same reason as adults do, for the pleasure of following rapidly unfolding events which avoid complexity, and therefore uncertainty, whether at a moral or merely narrative level.

Set moral frameworks, with characters placed clearly on the side of good or evil, characterize much, though by no means all, children's fiction, as well as related fantasy genres—adventure and detective stories and science fiction. Tolkien's *Lord of the Rings*, conceived and written for adults, gestures towards a moral complexity as apparently 'good' characters succumb to the lure of power offered by the ring, but their defections reassuringly flatten themselves out again, since if anything of good remains in them, they acknowledge their error at the moment of death. Above all, there are only two sides to choose from and allegiance is everything. There is a simplicity in this approach that appeals strongly in early adolescence, when one longs for the external world to perform a similar trick and resolve itself once more into the clear-cut two-dimensional morality of childhood. Yet some of the most appealing children's writers of the last fifty years have taken the moral difficulties and confusions of existence as their central themes, offering complexity, rather than the 'certainties' promulgated by a writer like C.S. Lewis: E.B. White, Mary Norton, Philippa Pearce and Alan Garner come to mind.

I once assumed that it was the moral simplification that drew adult readers back to reread childhood favourites—Kenneth Grahame, E. Nesbit, even Enid Blyton—when they are feeling tired or ill, but there could be other explanations, and the mere pleasure of reliving childhood experiences plays some part: children's fiction offers a retreat into an ideal world, a world of pastoral (as Empson suggested, but scarcely attempted to justify, when he included *Alice* in his book *Some Versions of Pastoral*, 1935), where the intolerable logics of duty and possibility do not exactly die, but are at least temporarily suspended. Writers for children are consolingly adept at combining power and liberating freedom with a sense of security, whereas serious adult fiction is more likely to concern itself with defining the nature of the conflicts between them. But perhaps the most comforting aspect of 'classic' children's fiction (and the telling mark of its adult origins?) is the absence of any reference to sexuality. It may be that we revert to these texts when we are ill because that most troublesome gauge of the body's vulnerability, its unpredictable response to others and its own involuntary life, is here comfortingly concealed. The suppression of sexual themes clearly reflects adult prohibitions, and the repression of (guilty) memories of childhood sexuality, impulses that re-emerge, now disguised beyond recognition, in the adult writer's invitation to his child reader. This evasion may be a reassuring one to all concerned. Sexual desire is itself one crucial source of difference between adult and child, since it changes its nature so radically at puberty. As an appetite, it is absent, perhaps displaced by that other primal and atavistic pleasure of eating; in children's books, the appetite for food is frequently and sometimes expansively indulged:

> 'What's inside it?' asked the Mole, wriggling with curiosity.
> 'There's cold chicken inside it,' replied the Rat briefly; 'cold-tonguecoldhamcoldbeefpickledgherkinssaladfrenchrollscresssand-widgespottedmeatgingerbeerlemonadesodawater—'
> 'O stop, stop,' cried the Mole in ecstasies: 'This is too much!'

But no appetite is so innocent that it cannot prompt forbidden desires—from the fright over the apple that begins Sarah Fielding's *The Governess* (1749, and the first serious fiction written for children) to Peter Rabbit salivating over one more radish or Edmund's perverse hunger for Turkish Delight in *The Lion, the Witch and the Wardrobe*.

The practice of active censorship carries implications concerning the power of fiction to affect its readers which may be positive as well as negative. Strong claims have been made for the therapeutic power of certain stories for children, most notably by Bruno Bettelheim in his delightful book *The Uses of Enchantment* (1976). He proposes that fairy tales can play a valuable part in children's development because they provide relief from inner pressures, release from painful or threatening situations and hold out the hope of a happy outcome. Particular fairy tales, it is argued, dramatize characteristic problems experienced by the child during the process of growing up; they afford imaginative escape routes that encourage readers to trust and believe in their own powers of luck, perseverance or native wit. Bettelheim's account of the healing nature of fiction is bound to be deeply attractive to those such as teachers, librarians or academics, who have an investment in it. It is scarcely surprising, then, that this approach has been taken up and extended to include more recent fictions for children, for example by Margaret and Michael Rustin in *Narratives of Love and Loss* (1987); here E. Nesbit, C.S. Lewis, Philippa Pearce and E.B. White are praised for reconciling their young readers to painful personal experiences.

But important objections can be raised to this line of argument, and especially to Bettelheim's account of what fairy tales are, where they come from and how they affect their young readers. Some of these are particular and historical: fairy tales were not composed for children in the first instance, do not exist in definitive ('pure') versions, and a number of their early analogues (for example, those of 'Bluebeard') are so savage that their aptness as consolatory fables must be assumed to have been developed at a later stage, if at all, and cannot therefore be regarded as fundamental or innate to them. There may be a more general objection to the process of taming or sanitizing literature, of regarding it as health-giving. Once its dangerous corners are straightened out, its seductive transgressiveness smoothed away, something of its vitality has gone.

'Little Red Riding Hood' provides an obvious example of a story that has been moralized in more ways than one, since it has at least two different endings: in both, Red Riding Hood is eaten by the wolf, but only in one (recorded by the brothers Grimm) does she survive and the wolf die. Bettelheim condemns Perrault's harsher version and Perrault's trite and prudential moral ('Little girls shouldn't speak to strangers'), since it is not at all in keeping with his theories about the ways in which fairy tales teach constructively. But in their *Classic Fairy Tales* (1974) Iona and Peter Opie, unconcerned to teach any particular lesson, reprint the version that ends with Riding Hood's death. The whole question of the status of fairy tales, and their reshaping by the society that perpetuates them has been illuminatingly investigated by Jack Zipes in *Fairy Tales and the Art of Subversion: The Classical Genre for Children and the Process of Civilization* (1983), and more recently in *The Brothers Grimm: From Enchanted Forests to the Modern World* (1988). In the latter Zipes shows how the brothers collected their narratives mainly from educated women with middle-class or even aristocratic backgrounds, how they edited out sexual elements that might offend the bourgeois susceptibilities of their readers and added Christian overtones and homely settings that served to reinforce their own society's ('*biedermeier*') values, since, in common with other children's writers of the day, they believed it their duty to contribute to the child's moral education. Zipes argues that their tales were conditioned both by their own psychological oddities and their society's preconceptions concerning family life, and goes on to suggest that, far from liberating their readers, these stories may work to reinforce existing hierarchies and gender roles and to repress or disguise themes of child abuse, though he adds as a rider that they may 'allow us to contend with these problems on a subconscious level'. His studies once again emphasise the primacy of adult beliefs and expectations in determining the nature of children's books.

One book that systematically explores many of the problems here touched on is Zohar Shavit's *Poetics of Children's Literature* (Athens, Georgia, 1986). Shavit sets out to free her subject from the child-centred approach of librarians, teachers and psychologists, to establish it as a legitimate field of research and a special branch of literature as a whole; she then attempts to identify the characteristic patterns and structures within it. Having acknowledged the problems created by the very marginality of her subject, she addresses herself first to the protean nature of the texts involved: she discusses the remoulding of fairy tales by their editors, the rare reworking of an adult text for child readers by its own author (Roald Dahl rewrote his short story 'The Champion of the World' from *Kiss Kiss* as a Puffin, *Danny the Champion of the World*), as well as the adaption and abridgement of classics such as *Robinson Crusoe* and *Gulliver's Travels*. Lacking serious literary status, children's books often exist in several versions, more than one of which may be authorial, and while such variants often reflect differences in the conditions of production or the audience addressed, they further add to the scholar's problems. The second part of Shavit's enterprise is to explore the relationship between the autonomy and self-perpetuation of children's literature, and its determining moment. Her examples here are largely drawn from the history of British children's books, since this is the fullest and most extensively documented. It has, of course, also been the most influential and has thus become a dominating and possibly a determining paradigm. Whether we should infer that the particular sequence of development here described is somehow inevitable, or inevitable given the history of Western culture, or not inevitable at all, remains impossible to judge.

Shavit identifies patterns, but fastidiously avoids evaluation—Blyton and Dahl are thus as apt to her purpose as Carroll or the brothers Grimm. Bettelheim and Zipes, in common with the self-appointed custodians of the junior library, are agreed that childhood reading can make a strong impact, even if they are not agreed as to how and why it does so. Despite current concerns to chart anxieties of influence, the case of childhood reading is commonly overlooked. Juliet Dusinberre's *Alice to the Lighthouse: Children's Books and Radical Experiments in Art* (1987) endeavours to rectify this omission by arguing that the late Victorian flowering of children's literature promoted the development of modernism. Her thesis is fascinating and provocative, but virtually the only evidence she adduces for her arguments is stylistic: passages from James Joyce and Virginia Woolf are tellingly juxtaposed to passages from Lewis Carroll or Mark Twain, but there is no attempt to find out which particular books the modernists actually read as children, or whether their early reading has left identifiable traces upon their adult work, and the absence of this kind of detailed investigation weakens her case. Nevertheless the proposition that childhood reading may have a direct influence on the subsequent development of adult fiction is so interesting and so unexplored that her book has an importance beyond its achievement. Whether we accept the likelihood of direct influence or not, it seems clear that many key features of modernism such as surrealism, nonsense, parody and burlesque had entered children's literature before they entered into adult fiction, since the child's inner world was acknowledged to be fantastic, irrational and anarchic before the adult's inner world came to be seen in comparable terms. The very marginality of children in the nineteenth century allowed Edward Lear and Lewis Carroll to adopt a standpoint of irresponsibility and to mock faceless authority, with a freedom that they could not have found had they addressed a more socially integrated readership. Though Juliet Dusinberre scarcely mentions him, Dickens is once again a key figure here, bridging the gap between a stuffy establishment and the vitally destructive energies of anarchy, the world and the child, the adult conventions and the child's uncompromising gaze that recognizes the Emperor in his full nakedness.

Protecting Children's Literature

Natalie Babbitt

I feel protective about children's fiction, and I also feel protective about the pleasure it's supposed to provide. I think that a lot of what's happened to it lately threatens it. A great deal is being piled on it—things that don't have much to do with the joy of reading—and that's a worry. Fiction is a fragile medium. A good story can collapse if it's made to bear too much weight.

Many of us, in literature classes in college, had to go through the agonizing business of dismantling a novel in order to examine it critically. It was like taking apart a car engine and laying out the pieces on the floor of the garage. It utterly ceases to resemble a car engine and becomes a jumble of seemingly unrelated parts. Not that I've ever taken apart a car engine, mind you, but I once watched a clever niece do it, so I can claim some validity for the metaphor. Sometimes, in those literature classes, it was hard to put the novel back together again afterwards. I have seen stories put back together in such a way that the pleasure they gave in the beginning was lost forever. Still, it's perfectly true that once a piece of fiction leaves its author's hands, it becomes the property of each person who reads it, and each person will see different things in it, often things the author didn't necessarily intend. So there's no point in the author insisting on a single set of directions for assembly and operation. No point in being possessive. But feeling possessive about one's own fiction and feeling protective about the whole body of fiction are two very different things.

I know that there is a movement underway to stop using texts for the teaching of reading and to start using works of fiction. In the beginning that seemed to me to be a good idea. But now I'm not so sure. The texts had related workbooks with sentences to complete, quizzes, questions to think about, and all kinds of suggested projects. The feeling has been, as I understand it, that these texts and workbooks were making a dry and tedious thing out of learning to read at the very time when concern about literacy levels was growing more and more serious. So it seemed sensible to try using real stories in the classroom—stories that could grab the children's fancies and show them what the joy of reading is all about.

But what I see happening now is that these real stories are being used in the same way that the old texts were used. Every once in a while someone sends me something meant to accompany a classroom reading of my story, *Tuck Everlasting* (Farrar), and here's what I find: a related workbook with sentences to complete, quizzes, questions to think about, and all kinds of suggested projects. I worry that this will make a dry and tedious thing out of fiction. It's as if the same recipe for stew were being followed in both cases, except that chicken has been substituted for Spam. Stew is stew, and it gets tiresome in a hurry.

Well, I'm not a teacher, but I can imagine how painfully difficult it must be to try to teach a roomful of kids how to read. And not only how to read but what to read, while at the same time struggling to keep the process reasonably entertaining. The burden teachers have been forced to take on in the last decade or two is truly staggering. And now we've come reeling away from a governors' conference where the glad tidings were announced that we will have one hundred per cent literacy in this nation by the year 2000. What did they think they were doing? I found it all astonishing and, I must say, irritating. No mention of money being provided for such a horrendous undertaking. No mention of who would be expected to undertake it. Of course, we all *know* who's expected to undertake it: our teachers. But the governors didn't say how to do it. What the governors did, at least in the television reports I saw, was to emerge from their meetings flushed and starry-eyed with noble purpose and simply announce that in ten years there will be no more illiteracy. It seems to me you might as well announce that in ten years there will be no more salt in the ocean.

This is not to say that one hundred per cent literacy isn't something to strive for; but surely, in a sprawling democracy like ours, it's an impossibility. Isn't it? Well, perhaps it depends on what you mean by literacy. And there is something heartbreakingly American about the aspiration. We always have believed we could do anything if we just set our minds to it. Just pass a law, and the problem, whatever it may be, is solved automatically. When it doesn't work—and very often it doesn't—we are baffled and outraged. We want things to be perfect.

One of the paths we see as leading to a perfect society is to catch the children early and get them to think about things in the right way. We have all been struck with horror at the truly awful things some of our young people have been doing lately. Drug-dealing, murder, rape, random violence with nothing personal in it at all that anyone can see. They are doing things that are not so much immoral as amoral. The implication with immorality is that it is behaviour performed in opposition to morality, which implies an understanding of morality. But amoral behaviour implies no such understanding. Often it isn't even angry. It is behaviour performed in an emotional vacuum, and it makes chaos of society. Clearly something has to be done and done without delay if we are to save our children from growing up with no sense at all of social responsibility.

Social responsibility means, to me, caring about others, obeying the laws, keeping the wheels of society oiled and turning, understanding how our personal behaviour affects our environment. We learn the basics of it mainly from our parents and siblings, before we ever enter a classroom. I do not think literature can or should be expected to teach it, and I will try to explain why I feel that way.

Let us go way, way back to Oog and Mog, my favorite cavemen, at a time during the thawing of the Ice Age. Oog has just clobbered a musk ox. Mog comes along and wants the musk ox for himself. So he bops Oog over the head with a club. Oog is understandably annoyed. He bops Mog back. 'Ow!' says Mog to himself. 'That hurts! If I bop Oog again, he'll probably bop *me* again, and that will hurt, too. So if I don't want to get hurt, I guess I'd better not bop Oog.' And so social responsibility was born. But it was not born out of consideration for one's fellow man. It was born out of the desire not to get bopped. It appears to me, from this little prehistoric morality play I've just described, that social responsibility is a learned thing that arises from the instinct for self-preservation. Consideration for one's fellow man is not instinctive. It has to be demonstrated as wise and useful if one wants to be comfortable. It is, at bottom, selfish.

Now, you would think, wouldn't you, after all the centuries that have passed since Oog and Mog, that human beings would have adapted genetically somehow, and would now be born knowing they had better not go around bopping people. But, alas, this is not the case. My grandson is eighteen months old. He has all the external attributes of an angel, and this is not just the blind ravings of your average grandmother. But when he comes to my house to visit, as he does very often, and sees our middle-aged golden retriever, a certain unnerving light comes into his eye. He will give a laugh like that of an imp from hell, pick up a toy, and bop the dog with it. And then he will laugh again. He finds her funny to look at, and even funnier to bop. He has no conception at all of kindness and consideration. Not even as much as the dog has. He will have to learn it, like everyone else. It would speed things up if Rosie, our dog, were to bite him, but she won't. She's already learned about biting and bopping. And anyway, my grandchild doesn't know he's doing anything wrong. He is amoral, as we all were at his age. Oog and Mog and all of their descendants, down to you and me and my grandchild, have had to learn social responsibility for the most pragmatic of reasons: to preserve our own comfort and our own skins.

But what about the people who haven't learned it? What about that group of boys who raped the Central Park jogger? Why has their amorality survived well into their adolescence? We can only presume that it is because they have grown up in a place where people have been bopped whether they bop back or not. And there are, of course, all varieties of bopping. You can be bopped in the spirit, the ego, the heart, as well as on the head. If other people have never cared about you, you're not going to learn how to care about other people.

The Central Park rapists are an extreme example, of course. But our lives are full of minor examples. One of the least important but most annoying is that of the grocery store fast-checkout lane. 'Eight items or less' is the way it's labelled at my grocery store. But there are people who constantly go through with more than eight items. They go through with two times eight, three times eight. A time or two, I've mentioned the infraction mildly to the culprit, but the culprit is liable to turn surly if you say anything. Liable, in fact, to bop. Once I mentioned the situation to the check-out clerk. 'Come on!' he said. 'It's only a grocery store.' True. but where is the line between the eight-items violation and murder? I'm serious. There has to be a line somewhere, and I want to know where it is. When does it begin to matter whether you obey the rules or not? In my neighbourhood, it evidently comes somewhere beyond red lights and stop signs. I complained about Providence drivers once to a taxi driver. He drew himself up and said proudly, 'Rhode Islanders don't like laws.'

Clearly things are out of control around the edges, and something has to be done. Or else I'm getting old and cantankerous. Well, I *am* getting old and cantankerous. It's a sure sign of it when you can get seriously steamed over unauthorized vehicles parked in places reserved for the handicapped. In my grocery store parking lot, I once saw a motorcycle parked in a handicapped space. Still, I should save my steam for issues more worthy of the energy. Like, for instance, preserving what little is left of the pleasure of reading fiction. On the face of it, there wouldn't seem to be much of a relationship between eight-items-or-less and curling up with a good book. Well, that's the point. There isn't any connection, and if we try to create one, it's the book that will suffer. Or at any rate, that is my fear.

I don't believe in using fiction to teach anything except the appreciation of fiction. At least, not to children. It seems to me that there is enough difficulty getting them to read in the first place, and the more lessons you clog up reading with, the more of a lesson you make of it. Book discussions are a good thing because everyone needs help in learning to read critically—or, perhaps I should say, in learning to think critically. And if a given piece of fiction deals with a particular problem of being human, then it is only natural that the problem be dealt with in the discussion. I know that *Tuck Everlasting* suggests some moral problems, and it's perfectly reasonable to talk about those in a book discussion. But, you know, it's interesting to see, from the letters I get, which of those problems really interest the children. Curiously, no child has ever written to me about whether or not Mae Tuck should have killed the man in the yellow suit. They always write about whether or not Winnie Foster should have drunk the spring water and gone off with the fascinating Jesse Tuck. I suppose they feel that the man in the yellow suit, like the Wicked Witch of the West, needed killing, and so it's all right. The killing has bothered some grownups, but the children don't seem to turn a hair over it. They also do not write to me about whether Winnie did the right thing in helping Mae Tuck escape from jail.

Now, surely these two things, both genuine crimes in our society, are examples of social irresponsibility from which we scarcely want our children to learn. In fact, *Tuck Everlasting* demonstrates, if it demonstrates anything at all, the complicated moral ambiguities of social responsibility. I didn't think about demonstrating anything while I was writing it, though. I only wanted to tell a story and at the same time explore for myself the question of what eternal life might really be like. A lot of children write that they don't agree with me that it would be terrible. In some classrooms they write their own endings for the story. That's perfectly all right with me. What isn't perfectly all right is when they write to tell me, always rather woodenly, what they 'learned' from the story. I know these recitals are not from their own hearts. It's easy to tell. The most common expression of it I get is that a child will say, 'I learned that living forever would be a bad thing.' And then, in an impassioned postscript they will add, 'But why didn't Winnie drink the water?'

The best letters of all come from the children who got involved in the story, caught up in what suspense there is, and wanted to see what would happen next. Just normal, everyday fun from a story, the kind we all get with a book we like. Not, you understand, that I imagine they all like *Tuck*. It takes real persistence on the part of the teachers to get them past the beginning, which a great many children find boring and confusing, and don't hesitate to say so in their letters. But some do like it, thank goodness. And what they take away with them when they're finished it will depend on each child's personal needs and personal quirks. It does appear that a good many of the girls take away a desire to meet a Jesse Tuck, but that's all right. Nothing the matter with romance.

But I don't think any of them are coming away with a heightened sense of social responsibility. They could be made to, of course. You can come away from any book with that, if it's thrust upon you. But how sad for the book! Imagine teaching *Peter Rabbit* that way. Imagine teaching *The Secret Garden* that way. Or *Alice in Wonderland*, or any of the best-loved children's stories. Why do we remember these tales our whole lives long? What is it in them that endears them to us? Certainly it isn't because they taught us to be socially responsible.

I think the single most attractive quality to the stories that have lasted is that their heroes and heroines defy authority and not only get away with it but also create positive and happy endings thereby. To defy authority is to be socially irresponsible, isn't it? But, you see, children are small and surrounded by rules and restrictions and caveats and coercion. Their longing for independence and self-determination is very strong. So is their passion for justice, which they see little enough of in the world around them. If we leave them alone to identify with Alice and with Peter, and with Mary and Colin, and with all the other storybook rebels, we are allowing the books to work the magic of identification, and spread the balm of good therapy on their bruises. A good children's book says to the reader, 'Yes, Virginia, you *can* escape the pinches of your life and, for a little time, make a difference in the world, even if it is only vicarious.' If we turn children's stories into handbooks for proper behaviour, we will subvert their purpose and destroy their magic, and do the one other thing which is the saddest of all: make of reading a chore, a drag, just another lesson. And when that happens, the joy of reading evaporates.

I tried hard to think of a beloved children's story that demonstrates social responsibility as a natural part of its action, and I couldn't think of a single one. Every one of the most popular stories I could come up with demonstrated some kind of rebellion along with the need to destroy villains. This was not a surprise to me, and I suppose it's entirely possible that I couldn't find what I was looking for because I didn't want to find it. It's certainly true that children's stories have been written specifically to teach beneficial things. But mostly those stories don't last. Adults may see value in them, but children don't. Children are fundamentally pragmatic, and what they don't see value in, they will reject. I took a copy of my picture book *Nellie: A Cat on Her Own* (Farrar) to the four-year-old son of a friend the other day. 'Do you like cats?' I asked him as I handed him the book. 'No,' he said, and dropped the book on the floor. And the only emotion I felt from this exchange was envy.

I would like to say again, quite flatly, that I think social responsibility comes only from practical experience. I believe in Oog and Mog and the lessons about bopping. Oog and Mog did not have storybooks. I learned about bopping from my sister, not from reading. I read all through my childhood, but the only thing I learned from books was the joy of reading. I rejected stories, like *The Water Babies* and *Pinocchio*, that attempted to teach me how to behave. I relished the stories, like *Alice in Wonderland* and *The Secret Garden* and *Mary Poppins*, which confirmed my belief that breaking other people's rules is a fine thing when good things come of it. But I didn't go around, therefore, in my real life, breaking rules. As children go, I was a very good child. If my mother had told me to stay away from the secret garden, it would still be a tangle of weeds today. But I broke rules along with my stories' heroes and heroines on a regular basis and got a great deal of vicarious satisfaction from it.

Yes, our society is messy; yes, our children need to learn to care for each other and to be, in short, socially responsible. But in all our zeal, I hope we can find a way to teach them without destroying more than we create. I hope our teachers will find a way to keep on reading great children's stories aloud in their classrooms for no other reason than the joy those stories will bring. I hope the subsequent book discussions will stick to the questions raised by the stories themselves and not get guided uncomfortably down other paths. Because if we weigh the stories down with the baggage of unrelated lessons, they will sink and disappear. And then there will be a lot of lamentation in the children's book section of that great library up in heaven where, I like to imagine, Lewis Carroll and J.M. Barrie and E.B. White and Beatrix Potter and Arnold Lobel and Arthur Rackham and Margot Zemach and all others who have added so much to our lives meet every morning for milk and cookies and have a good time talking shop.

A good story is sufficient unto the day. It is complete as it stands. If it has something to teach, let it teach in its own sufficiency. Let it keep its magic and fulfil its purpose. In other words, let it be.

THE IMAGINATIVE USES OF SECRECY IN CHILDREN'S LITERATURE

John Daniel Stahl

Secrecy in children's literature is an enlightening conspiracy between adult author and child reader. In the process of creating, discovering, and keeping secrets, the child reader finds ways to grow as an individual and as a social being. To the adult author, the writing of stories about secrets and secrecy offers the dual pleasure of recapturing childhood states of mind and of commenting on the limitations of childhood. Children's literature that deals with secrecy therefore frequently reveals a dual perspective: the naive but authentic internal perspective of childhood, and the experienced though also limited external perspective of adulthood, sometimes indulgent or ironic, frequently affectionate or nostalgic.

The idea of secrecy appeals to adults occasionally, not only to children. What then are the distinctive functions of secrecy for the young reader? It is clear that secrecy and mystery have for young readers the sort of universal appeal that can be exploited by formula fiction. Witness the many books of the Hardy Boys and the Nancy Drew series, as well as many of the books on the mystery shelves of the juvenile department of our libraries. But secrecy is not the province only of cheap mysteries, just as romantic love is not the subject matter only of shallow romances. Secrecy, like initiation or death, is a theme capable of being treated banally or brilliantly. It has the special quality of paradoxically symbolizing not only the author's relation to the reader (reading is an act of entering into a shared consciousness with the writer—a shared 'secret'), but also the adult author's relation to the child as character and as reader. The author of a children's book re-enacts the mysterious truth that one consciousness can contain another. The child's secret becomes the adult's stated truth.

Secrecy is often the child's method of declaring and developing his or her individuality and independence. Louise Fitzhugh's treatment of a child's secrecy is particularly trenchant in part because her narrative perspective is free of condescension. The narrator in *Harriet the Spy* approximates Harriet's point of view, as Virginia L. Wolf has pointed out.[1] Harriet's 'spying' is really curiosity masked in secrecy; Harriet wants to find out without being found out. Her explorations of various people's lives serve the function of helping her to grow in awareness of the options of adult identity, of what directions she can take in the process of becoming. Secrecy, especially the privacy of her notebooks, is important to her because she needs the opportunity of judging without shaping her responses to the expectations of others, adults and peers. Her notebooks allow her to assess potential adult role models and to criticize cowardice, stupidity, and other faults in her classmates and friends. Fitzhugh emphasizes this function of secrecy by satiric portrayals of adult foibles.

As long as Harriet's thoughts remain secret, she can be honest. The loss of the protection of secrecy leads to a compromise of her integrity. She must pretend to be sorry for what she wrote in order to win back her friends. Though the repudiation of the honesty of her confidences to herself is a necessary compromise for the sake of social growth, through her notebooks Harriet is able to develop her skills as a writer and to explore her perceptions and emotions through her secret dialogue with herself. Many readers of *Harriet the Spy* report starting a journal like Harriet's after reading the book as children, which suggests that the secrecy of Harriet's writing offers children a form of self-realization to emulate.

'Secret' can be synonymous with knowledge. When Harriet is spying on the bed-loving Mrs Plumber, she overhears the following conversation:

> 'Well,' Mrs Plumber was saying decisively into the telephone, '*I* have discovered the *secret of life*.'
> Wow, thought Harriet.
> 'My dear, it's very simple, you just *take* to your *bed*. You just refuse to leave it for *anything* or *anybody*.'
> Some secret, thought Harriet; that's the dumbest thing I ever heard of.

Harriet is disappointed. She recognizes that this adult's knowledge is clearly affectation or stupidity or both. On the other hand, Mata Hari is a model Harriet is eager to imitate, even when it means learning the—to her—odious skill of dancing. Mata Hari's secret identity and activities guarantee the integrity of her character for Harriet. By testing adults' various kinds of knowledge against her own judgement, Harriet approaches, very imperfectly, to be sure, the Dostoevskian command to love everything and perceive the divine mystery in things.

Through secrecy, children may seek a knowledge of their own which is sometimes forbidden or in danger of being abused by adults. In Frances

Hodgson Burnett's *The Secret Garden*, the garden is a place of privacy which needs to be hidden from adults. The garden is directly connected to the awakening of Mary's imagination, and with the development of her own personality:

> The Secret Garden was what Mary called it when she was thinking of it. She liked the name, and she liked still more the feeling that when its beautiful old walls shut her in no one knew where she was. It seemed almost like being shut out of the world in some fairy place. The few books she read and liked had been fairy-story books, and she had read of secret gardens in some of the stories. Sometimes people went to sleep in them for a hundred years, which she had thought must be rather stupid. She had no intention of going to sleep, and, in fact, she was becoming wider awake every day she passed at Misselthwaite.

In the garden Mary discovers for herself purposeful activity and fulfilment. 'If no one found out about the secret garden, she should enjoy herself always,' the narrator says, from Mary's perspective. The garden is imaginatively transformed into a magical realm, a place where Colin eventually grows toward healing. Identification with Mary and Colin's pleasure in preserving and enjoying their secret paradise can be a cathartic experience for readers of the book, because the garden is synonymous not only with growth in nature and of personality but with liberation from adult restraints and inner bonds of self-pity and defeat. Burnett achieves a complex rapport with the reader partly because she shows us Mary and Colin truthfully as they appear from an external perspective ('she was a disagreeable child') and sympathetically from within.[2]

Often secrecy in a children's story is not created by the children who are the main characters. In many mystery stories the secret lies in the outside world and presents itself as a puzzle to be solved. Both the inner secrecy (the child's creation) and the outer secrecy (a mystery in the larger world which calls for the child's discovery or quest for discovery) represent ways of ordering experience into meaningful patterns. To give an example of what is here meant by outer secrecy, in the story *The Horse Without a Head* by Paul Berna, a band of children lose their beloved three-wheeled metal horse to mysterious and threatening thieves who apparently place an extremely high value on the battered old toy. The question which the story's events pose and around which the book is structured is, why do the thieves want a seemingly worthless rattle-trap tricycle? The adults are not overly concerned about it all, until it turns out that the horse contains (literally) a key which leads to the solution of an adult mystery. The presence of something unexplained, the effort to find clues about the explanation, and finally the discovery of the desired answer: this sequence in a story is appealing because it is in fact the pattern of such a large part of growing up. Moreover, in recapitulating and symbolizing processes of learning and of the formation of purposeful, goal-oriented activity, the unriddling of mysteries offers a variation of the 'principle of hope' (Ernst Bloch's phrase). Like the punishment of evildoers or the successful performance of a trial task in the folktale, the pursuit, discovery, or protection of secrets of literary stories for older children have hermeneutic potential.

Often children who are concerned with secrets will form clubs or gangs at the same time. Private secrets represent the development of an individual identity; shared secrets often denote a shared identity. In *Huckleberry Finn*, Tom Sawyer organizes a band of boys, to be called Tom Sawyer's Gang, which requires an oath and one's name written in blood for admission.

> Everybody was willing. So Tom got out a sheet of paper that he had wrote the oath on and read it. It swore every boy to stick to the band, and never tell any of the secrets; and if anybody done anything to any boy in the band, whichever boy was ordered to kill that person and his family must do it, and he mustn't eat and mustn't sleep till he had killed them and hacked a cross in their breasts, which was the sign of the band. And nobody that didn't belong to the band could use that mark, and if he did he must be sued; and if he done it again he must be killed. And if anybody that belonged to the band told secrets, he must have his throat cut, and then have his carcass burnt up and the ashes scattered all around, and his name blotted off the list with blood and never mentioned again by the gang, but have a curse put on it and be forgot, for ever.[3]

Mark Twain had captured with comic accuracy the intense seriousness of children's preoccupation with cementing social ties of their own creation, in fantastic mimicry of romanticized adult models. But the very straightforwardness of Huck's—and Twain's—reporting of these activities itself signals an adult amusement at childish innocence, and invites knowing hilarity without deflating naive identity. The contradiction of thinking of themselves as robbers and murderers (i.e., outlaws) and yet wishing to have recourse to suing in a court of law if their sign is used improperly, of forming an antisociety, may or may not be evident to any particular child reader.

The gang is the juvenile replica of adult society, on a smaller scale. Often the gang requires that its activities be clandestine because it seeks to elude adult supervision. Erich Kästner's classic German children's novel *Emil and the Detectives* furnishes an example. Kästner recreates the state of mind of the child who cannot confide certain difficulties to any adult. When Emil wakes up in a train and finds that the money which was pinned inside his coat pocket has been stolen, he is terrified, because he feels he cannot call the police to aid him even though the loss of the money is a very serious matter. Emil has a guilty conscience because he defaced a monument in the park, and expects to be accused and jailed if caught. This is what he thinks:

> Now, to top it all, he had to get mixed up with the police, and naturally Officer Jeschke could keep silent no longer but would have to admit officially, 'I don't know why, but that schoolboy, Emil Tischbein of Neustadt, doesn't quite please me. First he daubs up noble monuments. And then he allows himself to be robbed of a hundred and forty marks. Perhaps they weren't stolen at all?
>
> 'A boy who daubs up monuments will tell lies. I have had experience with that. Probably he has buried the money in the woods or has swallowed it and plans to go to America with it. There's no sense trying to capture the thief, not the slightest. The boy Tischbein himself is the thief. Please, Mr Chief of Police, arrest him.'
>
> Horrible! He could not even confide in the police!

But he can confide in other children. In the metropolis of Berlin, he meets a gang of boys and girls who, once initiated into the difficulties of the situation, organize into a spy ring which eventually tracks down and delivers the thief to justice. All of this happens without adult assistance, and on the sly, of course. The book is the adventurous history of Emil's voyage away from home, alone, into independence from the adult world through the assistance of his peers. The reader's imaginative participation in fictional gangs such as Emil's can be a form of vicarious socialization. The secrecy and self-sufficiency of clandestine children's groups in stories is a form of empowerment of the younger generation. Kästner recognizes and, like Twain, affectionately mocks the tendency of children to mimic adult behavior, for instance in nicknames such as 'Professor' and in Emil's cousin Pony Hütchen's ironic formality.

The gang and the secret code are not, of course, desired by all children. In Nina Bawden's *The White Horse Gang*, despite the title, the gang is a loose organization with plenty of internal conflict. Bawden presents the variety of attitudes children at different stages of social development have toward secret organizations. The gang is begun at Rose's suggestion, and neither Sam nor Abe (her friends) are enthusiastic.

> They both looked at Sam. 'All right,' he said. 'We'll call it the White Horse Gang. And we got to have a secret sign.'
>
> Giggling, Rose placed her left forefinger against the side of her nose. Sam suggested that they should use the other hand at the same time, and pull the lobe of the right ear, but Abe said they didn't want to make it too obvious.
>
> 'And we'll sign our names backwards,' Rose said. She looked blissfully happy, so happy that neither boy could bring himself to protest that this was a childish device. They practised with a pencil stub on an old bus ticket Sam had in his pocket. Esor and Mas and Eba. 'That's lovely,' Rose sighed. ''Course, we ought really to sign in *blood*.'
>
> 'Blood's for kids,' Sam said. He had once got a septic finger from pricking and extracting blood for this purpose. 'What we want more is a *reason*.'

In its portrayal of the conflicts that separate and distress the members of the White Horse Gang, Nina Bawden's book is more psychologically realistic than Erich Kästner's smooth-working, effective Robin-Hood-style gang; Kästner's book is in this respect closer to fantasy. But whether in realistic or in mythic guise, the fantasy is of a kind very appealing to children; it has a great deal of resonance in children's experiences. The secret club or gang appeals to dream-wishes for group identity, and represents an early recognition of the truth that there is strength in numbers. The secret organization provides readers with fantasy versions of substitute families and of social roles among one's peers which are not determined or monitored by adults.

Secrecy is a means for fictional characters to create a meaningful sense of self, frequently in productive, not necessarily hostile, opposition to grown-ups or rivals. One value of such themes lies in children's being encouraged to imagine similar sources of self-awareness in their own lives. In Astrid Lindgren's *Bill Bergson Lives Dangerously* some of the appeals of secret signs, secret languages, and secret organizations are made more explicit than in many books for children, surely one of the reasons for the popularity of Lindgren's work. The book opens with the war of the Red Roses against the White Roses, and it becomes clear that the war and the mystery surrounding it, especially the secrecy about the totemic object called the Great Mumbo, are ways of introducing purpose and entertainment into random, dull experience: 'Bill grinned contentedly. The War of the Roses, which with short interruptions had been raging for several years, was nothing one voluntarily denied oneself. It provided excitement and gave real purpose to the summer vacation, which otherwise might have been rather monotonous.'

The Whites (with whom the story is primarily concerned) have a secret language, which involves doubling each consonant and placing an 'o' in between. The Whites can flaunt their identity with their secret language: 'There was no surer way of annoying the Reds. Long and in vain they had tried to decipher this remarkable jargon which the Whites spoke with the greatest facility, chattering at such insane speed that to the uninitiated it sounded like perfect babel'. When the Reds capture and interrogate Anders, the leader of the Whites, he does not reveal any secrets under 'torture'.

Lindgren's narrative perspective does not disguise adult awareness of children's maintenance of secrets. In fact, it acknowledges secrecy as the child's way of creating self-identity; but the open, indulgent attitude of the adult narrator defuses potential conflicts between generations. Eva-Lotta, a member of the Whites, meets her mother in the market place. When asked where she is going, Eva-Lotta says, 'That I must not tell. . . . I'm on a secret mission. Terribly secret mission!' Despite Eva-Lotta's refusal to tell, the exchange between mother and daughter is affectionate and amusing:

> Mrs Lisander smiled at Eva-Lotta.
> 'I love you,' she said.
> Eva-Lotta nodded approvingly at this indisputable statement and continued on her way across the square, leaving a trail of cherry stones behind her.

Her mother's acceptance of Eva-Lotta's rights to have secrets is a liberating, loving attitude. That the secret mission represents the development of an independent personality is suggested by Mrs Lisander's concerned thoughts about her daughter: 'How thin the girl looked, how small and defenceless somehow! It wasn't very long since that youngster had been eating biscuit porridge, and now she was tearing about on "secret errands"—was that all right, or ought she to take better care of her?'

But Eva-Lotta's experiences are narrated also from a perspective that implies the child's need and ability to face danger on her own. For a while, a secret box, containing mysterious documents, is the object of an entertaining struggle between the Reds and the Whites. But secrecy only comes into full play in a dangerous situation when Eva-Lotta is alone with a murderer in an abandoned house. The murderer has every reason to kill her: she holds the key to knowledge of his guilt. When Anders and Bill arrive in this frightening situation, she communicates with them through secret signs: with the danger sign, then with a song in secret codes that tells the boys that the man is a murderer. The boys respond with another secret sign (pinching the lobes of their ears) which means that they have picked up the information. Here, quite explicitly, children have to protect themselves from harm from the adult world through the code they have created. Secrecy is necessary for self-preservation, just as in *Nobody's Family Is Going to Change* the 'Children's Army' has to conceal its existence from adults in order to function effectively as a children's rights advocacy organization.

Lindgren, like many other of the best of children's authors, is able to convey the comic incongruities of childhood experiences without diminishing their significance. In the final chapter of *Bill Bergson Lives Dangerously*, after the murderer has been captured, the Whites teach the Reds their secret language. Bill explains why: 'We can't have it on our consciences, letting the Reds walk about in such dreadful ignorance. They'll be absolutely done for if they ever get mixed up with a murderer.' Though that statement may strike an adult reader as comic, murder is not minimized in the book. Eva-Lotta's reaction to finding the body of the murderer's victim is a state of shock that realistically lasts several days. Despite the implausibilities of the plot, the theme of secrecy is treated with a seriousness that does justice to its importance as a means of achieving identity and as a defense against the danger of harm by powerful adversaries.

Secrecy in children's literature, in a variety of forms, emphasizes the ambivalent consciousness of the adult author writing for children. The adult, having once been a child, has access to memories of childhood in the form of internalized experience—the alter ego that always remains a child within us. But the adult writer also has a mature and sophisticated consciousness that analyses the child's experience and the child's placement in many contexts of family, society, psychological and moral development, inheritance, and environment. The triumph of the spirit in children's literature that reflects children's preoccupation with secrecy lies in skilled authors' ability to combine the dual perspectives of childhood and adulthood in an instructive tension. At the root of this illuminating tension lies respect for the development of the child's personal and social identity. Sympathetically conceived works of fiction invite imaginative participation in the experiences of fictional characters who create and discover secrets. Like fairy tales, stories about secrets and secrecy have imaginative connections with children's psychological and social development which go beyond the literary qualities of particular stories. But the artistry of works such as those discussed here connects the private world of the child's imagination with the reality of experience and with the realm of all great literature.

Notes

[1]'The novel does not attempt to portray reality fully or journalistically. It is rooted in Harriet's experience, and that is a limited experience. If, then, characters seem like caricatures or types, this is justified. We can only experience them when and as Harriet does. The merits of this limited point of view result from the distortion it causes.' Virginia Wolf, 'Harriet the Spy: Milestone, Masterpiece?' in *Children's Literature* 4 (1975), 123. See also Wolf's article, 'The Root and Measure of Realism,' in *Wilson Library Bulletin* 44 (1969).

[2](Philadelphia and New York: J.B. Lippincott, 1911). In a symbolic and disappointing way, the garden eventually opens up to include not only virtually every character previously outside it but also the gender and class values of élite Victorian society. See Elizabeth Lennox Keyser, '"Quite Contrary": Frances Hodgson Burnett's *The Secret Garden*,' in *Children's Literature* 11 (1983). As U.C. Knoepflmacher's discussion of Burnett's 'Behind the White Brick' suggests, secrecy in Victorian children's stories can exist in a subversive association with aggressions sublimated into dreams ('Little Girls without Their Curls: Female Aggression in Victorian Children's Literature,' in *Children's Literature* 11 [1983], 26).

[3]In a discussion of children's oaths, Iona and Peter Opie write, 'it should be emphasized that the asseverations in the following pages (mostly collected from ten- to eleven-year-olds) are not treated lightly by those who use them. An imprecation such as "May I drop down dead if I tell a lie" is liable to be accorded the respect of its literal meaning, and distinct uneasiness may follow its utterance, even when the child concerned is fairly certain that he has not departed from the truth' (*The Lore and Language of Schoolchildren* [Oxford: Clarendon Press, 1959], 121).

An Eye for Thresholds

Tim Wynne-Jones

In Peter Dickinson's award winning novel, *Tulku*, there is a tense moment when bandits catch up to young Theodore, the book's protagonist, and his two companions, backing them up against a deep gorge over which a rope bridge leads from China to Tibet. The bridge is in use, blocked by a Lama and his party coming over into China. As it turns out, through the Lama's intervention, the bandits are scared off. But there can be no going back for Theodore and company. They must cross the bridge into Tibet leaving everything behind. Theodore has little enough substance to go back to but he is leaving behind his adopted home and his past. It is a passage, then, of some moment. Dickinson writes:

> The Yak-drivers they had met on their way to the valley had said that there was no real border. The Lama waved a vague hand eastward and explained that two whole provinces had been stolen by China a hundred years before, so Theodore's party had really been travelling in Tibet for many days. But for Theodore the border lay, sharp as a shore-line, at the bridge. *From then on the grammar of all things, large and small, changed.* [my italics].

Crossing the bridge, Theodore enters 'the enormous sharp-seen distance'. He will never be the same again. The grammar of his life, the seemingly insignificant little events, the units of time with which we measure off the diurnal cycle—all this has changed; he will see everything in a new light. He has crossed a very real Threshold. Had Dickinson not pointed this out to us, the adolescent reader would have been very likely to recognize it as such. Threshold recognition is one of the joys of literature. 'Hark! We are this very minute entering a new stage in the life of the character or the drama (and, most likely, both).'

In addressing the notion of 'Somewhere meant for me', I have chosen to hover on the Threshold, looking forward and backward, furtively, and considering the nature of boundaries and limits, real or imaginary.

'How concrete everything becomes in the world of the spirit when an object, a mere door, can give images of hesitation, temptation, desire, security, welcome and respect,' says Gaston Bachelard in *The Poetics of Space*. He adds: 'If one were to give an account of all the doors one has closed and opened, of all the doors one would like to re-open, one would have to tell the story of one's whole life.

'But is he who opens a door and he who closes it the same being?'

That is what Thresholds are all about in literature. A Threshold is the physical manifestation of change. Inasmuch as the image of the Threshold is stoutly conceived, it is as physical—as real—as any doorway of wood or steel, for the memory is reductive; the real and the fictional are rendered down to impulses. One must 'imagine' the real doorways of one's life and as such they end up being stored alongside the ones we read about in books. The past renders them equal in substance though one is more likely to recall the literal doorway more vividly for, assuming the writer/creator had some gift of style, these doors were probably built to be remembered. Art is like that.

The Poetics of Space is a book of philosophy which has had the most profound influence on me as a writer. It is, among other things, about the space occupied by memory, a space not measured in brain cell dimensions, or hiatic gaps. Memory, according to Bachelard, is stored in rooms and cupboards and playing fields. Bachelard sees one's life as a series of rooms, of places to put things, or to curl up in, or to carry a candle to. He talks about nests and shells and corners and in the next-to-last chapter, he looks at 'The dialectics of outside and inside'. It takes Bachelard nearly a whole book to get to the subject of Thresholds. He quotes Georges Spyridaki: 'My house is diaphanous, but it is not of glass. It is more of the nature of vapour. Its walls contract and expand as I desire.'

From the time I was about eight I wanted to be an architect. I discovered, to my horror, about by my third year at architecture school, that to be an architect was to put up walls, to disconnect spaces, one from the other, to remove the possibility of getting from here to there. All along I had liked most those rooms one occasionally finds in the woods, if one looks hard enough. Rooms constructed by a geometry of leaves and dead logs and light. One leaves such a found-room only after having absorbed the sense of it and one leaves only the sense of it behind. The next woods-walker might pass through the room without knowing it there at all. Walls which contract and expand as I desire.

I realized by my third year at architecture school that I was interested mainly in an architecture of the spirit. There was a time after I left architecture school to become a musician, then an art student, and finally a lecturer in art, when I would turn to architecture for solace in times of despair. I would design a house on paper, in greater and greater detail depending directly on the length and breadth of my depression. It was in just such a state that I 'built' *Odd's End*. I actually did build it, ⅜"-to-the-foot, but I still could not dispel the gloom of a failing relationship and having just served a two-year term at York University Penitentiary getting my MFA. I needed to inhabit the house I had made and since I could not make myself small enough—not quite—I wrote a book and moved in. It is a book about a couple predisposed to distrust one another and an intruder, a Mr X., who capitalizes on this and comes between them. He wants their home to himself! The German title for the book was *Der ungebitten dritte*— the uninvited third. But there are really four characters in *Odd's End*: Mary, Malcolm, Mr X., and the house itself. I've been writing ever since I built Odd's End and everything I write has to do with architecture. Indeed, my next picture book, to be illustrated by Ian Wallace, is entitled *The Architect of the Moon*. It takes place in a child's bedroom and then in the room where the moon lives.

Doorways are no less crucial in stories than in the architecture of stone and wood. Indeed, as I have mentioned, we are inclined to notice the fictional threshold more readily than the real ones we cross for granted. Let us look at some solidly built doorways in children's literature. There is the doorway in Shirley Hughes's *Alfie Gets in First*, for instance. Nothing could be more solid, more familiar, or more threatening than that door to Alfie's own house! Alfie has raced Mom and Annie Rose home. Mom brings up the groceries to the hall and goes back to retrieve Annie Rose from the stroller, when, with the winner's zeal, Alfie closes the door—slam, bam! Mom's keys are inside with Alfie. He cannot reach the door knob. He cannot reach the letter-chute; he is locked inside and his own house home is quite suddenly a jail. Well, he gets out. Half the neighbourhood congregates on the front stoop to solve the problem, but Alfie figures out his own escape and in so doing crosses a Threshold of signal importance. With the help of his chair he reaches the lock. He is taller for the experience. The real Threshold coincided with a symbolic crossing-over, as well it might.

In my own book, *I'll make you small*, illustrated by Maryann Kovalski, when Roland finally has the nerve (and the excuse) to visit the crotchety and reclusive Mr Swanskin, his next door neighbour, he finds the door opens easily—a little too easily, on a rusty hinge. Faced with an open door, it is difficult to turn back. It is a long way through Swanskin's house to the room where the old man works but the light shining in the workroom doorway draws little Roland forward like a beacon despite his growing trepidation. He wants to cross the Threshold.

We come across a door as seemingly impenetrable as Alfie's in John Rowe Townsend's *The Intruders*. The whole book has a lot to do with home and hearth and belonging but the Threshold to which I refer is not the one to the protagonist's threatened house. The doorway of which I speak is not met until the climax of the book. Arnold Haithwaite has narrowly escaped death at the hands of the intruders of the book's title but now faces the equally awful prospect of death by drowning in the mounting tide of the Skirl estuary. He has made it as far as Saint Brendan's church, once on an island but now 'the church in the sea' and long since deconsecrated and deserted. There he finds Jane, who herself is cut off from the mainland. She is a powerful swimmer but the storm and the tide have made swimming to safety impossible. As the water rises around them, Arnold casts back in his mind for an image:

> . . . a fleeting image from years before . . . Ted Whitson, the council bricklayer, surrounded by children—Arnold one of them—and filling in the archway, the archway to the stumpy useless [church] tower.

To find that bricked-in entranceway in the 'blank unyielding wall' of the tower is their only hope. Having found it, Arnold must bust his way in with a boulder, hurling it at the wall, again and again, and hurling abuse at the sea and the rock and the church as he does so: 'He swore between blows, swore at the top of his voice, swore and hit, swore and hit.'

They get in, Arnold and Jane, and are saved. Arnold breaks a hole clear through the storm. There is some tenderness between them—the tenderness of thankfulness. But in rupturing the walled-in Threshold of that tower, Arnold has forever revealed to Jane who he is and he is not someone she can ever really know; nor she him. The tower is a powerful image of Arnold's angry solitude.

Mr Townsend says something wonderful as Arnold rescues Jane: 'Arnold was dragging her through the hole, through water, through panic and despair and death and resurrection all in a second.' There is this about Thresholds: one is born through them and one dies through them. And it all happens in an instant.

There is a sensational birth in Jan Andrews's and Ian Wallace's *The Very Last First Time*, which, incidentally, takes place at the rising of the tide. Eva Padlyat, an Inuit girl, has gone below the ice at low tide to collect mussels. The netherworld beneath the ice captivates her, she loses her way, drops her candle, hears the tide coming in—is panic-stricken. But then she finds the hole she has cut through the ice and her mother drags her out. It is a rebirth, an apotheosis crowned by the sun in Ian's breath-taking illustration.

Death appears at the doorway, not always in black with a scythe; sometimes as radiant with light as Eva on the ice under the midnight sun. In Jill Paton Walsh's *A Parcel of Patterns*, death is everywhere, the town of Eyam is under the siege of the plague. Apart from laying her family in the grave, the plague has kept apart our narrator, Mall, from her beloved Thomas, who lives in the next village. Believing Mall to have died, Thomas crosses the border, crosses the brink: 'Then he plunged over the scarp, and lurched like the land, downwards, running, arms spread like a bird starting into flight. . . .' He finds Mall very much alive and since he is there and cannot cross back over the boundary which quarantines the dying village, the two are married, finding something of joy in the desperate little valley town. In the brief happy period of their marriage, Mall describes Thomas arriving home:

> He would be rimmed with gold, for the setting sun would catch upon his golden head and the red-gold hair upon his wrists and arms, and bleach his shepherd's smock, and dazzle me. But though he stood in shade, or in rainlight, or in the summer darkness in the gardenside, I saw him always as apparelled in celestial light, and I warmed like a sunlit stone when he drew near me.

What could be more beautiful or sensual than this description of her lover returning home and framed in the doorway? It is foreshadowing. And how horrifying it is when that same wreathed figure arrives at the same doorway only a few pages later and says to Mall: 'Sing me that air again, sweet Mouse.' And Mall looks up, startled, for she had not been singing and a deadly calm engulfs her as she tries to sing the song he has thought he heard her singing all the way down the street, drawing him home. But of course the song he heard was not one for which Mall knows the words. She and the reader recognize the signs. He is dying. Mall does not waste much of her journal or the patience of the reader describing her last week with Thomas. The image we are left with is of Thomas on the brink of death, apparelled in celestial light. Almost an angel.

Not all boundaries are as visible as a deeply cut gorge in the Himalayas or, for that matter, as visible as a simple doorway into a cottage. I would like to give a rather disturbing image, not from fiction but from my adolescence (which may very well prove to have been a fictional time in the final reckoning of things!). I recall the rather extraordinary home of my high school girlfriend. Physically it was very plain though it had flat roofs, which for Ottawa was different, which is to say, not very sensible. When it snowed too much someone would have to get up on the roof and shovel off the snow and when it was icy the ice on the roof would crack like a gunshot. I remember this as a deterrent to advanced amorous activity. There was a very old grandfather in the house who might have been fascinating had he ever spoken. I recall only one such occasion over Campbell's Scotch Broth and a cheese sandwich on plain-white store-brought bread.

My sweetheart proved to be far too smart for me: she became a professor of statistics. But there was one thing about the memory of her and that time and that flat-roofed house that will always remain enigmatic for me: an older sister who had suffered a nervous breakdown. I was then, as I am now, drawn to psychological dysfunction. This sister did not manifest much in the way of hysteria but she did exhibit a marked inability to walk through doorways. I recall vividly watching her enter the television room off the dining room. It had double glass doors, both wide open, but she stood on the Threshold for several moments, swaying, held back, before at last breaking through whatever barrier there was there for her. I could not see her face from where I sat but I'm sure she must have squeezed her eyes shut before she could take the step. It is the kind of step one takes in a dream, like Alice down the rabbit hole. Doorways required a major commitment from my sweetheart's sister. Perhaps for her, each doorway represented a little death.

From an early age I sensed with mingled dread and delight those little deaths which are everywhere to be found in children's books. I am not the only one who has commented on this but for a long time I was sure that it was a morbid obsession peculiar to myself.

Particularly I recall George MacDonald's *The Princess and the Goblin*, when the princess, bored, finds a stairway she has not seen before. She mounts the stairs and goes up and up until she arrives at a place where there was 'nothing but passages and doorways everywhere!' After travelling in circles and crying her eyes out she finally does notice a door to a stairway around a corner, half open. 'But alas! the stairs went the wrong way. They went up!'

Uh oh! There was and is only so far you can go upstairs before arriving in Heaven or a reasonable facsimile thereof. Perhaps, unconsciously, I was alerted to the special nature of these stairs by the lack of description MacDonald provides the reader. The stairs don't have a colour; the light is not described as falling on them in any particular pattern, if there is light at all. They are not made of any material. The stairs don't squeak or creak. Not a good sign. Mind you, I was not displeased or even frightened. I took it calmly. I hadn't known the princess long enough at that point in the story to mourn her passing. The fact that she returned to the nursery didn't fool me for a minute. She was dead; the rest was but a dream. There are certain passages in fiction, movements into certain places which strike me with unexpected force and which I can only assume represent a kind of modified dying. The death may be only the death of innocence.

In Maurice Sendak's *Outside Over There*, Ida's baby sister is carried off by goblins. Ida must think quickly and, as it turns out, she thinks too quickly:

> Now Ida in a hurry
> snatched her Mama's yellow rain cloak,
> and made a serious mistake.
> She climbed backwards out her window
> into outside over there.

'Outside over there' sounds remarkably like the end-of-the-line to this ear for Thresholds. In an extensive interview in Jonathan Cott's *Pipers at the Gates of Dawn*, Sendak says: 'If I had died of a heart attack in 1967, my career would have ended with *Higglety Pigglety Pop!*—a book that's all about death. And even in a comic work like *Really Rosie*, all that the characters talk about is death—the whole thing is a theme and variations on how many ways you can die.'

Sendak goes on to talk about how characters in the works of Kleist confront an overwhelming situation by fainting or swooning. He says 'And in a sense, this blacking out is a form of dying. Something happens which is so terrible—it's like a Gorgon's Head—that when you look at it, it kills you. But you wake up as if in another life, refreshed—you wake up better for having died.'

Sleeping, dreaming, dying—writers can be frustratingly gratuitous about using these terms interchangeably. But then if one is not the same person who closes the door as the person who entered it then that other person must have died. And, come to think of it, wouldn't you die rather happily if in so doing you could fly to Neverland and never grow up? And isn't it true that in order to stop growing up or older one must stop altogether?

What, I can't help wondering, would Bachelard have made of *Outside Over There*? Ida's journey takes her out and down and through and in and back. Sendak himself says it is such a spatially convoluted story it might as well be called 'Inside in here'. There is about Thresholds this ambiguity of which way is in and which way is out. Ambiguity, as Carl Jung has pointed out, is the nature of the true symbol. Arnold Haithwaite and Jane are prisoners *outside* the tower. Alfie is a prisoner *inside* his own home, because a good deal of what makes home home to a child—*mother*—is outside.

These words, from Pierre Albert Birot's *Les amusements naturels*, stand at the Threshold of Bachelard's opening chapter in *The Poetics of Space*:

At the door of the house who will come knocking?
An open door, we enter
A closed door, a den
The world pulse beats beyond my door.

A pulse outside of oneself. As if one were in the womb surrounded by the pulse of an all-engulfing mother one has never seen but upon whom one depends entirely for sustenance. One is poised on the Threshold of life waiting to be born. It's an ongoing process. Some of us are not happy unless we are born over and over again, still trying to get it right. In *Outside Over There*, Sendak was born again. It was for him a story about 'dissolution, the eradication and conquest of fear and depression, of hallucination, of obsessions, of neurosis—breaking through and making it literally disappear by one's own act. . . '. In the five years from the conception of *Outside Over There* to its birth, Sendak was able, through therapy, to overcome a long-standing depression. It took him a great deal longer than Ida who made her trip in the twinkling of an eye.

Thresholds. Boundaries. Kathy Lowinger at the Canadian Children's Book Centre made an interesting point when I mentioned the topic of my paper. In an immigrant nation, she suggested, Canada, itself, is a Threshold. Having crossed a Threshold is an integral part of our collective consciousness. Needless to say, this sense of a new arrival finds its way into the literature of the country. In Barbara Smucker's *Underground to Canada*, there is a Threshold early in the story as young Julily decides to make her break from slavery. It is a Threshold which might lead to death or freedom, but these were precisely the choices to many early Canadians and some very new immigrants, it would seem. So, like Theodore in *Tulku*, who had been travelling in Tibet for many days without knowing it, Julily had been travelling in freedom for many days, but needed that second tangible Threshold, the border, in order for the grammar of her life to change in some meaningful way. A political boundary as insubstantial as it may be when it is not walled or patrolled by armed soldiers still makes real the abstract quality of Freedom.

The experience of the immigrant once he is safely landed is another kind of Threshold: the Threshold of non-acceptance/acceptance, of not being understood/being understood. Social mores and customs come complete with walls which must be breached. It's a two-way street, this doorway. In this country's children's literature, if the truth be told, there is a great deal of tokenism with regard to mutual awareness between people of differing ethnic, racial, or religious backgrounds. There are by now a great number of token Sikhs and Greeks trapped in styleless tracts sitting about on high school book shelves waiting for a sensitive and well-informed teacher to lend life to their tales. Didactic literature depends on a support system in order to breathe. However, there are very moving exceptions to this triviality, notably, Joy Kogawa's *Naomi's Road*, which deals with the experience of a Japanese Canadian child interned during the Second World War. Kogawa is a fine writer, which is the difference between her book and those written by good-hearted, well-intentioned moralizers.

Another quite good exception to the rule of mediocrity in the immigrant experience is one of the short stories in Nazneen Sadiq's *Camels Can Make You Homesick*. In the story, 'The shonar arches', Amit, a Canadian child born of Indian parents, is disenchanted by the visit of his grandmother from Bengal and especially by the traditional cooking the visitor and his mother end up doing. Then he is given the golden opportunity to choose where the family might go to dinner one evening. He takes her, as you might guess, to McDonalds, 'the golden arches'. Grandmother is impressed: 'So soft!' she exclaims of her Big Mac, and insists on congratulating the boys and girls behind the counter who have cooked this delicacy. Young Amit's chest swells with pride. The story is called, in a beautiful pun, 'The shonar arches', for grandmother has described, lovingly, the burnished colour of the sun on the fields in her Bengali homeland as 'shonar'. A Threshold is crossed. 'The stranger is invited in.'

Then there is, in this country, the Threshold between the civilized, of which there is very little, and the wilderness, of which there is an enormous lot! This theme is so popular as to have given rise to one of the country's most important critical literary studies, Margaret Atwood's *Survival*. As I said recently in my column in *The Globe and Mail*, 'Writers addressing teen readers seem to find endless inspiration from stranding a youthful protagonist or two in the "monstrous" wilds, there to come to better terms with themselves.' In that same column I reviewed Monica Hughes's *Log Jam*. In *Log Jam* Isaac Manyfeathers

> . . . escapes from a medium-security prison and sets out to find the
> home of his grandmother many hundreds of miles to the north. His

trek becomes a spirit hunt in which, through fasting (literally going out of his mind), Isaac hopes to get in touch with his animal self. Lenora Rydz, 14, is on a different kind of trip altogether, an agonizing camping holiday with her mother, her brand-new stepfather and his two sons.

Chapter by chapter the paths of these two alien beings approach one another, until on the banks of the lonely Brazeau River, where Lenora has been washed ashore after a canoeing accident, they finally meet. The meeting is brilliant and strange, for the memory of both these babes in the wood is compromised; one by starvation, the other by a bump on the head. The surprising series of events that then take place leads each of them to examine the log jam in his or her head, as dangerous as the one which spilled Lenora on her nightmare ride down the Brazeau.

Lenora is 'born[e] down the river'.

Now there are distances which are a great deal larger than the distance between the cities of the east and the great expansive boreal forests of the northwest, and there are lands further apart than India and Canada. Worlds apart. Separated by light years of space or the more impenetrable barrier of Time. Fantasy is all about Thresholds. For, as Sheila Egoff has said, 'Fantasy is a literature of paradox. It is the discovery of the real within the unreal, the credible within the incredible, the believable within the unbelievable. Yet the paradoxes have to be resolved. It is in the interstices between the two halves of the paradox, *on the knife-edge of two worlds, that fantasists build their domain.*' [my italics]

It would be quite easy to write an entire book about the notion of Thresholds in fantastic literature. In time-travel, for instance, it is the manipulation of the mechanism of travel, whether it be a machine, a door, or a watch ticking off the hours of a summer long past, as in Kit Pearson's recent *A Handful of Time*—whatever the mode of transport may be, the manipulation of the Threshold device is so critical as to determine the success of the book regardless of the writing talents of the author. Logic must be seen to be done justice in the crossing and re-crossing of the Threshold which separates now from wherever it is the writer has spirited us. It is a generalization but I think a safe one that there are always two critical crossings of the Threshold in a time-travel fantasy: the first time the protagonist crosses into the new world and the last time. If loneliness or illness has provoked him or her to cross the Threshold in the first instance, there is inevitably a greater dilemma in store, compelling the protagonist to go or stay behind, stranded in the past or the future. Time-travel is, structurally, a literature suspended between Thresholds.

In 'straight' science fiction, Thresholds are often described in great technological detail, from the decorous Second Empire furnishings of Jules Verne's *A Journey to the Moon and a Trip Around It*, right down to the cockpit of a starship about to go into warp-drive. But there are more interesting modes of transportation across the great divide. I myself am partial to the means by which the young Lord Tomi Bentt is forced to leave ArcOne in Monica Hughes's *Devil on My Back*. A shortlived revolution of the slaves in the domed city finds Tomi hiding and then falling down a garbage chute into the wild river (which just might be the Brazeau) and the wilderness outside the city. Tomi tumbles into—well—outside over there. Once again we see the theme which Monica hammers home again and again with great gusto and invention: the necessity of knowing the interface between the wilderness and civilization, between our past and our future, of knowing the interface and establishing intercourse across that border at all cost however inviolate that border may seem to be.

I would like to look now at what Thresholds mean to the writer in the thick of the 'creative process'—or should I say, what Thresholds mean to *this* writer during the fragile period of early gestation when the threat of miscarriage is imminent, when the idea can only sit there in the mind and coaxing it to move anywhere at all is a delicate business, let alone getting it to go 'Somewhere meant for me'. It is from chance bits of dialogue or narrative which occur to one out of nowhere, or snippets of conversation, overheard, or bits of paper which float into the collage of our lives, and which the artist notices and *grasps*—it is precisely from these disconnected and oft-times feeble but nonetheless, to the ready mind, startling discoveries that the artist or writer *begins*. Thresholds are necessary in the creative process in giving an idea somewhere to go. There are doors, of course, windows, and railroads—all of these are Thresholds, *connectors* to other places. And then there are books, and last of all, launching pads—books and launching pads are Thresholds to places of great distance—as far as the mind can see.

I would like to talk about three doors of my own devising: the big front door upon which Zoom knocked in *Zoom at Sea* which was opened by Marie; the little door signposted 'The Northwest Passage', through which Zoom made his way to the Arctic ocean, but which was too small for Maria; and finally, the door through which Zoom is to enter upon his third and last adventure in the book, *Zoom Upstream*, a book for which the bones, the scaffolding, exist—which is to say, the words—waiting only for Ken Nutt (or his friend) to flesh out.

When one is writing one must make certain never to be far from a doorway, or preferably a hallway lousy with doors. How else can your characters get in? There is a gorgeous picture of Edward Gorey's *The Unstrung Harp*, a book all about writing books, in which the author meets one of his characters at the top of the stairs. Presumably he let himself in.

The Obvious is the great bane of the writer, no matter how good he might be. It is like a giant lump and it is in the room with you as you write only waiting to be tripped over. The word comes from the Latin: *ob viam*— that which gets in the way. It is a stifling great pile of a blanc mange, always whispering suggestions: 'Pssst! If this Zoom-cat likes water so much, why don't you take him to the sea and he can rent a fishing boat and. . . .' Sometimes the Obvious oozes in so close, crowding you up against your desk, that 'making leaps' becomes an impossibility. That is when a doorway comes in handy. One simply paints a door on the side of the great white amorphous lumpy Obvious, as does the roadrunner in the cartoons, and runs through it.

When I was writing *Zoom at Sea*, at a crucial moment, with the gooey Obvious already trickling down my shoulders, I recalled Ken Nutt's gorgeous not-so-still-lifes which I had seen in art galleries: large drawings of familiar objects and their shadows rendered in equally intricate detail on spatially shallow shelves where you could keep your eyes on them. I knew that the sea for Zoom, if Ken was to illustrate Zoom, could not be anywhere near any obvious open-ended sea. And simultaneously, I realized that the *right* sea must be contained. From that second the sea was not far really. Zoom could take a bus. I always tell that to writing students: if you are having trouble describing how to get from A to B, maybe you should just take a bus, and have done with it.

Anyway, in climbing off the bus to the sea, Zoom was confronted by a big door. We, me and Zoom, knocked on it together, three times, for all magic comes in threes. We did not have the foggiest idea who would answer. When the door opened, Maria was there. I had the feeling she had been waiting a long time and that her bit of business about having to put her hair up was just a ploy. Ken must have sensed this and consequently never shows her hair undone in the first place!

I cannot say this with more sincerity. The mind of the most boring of God's human creatures is fairly bursting with images to offer up if he or she can find the door behind which they reside. This requires believing in the door and recognizing it when one sees it and then, having the courage to knock on it.

Zoom required considerable courage to enter the door called the Northwest Passage. He has to do it alone, a point I didn't realize in my first draft but which Ken made clear to me. Of course Maria could not reach the North Pole by the same route as Zoom; she is a grown-up, she will have to find her own way, which, of course, she does. She will be there when Zoom is tired. How she gets there is not important to the story any more than how we, as parents, are there when our children need us is important to them. They take us for granted. How she got to the Catship is Maria's story, and might be an interesting one at that, but *Zoom Away* is Zoom's story.

In *Zoom Upstream*, the last of the trilogy, Zoom and Maria are such old friends that the story opens with them together in the backyard on a fall day, raking leaves and planting lily bulbs for the spring. The sun is warm and Zoom takes a nap. When he wakes up, Maria is gone. Luckily for him, she has left muddy footprints back into the house. To the library.

I experimented with other places. I knew the only route left for Zoom was down since we had already sailed over the first floor and hiked to the attic. The question was: how to get down? I didn't want Zoom going into the closet! It seemed far too obvious to march him down to the cellar! And then I realized what the final Threshold *had to* be. A book, or better still the place behind a book, the place where a book was: 'Zoom followed Maria's footsteps to the library. The footsteps ended at a huge book which lay on the carpet. There seemed to be a light coming from the space on the shelf where the book had been.'

Every book is a Threshold. But it must first be taken from the shelf. In Zoom's case, the shelf is high and the book is a step-up. 'This must be the way,' Zoom realizes and sure enough behind the bookshelf is a staircase made entirely of books.

For the young child, the preliterate child, there are really only two kinds of literature as far as I can tell. Those books which mirror the child's life, his environment and expectations, and therefore give him a secure sense of belonging to a society. And those books which are Thresholds to the world beyond the home and his day-to-day experiences: The Arctic Sea, The Nile, The Moon, the house of one's crotchety next-door neighbour—all places about equally as far away for the pre-schooler. This second kind of book is a Threshold book. Just about everything is a Threshold for a six-year-old. And the Threshold is an important concept to get firmly in mind. The Canadian scientist and Nobel laureate, John Polanyi, said recently in an interview: 'It takes a very trained mind to recognize when you have made a discovery. When you cross a Threshold no bells ring.' The real world does not readily reveal its patterns. Fiction, the *shape* of fiction, with its literal Thresholds, trains the mind to recognize Life's invisible truths and thus lends form to the chaos of living. 'Somewhere meant for me' is only reached through many such doorways, both real and fictional. It would seem to be advisable to create picture books for children which ring the bell loudly, that the child, grown-up, might hear the echo down through his life and stop and look around and step forward with courage and cognizance across otherwise invisible Thresholds into Discovery.

Interpreting the Past: Reflections of an Historical Novelist

Joan Aiken

What can we do with the past, that marvellous lumber-room of unused treasures? We can forget it; we can fantasize about it; we can try to recapture it with fidelity.

Our generation is in danger of forgetting it—and, paradoxically, becoming obsessed by it. Children, in particular, need what it has to offer. As a writer of historical novels for children, I believe that fiction can help.

People write historical fiction from a number of different motives, two of which seem primary. One is a true wish to interpret the past and make it visible, intelligible, coherent. The other is to take refuge from the present in a region where the writer may be secure from interference. A number of writers have been activated by both motives—or, in the course of their work, have moved gradually from one to the other.

Like the subconscious, the past lies all around us; and we ignore it for most of the time. In fact, insofar as the subconscious is the aggregate of all our former wishes, experiences, and frustrations, it could be said that history forms the mass subconscious, the underlying source of all our actions.

Yet our own late-20th-century culture is probably less aware of the past, more separated from it, than any previous epoch. True, we have magnificent, unprecedented opportunities for learning about history, geology, and archaeology: we have X-rays and radio-carbon dating and countless erudite and skilful investigators, aided by computers which can collate the result of their researches far more quickly than any human brain. A small percentage of the population knows an enormous amount about the past—more than was known by anyone except those who lived in the period under study, and in some respects even more than they. But knowledge is not always the same as understanding and feeling.

In 'primitive' societies, traditions live on. Peasants in the Indus Valley in present-day Pakistan, for example, make pots, spin, weave, and grind corn exactly as their forebears have done for the past 4,000 years. In the American desert, some tribes of Indians still laboriously collect nuts, bake them, hull them, re-bake the kernels, grind them into paste, and finally cook them into cakes as their ancestors have been doing since the beginning of recorded history.

Most of the industrialized world, by contrast, lives in surroundings that are largely man-made, urban, and brand-new. Many of us give hardly a thought to the past. We are not reminded of it by ancient buildings, family heirlooms or ceremonies, group traditions, domestic or local practices, religious or social rituals, or immemorial landscapes with their trackways and fortifications and boundary marks. Most of us have little information about our ancestors: who they were, where they came from, how they behaved. That is of antiquarian, not practical importance. We don't go into trances and consult them in times of trouble, or look up records to discover how they might have acted in a crisis.

And this is very unnatural. It is the human tendency to imitate one's parent. After the initial rebellion and breakaway in adolescence, most people slowly converge back towards parental habits. As a race, however, as a civilization, we are hardly able to imitate the habits of our predecessors—partly because we are ignorant of them. There is no oral tradition to remind us; and there is a very broad and deep technical gulf.

When Shakespeare wrote *Julius Caesar*, he was portraying a way of life not wholly remote from that of the Elizabethan age. There were climatic differences between Rome and England; the Romans wore togas, not ruffs and doublets. But the Elizabethan audience could envisage Caesar as easily as it could the Merchant of Venice. Both Romans and Elizabethans travelled on horseback or by sailing-ship; they fought their battles mainly with swords, bows and arrows, and spears; they were dressed in wool, linen, and fur; they cooked over wood fires; they wrote with quills; they believed in astrology; they used candles or oil lamps if they worked at night. From 55 BC to 1564 AD—one thousand, six hundred and nineteen years—the circumstances of life changed at a very moderate pace. Add only another four hundred years, and the graph of human discovery has suddenly shot straight upwards. Electricity has arrived; so have radio, television, the telephone, computers, air travel, electronics, and the thermonuclear bomb.

The past has been snatched away. Our daily habits now are the product of this century, or even of this generation. Fashions in living, art, clothes, eating, thinking, medicine, architecture change with such formidable speed that anything two years out of date may seem as archaic as a bygone. 'Dated' has become a term of contempt, not veneration. Machines and utensils are obsolete almost as soon as we have learned to use them.

This notably affects our children. Reared in contemporary surroundings, and on visual images—not those they have read or heard and therefore formed for themselves—they are hardly aware that the past exists, unless they see it artificially preserved behind glass or across neatly mown lawns, on a duty visit to Battle Abbey or Hampton Court.

Yet the landscape of the past is huge, and keeps expanding. As our lives proceed, as we plod through jobs and birthdays and relationships, write a book or a few letters, always growing a little older, the past surges forward to encompass more territory, turning our memories into history. World War II is now thoroughly colonized. The Fifties, the Sixties, the Seventies are fixed, glamorized, and designated as historical periods, like listed buildings or nature conservancy areas. The past is growing behind us faster than we can keep up with it. There is more history than we can ever hope to learn.

This has always been so, in every generation. But I am inclined to think that it is especially true of our own, because we lack routine or ritualistic connections with the past. Like bereaved people who have been allowed no funeral rites, we have become depressed, dispossessed, obsessed. The past we have failed to mourn has returned to haunt us.

Children, in this respect, behave differently from adults. They are less prone to depressions after the death of someone they know or love. Their grief and pain are sharp and overwhelming at the time; but their memories are short and their power of recovery is strong. So, while many adults have an addictive devotion to the past, children may be almost wholly unaware of it.

As adults, we imagine past scenes with intense nostalgia because they have the radiance of unchanging fidelity. They cannot be swept away from us. That convivial lunch party in Hampstead with Wordsworth and Keats, when Charles Lamb got drunk and was so rude to the stamp officer; Cassandra Austen's funeral, when the gusty autumn wind blew beech leaves all over the coffin; the painful, last, silent meeting between those estranged friends, Beau Brummell and the Prince Regent—descriptions of such scenes have wonderful luminosity for us. What scenes from our own time will survive in such lustre? Will there *be* any posterity to contemplate them? Are we the first generation to have wondered that?

Part of the attraction of the past is its safety, its unalterability. It can seem almost cosy, even in its horrors—even the Black Death, the Hundred Years' War, or Buchenwald. It is safe because it is all over now. We know what happened; we can chart it, assess it, turn it into statistics and patterns. It can't get any worse. And even the Spanish Inquisition, the Massacre of St Bartholomew, the Children's Crusade, the Black Hole of

Calcutta, the Charge of the Light Brigade, the Amritsar Massacre, or Auschwitz; none is quite so appalling or terrifying as the possibility of a nuclear holocaust.

Could a better contact with the past make us behave more wisely? Education is in part a system of inoculation with history—absorbing small, homoeopathic doses of what former generations have learned, discovered, said, thought and done. In theory, it should teach us not to repeat our ancestors' mistakes. But there is always room for new mistakes. Can history protect us from one which might be final?

It can at least give us and our children a sense of context; it can show us where we belong in the pattern, what came before, how everything connects. The main symptom in some forms of mental illness is blankness, a loss of the personal past. If one can't remember, one can't act intelligently, because there is no springboard for future action. Children reared without knowledge of their own family past, their local, social, or historical past— and particularly children reared on television and computers, which cast a blank uncritical eye on certain areas of the present—such children have inadequate resources with which to face formidable choices ahead of them.

Adults in search of the past in fictional form read Barbara Tuchman, Mary Renault, Ellis Peters (or Edith Pargeter), or Georgette Heyer and her successors. They watch *Pride and Prejudice* on television, or *The Jewel in the Crown*. But few children pursue such a quest. Historical novels, it used to be said, sold less well than other Puffin Books; the only historical figure to whom children seem unfailingly attached is Robin Hood.

How, then, can the past be made palatable to children—if, reared among tower-blocks, they can hardly imagine it; if they have no incentive or stimulus from their day-to-day surroundings; if they can't even look along the High Street and see the Georgian frontages behind the chain-store façades? How can we persuade them that history ever really happened?

One of the few habits we still share with our ancestors is reading. Holding a book, we still behave in much the same way as people have done since the invention of written records. If for no other reason, we should try to make sure that reading does not become a lost art.

To keep children reading, and to encourage their slightest interest in the past, we have to be wily. Mercifully, children do take a natural interest in their own personal history. 'What was I like when I was a baby?' they ask. 'What did you give me for breakfast? What did I wear?' This self-oriented curiosity about what their environment was like before the

'At this she cried that I was a Norman thief'

H.R. Millar's illustration for a tale in Rudyard Kipling's *Puck of Pook's Hill* (Macmillan, 1906) recreates a Norman and Saxon confrontation post-1066.

present can by strategy be expanded into a general curiosity—about how people drew before pencils were invented, how they kept clean without soap, electricity, or piped water, how they despatched news before the foundation of the post office. Children enjoy such details; they also enjoy the discovery that there were periods in the past when adult knowledge was scantier and flimsier than it is now, when adults held beliefs we now know to be fallacious, as that the earth was flat or that trolls lived in the mountains. The logical and hopeful corollary, for children, is that if adults could be so mistaken then, today they need not be infallible.

When I was a child, history was still told in stories. Fair Rosamond, the White Ship, Richard and Blondel; such tales trip the imagination, and stick in the mind long after statistics and dates have slipped away. The teacher's task is to ensure that they encapsulate nuggets of reliable information. The romantic legends in *Our Island Story*, my first history primer, were fairly weak on fact and strong on sentiment; but I was also lucky enough, learning history at home with my mother, to be given two charming little books by Rhoda and Eileen Power, *Boys and Girls of History* and *More Boys and Girls of History*. These described the daily lives of such young people as 'Lucius', a Romano-British boy; 'Olaf', a Dane; Salathiel Pavy, an Elizabethan boy actor; a little Stuart housewife; and then, travelling overseas, Pocahontas; a New England boy involved in the Boston Tea Party; a Maori boy; and an Aborigine girl. The books not only recounted stirring tales; they gave practical details of food, clothes, lessons, and toys. I remembered them vividly for forty years. In their strength and simplicity, they awakened a lifelong fondness for history.

Only fiction, or truly perceptive biography, can communicate this real appreciation of how the past looked, sounded, felt and smelt. 'The peasants lived in squalor' is a flat, unmemorable statement. The reader, and especially a child reader, needs to picture an actual peasant lying down to sleep in a mixture of mud and straw, by the side of his pig.

Contemporary fiction, written during the period it depicts, can be disappointing as an historical source. Those who wrote it neglected the needs of posterity, prying between the lines, puzzling over every nuance; they omitted what their readers took for granted—and what we are longing to know. Jane Austen's novels, despite their domestic setting, contain very little about the details of daily life. We pounce with excitement on the fact that Mary Crawford's harp has to be brought from Northampton in her brother's carriage because during the hay season a farm cart cannot be had. We note that Frank Churchill rides to London to have his hair cut, and secretly buy a piano. We are delighted to see Kitty and Lydia treat their elder sisters to a lunch of 'such cold meat as an inn larder usually affords'; they borrow money for it, and are busily employed beforehand 'dressing salad and cucumber'. What dressing did they use? I have a 'Jane Austen' recipe book, but it is dumb on the subject of salad dressings. Charlotte Brontë was better at describing stoves, costumes, domestic interiors, and culinary processes—either because she was consciously reporting for more metropolitan readers or, one might fancy, because she guessed what future generations might be itching to know.

Historical writers now, of course, take immense pains to include all such details. Georgette Heyer's notebooks were packed with information about costumes and carriages, 18th-century slang, and the Battle of Waterloo. We are grateful, but one salad and cucumber in *Pride and Prejudice* carries more conviction than all the products of careful research.

We should encourage children to engage in lateral sleuthing: to read *Henry IV, Part II* in order to find out how men-at-arms kept their stockings up; *Lycidas* to discover what were Milton's favourite wild flowers; *Tom Brown's Schooldays* to ponder the embryonic rules of Rugby football; the 'Ode to a Skylark' to decide how Shelley must have pronounced many of the words in it, differently from the way they are spoken today. Such odds and ends of fact-finding make one far more attentive—to one's own surroundings as well as to the text. The experience is like hunting through a town for Tudor houses, or through a valley for the old course of a river. The searching eye lights on orchids and milestones and old notices and all kinds of unexpected treasure trove.

When I was a child, my mother and I worked our way through great quantities of Scott, Dumas, Victor Hugo, Charlotte Yonge, Stevenson, and so on. We read *A Tale of Two Cities*, *Lorna Doone*, *The Cloister and the Hearth*, Kingsley's *Westward Ho!* and the 'Conscript' books by Erkmann-Chatrien. Some of these books, I know now, were good, some so-so, some downright bad: yet I learned a great deal from them. I may never read *Quentin Durward* again, but I remember with pleasure Scott's portrait of Louis XI, disguised for some obscure reason as a merchant, having dinner at a French inn. For good or ill, it fixed in my mind an image of that monarch—canny, crafty, stingy, yet not wholly dislikeable.

Listening to such novels, then reading them myself, I began to notice connections and cross-references. My father owned a 19th-century French history picture-book. The captions might be in French, but the pictures were luridly dramatic. I gazed with eight-year-old fascination at a ladder, laden with horror-struck soldiers, being thrust back from the battlements of a besieged castle; at Napoleon, gloomy among his frostbitten, dying men, on the way back from Moscow; and there again, recognisably, was Louis XI, already familiar from *Quentin Durward* and *The Hunchback of Notre Dame*, this time on his ghastly deathbed, haunted by the ghosts of tortured victims.

These cross-bearings from novels began to give me, as a child, the confident feeling that history was real: that Scott and Hugo and Dumas were not just inventing. The disparity between rival portraits of Charles II's younger sister made me understand that, although the people in history were solidly there, everyone had a right to an individual view of their motives. Was St Joan a noble, simple, inspired girl, as in Shaw's play? Or a witch, consorting with fiends, as seen by Shakespeare? Was Richard Crookback a monster, as in Shakespeare? Or a shrewd, ruthless, but not unsympathetic young general, as in Stevenson's *The Black Arrow*?

Children can be a difficult audience—especially in these days of exposure to the audio-visual media. Accustomed to television, they have a shorter attention-span; they will no longer accept two-page descriptions of a knight's armour, as in Walter Scott. And there are gaps in their knowledge—as there are, too, in the author's picture of the past.

Recently, writing a series of playlets for the BBC about emigrants to Virginia in the 17th century, I planned to make my colonists Cavaliers escaping from Roundheads in the Civil War. The producer told me that this wouldn't do: the nine-year-old audience would never have heard of Cromwell. Could some of the characters be Quakers? No again, because the nine-year-olds didn't know about Quakers, and only a limited amount of explanation could be crammed into a twenty-minute script.

Still more fundamental are the gaps in the author's knowledge. Everyone has his strategy for dealing with them. He can leap nervously across from one solid fact to another, using only those of which he is certain. That method is ethical: but it leads to rather bloodless writing. Flaubert lamented, when he was working on *Salammbô*, that his material knowledge about the lives of the Carthaginians was so scanty that he had to spread it thin to make it last. Yet when Tolstoy tells us, in *War and Peace*, that Napoleon had a bad cold before the battle of Borodino, and that he grumbled because the lozenges his doctor prescribed made him unable to enjoy his glass of punch, we believe the story implicitly. Was it guesswork? Perhaps: but Tolstoy had taken pains to study the battle, which had occurred sixteen years before he was born. He had looked at maps, read all the available accounts, and explored the site for several days.

"Here, Camilla, girl, unlace my helmet! What, know'st not how?"

Illustration from Charlotte M. Yonge's *The Dove in the Eagle's Nest*, a historical romance for children, set in Huguenot times (Appleton, 1883).

Clearly, the writer of historical fiction has the duty to take such pains as he can. But what next?

Having acquired the information, he should try to forget that he ever had to seek it. Nothing is so tedious as Scott's two pages about the knight and his armour—as if he were boasting about how much he knew. Another strategy is to offer links of comparisons with one's own time. Sometimes, a writer will do this unconsciously, anachronistically; and the canny reader can detect, say, the Romantic Movement stirring in Scott's Middle Ages, the English Labour Party of the 1920s in Naomi Mitchison's Sparta, or Keble and the Oxford Movement in Charlotte M. Yonge's Huguenots. Writers today no doubt do the same and are unaware of it, as one tends to be unaware of the contemporary slang that infiltrates one's prose. In one sense, we can interpret the past only from our own viewpoint: but perhaps we should try to take as many bearings as possible from different points of view. What did Queen Elizabeth think of Caligula? What did Alexander Borgia think of St Paul? History, said Gibbon, is 'little more than the register of the crimes, follies, and misfortunes of mankind.' And Mrs Markham, whose best-selling *History of England* was published in 1823, declared that 'It is one of the great drawbacks to the pleasure of reading history, that it is such a painful record of human crimes.' Nowadays we take the opposite view. Crime is an economic asset on any publisher's list.

Questions of accuracy and viewpoint apart, the writer of historical fiction faces three broad choices. The first is Shakespeare's option: to adopt as one's protagonist an historical character, and shape the story to follow historical events. The second, used by Rosemary Sutcliff, Leon Garfield, Alan Garner, Jill Paton Walsh, Barbara Willard and many more, is to tell a story of fictional characters against a background of fact. The third, adopted by Saki in *When William Came*, E.L. Doctorow in *Ragtime*, T.H. White in his Arthurian trilogy, and Kingsley Amis in *The Alteration*, allows scope for even more variation. The writer reshapes the course of history, using the past as a springboard for invention, faithful to the spirit of the age in question, but departing where need be from the letter. So doing, he can tease a young reader's interest into wakeful attention.

For example, the combat between Sir Grummore and King Pellinore in *The Sword in the Stone* is a memorably funny scene. T.H. White vividly conveys the weight and awkwardness of knights in full armour, the clumsiness of caparisoned horses, the narrowness of visored vision; and he strengthens the point by turning his combatants into 19th century huntin' and shootin' county gentry. The device is legitimate, since that is what local lords would probably have been in the Arthurian period—supposing there to have been an Arthurian period. The author's extensive knowledge of chivalry, falconry, and castle life entitled him to such flights of fancy. They certainly recruited more readers than many a serious historian's conscientious sobriety.

I too, in some of my books, make use of this fanciful, looking-glass approach. Suppose, as James Thurber said, that Grant had been drunk at Appomattox; that Bonnie Prince Charlie had not turned his army back halfway down England; that the marital problems of Henry VIII had not brought about the Reformation—as, in *The Alteration*, Kingsley Amis suggests. Or suppose, as I have, that all Queen Anne's children had not died, that the Stuarts had remained on the throne of England.

To try out these hypotheses is fun: it can also be a useful exercise, making one think about the strands of causation and the formative elements in real events. In my own books, I encourage readers to understand that this is fantasy—not serious history—by exaggeration and nonsense, such as making rich girls wear seventeen silk petticoats, dukes have billiards cars on their private trains, conspirators plan to put St Paul's Cathedral on rollers and run it into the Thames, Phoenicians (employed by the Romans in Welsh gold-mines) go underground and remain there for 2,000 years, or Roman Britons emigrate to South America, where they establish an Arthurian society.

Not all my books take such liberties with history. The two Spanish stories, *Saddle the Sea* and *Bridle the Wind*, were based on things I had seen for myself or learned from factual accounts of Spain, with an external story added. A reader wrote to me about *Saddle the Sea*, taking exception to my description of the rigging of a Basque felucca—an arrangement which had seemed so strange that I had taken pains to check it, twice. That confirmed my feeling that the outline of the story is more important than recondite details, on which some expert can always cast doubt. Of *Midnight is a Place*—another seriously researched story—reviewers said that the factory scenes were convincing, but not the goings-on of the sewers. I had taken the sewer details from Mayhew's *London Labour and the London Poor*— whereas the carpet press in my factory was the product of a nightmare I had had before writing the book. Later, when facts were being checked for the television adaptation of the story, I discovered that carpets had, in fact, been made in the way my dream suggested.

Writers of fiction make a profession of projecting themselves into other people's minds and positions. Their imaginative grasp can help make a reality of the past—when hell-fire religion was part of daily life, when most communications were by word of mouth, when so much hair must have lain about on the floor because women wore it to their waists and there were no vacuum cleaners. This is what I really enjoy learning about the past: what it felt like to sit down in a crinoline, or wear armour, or share a bed-place with three other passengers in a transatlantic ship in the 18th century.

As historical writers, we have a twofold task. First, to bring an awareness of the past to children who are often reluctant readers, their ability to concentrate on the printed word impaired by too much screen-watching. Secondly, to make them aware how much we owe to the past.

When I was at school we used to sing, at the beginning and end of every term, G.W. Briggs's hymn 'Our Father by whose servants our house was built of old'. It was a reminder of previous school generations. As twelve-year-olds, we used to feel cynical: we knew that these North Oxford buildings had not actually been constructed by the alumni listed on the boards which flank the stairs. Only later did we come dimly to understand that what they had contributed was the essential character of the school itself. Likewise, we intermittently remember our debt to former generations who passed factory acts, dug sewers, established public transport, and all the other benefits we now unthinkingly enjoy. Briggs's hymn continues:

They reap not where they laboured:
We reap what they have sown.
Our harvest may be garnered
By ages yet unknown. . . .

We too can contribute to the storehouse. The first and simplest way is to make for the nearest ninety-year-old, put questions, take notes, use a tape-recorder. But our fundamental duty is to match, to build upon, to develop, and to preserve the riches that our ancestors have left us. To do that, we have to respect and understand them; and the way to understanding is through the creative imagination. Historical fiction for children is one lifeline to a world they are in danger of losing.

Progressive Utopia: Or, How to Grow Up Without Growing Up

Perry Nodelman

A solitary young girl is travelling—in an old stage coach on a dusty road, or an open buggy on a pretty street, or another buggy on a road 'fringed with blooming wild cherry-trees and slim white birches'. Maybe she is in a railway carriage, or just on a footpath where 'the air is fragrant with the scent of mountain flowers.'[1] The girl may be five or nine but is most likely eleven. She probably has remarkable eyes—'big blue eyes' (Pollyanna), 'big eyes . . . full of spirit and vivacity' (Anne), 'eyes like faith' that 'glowed like two stars' (Rebecca). Her other physical characteristics are less imposing. She is 'a small dark-haired person in a glossy buff calico dress' (Rebecca) or 'a slender little girl in . . . red-checked gingham' (Pollyanna) or in 'a very short, very tight, very ugly dress of yellowish grey wincey' (Anne). Perhaps she is just 'a plain little piece of goods' in a black dress (Mary), or perhaps she is 'wearing two frocks, one on top of the other' (Heidi). Whatever she is wearing, the people she is travelling towards will probably not approve of it.

Those people will be old, or they will act as if they are old. They will be stiff and unfriendly, very strict about themselves and others. They will have suffered greatly in the past, probably because of thwarted love, and they will be unmarried or widowed. They will probably have a strong sense of duty. And the child who is about to descend on them will transform their lives and make them happy.

This is the warmhearted world of the traditional novel for girls. While such novels are no longer written, many of the ones produced decades ago are still widely read. The continuing popularity of these novels is surprising, given the great differences between ourselves and our grandparents; but even more surprising is their likeness to each other. Heidi, Anne of Green Gables, Pollyanna, Rebecca of Sunnybrook Farm, Mary of *The Secret Garden*—they live in widely separate countries, but their similarities outnumber their differences. They all live the same story, and they come to seem like variations of an ideal of female childhood that transcends national boundaries, and even the boundaries of time—for we still find the story enticing.

This is the story. The young girl, an orphan, arrives at her new home, which belongs to a relative, an aunt or a grandfather who has probably been living alone for a long time. Her sensible or faded clothing does not suit her character; she is a spontaneous and ebullient child, quite unaffected by her previous history of misfortune and deprivation. (Mary Lennox of *The Secret Garden* is an exception—her spontaneity and ebullience don't emerge until later in the novel.)

Luckily, our heroine's new home is a place of some physical comfort—a refuge from the deprivation she has suffered so far. There is enough food, and she will have a room of her own for the first time. The room is sparsely furnished, but it has a window. Through the window, she will see beautiful prospects of trees or flowers or mountains, and probably think of them as 'delicious' (*Rebecca, Pollyanna*).

But as it turns out, the physical comfort of the new house is not matched by its emotional atmosphere. Its current inhabitants, who are old and solitary and unhappy, make it a bleak and sterile place. It is quite cut off from the beauty to be seen from its windows. There is little evidence of love, and there are many hard rules for a young child to learn.

Nevertheless, our heroine usually loves her new home. So she tries to love the people who live there, and to live by their rules. Sometimes she *does* love them, because she is too innocent to see how unlovable they are. Sometimes she finds them hard to love, but manages it anyway.

In fact, her almost magical qualities seem to triumph over every bad circumstance. She does not change much in the course of the events that follow—she manages somehow to age without becoming terribly different. But the wonderful qualities she starts with and never loses have remarkable effects on other people, who change miraculously.

Bad ones become good ones; nasty people turn nice, uncharitable people give things away, potential divorcees decide to stay married. Or perhaps bad people are replaced by good ones; both the unsatisfactory minister and the unsatisfactory teacher Anne Shirley finds ensconced in Avonlea on her arrival are magically replaced by people she likes.

But most frequently, it turns out that the bad people were not really bad at all; while they have been soured by experience, they only need the presence of our remarkable heroine to rediscover their goodness. As Pollyanna tells an apparently nasty man, 'I'm sure you're much nicer than you look,' and he is, of course. Our heroine's major talent is the ability to restore the past—to return grown-ups to the happiness they felt in their youth. 'That man is waking up after being asleep for over sixty years,' says Rachel Lynde of Matthew Cuthbert.

Matthew is not the only grown-up awakened by the magic touch of youth; it happens to Aunt Jane and Aunt Miranda and Aunt Polly, to various friends and other people in the environs, to Heidi's grandfather, and so on. The process is carried to the extreme in *The Secret Garden*. Not only does the coming of spring and the resurrection of the garden change a desolate and decaying place into a lovely one; it also seems to cause human beings to spring up from nowhere, almost as if they had been hibernating. An apparently almost deserted house containing only a few unhappy people turns out to be a surprisingly populous one, and the people are all happy ones.

But despite, or perhaps because of, our heroine's magic ability to awaken dormant joyousness, this is a story without a plot. There is no suspense, no one action that gets more complicated as the novel progresses and is resolved at the end. In emotional terms, each episode merely repeats and amplifies the episodes preceding it; it causes an increase in the available amount of happiness, which gets larger as the novel gets longer.

In fact, there can be as many episodes as the novelist can think of, without much change to the texture or meaning of the whole. Entire chapters, like the one about Pollyanna's encounter with a minister in the woods, are quite separate from anything else that happens, and could easily be left out. Other chapters could be added, and perhaps that is why so many of these novels have sequels. The important thing is that each episode ends with someone feeling better about himself and the world he lives in. The same thing happens again and again; if we are entertained, it is not because we want to find out what will happen, but because we know what will happen, and like it happening, and want it to keep on happening.

What each episode consists of is this: our child heroine shocks, and then delights, repressed or unhappy grown-ups with her childish spontaneity and lack of artifice. In acting 'naturally', she makes them more natural, and brings an end to the artificial repression of their overcivilized values. She restores them to what they once were. This is made particularly obvious in *Rebecca of Sunnybrook Farm*. Rebecca's Aunt Jane, who responds immediately to her, says, 'I remember well enough how I felt at her age.' Aunt Miranda, who is more rigid, and who never admits to the degree to which her contact with Rebecca has transformed her, says, 'You was considerable of a fool at her age, Jane.' Jane's answer reveals the heart of all these novels: 'Yes I was, thank the Lord. I only wish I'd known how to take a little of my foolishness along with me, as some folks do, to brighten my declining years.' Fortunately, she *has* brought it along, and Rebecca reveals it to her.

But there is some ambiguity about the 'foolishness' of childhood. Our heroine does things that are meant to make us laugh. She dyes her hair green, or saves dinner rolls in her closet, or invites missionaries to dinner on the spur of the moment. Since she is too innocent to know what she ought not to do, her life is a series of comic disasters, in which her spontaneity and her ignorance of the ways of the world get her into trouble at the same time as they endear her to us. And while we are meant to find her actions delightful, we must also realize that spontaneity has its dangers.

Consequently, each time our heroine displays her innocence, she learns to be less innocent. As the grown-ups become more like children, the children become more like grown-ups. As the young Rebecca says to her friend Mr Aladdin, 'If you don't like me to grow old, why don't you grow young? Then we can meet at the halfway house and have nice times. Now that I think about it . . . that's just what you've been doing all along.' In fact, that is what happens to the characters in all these novels. They start at opposite extremes, and gradually change until they are much like each other; old people find their sobriety balanced by joy, and young people have their spontaneity balanced by discretion; the old rediscover the pleasures of imagination, and the young discover the virtues of common sense.

Finally, because our heroine is learning something important, she is tested. We must see that she can apply her magic gifts of healing to herself—that she can act on her own teachings. So the even tenor of her life, the continuing ebb and flow of not particularly significant events, is interrupted. Something serious happens, usually in the second chapter.

Not always, however—Heidi confronts her problem earlier, in her imprisonment in Frankfurt, and Mary Lennox's problems end as the novel begins. But in these two novels, the story is not complete; their heroines do not grow old enough to complete it. There is no test at the end, for the test seems to signify the end of childhood, and Heidi and Mary remain triumphantly young, triumphantly magical. This is not to say that the myth expressed by all these novels is not complete in *Heidi* and *The Secret Garden*; it is. Other people in these novels *do* pass the test and manage either to retain their youthful spirits or to rediscover them.

For the heroine who gets older, the test is hard indeed. She becomes seriously ill; perhaps, even, unable to walk. Will she have the strength to heal herself as she healed others? Or perhaps a loved one dies. Will she be able to accept death and still be joyful? Or her glorious plans for the future are thwarted. Will she be able to accept it? She will, of course. She will feel what L.M. Montgomery in *Anne of Green Gables* calls 'the cold, sanctifying touch' of sorrow, and be sanctified by it. All ends happily; happiness has progressed to its point of perfect ripeness.

That is the story. The question is, why is it so consistent? Why are these novels so similar to each other, and so satisfying in their consistencies?

To begin with, the setting of these novels, a house in a pleasant rural location, is important. Such a place offers the pleasures of nature without its wild savagery, and the pleasures of civilization without its urban constrictions. It is a place to relax in, something like paradise. Clearly nothing very unpleasant will happen here.

In fact, nothing unpleasant does happen. The classic novels for boys always start with their heroes leaving home, and describe their exciting confrontations with hardship and evil in wild, uncomfortable places, until they finally come home again. These novels for girls start with their heroine's arrival at what is to be her home, *after* a series of unsettling adventures which are glossed over rather than described; once she gets home, she does nothing but grow up quietly. In boys' books, things start badly and get worse, almost until the very end. In these girls' books, things start well and get better, almost until the very end. The pleasure offered readers is something not usually considered desirable in fiction—lack of suspense, lack of excitement, lack of conflict; it is a pleasure we might associate more with our indulgence in utopian dreams than with our love of a good story.

But not quite; the place may be perfect, but the people who live there need working on. In fact, that is why these novels might best be called progressive utopias. They begin with a heroine's arrival at an almost perfect place; and after that, the heroine's action on the community makes it an even more perfect place. Sympathetic readers can partake in the creation of heaven on earth and be satisfied in realizing that heaven on earth is the world one already lives in—not a deserted island in the South Seas, not a lost corner of Africa, not the exciting past or the glorious future, but home. The growing happiness of the inhabitants of utopia is their growing understanding that home is in fact utopia.

The children who bring them to that satisfying awareness share some important characteristics. They are all girls, of course, and therefore ideally suited to the unexciting pleasures of home—or so these novels assume. And they are all orphans. Without parents (or in Rebecca's case, with only one parent) to guide them and restrain them, they have not been spoiled by grown-up attitudes—they are purely and essentially childlike. In fact, they are symbols of childhood and its virtues, pure manifestations of qualities that would be muddied in less detached children. These girls all transcend the specifics of their situations and develop almost mythic intensity. Their novelists adore them, and expect readers to adore them too. Rebecca is called 'a little brown elf', and Anne 'some wild divinity of the shadowy places'. Such divinities clearly represent something of importance.

That thing is best expressed by the poet Wordsworth; as Kate Douglas Wiggin says in *Rebecca of Sunnybrook Farm*, 'Blessed Wordsworth! How he makes us understand.' What Wordsworth made the generations who followed him understand and take to heart is that childhood innocence is automatically sympathetic with the healing beauties of nature, which are themselves divine, and which we become blind to in maturity. 'Heaven lies about us in our infancy,' and as children, we perceive 'splendour in the grass . . . glory in the flower'. Grown-ups usually can't do that. But Anne says, 'If I really wanted to pray I'll tell you what I'd do. I'd go out into a great big field all alone, or I'd look up into the sky—up—up—up—into that lovely blue sky that looks as if there was no end to its blueness. And then I'd just *feel* a prayer.' Heidi feels the same way about mountains: 'everything seemed more beautiful than she had expected. . . . It was so lovely, Heidi stood with tears pouring down her cheeks, and thanked God for letting her come home again.' Both Rebecca and Pollyanna escape restrictive houses into 'delicious' landscapes, and in *The Secret Garden*, the most symbolic of these novels, God's 'Magic' expresses itself best in natural landscapes. Colin says, 'Sometimes since I've been in the garden I've looked up through the trees at the sky and I have had a strange feeling of them being happy, as if something were pushing and drawing in my chest and making me breathe fast. Magic is always pushing and drawing and making things out of nothing. . . . The magic in the garden has made me stand up and know I'm going to be a man.' In fact, spontaneous feelings are prayer, and Nature is God's cathedral; L.M. Montgomery tells us how 'a glimpse of painted sunset sky shone like a great rose window at the end of a cathedral aisle.'

Children, being unrepressed by social values, are naturally responsive to the divine joys of Nature. As Wordsworth said, a child is the

. . . best Philosopher, who yet dost keep
Thy heritage, thou Eye among the blind,
. . .

    Mighty Prophet! Seer blest!
On whom these truths do rest,

Which we are toiling all our lives to find,
In darkness lost. . . .

Our orphans are all 'seers blest'. And because these novels give us, not the real world but an idealized one, all of them show the way to those older than themselves who are 'in darkness lost'.

They are lost in darkness because they feel a strong sense of 'Duty'—a virtue Wordsworth called the 'Stern Daughter of the Voice of God', and opposed to natural, childlike spontaneity, for it made him act against his own natural feelings. Wordsworth eventually got tired of 'uncharted freedom' and 'chance desires', and gave in to Duty; but as a poem by Rebecca suggests, that is not the case in these novels of child worship:

When Joy and Duty clash
Let Duty go to smash.

Not that Duty isn't important. Children do grow up and have to face responsibility, and in any case, natural spontaneity is not always a virtue, despite our wistful admiration of it; it is self-centred and antisocial. In fact, the authors of these novels even pretend to dislike it. Rebecca, we are told, 'never stopped to think, more's the pity,' and we are expected to see that our heroines get into trouble whenever they don't stop to think. But we cannot really take that seriously, for it is their spontaneity that makes these girls adorable. While our heroines do look Duty in the face, their spirits are not quenched by it. They age without losing their childlike qualities, grow up without actually growing up; that is the heart of the appeal of these novels.

Even from the beginning, our heroine's spontaneous joy in living has not been destroyed by circumstances that ought to have destroyed it. Only Mary Lennox begins depressed, and she soon regains her happiness and her innocence. So does her friend Colin; apparently one *can* go home again. The other girls have suffered before the novels begin, but show no signs of it; the message is that bitter experience does *not* quench true childish joy. In fact, Anne and Rebecca, who do eventually grow up physically, never lose their childlike qualities. That is why they are tested—tested and found to be unresponsive to experience, terminally incapable of not being, as Pollyanna insists, 'glad' no matter what. They are only slightly restrained by the women's bodies and lives they inhabit. The mature Rebecca is still a 'bewildering being, who gave wings to thoughts that had only crept before; who brought colour and grace and harmony into the dun brown texture of existence.' And as Anne tells us, 'I'm not a bit changed—not really. I'm only just pruned down and branched out. The real me—back here—is just the same.' They are still childlike divinities of the shadowy places, just as Mary and Heidi and Pollyanna are.

Contemporary feminists might well find these novels objectionable. Their central message is that a comfortable home is heaven and that the perfect divinities to occupy that home are women who act much like children. The utopia these novels progress towards is actually a regressive world of perfect childlike innocence. But despite our revised ideals both of childhood and femininity, many readers are not revolted. In growing up, or merely in allowing people who have grown up to become children again, our heroines perform a miracle that readers apparently would still like to believe in.

One of the ugly things the philosophy of the Romantic movement accomplished for us in its admiration of childlike qualities was the divorce of childhood from maturity. Until the early nineteenth century, children weren't thought to be much different from grown-ups; they certainly weren't thought to be better than grown-ups. But Blake and Wordsworth changed all that, and we still believe that children think differently, see differently, and feel differently from the way we do. While this conviction helps us immeasurably in our dealings with children, it does create problems. It separates us from our own past selves, and it makes children into strangers in our midst. Worst of all, it makes childhood, which inevitably passes, agonizingly enticing to us—somehow better than, richer than, realer than the maturity we are stuck with. It forces us into a fruitless nostalgia—a lust for something we simply cannot have anymore.

But in the wish-fulfilment world of the novels of progressive utopia, we can have it again. Childhood never really ends; the most childlike children never really grow up, and even terminally mature people can become childlike again. It is the secret desire of grown-ups to be children again that makes these novels so appealing to grown-ups, and it may be the secret desire of children to never grow up that makes these novels appealing to them. Apparently these desires transcend both place and time.

Furthermore, these desires are just one version of a central concern of children's literature, no matter where or when it was written—how to grow up, as one inevitably must, without losing the virtues and delights of childhood. This is the subject of *Harriet the Spy* and *Tom's Midnight Garden* and *The Little Prince* just as much as it is the subject of *Treasure Island* and *Tom Sawyer* and *Swiss Family Robinson*. As long as we produce books especially for children because we are convinced that childhood is quite different from maturity, it may be the only thing a good children's book is ever about.

Note

¹The novels the solitary young girl travels in are, respectively, *Rebecca of Sunnybrook Farm* by Kate Douglas Wiggin, *Pollyanna* by Eleanor H. Porter, *Anne of Green Gables* by L.M. Montgomery, *The Secret Garden* by Frances Hodgson Burnett, and *Heidi* by Johanna Spyri. The popularity of these books over the decades means that they have been available in many different editions. The translation of *Heidi* that I have used is by Eileen Hall (Penguin-Puffin, 1956).

ALICE, HUCK, PINOCCHIO, AND THE BLUE FAIRY: BODIES REAL AND IMAGINED

M.L. Rosenthal

The three authors whose book-bodies I am about to violate were born within a decade of one another: the Italian Carlo Lorenzini in 1826, the Englishman Charles Lutwidge Dodgson in 1832, and the American Samuel Langhorne Clemens in 1835. The titles of their masterpieces all dangle the appeal of adventure, literally: *The Adventures of Pinocchio: Tale of a Puppet; Alice's Adventures in Wonderland*; and *The Adventures of Huckleberry Finn*. All used pen names: Carlo Collodi, Lewis Carroll, Mark Twain. The books themselves were born within the same generation, between 1865 and 1883. Apart from being masterpieces, then, what the three books have in common is the era in which they were written, their effort (however conventional) to hide their makers' real identities, and the grown-up assumption that books for children should promise adventure—an assumption that almost inevitably implies dangerous risks overcome, within a probably picaresque context. The characters imagined in them, like the 'bodies' shaped by language in all fiction, bear a special relation to the real memories and personalities of their authors. An obvious but most important corollary therefore suggests itself: every sensation, emotional state, and thought in such books is imbedded in a verbal palimpsest, a necessarily ambiguous layering of imagined childhood experience and attitudes, authors' memories and preconceptions, and traditional motifs.

Thus, the presumed subjective life of Alice can't quite be sorted out from the Reverend Dodgson's understanding of how those delightful, intriguing creatures, middle-class British schoolgirls aged about seven or eight, behave at their best. (For one thing, they can be charmingly saucy, but they do know their manners and worry about giving offence; for another, they love riddles and wordplay; and for another, they shy away from almost anyone's touch and yet—like Alice's creator—move imperturbably among grotesque and cruel images and ideas.)

Similarly, Huck Finn, the tough, wily, barely literate pubescent son of a southern village drunk, is also the innocent carrier of his author's humane decency. Reared in squalor and basically liking it (though detesting his besotted father), he nevertheless is sentimental and chivalric, sometimes even worshipful, toward girls and women. A keen observer of the way coarse men behave when the chance arises, he himself never has an unbecoming adolescent thought—even when he dresses as a girl and clever Mrs Loftus explains how she saw through the disguise. Nor does nicely brought-up Tom Sawyer, whom Huck accepts as his natural leader, ever have a naughty thought. Tom, Clemens's flamboyantly idealized vision of his own boyhood self, serves as the *deus ex machina* who rescues the plot from existential wreckage unfit for children. But it is Huck, that youthful voice of a despised class, who is the main conveyer of the author's memories and observations. Never was there a more realistic, straight-faced portrayal of the organic body of a social region than the one which he provides us. Yet Clemens's sexual self-censorship, his indulgence in literary horseplay, including puns, and his gift for beautifully evocative prose poetry are grafted onto this humourless, literal-minded character.

Huck's increasing sympathy with the runaway slave Jim, despite his guilt at helping him, is another matter. It is a blending of Huck's psychologically believable maturing with Clemens's own sensibility. The book's stabbing satire against the assumption of a slave culture (outlawed but hardly dead sixteen years after the Civil War) that a black body is worthless except as chattel has the power of great art. Huck's comic struggle with his conscience—like his ignorant father's comic diatribe against a 'gov'ment' that respects an accomplished black man—is the vehicle of this satire, which carries the book into Dostoyevskian territory. But its underpinning is the episodes revealing Jim's qualities of courage and compassion.

As for Pinocchio, the wooden puppet fashioned by the impoverished old artisan Geppetto, he too is a politically liberal author's vehicle of satire against injustice and, like Huck, is awakened to compassion. He is enslaved at one point, imprisoned at another, almost executed at another, changed into a donkey and cruelly misused at another, and so humanized internally that at last he becomes a real boy. In this dimension of the book—the major one—Lorenzini's gift for pure fantasy is livelier and happier than Dodgson's and less ruthlessly grim than Clemens's. He was a master of short-term suspense, so that he could put Pinocchio through a hundred perilous hoops and worry young readers just . . . long . . . enough before the mischievous, forgetful, naïvely sly little hero is miraculously rescued again.

Pinocchio is a startling creature, a wooden being who cries out with pain as he is being carved from what at first seemed merely 'a plain log'. At first he struggles only to be his own wild uncontrollable self: a tree-spirit

HUCKLEBERRY FINN.

E.W. Kemble's Huck Finn, rendered for Mark Twain's *Adventures of Huckleberry Finn* (New York: Charles L. Webster & Company, 1885).

given body by an unwitting artist. He finds his supreme moment of puppet happiness when he is welcomed by other marionettes he encounters in a puppet theatre. But Lorenzini, a sophisticated writer making use of antecedents from Dante to Stendhal and Balzac, gives him another objective. In certain respects he is not unlike Stendhal's Julien Sorel. Naturally, there is no room for the sexual torments, conquests, and strategies of a Sorel in little Pinocchio's life. Yet we could perhaps find parallels—I think we do—in the way the Blue Fairy comes to Pinocchio's rescue and then lets him go, but reappears at strategic times after making him grieve over her supposed death; while he, for his part, constantly betrays the very devotion to her that is his chief inspiration. Sorel tries to find his place as a man, and Pinocchio as a human boy, and the self-transformation in both instances means death: literal death for Sorel, who has betrayed his deepest needs and convictions all along the way despite his inner knowledge; and the death of the old, wayward Pinocchio as a puppet whose free spirit kept violating the ways of the workaday world. Julien is a revolutionary spirit in an impossible reactionary period; Pinocchio is humbled into accepting the fatalistic, self-denying standards of the virtuous, hardworking poor.

Adult consciousness of life's physical terrors and ecstasies is always present, though usually in repressed form, in children's literature that approaches greatness. Often it is concealed in whimsy or grotesque detail. Take that famous nose of Pinocchio's. What a surprise, if you actually read the book—by which I don't mean anything touched by Disney. The first time we see the nose growing uncontrollably is when Geppetto carves it into existence—nothing to do with lying. The second time it is because Pinocchio is so terribly hungry. Only twice more, actually, do we see it growing again: when Pinocchio lies to the Fairy and when he lies to a kindly old man. A forceful image, associated with wild, natural disposition and then with guilt and embarrassment, its inevitable symbolism is at once earthily phallic and social—no doubt part of the buried sexual fantasy that also involves the Fairy's change from little girl to woman. As with much else in his tale, Lorenzini was content to inject these notes of combined elemental and sophisticated awareness into the text without pursuing them unduly.

Pinocchio abounds with primal life forces, presences out of myth, and magical elements, all of which give it a vitality beyond that of any other children's book of comparable length. The irrepressible wooden log that keeps tormenting Mr Cherry and Geppetto; the puppet-actors seen as tree-people ('*quella compagnia drammatico-vegetale*'); and the ogre Fire-Eater and the Green Fisherman, both right out of the hoariest mythology—these,

Title page of Carlo Collodi's *Le Avventure di Pinoccio* (Fierenze: R. Bemporad & Figlio, 1883).

along with the talking animals, both the gentle and the viciously hostile ones, charge Pinocchio's zigzag progress toward rebirth as a human being with terror and delight.

The parallel figures that Alice encounters have a more ponderous quality in their physical ugliness, rudeness, and endlessly down-putting attitudes. Alice has followed the very bourgeois-looking White Rabbit into a fantasy world of grown-up authority and power. At first she is baulked at every turn, in a series of details that suggest a grown man's nightmare of symbolic sexual failure rather more than they do a little girl's frustrated effort to learn more about life. The long passageway, the locked doors, the key to a little door that opens onto an entrance too small to pass through, the changes in size, and the Dantean Pool of Tears—really! If you add the gross scene of the Duchess and her baby who turns into a pig while the cook tries to kill them both, the long murderous 'tale' of Fury and the Mouse, the haunting grin of the Cheshire cat (echoed in other hideous grins), and the play on the idea of madness, it is no wonder that Alice is glad to awake from that world into her older sister's arms. (These effects are echoed and intensified in many ways in the later *Through the Looking-Glass, and What Alice Found There*.) Fear—both of life's challenges and of death, and also of the violently competitive Victorian world beyond the protected realm of his Oxford chambers—seems to pervade the tale Dodgson has to tell. The marvellous wit and wordplay and comic turns try to hold all the terror at bay, but who that gives the book any thought can help seeing it?

The pressure of death and suffering in all three books is really remarkable. *Pinocchio* handles it by making death only temporary after the morbid pall cast over the story by the Blue Fairy's supposed mortal illness and burial fairly early on. The book's zest, humour, and speed make it impossible to linger over its darker side. But consider all the supposed deaths that must wring a child's heart on the way to final triumph: the Fairy's, the Talking Cricket's, Eugenio's, and even Pinocchio's—and beyond these, the actual death of Candleflame, Pinocchio's alter ego, and the misery of the little donkey that tries to warn Pinocchio and whose ears the horrible Little Man bites off. As for Huck Finn, the shooting of Buck Grangerford and of Boggs, and the death of Pap Finn, carry his story far beyond the limits of painful knowledge observed by most children's literature. If not for its comic digressions and the idiotic foolery at the end, the book would have become a tragic work.

That possible outcome, indeed, shadows the denouements of each of these three children's classics. The ending of *Pinocchio* is a beautiful instance. There the former puppet exclaims, as he well might: 'How strange I was when I used to be a puppet! And how glad I am that I've become a real little boy!' But how glad the rest of us are that he *was* a puppet for all those pages, and what a twinge it gives us to read the description of his now-abandoned puppet-form. This is the true death in the book. All the intensity of the excitable being we have known is chillingly distanced by the picture of the figure's utter, unwonted lifelessness: 'its head was twisted to one side and drooping down, its arms were dangling, and its legs were so bent and crossed that it was a miracle the puppet was still upright at all.'

This language is a pang of regret for the lost freedom of unselfconscious childhood. In this respect it parallels the feeling of the other two volumes. Pinocchio's body has been co-opted. Alice is happy to return to what she was before Dodgson's fearful vision was superimposed on hers. Huck is going to 'light out for the territory ahead of the rest, because Aunt Sally she's going to adopt me and civilize me, and I can't stand it. I been there before.'

Of Style and the Stylist

Eleanor Cameron

When I read Katherine Anne Porter's response to an interviewer who said that she had frequently been spoken of as a stylist and who asked if she thought a style could be cultivated, or at least refined, her answer brought an assault of three recollections. The first was of a friend sitting at our dinner table saying, with an impatient flick of the hand, 'Style is of no importance,' at which I was so stunned that the quick give-and-take of conversation surged on without my answering. The second recollection was of a librarian friend handing me Isak Dinesen's *Out of Africa* with the words, 'How I despise fine writing!' The third was of an article on fantasy I had written in which I expressed my pleasure in the prose styles of Grahame, Kipling, Farjeon, Thurber, and Godden and spoke of Rebecca West, Colette, Isak Dinesen, Elizabeth Bowen, and Virginia Woolf as 'great women stylists'.

What Miss Porter replied to the interviewer, in part, was this: 'I've been called a stylist until I really could tear my hair out. And I simply don't believe in style. The style is you. Oh, you can cultivate style, I suppose, if you like. But I should say it remains a cultivated style. It remains artificial and imposed and I don't think it deceives anyone.'[1]

In these words lies the whole argument of style and the stylist. There is the confusion of it: the librarian's equating style with fine writing (meaning to him, apparently, preciousness and self-consciousness), and Miss Porter's saying in one breath that she doesn't believe in style, in the next that it is you, then using the words 'artificial' and 'imposed'. As a matter of fact she has told Glenway Wescott that she spends her life thinking about technique and method and style and that the only time she does not think about them at all is when she is writing. My friend at the dinner table no doubt equates the word style with something objectionable in writing that is worked in only to impress and is therefore of no importance compared to meaning, to the meat of the writing; something, in fact, which might simply get in the way of meaning.

There is given off from any piece of writing, be it prose or poetry, what can only be described as a certain sound (meant figuratively, as something that rings on the inner ear). Maxwell Fraser, speaking of the romance of

Tristram and Yseult, says that it has 'a particular sound which hardly is to be found elsewhere in medieval literature, and only to be explained by the Celtic origin of the legend'.[2] Far from being ornament, embellishment, anything artificial which is self-consciously woven into or impressed upon the natural expression of the writer, style in its simplest definition, it seems to me, is sound—*the sound of self*. It arises out of the whole concept of the work, from the very pulsebeat of the writer and all that has gone to make him, so that it is sometimes difficult to decide definitely where technique and style have their firm boundary lines. Each mingles with the other to create a final effect, as in the following passages from some of the best-loved children's books:

> At last the cart stopped at a house, where the hamper was taken out, carried in, and set down. The cook gave the carrier sixpence; the back door banged, and the cart rumbled away. But there was no quiet; there seemed to be hundreds of carts passing. Dogs barked; boys whistled in the street; the cook laughed, the parlor maid ran up and down-stairs; and a canary sang like a steam engine.

> It was indeed a Superior Comestible (*that's* magic), and he put it on the stove because *he* was allowed to cook on that stove, and he baked it and he baked it till it was all done brown and smelt most sentimental.

> Old Hank Bunker done it once, and bragged about it; and in less than two years he got drunk and fell off of the shot-tower, and spread himself out so that he was just a kind of a layer, as you might say; and they slid him edgeways between two barn doors for a coffin, and buried him so, so they say, but I didn't see it.

> He watched the fox as if she were on a stage. She walked over the grass like a dancer: each leg had its attendant pointing shadow; the Gill still made rippling music. The fox made her own ballet, pointing each silent foot, and reached the shadow of the wall. Under the tractor shed the moonlight moved: a straight gleam pointed to the fox; the night burst round the moving moonlight: twice there was thunder in the air; the fells sent the double report back from bank to bank and scar to scar. Every creature that heard crouched low and fearful; but one crouched animal heard nothing: shot moves faster than sound, and the fox was dead before she fell.

As a first requirement, each of these writers can handle the language. What is more, each loved intensely what he created with his 'feeling mind and his thinking heart'. Literary excellence goes deeper than prose. It is the writer's involvement, suffusing his particular idiom and voice, which makes what he has to say unforgettable.

But what distinguishes his particular idiom and voice? Apart from an atmosphere, a general tone, what gives each of these excerpts away? Always, for one thing, it is a certain rhythm. In the first, from *Johnny Town-Mouse*, it is the quick succession of stroke upon stroke, short phrases often separated by semicolons that call up pithily, sparely, yet vividly the whole busy scene, and then the final wry touch about the canary, that reveal the author. These few lines speak at once of Beatrix Potter, who happened to be a shrewd, ironical, tempery, tender woman who could drive a hard bargain over sheep or land on the one hand, and who, on the other, loved deeply every visual and human aspect of life in the little village of Sawrey.

As for the next, this is only one of Kipling's styles, which varied from the *Just So Stories* to *Puck of Pook's Hill* and *Rewards and Fairies* to *Kim* and *The Jungle Books*. For he was one of those rare few who are always breaking the mould but who manage to mark the new with their distinctive prints. In each apparently different style there is always the inescapable tone or rhythm which to one familiar with that writer's work is instantly recognizable. Here, in this bit from a *Just So* story, 'How the Rhinoceros Got His Skin', the 'Superior Comestible' betrays Kipling, for a peculiar and particular choice of words is a part of style. He offers innumerable swift-rolling treasures for the tongues of children, like 'more-than-oriental-splendour' and 'Exclusively Uninhabited Interior', and his own pleasure in them is so great that it seems plain it never entered his head to bother whether children would understand them or not. That wasn't the point; it was feeling and sound and overtone. He is revealed too in the easy, conversational underlining of 'that's' and 'he' and the delicious unexpectedness of something good smelling 'most sentimental'. Only Kipling would have thought of those words to describe a smell.

In the third passage, Mark Twain is speaking with the voice of Huck, his alter ego, the rebellious, civilization-hating, uneducated boy whose powers of observation, depth of feeling, honesty, and sensitivity to his surroundings constantly emerge in the often ungrammatical sentences. Nor is this, given Huck's lack of education, either contrived or impossible, for education and culture have nothing to do with richness or individuality of expression; indeed, they often inhibit it (take a few PhD monographs off the library shelves and try to read them). In Edmund Vale's *The World of*

Wales, he tells of a young Welsh labouring man describing a dirigible, 'Well, it was like a salmon leaping in the sky.' The rhythm of Huck's sentences is suggestive of the flow of the river with its long smooth stretches, sudden purling over pebbly shallows, its swerving around stones to the curving bank: '. . . and buried him so, so they say, but I didn't see it.' This rhythm and the dry, wry, understated humour with which he speaks of old Hank Bunker's final state are Huck's thumbprints, and Twain's.

In the final except, what one feels above all in these lines from William Mayne's *A Grass Rope* is their taut economy. Here we have Beatrix Potter's tendency to the quick succession of stroke upon stroke, the short sentences, or the short phrases within the longer sentences separated by colons or semicolons, and each a compact, vivid expression of a visual, emotional, or active progression. As Mayne does in the structure of his books, he works the phases of development of a paragraph toward the final effect by gradual release, with full attention to timing, to pace. Mayne is a master of the art of exquisite control, of the disciplined paying out of his line, be it within the structure of his plotting or within the structure of his sentence or paragraph. One feels the mounting tension of movement conveyed fully as much through sentence structure as through the tightening of action.

Mention of the economy and tautness of Beatrix Potter's and William Mayne's usually short sentences and their short phrases within longer sentences brings me to a kind of writing which, if it is not a reflection of lack of ear, is a sad, drab diminishment of the Hemingway style. It is a kind of writing having only the shortness of sentence or phrase in common with Potter's and Mayne's. In this writing there is no variation in texture, none of their sensitivity to rhythm, to sound; one presses one's way in sheer desperation through an endless swamp of short, choppy statements, graceless and all of approximately the same length, so that after a chapter or two one's nerves are numbed and exhausted, as if they had been submitted to a series of blows, so insulted that a pain begins to be felt in one's middle that sharpens until one could throw the book across the room in sheer rage and disgust. The very worst examples are to be found in books put out by departments of education on certain projects they have planned for their elementary students, books on local subjects which would not find a wide circulation. They are often written by committees, and the awkwardness of the prose is often beyond belief, an awkwardness arising out of utter lack of feeling for the architectural harmony of a sentence, its rise and fall, its sound within a paragraph. But of course it results not only from lack of feeling and ear but from the conviction that the shorter the sentence, no matter what kind of sentence, the clearer will be the meaning. One can only suggest that those who wish to write simple prose for which the critical reader can have respect should consider that of the finest picture books—those of Marcia Brown, Barbara Cooney, Virginia Lee Burton, Wanda Gág and Robert McCloskey, for instance, and books for slightly older children by Rebecca Caudill, Beverly Cleary, Eleanor Estes and Clyde Robert Bulla. The clear, quiet dignity of Bulla's best prose is to be found in *The White Bird*.

Stilted, dreary, one-dimensional prose is what Truman Capote calls, not writing, but typing. It is the kind prevalent in much of the realistic fiction being turned out for children in answer to the accusation that not enough is being published on integration, on the ghetto, the poverty-stricken. But surely if fiction is to bring children of this environment what it should bring them—release, extension, understanding, illumination, an appreciation of and hunger for the written word, a feeling that someone is aware of their existence in the realm of literature—then they must be shown the highest possible respect by the publishers; they especially require only the best in prose (admittedly, there are many different kinds of best). If this best is not available in the kind of realistic fiction we say they need, if what they find in books about themselves is colourless, dead, full of the dry taste of duty, then it might be they could find more joy, more release and extension in fantasy. Here, children of all colours and backgrounds can find unself-conscious identification, and for the young child, fantasy can say what books of reality do not say, in words often more sensitively chosen than in the prose of realism.

But realism that arises out of a writer's *need* to tell a story, knitted into the kind of background he knows, is an entirely different matter: Nat Hentoff's *Jazz Country*, Mary H. Weik's *The Jazz Man*, Louisa R. Shotwell's *Roosevelt Grady*, Mary Stolz's *A Wonderful, Terrible Time*, Karen Rose's *There Is a Season*, Eleanor Clymer's *My Brother Stevie*, Frank Bonham's *Durango Street*, Paula Fox's *Maurice's Room* and *How Many Miles to Babylon?*, Zylpha Keatley Snyder's *The Egypt Game*, and Joseph Krumgold's fine *Henry 3*, a novel which takes us with ironic insight into a social structure entirely different from the others. All of these books, in varying degrees, are written and felt and not simply typed out in answer to the demand for a certain kind of fiction. (Compare the kite-flying scene in *A Wonderful, Terrible Time* with that in *Henry 3* and both of these with the scene near the end of Rumer Godden's *The River* to discover how an activity beloved of childhood is handled by writers of three quite different sensibilities.)

But book after book of the urban-sociological kind is put down utterly without luminosity, without that overtone that is the signature of the poetic imagination (*How Many Miles to Babylon?* is a beautiful example of a story

having its background in the grey ghetto which *is* put down with luminosity, and that *does* bear the signature of a poetic imagination); it is as if
the drabness of city cement is infecting the prose telling about it. Rarely are
we given a view, rarely the feel of things, the sound, the smell—rarely the
sense of anything, the astonishing recovery. All is action and conversation,
going in and out of buildings, up and down streets, getting on and off
bicycles and to school and back. They're telling it like it is and, more often
than not, in the first person so as to make absolutely no mistake about
giving an impression that this all really happened. But there is a chasm
between Twain's and Krumgold's first person (Krumgold has used it in all
three of his books, to the best effect, I think, in . . . *and now Miguel*) and
what usually tries to pass as fictive art in the first person. For a writer who
has not yet fully developed either himself or his control of language, the
use of the first person means, apparently, that the story can go down
without discipline of style—because, after all, this is a person talking. This
is life, not book-stuff. Life it may be, but it is not art. It is an echo, perhaps,
a reflection, but it is not creation. Getting on with the plot or the action is
one thing, but investing the telling with innumerable dimensions and associations one can never analyse or explain is quite another.

In these books of telling like it is, either in the first person or not, I
look in vain for anything of the quality of Philippa Pearce's 'Mr Moss said
nothing, nor did he smile, but David knew from a certain delicate
rearrangement of the lines of his face that he was pleased'; or 'Then she
rapped on the driver's window and they set off—the five miles from Castleford to Great Barley, and straight through Great Barley, and bouncing over
the two bridges into Little Barley, and through that, and well ahead of time,
and everyone looking forward to early teas'; or anything remotely like 'He
could not say why, but this was what he most looked forward to on his
visits: a fine day, and going along, but not in a hurry, a stem of grass
between his teeth, and the company of a dog that snuffled and panted and
padded behind or to one side, or suddenly pounced into the hedgerow, in
a flurry of liver-and-white fur, with the shrill bark of "A rabbit! A rabbit!"
and then came out backwards and turned round and sat down for a
moment to get her breath back and admit: "Or perhaps a mouse."' But
surely, some might protest, these last two sentences (from *A Dog So Small*)
are needlessly long, especially for children, especially when they could so
easily be made into several short ones. Furthermore, the constant use of
'and' to join a series of thoughts is an extremely careless practice.

But listen to the sound of journey given off in that sentence about the
bus as it bounces gaily over the miles from Castleford to just beyond Little
Barley, with something in the progression of the phrase evoking the

passengers' feelings as they gaze contentedly toward the home fields drawing ever nearer. Chopping up wouldn't have given us this; it is the very 'ands' that convey the sense of journey, of alternately flowing and bouncing haste toward early teas, just as they give the sense of Young Tilly's darting forays after the rabbit in the last excerpt. And that final 'Or perhaps a mouse' would not have been nearly so comical or satisfying in effect had it not been an ending fall made possible precisely by the series of 'ands' that precede it. Yes, these are dangerous sentences, I suppose, to give as examples of something missed in the run-of-the-mill book. But what I mean by quoting them is that we need the ear of the artist and that we cannot make rules about sentences if it is an artist writing them and not a careless amateur joining phrases with 'and' because he is too lazy to find another, possibly more compact, way of gathering and releasing his thought.

As a final example from children's fiction of a sentence which evokes by its very architecture and pace the image of the thing it is talking about, I offer these lines from *Henry 3*:

> And then the roar began while the picture tube looked like it was folding in on itself to show the shape of an atom bomb growing up lazy and slow, turning its insides out and climbing to a stop that reached higher again while inside the fog a faint circle of the sun began to hatch and grow brighter, forcing its way through the ring of clouds that gently rose as the white hot sun stood sure and bright and growing until it filled the twenty-one inch screen with glitter to sprout, suddenly, another cyclone shooting higher still that spread a slow smoke wave which hung there, dead and still and cold. Our playroom was filled with the thunder of it.

Chilling are those three single-syllabled adjectives that end the slow rise and swell and final wavering spread of the cloud, and then the short sentence, 'Our playroom was filled with the thunder of it.'

In Mayne's writing, 'the night burst round the moving moonlight,' as well as in the paragraph above from Krumgold's, is expressed a fourth quality common to memorable prose aside from control of language, distinctive rhythm and the involvement of the writer: poetic vision. The word 'poetic' is, I realize, as dangerous in its way as those long sentences are dangerous in another. Flannery O'Connor advised a young woman whose work she was criticizing not to get poetic when she was writing prose, not even to get poetic when she was writing poetry, because only bad poets are poetic. A friend of Colette's labelled her tendency toward excess, toward an emotive extravagance, as 'rustic poetics'. However, Harriet Zinnes, a poet, says of a book on Robert Owen that the author wrote 'with poetic understanding of the complexity of the man's motives'. Clifford Odets speaks of having, in the rehearsal of *The Silent Partner*, to sacrifice some of its poetic quality because 'the texture was very dense as originally written'. Further along he says that John Howard Lawson's *Success Story* showed him 'the poetry that was inherent in the chaff of the streets', and that he began to see how there was 'something quite elevated and poetic in the way common people spoke'. Margaret L. Coit, a biographer and historian, comparing Theodore H. White's *The Making of the President—1964* with *The Road to the White House* by the staff of *The New York Times*, says that while the *Times* volume is written with precision, the White book is written with poetry, and that the one is good journalism but that the other may well be literature. Finally, Emile Capouya writes of Harvey Swados's book of short stories, *A Story for Teddy—and Others*, that the force of one of his tales is to be found in the poetry of the narrative, and that 'it is a poetic gift that permits Mr Swados to slay dragons out of season.'[3]

We have, therefore, a use of the word 'poetry' and the word 'poetic' by a number of persons in a way which would seem to mean that, to them, there is something to be expressed through these words that is not quickly, or perhaps precisely, expressible in any other way. And I believe in each case that what is meant is an elusive, conjuring quality that for all its elusiveness is the powerful element in whatever is being spoken of: it may be its flavour, tone, atmosphere, or its force of association, all of which may have deeply to do with meaning.

Now here, in a way, we are getting mixed up with content, but it is difficult not to in talking about style, about Lucy Boston's, for instance. She is the kind of writer who gives no quarter to her audience, depending upon the extraordinary play of her vision, her deep delight in and knowledge of 'the richness and strangeness of childhood' and the compelling urge of her story to entice young readers through her phrasing: a phrasing that makes that of the average writer seem blind and tired by comparison. 'The sky was not crowded with cloud shapes; it was just pale, the water like tarnished quicksilver and the leafy distances like something forgotten. The canoe moved in a closed circle of silence, so that everything that was near enough to come within the magic circle was singled out for the imagination to play with.' Lucy Boston feels strongly about style, while at the same time she senses that 'people are unprepared to consider children's books as works of art.' Because children are artists themselves and transform whatever is given them, the writer for them can get away with almost anything, she says. All the same, 'they react to style with their whole being. I want to stress this. Style has an irresistible authority.'[4]

Of Colette, Glenway Wescott has said in his *Images of Truth*, 'When a manner is as fine and intensive as Colette's, it can hardly be distinguished from the action or emotion or thought it has to convey. On many a page her meaning really resides in the mode of utterance rather than in terms of statement; the nuance is all-signifying, as in poetry.' I very often feel this about Lucy Boston's prose, as I do about Mayne's, especially in his *Earthfasts*.

In the majority of those sociological fictions I was speaking of, there is an almost total lack of imagery—nothing beyond the flat, bare, unlifted telling of what happened. But 'plainness of manner is nothing unless there is lightning to puzzle over,'[5] and that is what the great plain writers have: that lightning. Wescott, in reading aloud thirty or forty pages from Porter's *Ship of Fools*, found only one image, a simile: freckles 'like spots of iodine'. He says of her prose that no one since Stendhal has written so plainly, but feels that her writing carries three times as much evidence of the senses as does Stendhal's. It is what I treasure: this evidence of the senses. It is subtle and powerful art which, in simplicity and plainness, can carry a burden of this evidence, as E.B. White's does, Rumer Godden's, Philippa Pearce's. Turn page after page of their writing and you will find few, very few images, but when you have read the last word of any of their books, you have a world.

There are writers, on the other hand, to whom imagery is a necessary part of their expression in doing the highest possible justice to the created universe, and our vision is quickened by the unique likenesses that spring to their minds. 'He was shrunken and frail, with a face as lined as the glaze of an old plate,' Humphrey Harman says in *African Samson*, and 'When he saw a guest . . . he would hurry forward, looking ragged and uncertain, like a bird that is learning to fly.' In an antiphonal image, its two parts answering and enhancing one another, he refers to a certain part of the African continent 'where the hills are rumpled like a skin tumbled from a bed and the clouds lie late in the morning'.

In extended imagery, Krumgold gives us in *Henry 3* the following inscape about losing, about the sensation of knowing you're losing, and here again, as in the paragraph about the atom bomb, the rhythm of these lines, their very flow, is an inherent part of Krumgold's meaning. (These lines, too, are a fine example of how a novel can be written in the first person, the person here being a thirteen-year-old boy, can reflect the disciplined and sensitive style of the author himself, and yet sound perfectly natural and unliterary, in the pejorative sense of the word 'literary'.)

> . . . losing became a part of whatever went on. There's even a color to losing. It's brown, like the one dead leaf on a full green tree is brown, twisting slow and waiting to drop. And the smell of losing is sour as a dirty T-shirt the morning after a ball game. There's a taste to it, too, that's dry and salty. You could be running a temperature, the way losing tastes. And the sound of it is far off. Losing is an echo of all the noises you pass through while you think only of what's wrong. It's brittle, losing, like the feel of toothpicks you snap between your fingers in Pirelli's Pharmacy, trying to answer questions.

But it takes a writer wholly at ease with himself, wholly certain of what he sees and knows and feels, to write like this, for imagery can be as dangerous as Philippa Pearce's skilled and purposeful use of 'ands'. In a children's book which was praised when it came out, we are told of birds skimming like cream off the lawn, and in another of this author's books, of a girl walking like a lot of sticks. Far from being given the sense of a window suddenly opened, we can only say to ourselves, 'But nothing can skim like cream, because cream is skimmed,' and of the second image, 'Walked like a lot of sticks doing what? Surely the author meant, "She walked as if she were made of sticks".' But still we are dissatisfied and are left, as we read on, with a sense of unfinished thought, the blurred vision, the effort not to use a cliché.

In another piece of prose, this time nonfiction for adults, I found, 'A wood thrush sings, its trill swelling suddenly to fill all the evening like a distended balloon.' But a bird song is at the very farthest pole from a balloon blown up. How can a bit of manufactured rubber be identified with beguiling sound? And a balloon is perfectly confining, while a thrush's song, in the open, in the quiet of evening, is pervasive. Furthermore, upon reading 'distended', one immediately begins visualizing, and it is more than likely that the word will bring to mind, not sound, but hunger: what it does to the bellies of starving children in India and Africa and China. Initially, the writer must have been led into this altogether unfortunate simile by the fact that he had just put down, 'the thrush's trill swelled.' 'Swelled' made him think of 'balloon', but having thought, he should have at once rejected. John Ciardi, in his meaty *Dialogue with an Audience*, says that nothing in a good piece of imagery resists comparison.

Possibly such examples as the above are what Flannery O'Connor meant by poetic prose and the badness of it. However, these are not really poetic sentences; they are prose trying to be poetic and failing. And Miss O'Connor did not deny her own writing its imagery. It is, in fact, many-dimensioned with it. In persons of great giftedness, the selfhood is over-powering and the deepest preoccupation of that self is quite often made known in the kinds of images used, if not throughout the entire body of work (as in Elizabeth Bowen's, where she continually refers to and creates images of light), then throughout one book in relation to its subject. For instance, Flannery O'Connor's *The Violent Bear It Away* is about a mad prophet, his death and his effect after death on the boy who is the central character (Miss O'Connor's deepest preoccupation was with the displaced, the lost, the misfits). To prophesy is to speak concerning that which is fore-seen, and there are at least one hundred references in a novel of two hundred and forty-three pages to vision and eyes and seeing, most of these references in the form of stunning imagery. We are never in any doubt as to the colour in each person's eyes, even those of the minor characters, how they appear, or their actions under emotional stress. And there are more eyes in the book than those of the human beings who act out the drama. 'He did not look up at the sky but he was unpleasantly aware of the stars. They seemed to be holes in his skull through which some distant unmoving light was watching him. It was as if he were alone in the pres-ence of an immense silent eye.' We remember, too, in relation to these many eyes, Flannery O'Connor's words about writing, 'The key word is see.' Every scene of hers is overwhelming testimony to her power of seeing, both physical and spiritual, and every image she uses is testimony to her poetic vision.

Nor is this quality of style to be found only in distinguished fiction. C.P. Snow, in his *The Two Cultures and the Scientific Revolution*, pleads for an effort at communication between the two worlds of science and literature. We are well aware that the private languages of the sciences, which are not words at all but signs, are simply unintelligible to the average layman, so that the only bridges left between the two cultures are those books which can excite us in our own language about what scientists are doing and believing and struggling toward. I can think of no better example of such a bridge than Loren C. Eiseley's *The Immense Journey*, which I should like to put into the hands of every scientifically minded young person who has never suspected that the English language, when used poetically, can serve to increase our understanding of the subtleties and implications of scien-tific effort and thinking. In each of the pieces collected here, whether the author is revealing how flowers changed the world, why he does not believe that man can ever create life, or what he learned from a captive bird and its escape to rejoin its mate, he has the power of making Time ring in the ears while one horizon opens dizzyingly beyond another. Eiseley's is the double power of the scientist and the poet.

Finally, there is in all of the books I have spoken of still another quality which must pervade the writing of any work we never entirely forget: a surging vitality, a sense of supreme assurance. It is present as fully in the airiest fairy tale by Eleanor Farjeon or the poetry of Robert Frost as in such a towering work as Rebecca West's *Black Lamb and Grey Falcon*. One feels it quickening every page; it is a power the writer cannot pretend to, for an inherently pale or weak or negative personality is betrayed in his style no matter what he says or causes his characters to say.

Which brings me back to my initial definition of style—that it is the sound of self—and to further words which Katherine Anne Porter had to say on the subject: 'You do not create a style. You work, and develop yourself; your style is an emanation from your own being.'[6] And when a high school student wrote, asking how she could develop a style, there was of course only one answer, 'By developing yourself.' For if one does not have a self, or only a weak or uncertain self, then one has nothing to refer to but grammar and usage. And both content and style (so closely related), the thought and the delivery of thought, are most memorable, most illuminating, when the writer is wholly at ease with himself and has neither the need nor the desire to cover up or avoid the uniqueness of that self.

Wescott tells us that after reading Katherine Anne Porter over a period of time, his own way of writing, with its impulsive images and emotional impressionism, puts him to shame. But he must continue to be himself. He might try to cut himself down if the impulsive image-making and the emotional impressionism dissatisfy him, displease his own ear. And yet, concerning Wescott's imagination and possibly because of that very emotional impressionism, Edmund Wilson said of his *An Apartment in Athens* that Wescott, who had never been in Greece and had not experienced occupied Europe, conveyed to him more of the constrained and suffocating life of the occupied city after defeat than did Vercors, who knew the occupation at first hand, in his *Le Silence de la Mer*.

Nothing is gained, then, and much is lost by going around among the books one admires most and attempting to shape one's style to theirs, for in echoing one is avoiding, even ignoring, one's own depths rather than discovering them. For Proust, style was 'like color with certain painters, a quality of vision, a revelation of a private universe which each one of us sees and which is not seen by others'.[7] There is the heart of the matter: the private universe not seen by others—and which can never be seen if the struggle is not engaged, honesty not given the upper hand over echoing others, over avoiding or ignoring the self.

In her continuous effort to make the delivery of thought hit the centre of the tone for which she was listening and therefore express most truthfully her inmost vision—the revelation of a universe as seen by herself and by no other person—Virginia Woolf wrote in her journal year after year until the end of her life. She commented in its pages upon the rough and random texture of it, crying out as it did to her, upon rereading it, for a word altered here, another there, but its vigour and slapdash and often unexpected bull's eyes compelling her to realize that the habit of writing quickly for her own eye alone was good practice. It loosened the ligaments of her style ('never mind the misses and stumbles') in making direct shots at her subject and thus *having* to lay hands on her words, choosing and shooting up on the instant of putting word to page, and then discovering in the year just ended an increase of ease in her style which she attributed to these half hours before tea when she quickly scribbled down, 'faster than the fastest typing', 'something loose knit and yet not slovenly, so elastic that it will embrace anything, solemn or slight or beautiful that comes into my mind'.[8] She writes there something about the look of things; which reminds us again of how the key word is 'see', of the enormous difficulty of fusing what the eye sees with what one feels about that perception, and of finding words which will convey, arrowlike, both sight and feeling.

In his 'An Appreciation' at the beginning of Beatrix Potter's journal, H.L. Cox comments upon the 'gradual refinement' of her style in its pages between 1882 and 1893, giving as examples of the early date these comments upon two pictures, 'the leopards very small and terribly spotty', and 'a most unpleasant subject, beautifully painted, especially the floor', and comparing them with the statement of eleven years later, 'There are only three almond trees in Torquay. I have seen them all and they are small ones.'[9] In these few words we hear unmistakably the essence of Potter: that tart, brief precision, which we associate with the prose of those little books that began to appear in 1900.

Style, then, whether it is plain or poetic, shrouded or luminous, knotted or lucid, would seem to be something that expresses the writer to his inmost core in more ways than he himself, possibly, is aware of, because it is the sound of himself, whether he knows it or not, that he is listening for as he writes. Of his own expression, William Carlos Williams has said, 'I wanted to say something in a certain tone of my voice which would be exactly how I wanted to say it, to measure it in a certain way.'[10] And apropos of Lytton Strachey's style, Michael Holroyd observes, 'For it is in the sound and complexion as well as in the stated opinions of a writer's work that one must look for a true revelation of his temperament.'[11]

So that there is a conviction in my mind which I cannot escape as I read the work of each writer spoken of in this paper. It is that these men and women would be opposed in every possible way to a writer of nonfiction for children who said to me some years ago, 'I tell my editor: Go ahead and change whatever words or sentences you like—you can probably say it a lot better than I can.' I had nothing to reply, for I realized we were talking about two entirely different kinds of effort. If a writer is concerned with more than getting his subject somehow or other onto paper, then *no one*, no dearly loved relative, no respected friend, no editor, even, can tell him how to say what is in him to say, any more than they can tell him what to say, or how he should shape his book from chapter to chapter. All this is not a matter of ego. It is a matter of art, or at least the struggle toward it, which requires a lonely searching and listening. The relative, the friend, the editor, can point out that he is troubled, dissatisfied, that he has not been made to see, hear, feel, know; he can say that words are getting in the way rather than serving as a means to seeing and hearing and feeling and knowing. But that is all. For a work of art, no matter how small and modest it may be, is nothing if not the expression of a single sensitivity, a single perception. I am not speaking of the mingling of prose and visual art which makes a picture book, and yet most of the great picture books are those which have been created out of the single vision. Wanda Gág would illustrate nothing but her own prose, or those stories which she herself had collected and translated.

Katherine Anne Porter told her interviewer that she had spent years in teaching herself how to write. 'But that,' she would probably say, 'still does not mean that I am a stylist,' for the word 'stylist' as opposed to 'style' troubled Miss Porter, bearing for her that connotation of something self-conscious, contrived, unnatural.

But perhaps we can define a stylist as one who is not only concerned with *how* he says what he says, with maintaining the upper hand over his material, exerting the discipline and control which, in the end, result in the effect of effortlessness, but as one, moreover, who writes so exactly about what he sees and feels and understands, that his pages reflect his thought and vision fully as much as they report his subject. With this definition in mind, I maintain that every one of the writers taken up here are of that company of men and women, writing either for adults or for children, who see all things with the continually astonished eyes of a child, yet who speak with the experience of the mature artist and who are sensitively preoccupied with how best to use the tools of their craft, which are words.

Notes

[1]Thompson, 'Katherine Anne Porter', *Writers at Work*, 2nd series: 158.

[2]Fraser, *Wales*: 15.

[3]Capouya, 'The Writer as Subject', *Saturday Review*, 14 August 1965: 35.

[4]Boston, 'A Message from Green Knowe', *The Horn Book*, June 1963: 264.

[5]Davison, 'The Gilt Edge of Reputation', *The Atlantic*, January 1966: 84.

[6]Thompson, 'Katherine Anne Porter': 156.

[7]Proust, *Letters of Marcel Proust*: 227–8.

[8]Woolf, *A Writer's Diary*: 13.

[9]Cox, 'An Appreciation', *The Journal of Beatrix Potter from 1881–1897*: xviii.

[10]Koehler, 'William Carlos Williams', *Writers at Work*, 3rd series: 9.

[11]Holroyd, *Lytton Strachey*, Vol. 2: 581.

FIN DE SIÈCLE

Roy Stokes

We are now close enough to the end of the twentieth century to be able to propose some kind of judgement on its achievements. A century of wars, revolutions and counter-revolutions, of famine amid plenty, of high hopes and hopes betrayed. But we can only begin to understand the past if we look at it through the perspectives of our own interests. What of books for children, young people past the great divide of 1900? What a century it has been! The first in history in which books written especially for the young have been a major part of the history of authorship, publishing, and therefore the dissemination of ideas. Dare we now go one step farther? Can we, individually—because there would be little consensus of opinion—make our lists of those books which have affected us most deeply and for which we predict a future in the twenty-first century?

The century opened triumphantly with Beatrix Potter as Peter Rabbit made his first, if private, appearance in 1900. There can be few better examples of lasting quality. Her assorted animals—rabbits, ducks, hedgehogs, squirrels, cats—are set against her exquisite paintings of the English Lake District. As the century ends they have lost none of their innocent charm; the small size which she designed for them, ideal for small hands, has made them perfect as 'personal' books. The major change in our appreciation of her work lies in our discovery of the superb nature painting which she did quite apart from the stories.

Time has dealt less kindly with A.A. Milne, largely because he has been seen as one of that group of writers, with J.M. Barrie and Kenneth Grahame, whose own relationship with children was difficult to understand. Nevertheless, one small boy and his bear, bumping up the stairs together, remains an indelible picture of childhood as it ought to be, even when reality is sometimes unfortunately different. And how few other writers have given us verse which can be sung, shouted, read aloud in unison? The new printing on a larger leaf size and with delicate tints applied to the original E.H. Shepard illustrations should take these four books from the 1920s into the next century.

In the 1960s, the two Gs burst upon the scene: one to be so prolific without ever compromising his standards, the other with a smaller, but magical output. Leon Garfield has done more to delineate the historical world of childhood than any other modern writer. With *Smith* in 1967,

Garfield began a series which has never seriously faltered. Is there an outstanding one or are there individual favourites? It is difficult to think of any better awakening to Christmas morning than to find *The Apprentices* under the tree, but I also find that time and again I go back to the first chapter of *The Drummer Boy* to re-read one of the great openings in modern literature.

Alan Garner's novels are less numerous than Garfield's but they reach superb heights. *Elidor*, now somewhat neglected, is a book of pure magic, combining Garner's interests in archaeology, history and folklore. The ruined, bombed-out church is one of the frontiers of human experience, on a par with the rabbit hole which led to Wonderland and the wardrobe which was the gateway to Narnia. Soon afterwards came *The Owl Service* which again united Garner's interests with accurate portraits of adolescents and one of the most successful attempts at portraying the inflexions of Welsh-spoken English.

It is not uncommon for members of the general public to wonder exactly what role is played by medievalists, especially if they live in Oxford, the home of lost causes. Living in a world remote from most people's imaginations, not unlike those cosy Tudors and Stuarts, speaking a language utterly remote from modern speech, they seem to have little bearing on the late twentieth century. Yet two of them, friends for many years, created worlds into which thousands upon thousands of people have entered. J.R.R. Tolkien created a whole new world with its own history, language and literature. He mapped it with precision, amended the language as new 'discoveries' were made and brought reality into a work of his imagination. The Third Age of Middle-Earth is not approached by any device from modern 'reality'; it exists in its own right as much as any place on the terrestrial globe. The three volumes of *The Lord of the Rings*, preceded by *The Hobbit*, are as complete a portraiture of a civilization as exists in imaginative literature.

C.S. Lewis' seven books in the Narnia Chronicles are on a completely different scale. They create a more intimate world, dominated by allegory as befits a scholar, one of whose outstanding scholarly works was *The Allegory of Love*. Lewis had a distinguished literary career, in at least four different directions, but Narnia seems to be as assured as any of survival.

The strides made in standards of book production throughout the century have brought about an absolute treasure trove of book illustration. Books, especially books for children, sell *because* of the illustrations. The roll call is almost endless and very distinguished. Margery Gill (nobody ever drew children more faithfully), Pauline Baynes, Antony Maitland,

Elizabeth Cleaver, Barbara Cooney, Maurice Sendak, Virginia Lee Burton, the list could go on and on. Occasionally, as with Edward Ardizzone and Robert McCloskey, they illustrated the world of their own storied imaginations and they did it brilliantly. But one artist stands apart for the contribution which he has made to the art of book decoration as a whole and not simply to illustrations. Brian Wildsmith used the whole opening of the book, with a large page size, and decorated it in vibrant colour. His sense of texture gave a richness to the page and his detail provided a feast for the eyes. His range of texts has tended to be along traditional lines of nursery rhyme, folklore, and legend but there is nothing that he has illustrated over his long career that has not brought fresh light and understanding.

Canada and the United States each have made contributions which would, on their own merits, make claim to prolong the longevity which they have already enjoyed. A freckled, red-haired eleven-year-old girl walked into the history of Prince Edward Island, by grace of L.M. Montgomery, when this century was only twenty-five years old and has stayed there ever since. South of the border, but further west, Laura Ingalls Wilder chronicled the life of a pioneer family with love and stringent attention to detail. Her stories are among the best of American writing in any category for the whole of the century. Surely they, with those about Anne, will survive the passage of time; but they face another challenge. They have both been subjected to the transfer to another medium. It is one which is very rarely successful; Tolkien was most displeased with a radio adaptation of *The Lord of the Rings*. Wilder faces the greater challenge because the TV series ran far beyond her books and introduced characters and incidents of which she was unaware. Many peoples' impressions of *The Little House on the Prairie* owe nothing to Laura Ingalls Wilder and she and they are both the losers. Anne is not yet under such serious threat, but the danger is there.

Passing all these and many others (Arthur Ransome, Rosemary Sutcliff . . .) through the memory, my mind kept harking back to one book which, ever since its publication, I have felt assured would endure. Hundreds of books have been written regarding the adventures of a small boy or girl who is sent away from home to avoid the illness of a sibling—usually measles. Ostensibly, Philippa Pearce's *Tom's Midnight Garden* is another run at the same theme. But what transforms it immediately is the style of the writing. It is old-fashioned to write of style or to admire it, but this is the quality which makes a text easy to read and to understand: the perfect clarity of good style.

The aunt and uncle to whom Tom is sent live in a large house, now converted into apartments, beyond the tower of Ely Cathedral and into the flat, unspectacular countryside of the Fenland. Tom is allowed no contact with people, even the milkman, in case he has already contracted measles and might 'pass it on'. The only books around are Aunt Gwen's old school stories for girls; Tom is bored and, through boredom, is sleepless when his uncle insists on ten hours in bed each night. Wide awake, he listens to the chiming of the grandfather clock in the hall. It belongs to old Mrs Bartholomew who used to live in the house but is now in an upstairs apartment and rarely seen. As Tom lies awake at midnight, the clock strikes *thirteen*. He goes into the hallway to investigate and opens a door at the back of the house which he had been told not to bother about because it opened only onto a small neglected area 'where dustbins were kept and where the tenants of the ground-floor flat garaged their car under a tarpaulin'. But at midnight it opens onto a large and beautiful garden, peopled with its previous inhabitants, Hubert, James, Edgar and above all Hatty. Tom has discovered the midnight garden and when he returns to the house, no time has passed.

The thin veil of time which both separates and merges the past and the present floats through this story as slender as a gossamer thread and as strong as a steel hawser. While Tom is in the garden each night, Mrs Bartholomew lies 'tranquilly in bed: her false teeth, in a glass of water by the bedside, grinned unpleasantly in the moonlight, but her indrawn mouth was curved in a smile of easy, sweet-dreaming sleep. She was dreaming of the scenes of her childhood.' On the day of Tom's departure to return home Mrs Bartholomew asks to see him and he goes up to her apartment. They are meeting for 'the first time'. His aunt has great difficulty in describing to her husband the nature of their parting. 'He ran up to her, and they hugged each other as if they had known each other for years and years, instead of only having met for the first time this morning. . . . Of course, Mrs Bartholomew's such a shrunken little old woman, she's hardly bigger than Tom, anyway . . . but, you know, he puts his arms right round her and he hugged her goodbye as if she were a little girl.'

PART II

MYTH
AND FOLKLORE

Runes to Ward Off Sorrow: Rhetoric of the English Nursery Rhyme

Joanne L. Lynn

These jingles of her skipping ritual
    Are runes to ward off sorrow. They must hold
When fallen leaves will mold against a wall
    And winter grows more cold.

Elias Lieberman, 1958

Nursery rhymes are an overfamiliar phenomenon. Speakers of English take for granted acquaintance with Little Boy Blue, Miss Muffet, Peter Pumpkin Eater, and a host of other figures who exist potently in rhythmic English verse. Despite television and video games, a large number of children in any classroom still 'know by heart' a surprising number of rhymes, although few have seen a well, and still fewer a pieman or a piper. The English nursery rhymes are full of archaic language ('Prythee, play me t'other little tune'), unfamiliar images ('What's a carrion crow, Mommy?'), and inexplicable behaviour ('Why does the barber want to shave a pig?'). And yet they endure. *The Real Mother Goose*, with its checkerboard endsheets, is still being reprinted; famous illustrators of children's books crown their careers with a splendid Mother Goose; parents still recite nursery rhymes on long car journeys and read them to sleepy children at bedtime. Even repeated attacks on their violence and amorality by well-meaning but overzealous parent groups and psychologists have failed to remove them from the scene of early childhood.

This endurance has been variously explained: The nursery rhymes are historically interesting. Perhaps they are caches of obscure political satire. Perhaps they refer to real historical personages. Surely they reveal a good deal of social history. Perhaps it's simply the usefulness of their didacticism that prolongs their life. Or maybe, just maybe, they are not trivia, cultural effluvia, but are after all, genuine poetry. Most of these explanations can be dismissed as irrelevant to the peculiar persistence of the nursery rhyme in our culture. Iona and Peter Opie's *Oxford Dictionary of Nursery Rhymes* supplies first publishing dates and subsequent publishing history for 550

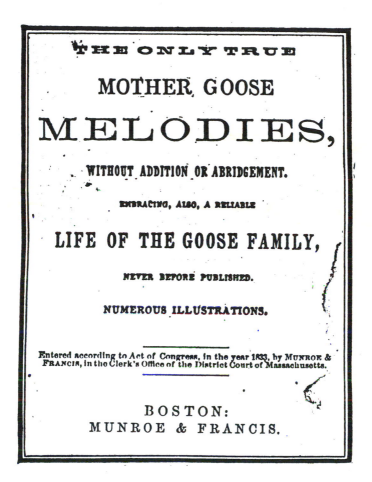

rhymes. Like the Baring-Goulds in their *Annotated Mother Goose* (which relies heavily on quotation from the *Oxford Dictionary*), the Opies approach the task with affectionate historical curiosity and responsible scholarship; but such works do not persuade toddlers to remember 'To Market, to buy a fat pig.'

Katherine Elwes Thomas' hopeful thesis that Mother Goose is full of veiled references to 'real personages' and political satire has long since been discredited.[1] More recently, William J. Baker quite rightly urges the study of the Mother Goose rhymes as social history not because they are still a living part of our culture, but because they reveal 'how vastly different the past was than the present'.[2] As for the usefulness of their didacticism, reflective reading of any fair-sized collection of nursery rhymes will produce a challenge to that position, if not refutation. What are the 'lessons' of 'Hickory, Dickory Dock' or 'Mary, Mary, quite contrary'? A minatory cause/effect relationship in these is tenuous at best. For every naughty Johnny Green who put Pussy in the well, there are ten unrepentant scapegraces who remain unpunished. A more fruitful means of explaining the viability of the nursery rhymes is one which considers the nursery rhymes as genuine poetry. Yet here, too, problems and loose assumption abound.

Before examining these explanations further, I should admit at the outset that not all English nursery rhymes interest me equally. Some are indeed trivial, some merely didactic, some primarily curious artifacts of literary archaeology. Nevertheless, in examining a large number of survivors as I have recently had occasion to do, I am led to observe that many are compelling enough for literary reasons to attempt a fresh accounting for their persistence in the culture. I propose that nursery rhymes—collected as they have been from a variety of sources—were selected by and for a specific audience of both children and adults, that they remain active in the culture thanks to a similar audience, and that the double nature of the audience has dictated the survival of a particular literary form. This form is characterized by compression, paradox, ambiguity, and a tension between form and content that is characteristic of genuine poetry.

Major children's literature texts purport to discuss the nursery rhyme as literature but base their discussions primarily on impressionistic observation, quotations from poets, and passing reference to the elements of literature. Sometimes poets can indeed be astute critics; certainly they can turn a phrase. Walter de la Mare's 'tune and runningness',[3] his 'tiny masterpieces of word craftsmanship', and Andrew Lang's 'smooth stones from the brook of time' appear predictably in texts, are quoted eagerly in student midterms. But quotability is not a measure of critical utility. Suggestive and perceptive as such phrases are, they do little to help us understand the real nature of the nursery rhyme.

Of 'quotable authorities', Maurice Sendak and Frances Clarke Sayers come closest to identifying essential qualities of the nursery rhyme. In his article on illustrating Mother Goose, Sendak describes their 'earthy, ambiguous, double-entendre quality', noting that they are 'deceptively simple', having 'a certain baldness' mixed with 'the subtle presence of elusive, mythic and mysterious elements transcending the nonsense . . .'. Frances Clarke Sayers finds in them 'an element that is in all great literature . . . the realization that in life there is a tragic tension between good and evil, between disaster and triumph, and it isn't all a matter of sweetness and light.'⁴ Both commentators note the chthonic suggestiveness that underlies their spare simplicity, their broad humour. Neither writer attempts or intends extensive poetic analysis. Helpful as these observations are as pointers, we seek explicitness.

Most children's literature text editors accurately note the obvious poetic features of the Mother Goose rhymes: strongly marked rhythms, repetition devices (rhyme, alliteration, incantations, incremental repetitions), and economy of expression. Unfortunately, these same authors assert that some of the chief literary strengths of the nursery rhyme are plot and character, a proposition that does not bear scrutiny. Five out of the seven texts sampled mentioned plot, character or 'drama' as important qualities of the nursery rhyme. Examples offered, however, fail to demonstrate the point. A typical case is Rebecca Lukens' citation of 'Three Wise Men of Gotham' as condensed story.⁵ The first two lines announce that the three went to sea in a bowl. The next, and last, two lines conclude: 'If the bowl had been stronger,/My song had been longer.' The comic impact of this verse depends not on condensation of story, but of suppression of it altogether. Likewise, 'Jack-A-Nory' exploits the reader's narrative anticipation, makes its effect by foiling it:

I'll tell you a story
    Of Jack-A-Nory
And now my tale's begun.
    I'll tell you another
    About his brother
And now my tale is done.

The comedy builds on the human need for narrative, gains its effect by frustrating it. This is not to argue that no nursery rhymes offer 'story,' but to establish that plot is not an essential component of the form.

Several writers mention 'memorable' characters. Certainly characters' names (Bo-Peep, Simple Simon, Boy Blue) are memorable; their situations are often memorable as gesture. Like figures on a Grecian urn, Bo-Peep eternally seeks her sheep; Jack Horner eternally sits, self-congratulatory, in his corner. But these are icons, not characters functioning in a fiction. Huck and Kuhn insist that characters in nursery rhymes are 'interesting likeable people'. In fact no characters in the English nursery rhymes exist in enough psychological complexity, actual or literary, to be called 'likeable'. One might as well complain that a lot of nursery rhyme characters are 'unlikeable': Georgy Porgy, the Knave of Hearts, Tom the Piper's son. Likeableness is not a test of character creation in fiction, and certainly not a test of poetic viability. The power of the nursery rhyme character is iconographic and poetic—the power to evoke, to suggest, even to mystify, rather than to satisfy with the illusion of deep acquaintance as one comes to know the characters of a novel.

This evocative power runs directly counter to the surface appearance of the nursery rhyme. On the surface, most are straightforward, good-humoured expressions of everyday events in a predominantly rural culture of householders, farmers, and tradesmen. The 'voice' of the English nursery rhyme is the voice of the sturdy English yeoman. The details of everyday life referred to in the rhymes are drawn from the life of the sixteenth, seventeenth, and eighteenth centuries.[6] Porridge and malt, tinkers and peddlers, barns infested with rats and mice, dairy cows, hens and roosters, sheep, tailors, and regional fairs all root the rhymes unmistakably in a specific culture. Regardless of subject matter, the point of view is always that of the small rural householder, subject to economic anxiety, but stubbornly independent. Pussy Cat may have been honoured by her London visit to the queen, but she is not awed; the queen sits in a chair, not on a throne, while Puss demonstrates her pragmatic skill ('I frightened a little mouse under her chair'). In 'Hark, Hark, the Dogs do Bark', the rural householder regards the gypsy beggars with ambivalence: he is at once attracted by their exotica and repelled by their irregular habits. The suggestion of class envy of the 'fine lady' on a white horse at Banbury Cross is countered by the speaker's healthy contempt for a similar lady in 'I Had a Little Pony'. He will happily forego the custom of the lady who mistreats her mount: 'I would not lend my pony now for all my lady's hire.'[7]

Iona and Peter Opie tell us that the nursery rhymes have come from a variety of sources: proverbs, songs, ballads, broadsides, mummer's plays, street cries, and so on (pp. 3–4; 19–30). Although the origins are varied and contemporary collections reflect this variety, survivors exhibit common qualities shared by the historical and by the contemporary rhetorical situation. 'The overwhelming majority of nursery rhymes were not in the first place composed for children; in fact, many are survivals of an adult code of joviality and in their original wording were, by present standards, strikingly unsuitable for those of tender years' (p. 3). A genteel principle of selection has excluded from popular modern editions such rhymes as:

Who comes here? A Grenadier.
What do you want? A pot of beer.
Where's your money? I forgot.
Get you gone, you drunken sot.[8]

Or this unromantic rhyme of courtship:

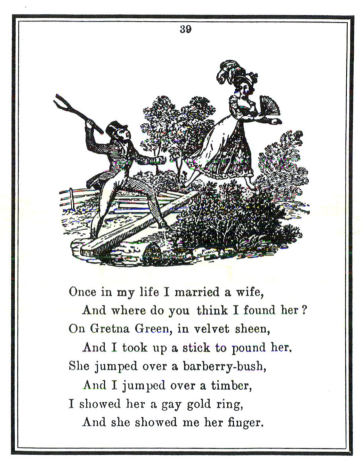

39

Once in my life I married a wife,
    And where do you think I found her?
On Gretna Green, in velvet sheen,
    And I took up a stick to pound her.
She jumped over a barberry-bush,
    And I jumped over a timber,
I showed her a gay gold ring,
    And she showed me her finger.

The financial embarrassment in the first rhyme is expressed as well in the more 'suitable' 'Simple Simon'. The hostility between the sexes and the difficulties of courtship and marriage of the second rhyme are implicit in the more 'acceptable' 'Peter, Peter, Pumpkin Eater'.

The original adult or general audience and the contemporary child share the frustration of social vulnerability in their necessary subordinate position, which may account for the oblique aggression and veiled hostility of a high proportion of nursery rhymes. In oral transmission, the compression and suggestion necessary to the original occasion of composition becomes a poetic virtue. Yet another, and perhaps more important, feature of the peculiar rhetorical situation in which the nursery rhymes survive may account for the dynamic tension between the matter-of-fact surface and the submerged darkness of hostility and aggression. The singer or sayer of folk poetry has chosen it from a large body of available material. In the case of the nursery rhymes the audience is double, a relationship best understood schematically:

S_1 = folk poet, composer
S_2 = adult (as caretaker)
R_1 = adult (as child, later as selector)
R_2 = child (tired? bored?)

I will use the semiologist's term 'sender' here rather than 'poet,' in order to emphasize the selective transmission process of materials in a folk tradition. Although many printed editions of Mother Goose rhymes exist, the persistence of nursery rhymes is due more to oral transmission than to print. The first sender is the original anonymous folk poet; the first receiver is the adult, who has heard nursery rhymes as a child, but becomes a selector—simultaneously now a sender and a new kind of receiver. The adult as caretaker becomes in turn a second sender, who retrieves rhymes from memory or selects them from books. The second audience is likely to be one very young child in an intimate relationship with the adult sender (S_2). The two audiences (R_1 and R_2) seek different satisfactions from the same 'message.'

The sender (S_2) sings or recites to amuse the child, simultaneously amusing him or herself. The Opies remind us that the nursery rhyme 'is resorted to by the mother for the soothing and amusement of the child . . .' (p. 3). The verb *resorted* implies stress in the transmitter (here, the mother) and stress in the receiver (the child). The two kinds of stress are different, the former being a product of the latter. In one common circumstance for recitation of nursery rhymes, the child is restless, irritable, tired or unhappy, exhibiting signs of stress. Even the most altruistic, patient parent will experience a conflict between the desire to nurture and comfort and the desire for emotional separation and getting on with one's own life, a conflict which produces its own stress. The nursery rhyme is a vehicle serving both audiences. Strongly marked rhythms and predictable repetitions reassure the child and free the adult to pay attention both to the child and to his or her own internal life. Matter-of-fact presentation of disparate images and paradigmatic daydreams or aggressions relieve the tension of the adult as audience and express the conflict of the adult as sender. Contained or cryptic aggression is perceived as comic by both adult and child.

The situation in which the nursery rhyme is chosen and transmitted is rhetorically unique. The person who repeats nursery rhymes to tired or vulnerable charges in a tightly circumscribed domestic environment speaks from a continual state of low-level stress, irritation, possibly even frustration at confinement with children. The Opies observe in passing that most of the rhymes were not originally composed for children, but that 'they enter the nursery through the predisposition of the adults in charge of it.' The mother or nurse chooses 'because in the pleasantness (or desperation) of the moment it is the first thing which comes to her mind' (p. 6). What comes to mind impulsively, intuitively, is bound to be 'selected' for emotional, aesthetic satisfactions probably more often than for didactic purposes.

This rhetorical situation has obviously influenced the choice and preservation of mnemonically easy verse—i.e., having short lines, compact stanzas, strongly marked rhythm and rhyme. What has not, to my knowledge, been noted is that the stress, frustration, or longing of the adult sender determines the selection of rhymes that can function as safe containers of sorrow, frustration, fear and anger in a situation in which direct expression of these emotions would be inappropriate. Thanks to Freud, we have grown suspicious of chance recall. What 'pops into the head' has often been found to have more or less demonstrable subterranean connections with internal needs. I submit that in the service of these needs, generations of transmitters of nursery rhymes have selected rhymes that are unsentimental and objective. A large group of them contain a high proportion of violence, both physical and symbolic. The deliberate choice of rhymes containing violence expresses tension by means of contrast between the illusion of everyday activity and jarring affronts to rationality.

The tone of the majority of nursery rhymes, regardless of form or subject matter, is objective, matter of fact. A lullaby ('Down will come baby, bough, cradle and all'), a tongue twister ('Swan swam over the sea. Well swum, swan'), a narrative ('Said Simple Simon to the pieman, "Deed I have not any"') all display the same dispassionate tone. Even nonsense has about it an air of no-nonsense:

Dr Foster went to Gloucester
In a shower of rain.
He stepped in a puddle up to his middle
And never went there again.

There is neither mockery nor lament for Dr Foster's plight, nor for the baby who falls 'when the bough breaks', nor for the man who 'scratched out both his eyes' in the bramble bush, nor yet for the man in the moon who 'burnt his mouth'. Although human situations are described or dramatized without editorial comment, conflict and anxiety are implicit: economic anxiety in 'There Was an Old Woman who Lived in a Shoe', domestic conflict in 'Peter, Peter, Pumpkin Eater', and in:

> Molly, my sister and I fell out
> And what do you think it was all about?
> She loved coffee and I love tea
> And that was the reason we couldn't agree.

The pain of frustration at confinement, of subordination, of humiliation, lies beneath apparent trivialities, as well as a constant wry awareness of the limitation of human existence.

The violence and amorality of nursery rhymes have been a centuries-long source of controversy, the contours of which are irrelevant here. Suffice it to say that the traditional moralists have had the better of the logical argument even as they have lost the real battle, since editions of Mother Goose have continued in dog-eared proliferation. Defenders of amorality and hostility in nursery rhymes have never found a satisfactory logical defence of these qualities as essential to the form. Yet these very qualities mark the nursery rhymes strongly, even poignantly: the longing of the speaker in 'Bobby Shaftoe's Gone to Sea' or the querulousness of the impatient speaker in 'Johnny's so long at the fair'.

The baffling violence of 'Goosey, Goosey, Gander' can be understood only in terms of symbolic tension:

> Goosey, goosey, gander
>   Whither dost thou wander?
> Upstairs and downstairs
>   And in my lady's chamber.
>
> There I met an old man
>   Who wouldn't say his prayers!
> I took him by the left leg,
>   And threw him down the stairs.

Whereas it is possible to give the entire poem a scatological reading, explicit sexual interpretation is not necessary to recognize the paradoxical tension expressed in the poem. The male goose's authority is challenged by the 'old man', who is not only poaching on forbidden territory, but is also impious, thus justifying his violent ejection (tossed, of course, by the left, or sinister, leg) by the 'goose' who here seems inexplicably linked with the 'I' of the second stanza. Displacement of the violent act onto an improbable agent (a gander) relieves the reciter (S_2) of responsibility for hostile and violent feelings. Containment of the violent image in a regular metre and predictable rhyme scheme defuses hostility, making it safe to express in the presence of children, whose need to feel secure is served simultaneously with the paradoxical need to be stimulated by gentle shock, and the reciter's need to find relief for inappropriate hostile feelings—confinement by class, or confinement by the caretaker role.

An even sharper contrast between the pleasant familiar surface of rhythmic refrain and the action of the poem is evident in 'Heigh Ho, the Carrion Crow', in which a tailor attempts to shoot the bird symbolic of death out of the Druidic oak, misses, and shoots 'his own sow quite through the heart', a real economic as well as a symbolic domestic tragedy. The disastrous situation is buffered by a jovial refrain: 'Fol de riddle, lol de riddle,/hi ding ho'.

In a dandling game, 'A farmer went trotting upon his grey mare' with his daughter behind him 'so rosy and fair,' but a raven, another emblem of mortality and decay, frightens the horse who breaks its legs, tumbling farmer and daughter, breaking the farmer's head. The gratuitously aggressive fowl flies off unrepentant and unpunished: 'And vowed he would serve them the same the next day.' The refrains, 'Bumpety, bumpety, bump!' and 'Lumpety, lumpety, lump!' provide an obvious rhythmic pattern for jouncing a child on one's knee, but they also relieve the adult's subliminal awareness that (as a bumper sticker motto puts it) 'Life is hard, and then you die.'

Eleanor Farjeon has said that for the child 'the prosaic and the wondrous are on equal terms'. Perhaps this is the quality of mind or developmental stage that allows children in the first place to entertain the incongruities of nursery rhymes unblinkingly, rarely demanding explanations. It is not the quality of mind that perpetuates them. The images of the nursery rhymes must serve the adult (the medium, the transmitter) as well, or die. For the adult the prosaic and the wondrous are most distinctly not on equal terms, and the juxtaposition of the two affords an attractive shock that relieves, amuses, delights.

What has prompted this extended analysis of verbal form that, like jokes, might better lie unanalysed, is the recognition that the nursery rhymes still do amuse and delight. More than mere historical curiosities, more than repositories of social history, more than didactic aids, more than vehicles for successful illustrators, nursery rhymes have a power that is both emotional and aesthetic. Nor are they simply the first rung on a hierarchical ladder to poetic sensibility. May Hill Arbuthnot says that the child 'progresses from jingles of Mother Goose to little poems by such poets as Robert Louis Stevenson and A.A. Milne'. This is not the place to argue the relative merits of poems written specifically for children and the folk heritage of the nursery rhyme. I suggest that Stevenson and Milne are culturebound in a way that Mother Goose is not, in spite of her archaisms. If I were taking bets on longevity, I'd put my money on Lucy Locket and Miss Muffet over Stevenson's 'heathen Chinee' and Christopher Robin's nanny's dressing gown. The nursery rhymes endure on their own terms because they encode vital concerns of their double audience. The concerns of the nursery are remarkably conservative and unchanging; the limitations imposed on those who care for small children today are much the same as those thus imposed when the rhymes first entered the culture. The need to find literary expression for the comfort and amusement of the subordinate and the vulnerable is, in Carl Sandburg's phrase, 'just the same as it always was'.

Notes

[1](Boston: Lothrop, Lee and Shepard, 1930). Astonishingly, Thomas' work is still cited frequently, although her scholarship has long since been discredited. Authors of texts on children's literature continue to quote Thomas as a horrible but amusing example. Two such references can be found in Charlotte Huck and Doris Young Kuhn, *Children's Literature in the Elementary School*, 2nd ed. (New York, 1968): 61; and in James A. Smith and Dorothy M. Park, *Word Music and Word Magic* (Boston, 1977): 31–2. In this last, a long passage recapitulates fanciful and erroneous interpretations with an appropriate disclaimer at the end, on the theory, I presume, that fiction is more interesting than truth.

[2]William J. Baker, 'Historical Meaning in Mother Goose: Nursery Rhymes Illustrative of English Society before the Industrial Revolution,' *Journal of Popular Culture* 9 (1975): 651.

[3]Quoted in most texts on children's literature, the phrase first appeared in Walter de la Mare, *Come Hither* (New York, 1923): xxxi.

[4]From an interview with Charles M. Wiesenberg, Public Relations Director of the Los Angeles Public Library, Spring, 1965. Quoted in Haviland, *Children's Literature*: 124.

[5]Rebecca Lukens, *A Critical Handbook of Children's Literature* (Glenview, IL, 1976): 157. Other discussions of the poetic appeal of nursery rhymes can be found in Mary J. Lickteig, *An Introduction to Children's Literature* (Columbus,

OH, 1975): 60; Nancy Larrick, *A Teacher's Guide to Children's Books* (Columbus, OH, 1962), 10; Eleanor Farjeon, in Edna Johnson et al., eds, *Anthology of Children's Literature*, 5th ed. (Boston, 1977): 83–4; Huck and Kuhn, 98; Virginia Witucke, *Poetry in the Elementary School* (Dubuque, IA, 1970); May Hill Arbuthnot and Zena Sutherland, *Children and Books*, 4th ed. (Glenview, IL, 1972): 114–17.

[6]Even if the Opies had not established the dates of most of the rhymes as belonging to this time period (pp. 6–8), obvious internal evidence supports the assertion. For further discussion see William J. Baker, 'Historical Meaning in Mother Goose.'

[7]*The Real Mother Goose*, illus. Blanche Fisher Wright. First published in 1916, it has gone through more than 50 printings. All citations will be from this edition unless otherwise noted, not because it is the most scholarly or comprehensive, but because it contains versions most familiar to American readers. In the interest of an uncluttered text, I have not cited page numbers for short quotations from familiar rhymes.

[8]*The Only True Mother Goose Melodies* (Boston: Lothrop, Lee and Shepard, 1905): 41. Subtitled 'An Exact Reproduction of the Text and Illustrations of the Original Edition Published and Copyrighted in Boston in the Year 1833 by Munroe & Francis.'

References

Baker, William J., 'Historical Meaning in Mother Goose'. *Journal of Popular Culture* 9 (1975): 651.

Baring-Gould, William S. and Ceil, *Annotated Mother Goose* (New York: Clarkson N. Potter, 1962).

Haviland, Virginia, *Children's Literature: Views and Reviews* (Glenview, IL: Scott Foresman, 1973).

Huck, Charlotte, and Doris Young Kuhn, *Children's Literature in the Elementary School* 2nd ed. (New York: 1968).

Lukens, Rebecca, *A Critical Handbook of Children's Literature* (Glenview, IL, 1976).

Opie, Iona and Peter, *Oxford Dictionary of Nursery Rhymes*.

Sendak, Maurice, 'Mother Goose's Garnishings' in Haviland, ed., *Children's Literature*.

Smith, James A. and Dorothy M. Park, *Word Music and Word Magic* (Boston: 1977).

WOODS AND CASTLES, TOWERS AND HUTS: ASPECTS OF SETTING IN THE FAIRY TALE

Joyce Thomas

Ever since *The Odyssey*, setting or landscape has constituted a vital element of Western literature. It is vital as well in children's literature—so integral to most, if not all, of the classic works of children's literature, that it is impossible to imagine them without first conjuring their respective settings. There is, of course, the fantastic, disturbing dreamscape of Wonderland into which Alice tumbles and the inverted, chessboard plane of the Looking-Glass through which Alice steps. There is the Wild Wood that patters, whistles, and peers with beady eyes to terrorize Mole; there is Rat's beloved river, 'The River', that swirls, sparkles, bubbles and chatters, lilts and lulls. There are the law-regimented jungle and superstition-riddled village Mowgli straddles, the savage frozen Wild that moulds White Fang, Oz's glittering Emerald City, Peter's eternal playground of Neverland, even Mr MacGregor's danger-laden, tempting garden. And coming long before these indelible settings, are those of the *volksmärchen* or folk fairy tales.

The first English translation of the Brothers Grimm's *Fairy Tales* in 1823 linked the Romantic and Victorian eras, and heralded the latter's golden age of children's literature. The influence of these and other tales upon that literature is clear; in one way or another, fairy tales affected the basic elements of plot, character, style, theme, symbolism, and setting. Even though the folk fairy tale is situated in a timeless, spaceless, quasi-mythic sphere—that familiar 'once upon a time'—it nonetheless has settings which serve crucial functions for countless tales. What is perhaps most intriguing about setting in the fairy tale is the ease with which a typical setting—for example, the green or dark woods—assumes heightened significance and thereby imbues its tale with a further, symbolic dimension, all the while that setting is presented with a minimum of narrative description. In itself the setting holds significance as a physical place while also providing a landscape that generates an appropriate atmosphere to the tale's action and theme. Further, setting often exists as one manifestation of the fairy tale's ongoing dialectic between matter and magic, between the material world and the marvellous forces that transcend, transmute it. Ultimately, setting functions as an external, tangible correspondence to things internal and intangible.

The four most common settings in traditional fairy tales are the woods, the castle, the tower, and the hut in the woods. Probably no landscape is so automatically associated with the faerie as is the woods; probably no amorphous locale is so often recreated as is that of the Black Forest. Innumerable tales, from 'Hansel and Grethel', 'Snow-White', and 'The Robber Bridegroom' to 'Rapunzel' and 'Little Red Riding-Hood', unfold their main action somewhere within the verdant wood. Where the wood waits, there wait all manner of magical beings, wish-granting crones, child-eating witches, trickster fairies, talking masquerading wolves. Almost always, when the wood is present, a character will either enter its dappled recesses or walk near its shaggy edge to encounter there the magical. The forest is an appropriate threshold to the supernatural. Its edge constitutes a literal threshold between man and nature, the cultivated and uncultivated, the tame and wild, the known and the unknown. Its lush, luxuriant vegetation well exemplifies the faerie realm. A place of towering oaks, whispering firs, lacy ferns, pristine streams, multifarious flora and fungi, a wealth of warm- and cold-blooded creatures, sun and shade, sable night and silver moon, the woods best embodies, best signifies the faerie, the wonder-full. It is a living, metamorphosing being, magically transformed by day and night and season. For the folk, it has always been the place where supernatural beings dwelt, and for ages its green was considered the fairies' colour.[1]

The spell cast by the woods is one with man's uneasy relationship with nature. No longer the familiar sphere of man's habitation, this is a place evocative of awe and wonder and an apprehensive discomfort, if not outright fear:

> The uncanny quality of woods is part of the lore of childhood. In the forest you are far from home, from fireside warmth and kindliness and the settled accustomed order of things. In the forest you are lost. In the forest the trees put out roots to trip you, and reach out for you with crooked, skinny fingers. In the forest, very often, lives the witch.[2]

More than any other setting in fairy tales, the forest intimates the magic inherent within mere matter. It is naturally an enchanting place, and easily becomes the setting of unnatural enchantments. In the forest, maidens sleep in glass, confectionery houses are nibbled by lost children, a plucked lily transforms the human into a raven, unseen wee folk titter behind splayed leaves, coiled ferns. Anything might happen once one has stepped onto the wood's yielding threshold, as even Young Goodman Brown and Sir Gawain discovered. The woods' unfamiliar, enchanting, eerie interior makes it an apt symbol of the unknown and the unconscious, so, too, is it an apt earthly translation of the labyrinthine night-sea journey. Countless tests, countless quests, are enacted in the wood. Countless treasures, countless deaths, wait there, somewhere. Thus, the wood sprouts in the fairy tale as conjoined matter and magic. The wood's presence immediately imbues a tale with an atmosphere of magical possibilities: one's imagination colours its fairy greenery with the full prismatic spectrum of marvels, threats, and benefices. The forest is both a physical setting as well as a transcending presence of that setting; ultimately, it functions as 'a psychic state', according to Gaston Bachelard,[3] a psychic space, which perhaps is why the narrator need merely state, 'There was a deep wood,' to set that wood's psychic aspects swirling within our imaginations.

The forest is nature's chamber. By contrast, the castle, tower, and hut are man's chambers, ones he has constructed to keep nature out. Even these familiar abodes when set inside the fairy tale prove to house the magical. Though many nondescript dwellings litter the tales' landscape, it is the solid, looming mass of the castle and the fragile, lowly nest of the hut which most emphatically speak to us, perhaps because they stand as polar extremes to each other. The castle, of course, rises as the apotheosis of all abodes. Its sturdy stone structure represents a type of architectural cosmos, ranging from the outer moat, battlements and gatehouse to the inner courtyard, keep, towers, interlacing chambers and heaven-set spires. It is, in fact, a community enclosed inside a fortress, and as such represents in one image both house and town, both individual and collective dwellings. It constitutes a macrocosmic rendering of the single house's function as family shelter and home; it is the hut magnified on a grand scale—so grand, that it looms less as any collection of dwellings than as a carved, Baroque mountain-top.

This is the fittingly impressive setting for royalty, a setting which seems always to have entranced those denied access to its sanctum. It is not difficult to appreciate the influence the castle on the hill would have exerted on the common folk below, nor to imagine how they might have spun tales about the 'beautiful people' sequestered behind its thick walls. As part of the fairy tale's landscape, the castle often functions less as a place per se than as a thing. Symbolic of royalty and ultimate success, it is the prize the hero or heroine gains at the end of her trials. It embodies all success within the tangible form of hewn stone: wealth and dominion, kingship and a royal marriage, safety, security, happiness. By extension, the castle's physical matter symbolizes the hero's absolute victory, more spiritual than physical. That the hero possesses the castle, its cosmos, at the tale's end suggests he now is in possession of the world and himself; similarly, he is assuredly secure, for his victory and happiness are ensured as much permanency as that of the castle's durable stone.

Despite that assurance, another function of this sturdy setting is to show that even the castle's fortifications cannot keep out the supernatural; even kings do not wield absolute power. Like the woods, the castle is so marvellous a place, now of human design, that marvels seem especially suited to it. Stories of royalty who must contend on their own grounds with magical beings readily demonstrate that the battlements only serve to shut nature and one's human foes out—they serve as much purpose as mist when it comes to preventing the supernatural from gaining entry. Thus the princess must admit and cater to the Frog Prince; thus the king, for all his fiery precautions, must yield to the prophecy of his daughter's hundred-years' sleep. The castle's solid mass also makes it an appropriate setting for enchantment because it is so fixed, so set, so protective. Briar Rose may have to endure the spell, but she dreams safely within the hard chrysalis of the castle's stone and its outer cocoon of the equally impenetrable bramble hedge. Enchantments transpiring inside the castle often partake of some form of frozen, suspended animation: a comatose sleep, being turned to stone. Both seem appropriate translations of the castle proper; its horizontal, winding walls and vertical, turreted towers create a geometric pattern which seems the very architecture of faerie, yet it is a fixed pattern and architecture, unlike the fluid woods; a solid image as unchanging as the cut blocks and hewn granite of which it is fashioned. With the castle, the ethereal element of faerie is crafted from a decidedly corporeal reality.

No matter the castle's material mass—it is not an especially distinct setting; after all, there is so much of it. It is more landscape than focused locale. Where closer focus is called for, some smaller part of the whole is used, such as the tower. Rising above the castle's other structures, the tower stands as the vertical locus of its landscape, and is therefore a more definite setting. In *The Poetics of Space*, Bachelard provides a fascinating perspective on both the tower and hut, and, indeed, the 'poetics' of various spaces and settings.[4] He notes how the tower seems somehow older than the structure of which it is a part; that it is akin to the attic in its association with the past, in the solitude it suggests, and in the steep stairs winding within it. Like the attic, like the attic's trunks filled with another time's objects and memories, the tower hints of marvels waiting inside its vaulted chamber; as it dominates space, so does it keep watch over the past, over the present and future. It is hardly surprising that Briar Rose should find her fate awaiting her inside an old tower. Indeed, her journey toward that destiny reads as if it were one made backward in time as she explores the castle's antechambers and secret recesses, corners and nooks, until at last,

> she came to an old tower. She climbed the narrow winding stair which led to a little door, with a rusty key sticking out of the lock; she turned the key, and the door opened, and there in the little room sat an old woman with a spindle, diligently spinning her flax.[5]

Ascending the tower's narrow stairs, she ascends into the past: a rusty key, an old woman, a forgotten spindle, the prophecy. Here, the tower is a symbolic construct of vertical space—like a stone obelisk, it rises as the narrative's focal point around which time winds and unwinds, around which the prophecy voiced in the past will be unspooled in the present and drawn out into the future, one hundred years distant.

Frequently the tower and its nimbus of the magical are linked to some aspect of time, of the past. As the tale 'Rapunzel' shows, the tower can exist by itself, without the castle's surrounding clutter. At the age of twelve years, Rapunzel is shut inside a tower 'in the midst of a wood, and it had neither steps nor door, only a small window above.'[6] Being the witch's edifice, the tower symbolizes her desire to hold time to the past, to keep Rapunzel forever in the role of a little girl. Unlike most towers, this one offers neither ready access nor a proper view of the outside world. Its small window suggests the witch's own restricted and constraining perspective as well as her attempt to hold the present and future—Rapunzel's budding adolescence, the outside world—at bay. The lack of stairs likewise reflects this denial of forward-moving time and outside influences. As a whole, the tower is reminiscent of an antiquated clock-tower whose frozen hands are fixed at some previous hour denoting Rapunzel's girlhood. Essentially, the rigid thing is a life-denying structure, less the architecture of a protective cocoon than a vertical coffin. Being separated from a castle, it rises as the landscape's physical focus and locus. Ironically, that landscape is one of the wood's lush, generative, changing vegetation; thus the tower is an unnatural setting in more ways than one, being an incongruous edifice for the wood and being severed from the castle's organic design and human community. As an image speaking of the witch's unnatural desires, it also anticipates her inevitable failure to sustain those desires.

Situated in the wood, designed by the witch, this tower is similar to other unique dwellings standing alone in the forest. Almost always, such abodes either house supernatural beings or are the place where supernatural events transpire. It is at a high hill in the woods that Rumpelstiltskin's 'little house' sits, just as it is a 'little house' in the glen where the seven dwarves live. The three little men in the wood, in Grimm's tale of the same title, prove to be magical agents. Hansel and Grethel need not meet the witch to know her food-house is something out of the ordinary, nor does the bride have to witness her robber groom's heinous crime to sense the ominous nature of his dwelling: 'she came to the middle of the wood, where it was the darkest, and there stood a lonely house . . . dismal and unhomelike.'[7] Even grandmother's familiar house in the woods metamorphoses into something unfamiliar when Red Cap walks in. Often the house is described as a hut, being small, solitary, simple, and fragile in appearance.

In contrast to the castle's massive body and appendages, the house-hut stands alone, automatically engendering interest in it and in whoever (or whatever) would dwell so reclusively. Bachelard associates the hut with the hermit's hut and what it suggests: a different life-style, a communion with nature and the supernatural, an absolute refuge. The hut seems the very 'taproot of the function of inhabiting',[8] whereas the castle is the exotic blossom. The hut's isolation and woods setting designate it as something distinct and therefore special, while its concentrated presence intimates an anthropomorphic being. Its panes blankly stare at the wanderer in the wood; its lit windows peer into the night, so that 'the house becomes human. It sees like a man. It is an eye open to night'.[9] Given the hut's concentrated presence, forest locale, and immediate impact when first espied, it more readily suggests the supernatural than does the castle, which more easily suggests what is humanly marvellous.

Within the hut, house, or castle proper, the forces of faerie predictably appear in the dark, hidden places of cellar and attic, recessed chamber and tower. Such places exist on the edges of a dwelling's interior. Whereas the kitchen, dining room, and bedroom glow with the light laughter of human company, the cellar, attic, and secluded chamber mutely wait in darkness for their occasional visitor. Such rooms delimit the house's physical boundaries; rarely frequented, they embody the unknown forces that exist on the periphery of human habitation—those same forces existing in the forest and alongside the woods' edge. Attic and cellar represent, as Bachelard terms it, the house's 'dual vertical polarity'.[10] As part of the house's total image, the attic peaks, the cellar submerges, each constituting the spatial counterpart to its opposite. Both are enshrouded in the dark past: the attic, previously mentioned, contains vestiges of man's past, while the cellar contains a deeper history, meandering back into the earth and primal time. Both have stairs leading to an unknown, perhaps nonexistent, centre, though each stairway speaks in a different voice to us. The attic's ascending steps seem less ominous and more promising than do the cellar's descending stairs that disappear into the very underground of all architecture. In that underground, as with any other, one might meet any and all subterranean forces hidden from day's light and earth's surface.

As the 'dark entity of the house',[11] the cellar sits in web-tattered shadows which themselves might assume an horrific life of their own. Thus, in 'The Robber Bridegroom', the bride learns of her groom's monstrous nature when she hides, crouching in the cellar. Thus, in 'Blue Beard', the forbidden room waits 'at the end of the long passage on the lower floor', and to get there, Blue Beard's most recent bride must descend a precipitous, private staircase. Each place provides an appropriate setting, literally and figuratively, for the man's deeds and natures. Each provides the perfect external translation of its owner's inner self—'cellar-psyche'—for each is a blood-clotted, violent place, strewn with the victims' decomposing remains. Here place reveals itself to be the true 'chamber of being'[12] wherein the worst of man's dark, unconscious side is disclosed and given tangible form. Again, setting functions as the external manifestation of the internal.

As the 'primer of the picture-language of the soul',[13] the folk fairy tale speaks to us in physical images and settings so as to convey truths beyond yet within them. This is part of their dialectic between things tangible and intangible, external and internal, between matter and mind. Little, if anything, exists in the tales by accident. As the 'bare bones' of narrative and of children's literature, the tales tend toward the essential, whether in plot, theme, character, style, symbolism, or setting. Physical matter especially is pared to crucial things—Rapunzel's lengthy golden tresses, a little girl's red hooded cloak, a talking mirror, poisoned apple, waiting spindle.

Such are the material things which plump and help sustain our lives as well, while all lives are played out against the backdrop of a landscape and within the personalized circle of a specific place. We flutter today from one dwelling to another, changing locales like disoriented migratory fowl; yet whenever, wherever, we temporarily settle, we reconstruct our personal nests, delimiting a tiny patch of earth or woods for our own castle, tower, hut. Despite our transience, setting remains a critical element contributing to our sense of self and that self's locus within the landscape of this Earth and this cosmos.

In that respect, setting yields the magical and is transmuted to much more than mere occupied space. This is part of what the fairy tale tells us in its use of setting. It is a message taken to the heart by writers like Lewis Carroll, Kenneth Grahame, Rudyard Kipling, Jack London, L. Frank Baum, J.M. Barrie, and Beatrix Potter. The faerie—that necessary wonder and magic—which sparks classic children's literature more often than not is rooted somewhere in setting. Once again, gold is spun from common straw; once more, both within and outside the story, we feel the value and magic and crucial meaning of place, whether it be the greening woods, stolid castle, lone tower, or humble, homey hut.

Notes

[1]Lowry Charles Wimberly, *Folklore in the English & Scottish Ballads*: 240

[2]*Encyclopedia of Magic & Superstition*: 60

[3]Gaston Bachelard, *The Poetics of Space*: 72

[4]Bachelard: 24

[5]'The Sleeping Beauty', in Lucy Crane, transl., *Household Stories by the Brothers Grimm*.

[6]'Rapunzel', in Crane, op. cit.

[7]'The Robber Bridegroom', in Crane, op. cit.

[8]Bachelard: 31

[9]Bachelard: 35

[10]Bachelard: 18

[11]Ibid.

[12]Bachelard: 138

[13]Joseph Campbell, 'Folkloristic Commentary', in *The Complete Grimm's Fairy Tales*: 864

UNKNOWN CHILDHOOD

P.L. Travers

The child from next door, once all the pancakes had been eaten, slipped from my knee, leaving behind him the battered first edition of *Little Black Sambo*. He was going into the garden to look for tigers.

Beside me, the young man who had been ushered in during the reading took up the book, looking through it almost greedily, I thought. Perhaps he had a liking for pancakes.

'I wonder,' he said, and there was a nostalgic note in his voice, 'if anyone ever read this to me.'

'Possibly. But it is exiled now from book shops and libraries lest it give offence to black readers. Yet it's a poem, with its rhythms and repetitions. And what white child was ever known to turn tigers into butter?'

'I wish,' he said—and again I thought, although I did not know him very well, that there was a sadness in him, 'that you would tell—not read me—a story or even, perhaps, a rhyme. There must be some about things that are lost.'

I laughed, not taking him seriously. 'Well, how about *Little Bo Peep*, which you've known, of course, since you were three.'

'I never was three,' he said shortly, turning his head away.

'Well, be three now!' I said lightly and recited the nursery favourite.

'Wonderful!' he said, softly. 'Even the tails come home.'

That pleased me. He had put his finger on the rhyme's capsule of meaning. Leave things alone and all will be well.

'And now,' he said, earnestly, 'what about the story?'

'But this is absurd!' I told myself. A young man in the prime of life, with all the things the prime can bestow, even a talent for painting, comes to my door demanding to be told stories, and stories, moreover, of a specific kind. Yet clearly, it was not a casual visit. The flowers on the table, still in their wrapping, were evidence of this. He had come of intention and, sensing a need in him, I felt the tales begin to gather. Perhaps we were even now in a story which, given time, would reveal itself. He was the hero out on a quest, and I the Toad, Dwarf, or Little Old Woman, come from Nowhere, the homeland of such characters, to say the word that would speed him forward.

I chose the Dwarf, feeling small and dwarfish in this situation but knowing from experience that if I stood under what I did not understand all would be made known. Leave it alone and it would come home. The Dwarf would know how to deal with it.

So I scurried around in mind for a story that carried the necessary theme and in no time was listening to myself telling of a princess playing with a golden ball, throwing it up, catching it, and then inadvertently letting it fall into a nearby well.

'Ha! So she lost it!' exclaimed a vibrant voice beside me with a note of bitter triumph.

'How can you say that?' the Dwarf within me reproached him. 'This is a very ancient story. You'll have known it since you were born—or almost.'

'I have never known it!' he said, fiercely. 'And I wasn't born, anyway, until I was fifteen.'

Was he joking? No, the tortured look on his face denied it. What, then, did he mean?

For a moment he was silent and then came a spate of disjointed words stumbling over each other.

'When I was thirteen, I was stricken with meningitis, which destroyed many cells in my brain and stole my childhood from me. I was two years in hospital remembering nothing. It took me ages to accept my mother when my mind began working again. My bonding was to doctors and nurses. Even now I hardly know my brother. Oh, I have been to analysts and psychotherapists, but none of them eased the ache in me or gave me what I needed. Not that I even know what I need. Then, this morning, I woke up with a longing that was like hunger for someone to tell me a story—childish of me who was never a child—and so I thought of you. But you're telling it, I warn you, to only half a man.'

His head went down into his hands.

I felt a shadow pass over my heart. What if this thing had happened to me, who all my life—at moments, naturally—have been accompanied by my childhood, that endless and beginningless time when I was free, and even amid the crowd, alone—except for the 'other', nameless, near, invisible, ever with me at the edge of the Known; that 'other' who was part of myself and yet belonged to what I than called and still call Something Else. All time was Now and nothing was explained; yet everything gave out intimations, meaning was everywhere. Oh, not to be aware of having looked for Moses in the bulrushes beside the local stream; of stepping carefully over ant and beetle less perchance they were princes in disguise; of listening to the trees communing, not knowing and yet almost knowing what was being said! Not to have all this at hand to turn to in my diurnal life would be, for me, disaster.

I could not look at the man at my side. My feminine nature inwardly wept as I cast around for words of comfort. The folly of it! There *are* no words. His mother—and I pitied her—would have done this for many years, exhausting all the dictionaries.

But the Dwarf was a sturdy little fellow. And, after all, we were deep in a story. He would know how to deal with heroes.

'Never believe,' he said with my voice, 'that the brain is the sole repository of memory. It knows the names, the lively facts, the palpability of things, the palimpsests of scripture and science, the endless torrent of information. In this way it serves its purpose. Even so, it is merely the handmaid of Mind which holds the key of consciousness and encompasses all things; runs in the blood stream, beats with the heart, carrying memory through the body. For the Mind the unreal has no being and the real never ceases to be.[1] Moreover, it understands that all that is lost is somewhere.'

The young man's head came up from his hands and he stared at me, surprised and thoughtful. The idea had caught him.

'Well, it can't fall out of the universe, I suppose.' Then he sighed. 'Even so, lost is lost, my childhood perhaps away in Orion, the ball at the bottom of the well.' And his head went down again.

'Wait! We are only halfway through the story. The ball, you must know, was not lost'—a faint moan sounded at my side—'for a frog leapt up from the dark waters, offering to rescue the treasure if the princess would make him three promises—to sit beside her at the dinner table, to eat from her little golden plate, and to sleep in her silken bed. Unwillingly, she promised. What had a frog to do with her? But she had to have her golden ball. . . .' The golden ball was her life. So she ran home quickly, holding it close, thinking to escape the frog. But her father, being a just man and hearing what had befallen her, was of another mind.

'What has been promised must be performed,' he told his daughter, sternly.

Thus it was that when the frog came splashing up the stairs she was forced to lift him to the table beside her where he ate from her golden plate.

'And now,' he croaked, 'let us go and rest.' So under her father's watchful eye she carried the slimy thing to her room and there thrust it into a corner.

---

[1] *The Bhagavad-Gita*

'No, no, Princess, you must lift me into your little bed according to your promise.' And that, for her, was the last straw. She took him up by two fingers and, promise or no promise, flung him—slam!—against the wall. Down he fell, splashing water from him, and in his place, to her surprise, there rose up a handsome prince.

'I was under a deep enchantment,' he told her, and his voice was no longer a croak, 'till someone should spurn me and set me free. You are my destined rescuer and now must be my bride.'

There was a long sigh from the man at my side. 'A pretty enough tale,' he murmured. 'But it hardly refers to my situation.' He was clearly disappointed.

'Ah, but you must let me finish. Faithful Henry is still to come. He carries the story's meaning.'

'Go on, then!' he said, grudgingly.

'Well, next day a carriage with eight white horses arrived at the castle to take the lovers, together with the golden ball, home to his father's kingdom. And driving it was Faithful Henry, the lifelong servant of the young prince. He wept with joy at the sight of his master and they embraced each other. . . .'

So they drove off. And after a time the pair in the carriage heard a cracking, metallic sound.

'Is the wheel broken?' asked the prince. 'No, Prince!' Faithful Henry answered. 'But when you were lost to the world of men, I felt such sorrow for your grief that I put three bands of iron round my chest to keep my heart from bursting. You have just heard the first band breaking.'

And again there came the same sound. 'Is the carriage wheel breaking?' asked the prince.

'No, master, but the thought of you dwelling in the deep dark waters and longing for the light of the sun was anguishing to me. You have just heard the second band break.'

And a mile or two further, the same thing happened.

'Is it a carriage wheel?' asked the prince again.

'No, Prince. But while you were so far from us, lonely among the creatures of earth, I, too, was lonely and suffered for you. The third band has now broken.'

And they drove home happily all together.

As the tale ended the room was so still I could almost hear our hearts beating.

'I am glad you waited for the ending.' I said, 'for the story not only assures us that all that's lost is somewhere but also that whatever is lost is longing for that which has lost it.'

For a long time he pondered what had been said, in silence.

'It is true,' he said quietly, at last. 'I knew it even as you spoke. If I need it then it also needs me. Why has nobody told me that before?'

He gathered himself out of his chair, took the wrapped flowers from the table, and thrust them at me, almost roughly. 'Thank you for Faithful Henry,' he said, and marched out of the house.

I watched him striding up the street. Not a man released from his burden but a man—and not merely half a man—carrying it, even holding it close.

The Dwarf slipped away, back to his province, and the child came in from the garden. He had found two tigers, it appeared. But I need not be afraid, he assured me. He was taking them home with him.

'But what if they threaten to eat you up? You have not got Sambo's blue trousers or his crimson slippers or his green umbrella.'

'I have two pairs of jeans. I will give them those.'

Blue jeans, I thought, were exactly right, the proper wear for a couple of Chelsea tigers.

And as he led them away, down my steps and up his own, I felt glad that his childhood was safe within him and hoped that he would keep it always, a strong vine, as my own had been, to sustain the wandering branches . . .

Whatever is lost is longing for that which has lost it.

A Dissolving Ghost

Margaret Mahy

The Lovers and the Shark

Two years ago it happened I found myself in a motel swimming pool in New Mexico. I like swimming. I swim quite purposefully and I had the swimming pool almost to myself. Not quite however. At the shallow end of the pool stood a young man and woman, passionately, indeed it sometimes seemed permanently, embraced. I didn't mind this while I was swimming away from them, but as I swam towards them I found myself filled with the embarrassment of someone who is intruding into a private space . . . a space which they have no right to violate. My shyness, my wish not to intrude on this couple, alternated with something less charitable—self-righteous indignation. After all this was a swimming pool and I was swimming backwards and forwards, which everyone knows is the proper thing to do in a swimming pool. Why should I be the one to feel intrusive and guilty? I felt like this swimming away from them. Then swimming towards them I began to think—ah but am I jealous of their youth and passion and so on (kicking regularly, surging to the other end of the pool). Yet who wants to be bothered with self-analysis when you are trying to shoot through the water like a silver arrow? As I swam backwards and forwards I began to dream of dressing up as a shark, and gliding up the pool towards them. I could see myself soundless, menacing and ruthless, my skin set with sharp close-set denticles, my silent crescent snarl filled with rows and rows of teeth. The lovers would suddenly see my dorsal fin approaching. They would leap out of the water screaming. I would have the whole pool to myself, free to be a silver arrow to my heart's content. It would be all *my* space, and deservedly so.

After I left the pool I found myself haunted, not by the lovers themselves but by the one who had wanted all the space in the swimming pool, this person usurping the primitive power of the shark, the fin cutting through the water, the huge mouthful of teeth rising up over the back of the boat . . . this temporary villain I had contemplated becoming, in order to have all the swimming pool to myself. It had in some way been a tempting and empowering persona, and one I recognized, although I had never met it in quite that shape before. My temporary shark began to make other sharkish connections. Sharks have been part of my life for a long time. Though shark attacks are almost unknown in New Zealand, we all know the sharks are there. Parents sometimes warn their children: 'Don't go out deep! There might be sharks!' Of course the children already know. Sharks!

Once, dramatically, I saw a shark caught on a hand line pulled up and left to die on the sand. It was only a small one, but it was a genuine shark. I stood over it watching it drown in the sunny air of a remote North Island beach. When it began to rot away, someone threw it back into the deep water where smaller fish flickered around it for a while, eating what was left, but even then its bones still glimmered mysteriously through the water if you knew where to look. It was the year I turned five. It was also the year I learned to swim. I couldn't write much in those days, but was already a slave to fiction. I talked aloud, waving sticks in the air, conducting unseen orchestras of stories remembered, recreated and invented, stories which I inhabited by temporarily becoming what I was inventing. That shark and the mystery and menace of the glimmering bones and what might have happened—that it might have been *my* bones glimmering there I suppose—were part of those stories in those days. It was certainly part of the first nightmare I can ever remember having: that my little sister vanished under the water and after a second or two her sunbonnet came floating to the surface. We were living in a caravan in those days. I woke up in the top bunk, crying and bewildered, to find that something which only a moment before had seemed so utterly real had dissolved into nothing. I think it was that same shark, flesh on its bones once more, that came out of the past to inhabit me and swim up and down the motel swimming pool. It's just as well I didn't have my shark suit with me.

I like to swim in deep water. I like to be where I can't feel the bottom and I have always liked that from the time I was very small, but there is always the fear of the shark sneaking up from the darkness below, and grabbing your foot. After you've been frightened of the shark for a while, you begin to tell stories about it, to take it over . . . and in odd moments of life, when you have a little go at being a shark yourself, you recognize an old truth in what you are doing.

A Marvellous Code

I am going to propose that there is a code in our lives, something we automatically recognize when we encounter it in the outside world, something personal, but possibly primeval too, something which gives form to our political responses, to our art, our religious feeling, sometimes to our science and even to the way the weather forecast may be presented as a little drama. It is something eagerly recognized in children, so perhaps there is no first encounter. Perhaps it is already in them. My own experience of it has been that, by giving experience a recognizable structure to mould itself around, it makes it easier to recall and to use. This code makes use of cause and effect, though sometimes it precedes and transcends this necessary relationship. It can be suspected or duplicated but I don't think it can be really dismantled. Broken into bits, it starts to reassemble itself like the Iron Man described by Ted Hughes, and creeps back into our lives patient but inexorable.

I am referring to *story*, something we encounter in childhood and live with all our lives. Without the ability to tell or live prescribed stories we lose the ability to make sense of our lives.

A Misleading Question

Many years ago I read for the first time a novel by Noel Streatfield called *Ballet Shoes*, possibly the book for which she is best known. It is a story for and about children; about three girls, Pauline, Petrova and Posy Fossil, who took this surname because they were all adopted by a kindly archaeologist, Great Uncle Matthew or GUM. It tells of their childhoods, as part of an oddly random but united family obliged to make a living. The living they make, in their various ways, is on the stage. Some years ago when I was working as a librarian in the National Library Service I found another novel by Noel Streatfield call *The Whicharts*, which tells the same story as *Ballet Shoes*, but tells it for adults. The three girls are now revealed as half-sisters, all illegitimate daughters of a charming but irresponsible, well-born Englishman. They are cared for by a woman (the Sylvia of *Ballet Shoes*), who had loved him deeply in spite of his facile character and who grows to love his daughters as if they are her own. He dies leaving them in difficult circumstances and in an effort to make a reasonable middle-class living, the girls become involved, as in the children's book, in life on the wicked stage. The story pursues them through childhood and adolescence, tells us how the girl who corresponds to Pauline in *Ballet Shoes* is seduced, I think by a theatrical director, and how the one who corresponds to Petrova actually locates their mother after their loving guardian dies, and finds herself shyly welcomed by a woman as odd and adventurous as she is herself. The family in this book is not called the Fossils, but the Whicharts (a name which also involves a play on words however, coming as it does from their mishearing of something in the Lord's Prayer, *Our father, which art in heaven* . . . words eloquent to children who had been told, on debatable evidence I must say, that heaven was where their father was). I was fascinated by all this new information which suggested that Noel Streatfield certainly knew more about the family than she had revealed in her children's book and I gave *The Whicharts* to a friend of mine who had enjoyed *Ballet Shoes*. She read it and, feeling betrayed in some intangible way, became angry. 'It just made me wonder how much truth we tell children?' she said. 'How much should we tell?'

She was asking leading questions, but questions which are also misleading. It is an old debate with many answers. For instance I don't think Noel Streatfield would have been allowed to tell everything she knew about the Fossils in a children's book back in 1936, though she certainly would be permitted to tell more today, since our interpretation of childhood has altered since then. However, as an adult reading *Ballet Shoes* I am now always aware of that ghostly *other* story, that extra truth, and something about the nature of my adult experience makes me think that *The Whicharts* is the truer story. I think *Ballet Shoes* a better book for what it is than the *The Whicharts* for what *it* is, and yet for all that I feel I have unfair knowledge, for I can't help including what I know of the adult story as part of the truth of *Ballet Shoes*. I say to myself, 'This is what was really happening, but we couldn't tell the kids.' Unlike my friend I don't think Noel Streatfield should have either insisted on telling the full truth or not told any of it. No one tells the full truth anyway, and children's literature would have been the poorer for not having *Ballet Shoes*. Nevertheless, I have never forgotten my friend's question, and there is a dislocation in my feelings about it all—a sort of puzzlement which I am perhaps unfairly trying to get rid of by passing it on to others.

How much truth do we tell children? We certainly encourage them to tell all the truth themselves. I impressed on my children what my mother impressed on me, that we should always tell the truth. (Funnily enough, now they're grown up I quite often find that I wish they wouldn't tell so much, and I know my mother often wishes I would shut up.)

How much truth we choose to tell children is an important question, but not a fair one. How much truth should we tell grown-ups for that matter? After all, children often want to know about things and adults often don't. Many people want to protect the innocence of childhood but isn't it also a pity to disturb security and innocence in adulthood? Sometimes we just don't like to see people living happy lives for what we perceive as wrong reasons. We tell them the truth, as we see it, and if they choose to ignore it, we tell it again and try to force them to listen to it. This poor single word 'truth' has to bear a heavy burden. It is not fair to ask one word to do so much work when, unlike Humpty Dumpty, we exploit our labour force. We don't pay words extra when we ask them to carry a heavy weight on our behalf.

Fact and Fiction

I was born in 1936, the year *Ballet Shoes* was published, and from the time I was very small I was encouraged to listen to stories. I began as a listener, and then, since I wanted to join in that particular chorus, I put together stories of my own as I have already mentioned, telling them aloud to walls and trees. Because I couldn't write, back then, I learned them by heart, as a way of containing them, but I went on to become a reader, and very shortly after that learned to write and began to set them down in note-books complete with titles and a few illustrations. I began as a listener, became a teller, then a reader and then a writer in that order. Later still I became a librarian, which in some ways is the ultimate result of this evolu-tionary process, since a lot of library work is concerned with orderly containment. (But I must advise you to beware a little of my description of myself which is automatically starting to gather the elements of a romantic story around it.)

Being a librarian forces you to think a lot about truth and to pretend you have got over any confusions you might ever have had about it. You have a book, it has to go in some particular physical place in the library shelves. It can't really be both here and there. Even if you have a big enough book grant and can afford to buy two copies of the same book and put it in two different places, a book like *The Endless Steppe*, say, is not quite the same story in the non-fiction shelves as it is in the fiction—where it was rather more likely to be read in our library at least. If you are a librarian (allowing for the general advice we get about putting a book where it is going to be looked for and best used), you have fiction on one side of the library and non-fiction on the other. Ask a child the difference between fiction and non-fiction and the child will often answer that non-fiction is true and fiction is not true. 'That's right,' we say. 'Fiction is not true and non-fiction is.' But sophisticated writers and readers often dispute this simple division, and I'm sure that there must be many librarians like me . . . librarians who suddenly find themselves staring around wildly at their library walls (all that *knowledge*, all that *emotion*, all that *astonishment!* What am I doing here at the intersecting focus of all these great fields? I am trying to *shelve* it!), their own sense of reality terminally eroded by service for others. Making books available in the most sensible way makes us aware that in serving one function we are distorting others. We are standing astride the line of a great dislocation.

Dislocations in a True Landscape

I am used to dislocations. I have more than one running right through me. Dislocation is in some ways an image of the country I grew up in, even if we agree to call it diversity. If dislocation wasn't the *source* of my sense of things not matching up, of them rushing together and immediately beginning to fall apart, it is to some extent the mirror of them.

New Zealand, the country which is in every meaningful way my home, is a country in the Pacific Ocean but my family were European, not Polynesian, and consciously and unconsciously regarded European and more specifically British culture as the highest form of civilization in the world. The result was a big imaginative displacement, for, though there were a few children's books written in and about New Zealand when I was a child, the majority of stories, including those that inexorably fixed me, came largely from Britain with a few, a very few, from the USA.

Coming in from swimming on Christmas Day I would sit with my sun hat on, reading stories of snow and robins and holly, and though I have never spent a Christmas in the Northern Hemisphere, those things are now part of my Christmas nostalgia. The imaginative truth and the factual truth may be at odds with each other but personally I still need those opposites to make Christmas come alive for me . . . the sunny sea in front of me and the simultaneous awareness of short days, long cold nights and snow on dark bare branches.

But containing and synthesizing such contradictions is easy for an imagination nourished on stories in which so much becomes possible. I did indeed grow up with a fault line running through me, but that is a very New Zealand feature when you consider that it is a country of earthquakes and volcanoes. A fault line ran right through the town I was born in so perhaps my disjunction is part of what makes an essential New Zealander of me after all—perhaps the country has imposed its own unstable geography on my power to perceive. I don't mind. I regret it only in the sense that one always regrets not being able to be everything all at once. Dislocations can expose the secret nature of the land. They can make for an intensely interesting landscape, provided one does not come to feel that a landscape full of fault lines is the only legitimate kind. Dislocations made me a world reader rather than a local one: they made me contingent rather than categorical.

New Zealand at the present is celebrating in a small way the development of a more indigenous children's fiction than at any time previously. Having at last got a foothold in the imagination of its writers, New Zealand is now an innate part of most of its indigenous children's books, which are increasingly free of unnaturally deliberate reference, of the self-consciousness that marked the first attempts to have *I am a New Zealander writing about New Zealand* as a sort of subtext. There is a certain relieved mood of congratulation within the writing community, and a lot of talk, some of it meretricious I think, about 'relevance'.

I think it is most important that a local literature should exist, so that the imaginations of children are colonized in the first instance by images from their immediate world. I am not in favour of dislocation for the sake of dislocation. But I am curious too about why I should have become such an enthusiastic reader myself when so little of what was immediately relevant was offered to me, and why, later on the rare occasions when I did encounter books presenting my own street and my own idiom, I tended to pass them over in favour of exotic alternatives. Why was it that what seemed truest to me had nothing to do with the facts and images of my everyday life, which, mistakenly enough, I came to regard as inadequate stuff for a story?

Truth and Desire

In his celebrated essay *Tree and Leaf* Tolkien speculates as to why Andrew Lang turned his adult story of myth and folklore into a series of stories for children.

'I suspect,' Lang writes, 'that belief and appetite for marvels are regarded as identical or closely related. They are radically different, though the appetite for marvels is not at once or at first differentiated by a growing human mind from its general appetite.' Lang, according to Tolkien, may be implying that the teller of marvellous tales to children trades on the credulity that makes it less easy for children to distinguish fact from fiction, 'though,' Tolkien says, correctly I think, 'the distinction is fundamental to the human mind, and to fairy stories.' All the same, I think that the appetite for marvels may reinforce some aspects of truth that the fact or fiction dichotomy obscures.

Talking further about the appetite for marvels, and his own appetite for reading, Tolkien then says of himself:

I had special wish to believe. . . . At no time can I remember that the enjoyment of a story was dependent on belief that such a thing could happen or had happened in real life. Fairy stories were plainly not concerned with possibility but with desirability. If they awakened desire, satisfying it while whetting it unbearably they succeeded.

I think that, like Tolkien and many readers before and since, I was filled with an appetite for marvels, and desire alone seemed to me to be a sufficient justification for a story, even though longing for what is not true has been seen as a wicked thing to do, particularly by those readers who also strenuously maintain that we should not disturb the innocence of children by telling them all the truth. I tend to think, since the appetite for marvels appears to be so much part of humanity, that it exists in us for a reason, and that in an odd way it may be connected with truth. My enjoyment of a story certainly did not depend on belief while I was *reading* the story, for the story generated its own belief, but afterwards I would often try to adjust the world so that the story could be fitted into it. To find something that was marvellous was wonderful; to find something that was wonderful and true was ecstasy; for it meant wonderful things might be possible for me too.

'The function of the story teller is to relate the truth in a manner that is simple, to integrate without reduction, for it is barely possible to declare the truth as it is because the universe presents itself as a mystery,' says Alan Garner, after saying that the true story is religious and adding that he is using the word 'religious' to indicate concern for the way we are in the cosmos. All the vital processes of our lives (like eating and reproducing) are reinforced with powerful pleasure principles. We take pleasure in stories, we *desire* them, because we need to know about them and to be able to use them. Stories enable us first to give form to, and then to take possession of, a variety of truths both literal and figurative. Once we have part of the truth caught up in a story, we can begin to recognize it and get some sort of power over it. But of course we have to be careful about the way we believe stories. They can make us not only into temporary heroes and wizards, but temporary villains too . . . even into temporary sharks.

Poor Judgements

When I was a small child and read *King Solomon's Mines*, a book inherited from my father, I knew it was an invention. And when I read in another of my father's childhood books (volume one of an Edwardian edition of

Arthur Mee's Encyclopedia), that the earth had once been a fiery ball and that it had dropped off the sun, I knew it was true. The encyclopedia was true and *King Solomon's Mines* wasn't. Nevertheless, at one time I tried to tell a cousin of mine that the events in *King's Solomon's Mines* were historical facts even though I knew they weren't, trying by powerful assertion, by faith alone, to drag the story through to sit alongside the fiery ball which had fallen off the sun. Well, it wouldn't go. I needed an identical act of faith from other people to give it even the semblance of this other truth, and no one else would agree to play that game with me. I was alone with the story and with my desire for it to be true. It wasn't the only attempt I made to bring a marvellous fiction through into the real world, to force a general agreement that I was in charge of truth and not the other way round. From the time I was seven until about ten I publicly maintained and defended the proposition that I could talk the language of the animals. The immediate source of this assertion was *The Jungle Book*—not the book but a film of the book, the one starring Sabu and a variety of real animals. It absolutely overwhelmed me. My mother must have enjoyed it too, because, for the only time in my childhood that I can remember, I was taken to see a film twice. I couldn't bear that that particular story should remain in what I then perceived as the half life of fiction. Coleridge has described works of fiction as acts of secondary creation, and I wanted to make *The Jungle Book* primary. I wanted to make it as if it had been created by God, not by human beings.

In order to achieve this I publicly claimed and tried to demonstrate that I had the powers of Mowgli. Challenged, I would talk an invented gibberish that fooled nobody, least of all the passing dogs or birds, and not one of the lively knowing children round me. So I became more and more extreme in my attempts to demonstrate my oneness with animal creation. I ate leaves in public . . . all sorts of leaves . . . children came up to me in the playground and offered me leaves which I ate indiscriminately. I drank from roadside puddles as dogs do. Of course I was subjected to derision which I deserved for poor judgement if nothing else.

I knew all the time that I couldn't really speak the language of the animals in the world of primary creation, but I imagine now that I wanted people to agree to create the secondary world with me, a world in which I had already given myself a starring role. I also believe there were elements of the story existing in me already, that it was not that Kipling's imagination, filtered through the medium of film, imposed itself upon me, but that something already in me leaped out to make a powerful connection. Certainly at some levels I was powerless to resist whatever it was that came crashing in, or perhaps out. Nor am I suggesting that this susceptibility is a thing to be uncritically encouraged. I do think, however, that it is far from unique and in order for it to be understood it needs to be described. It certainly can be dangerous (after all I could have poisoned myself eating so much vegetation that unqualified way), but the same thing can be said of a lot of human obsessions including patriotism and love and even truth itself . . . they're all very risky indeed. Still, having received that story, I think I had to incorporate it, having incorporated it I had to discharge it, and, as I was young and simple, the discharging took a wrong turn—an inappropriately literal one.

Now oddly enough, at the same time that I was being teased about my claim to talk the language of the animals, I was subject to an equal derision, which once resulted in my being chased home by indignant children, some of them cousins of mine which seemed to add insult to injury. I publicly asserted that the earth had once dropped off the sun, that I had a picture at home that proved it, and I added on the same authority (that of *Arthur Mee's Encyclopedia*) that the world would some day, a million years from now, come to an end. I can remember running home with other outraged children after me, turning in at a strange gate, knocking on the door and saying to the astonished woman who answered it that the children were waiting outside to beat me up because I had told them the world had once fallen off the sun and that it would come to an end one day. I was confident that an adult would recognize and confirm the truth I was telling and rally to support it. Whether she believed it or not there was nothing she could do to help me.

Of course if you present certain facts too confidently it sounds as if you are taking personal credit for them, and perhaps I sounded as if I thought I was the one who had caused the world to fall off the sun in the first place and would one day will its end. And I certainly don't want to sound as if I'm whining because I didn't have the respect I should have had at school. I think I deserved all I got for eating leaves and drinking from puddles, which is not a sign of superior sensibility, only of poor judgement, tragically coupled with the will to be marvellous. I totally agree with the person who said that a difficult time at school doesn't necessarily entitle you to write a novel. But what I do want to record is that non-fiction could provoke as much derision, disbelief and resentment as fiction . . . and, just to make the situation a little more complicated, nowadays no astronomer seems to believe that the earth ever fell off the sun. The other children were right to suspect this fact, even if they suspected it for the wrong reasons. What I learned as truth back then was another mistake.

Variations on a Divine Gift

Because of the way science has developed over the last three hundred years, we do live in a time when we expect truth to be objectively provable. Measurement is a vital part of our lives today. We live, our children along with us, in a very mathematized society. In the past, before Tycho Brahe, if a minor detail did not fit into a major hypothesis it was easy to shrug it away. The idea that anyone might be accountable to *that* sort of truth was a foreign one. But Kepler, in computing the orbit of Mars, acknowledged as significant an error of eight minutes of arc which Copernicus had been able to ignore. Kepler wrote, 'But for us, who by divine kindness, were given an accurate observer such as Tycho Brahe, for us it is fitting we should acknowledge this divine gift and put it to use,' and what Whitehead describes as 'stubborn and irreducible fact' became increasingly important. Like Kepler I believe intricate and accurate measurement is a gift we are given by divine kindness, and that the inventive mind, coming up against stubborn and irreducible facts, has to capitulate and look for richness and amazement within that capitulation. Today 'stubborn and irreducible facts' seem paramount because of the kind of power that attention to such details confers, including the power to make money which often involves the power to get one's own way—very seductive powers indeed. So 'stubborn and irreducible facts' are frequently seen as coinciding with truth, or truth is seen as being the same sort of thing as the facts are and nothing more. It seems to me that deterministic accounts of existence never quite face up to the fact that they don't eliminate mystery but merely shift it into areas where it can be acceptably labelled. And history shows all sorts of aberrations built even into part of the truth we shelve in the 500s. For example, in the beginning of chapter sixteen of his book *New Astronomy*, Kepler, who thought of accurate observation as a divine gift, absentmindedly put three erroneous figures for three vital longitudes of Mars and then towards the end of the chapter committed several mistakes in simple arithmetic which virtually cancelled his first mistakes out so that he got more or less the right answer. At the most critical point in the process of discovering his law Kepler again made a series of mathematical errors that cancelled themselves out, allowing him to arrive at the correct result. What sort of truth was operating there? Perhaps something was so *determined* to be discovered that even mathematical error was forced to yield a true result? I recently read that Mendel cheated in recording the results of his experiments on genetic inheritance in peas and produced a nice pattern that illuminated what currently passes for truth and used to be taught as such in sixth-form biology in New Zealand schools. Perhaps something wants to be found. Nowadays it is suggested that even chaos has a structure.

Earlier this century, 1903 to be precise, at the time when there was much thrilling new information on radiation coming to hand, René Blondlot, an experienced physicist, discovered a new ray which he called an N ray, one of the characteristics of which was that it treated substances opaque to visible light, including wood, iron, silver, etc., as if they were transparent. Many notable scientists, particularly French ones, subsequently detected the same ray. But the American physicist R.W. Wood found he was absolutely unable to reproduce Blondlot's striking results. Blondlot and his colleagues then declared that it was the sensitivity of the observer not the validity of the phenomenon that was in question, but by 1905 only French scientists, and by no means all of them, believed in the N ray (though some of them still maintained that only the Latin races had sufficient sensitivity to detect the N ray, that fog had ruined the perception of the Anglo-Saxon observers and beer the perception of the German ones). Nowadays no one believes the N ray ever existed. The *Scientific American* May 1980, from which I got much of this good information, says that the times had psychologically prepared Blondlot to discover a new sort of radiation. I suggest that one might say with equal truth that he was imaginatively prepared to eat leaves and drink from puddles, but the way in which he did this matched up so closely with accepted reality or behaviour or desire that he temporarily did what I was not able to do—he actually altered perception for a while and won people to his side.

Scientific truths, which should be pure and objective, can stagger and sway on their way to becoming recognized as scientific truths, can be as bizarre as the plots of the stories they partly resemble, or the stories that are told about them afterwards. Yet though the scientists who advised the editors of *Arthur Mee's Encyclopedia* about the beginning of the world had made what I now take to be a genuine mistake, it was a mistake that fixed my attention in childhood, and (it is even tempting to think) enabled me to see something true which stayed true, even when the actual information turned out to be false. If so, the true thing was wonder . . . wonder which dissolves into Tolkien's desire, an aspect of our approach to truth which our physical systems are anxious to conceal. A perpetual state of wonder and desire (which seems to me the truest state with which to confront the universe) is certainly not the most practical state to try and live in. We are biologically engineered to have the wonder filtered out of our lives, to learn to take astonishing things for granted so that we don't waste too much energy on being surprised, but get on with the eating and mating, gardening, feeding cats, complaining about taxes and so on. We have the power to entertain visions, but operate most practically when life is mainly humdrum. When I first flew in an airplane it was an experience of amazement. Now I think of the flying time (a time when gravity is confounded, when a metal machine filled with people rises more or less safely into the air), as time when I am going to get a chance to read without any guilty feeling that I should be doing something else. To encounter the amazements, partly compounded of fear and beauty, which I recognized so eagerly when I was a child, I now have to give myself the space to achieve a rare and difficult mood, or search through the various disclosures of science and history, or, more frequently, read a story someone else has written.

I've certainly never had any trouble abandoning the falling-off-the-sun theory in favour of the Big Bang and slow condensation out of the stuff of the primordial universe. I know by now that facts, even marvellous ones, slide around, and that people get things wrong, and the truest thing in science is *wonder*, just as it is in story. And I never forget that story is as important to human beings as science, more powerful at times because it is more subversive.

A Fairy Tale Disguised

If any story I have told has the mark of social realism on it, it is certainly *Memory*, and in it I have told young readers a lot of truth I personally know about the metamorphosis of a rational human being replete with knowledge, memory and the power to make a cup of tea several times a day, into a demented old woman losing command of all the things in which self-respect is traditionally established, and driven to wear a tea cosy instead of a hat.

For a number of years I was in charge of my aunt, and though my aunt and Sophie are not the same person they are similar in many ways. Many of the happenings, many of the conversations in *Memory* are directly transposed from my life with my aunt, and if the story lacks the nastiness, the sheer fatigue of response involved in looking after a demented person it is partly because, though those elements were present, they were not a commanding part of my life with my aunt. Because I had a background of story to draw on she never lost her imaginative function. An English reviewer criticized the book because, somehow at the end, Sophie is tidied up rather too quickly, but there are two odd things about this tidying up. One is that in the real world, once I indicated I needed help, I got a certain amount. The support services were good, partly because I was sufficiently well educated to know where to go and what sort of things to say, and also because I had been prepared to cope with quite a lot before I asked for support. A district nurse and a housekeeper appeared, once a week things were tidied up quite quickly. In between times things went downhill rapidly, but neither my aunt nor I bothered too much about a certain amount of squalor. The other odd thing is that because *Memory* is full of factual experiences which are readily recognizable, and because it touches on a condition that, in New Zealand at least, enjoys a reasonably high public profile at present, it may seem to be intended as a book of social realism. However, for me it is a fairy tale of a sort. The fantasy of earlier books of mine is still present, but in the imaginative subtext rather than explicit in any happenings in the story. Because that fantasy is a part of the truth of my own life I cannot truthfully omit it. I didn't set out to write a fairy tale, but in an effort to convey truthfully the quality of the experiences I had had, I found myself telling the story of a young man who, having quarrelled with his father, sets out into the world with no blessing and no money to make his fortune. He meets a strange old woman needing help . . . a strange old woman who asks him a question, and, through giving her the help she needs, he answers the question and is strengthened by the answer. His response to her need determines the way he learns just as the kind responses of third sons or younger princes to the old people and animals they meet on their journeys result in them finding their fortunes.

These elements are recognizably fairy tale elements I think. Yet something like this fairy tale really happened in Christchurch once. A gang of rather derelict young people took over a house in which a demented old woman was living. Neighbours called in the social workers who found she was actually being looked after, though admittedly in a rough and ready fashion. She was being fed regularly and bathed, talked to and cared for. Her unlikely companions had grown fond of her, and after all there was no one else to look after her and nowhere for her to go, as all appropriate homes had waiting lists. I was told this story when I was already writing *Memory* by a social worker to whom I had described the book. And the first idea of the story came to me, as so many ideas do, from a haunting image seen from the window of a car in the early hours of the morning. Driving home through an empty city at about two a.m. I once saw an old man coming out of a supermarket car park pushing an empty trolley. The image stayed with me until I found a place for it.

Now I am not trying to suggest my story is true because it contains its share of irreducible facts, or even particularly good because of them. I mention the facts and associated anecdotes because they are eloquent in their own way, but just as much of the truth of this story, supposing it has any, lies in its form which seems to me to come from folktale, which has combined with it many other things to give me a code by which to decipher experience. I used it in part to interpret my experiences with my aunt, so when I came to tell the truth, as it were, about those experiences, I could not do so without conscious and unconscious reference to folktale. *Memory* has been described as tackling the subject of Alzheimer's disease, but it seems to me that it doesn't so much tackle it as recognize it, for the story is not in essence about Alzheimer's disease but about a magical encounter between two unlikely people, both of whom are possessed, in different ways, by a dissolving rationality. It is intended to be a serious story composed of many different sorts of truth, yet if I was asked to give a quick answer to the question 'Is it true?' I would have to say, 'No it isn't true.' All the same I have tried to make it tell part of the truth at least.

And so at last by fading paths I come back to a different sort of story . . . to the shark who wanted all the swimming space to himself.

The Great White Man-Eating Shark

As I have already indicated, an initial incident, true in the most literal sense of the word, began to hook itself into many others, some past, some present, some fantastic, some commonplace, but all a part of personal reality. The imaginative process involved is not so much an instantaneous flash of inspiration as an act—a series of acts—of synthesis, the ideas and associations forming a network, rather than a linear account, a network in which the spaces between the cords are as important as the irreducible knots that hold the whole thing together.

Fantasy writers are not noted for their adherence to truth. In fact often their books are seen as being ways of deliberately escaping from what is true into what is not true. However, to quote Angela Carter, imagination severed from reality festers, and writers of fantasy are often anxious to demonstrate that they are tied into real life in some way and to claim that they have a part to play there too. We may claim to deal with abstract truths rather than mere facts, or perhaps that we deal in metaphor. But behind the printed page crouches the story, looking out at us between the lines that have temporarily caged it, making it stand still so that it can be considered. First stories were approximations to history and science, though nowadays science and story are seen as separate and maybe even antagonistic, science being an outer adventure while story is an inner one, if I may anticipate something Walter de la Mare said about story which I will quote later.

As I thought about my temporary sharkness, it suggested a simple story which I would find entertaining to write. There are a lot of different sorts of sharks, many of them quite harmless, but I wanted to evoke the most sinister of all . . . the great white man-eating shark. I wanted there to be no misunderstanding about just what sort of a shark it was. This reminded me of a piece in Russell Hoban's novel *Turtle Diary*.

One of the narrators, Neaera, herself a writer for children, has read of an attempt by a rich man to photograph a great white shark.

> Eventually they found a great white shark which they attracted with whale oil, blood and horse meat. It was truly a terrifying creature and they very wisely stayed in their cage while the shark took the bars in his teeth and shook them about.

She then goes on to say that socially the rich man was out of his class.

> The shark would not have swum from ocean to ocean seeking them. It would have gone on its mute and deadly way, mindlessly being its awful self, innocent and murderous. It was the people who lusted for the attention of the shark.

Well, perhaps by reading and writing stories I too am guilty of trying to attract the attention of wonderful sharks. Locked in the cage of words I have stared out entranced while wonderful sharks took the bars of my cage in their teeth and shook it, and as I have already indicated I am capable to some extent at least of being a shark myself and worrying at other people's bars. Thinking of my own temporary sharkness I wrote a short story entitled *The Great White Man-Eating Shark*.

Like most stories I write, I intended it primarily as a story to be told aloud, but it has been produced as a picture book, and tells the story of a villain, a plain boy who happens to be a very good actor and who dresses up as a great white man-eating shark (a creature he resembles), frightening other swimmers out of the sea so that he can have it all to himself. He acts the part so well that a female shark falls in love with him and proposes something approximating marriage. He flees from her in terror. His duplicity is revealed and he is too scared to go swimming for a long time after. This is obviously didactic (but, I hope, ironically didactic), and seems far from true, since we all know that in real life firstly people do not dress up as sharks and secondly that the figurative sharks often go undetected because they don't allow people to see their dorsal fins. But in another way I have told the children all the truth I know from personal experience. Kurt Vonnegut says in the introduction to *Mother Night*, 'We are what we pretend to be, so we must be careful of what we pretend to be.' That turned out to be the hidden truth of my New Mexico swimming pool experience, but would that have been its hidden truth if I hadn't already read books like *Mother Night*, of if I didn't already know in a personal way that we become what we pretend to be? I did not learn to talk the language of the animals through eating leaves and drinking out of puddles, but I was chased and herded and treated like an animal for all of that.

But the story of the shark is a joke and this is how I expect it to be enjoyed, as a joke and only as a joke. It is only in the context of this occasion that I am bothering to tell of the experience compacted in it, offering it as a joke at my own expense and also as a part of a network, to a child who may one day read *Mother Night* or other books whose titles I can't guess at, and appreciate the truths in those books because they already know them. My own experience was real, funny, momentarily sinister and salutary, all at once, but someone else in that swimming pool on that day might have seen a different, a more anguished truth, might have realized that the lovers were saying goodbye, or that they were meeting after a long separation, or that they were honeymooners, or that the thought of being together without touching was unbearable to them. A thousand other stories were potentially there in the swimming pool with me, but my story was about the person who chose to become a shark.

Oddly enough, as I sat with *Turtle Diary* open in front of me seeing tenuous connections between my own childhood memories of sharks and my New Mexico fantasy, and Tolkien's speculations about desire, and the rich man lusting for the attention of the shark, I glanced at the opposite page where I was absentmindedly reading these lines:

People write books for children and other people write books about the books written for children, but I don't think it's for the children at all. I think that all the people who worry so much about children are really worrying about themselves, about keeping their world together and getting the children to help them do it, getting the children to agree that it is a world. Each new generation of children has to be told. 'This is a world, this is what one does, one lives like this.' Maybe our constant fear is that a generation of children will come along and say, 'This is not a world, this is nothing, there is no way to live at all.'

I can believe this but I think Hoban has told only half the story. After all we don't simply tell children what is and is not true. They demand to be told. When children write and ask, 'Do you believe in supernatural things?' they may be asking me to confirm that a story like *The Haunting* is literally true. But mostly they are asking, 'Just where am I to fit this story in my view of the world?' They want to be told what sort of world it is, and part of giving them the truest answers we can give also involves telling stories of desire . . . once there was a man who rode on a winged horse, once there was a boy who spoke to the animals, and the animals talked back to him, once there was a girl who grew so powerful that she was able not only to overcome her enemy but to overcome the base part of herself. Beware or the wolf will eat you and then you will become part of the wolf until something eats the wolf and so on. It is a gamble because we cannot tell just what is going to happen in the individual head when the story gets there and starts working. We can only predict statistically as we tell our children about hobbits or atomic fission, or that the earth fell off the sun, or about photosynthesis or that there was a lovable old archaeologist called GUM who once adopted three little girls. Perhaps that is why I was so fascinated, long before I began to think on these subjects by a line in Borges' story 'Tlon Uqbar Orbis Tertius'. He writes about a land brought into existence by a sort of assertion. 'The metaphysicians of Tlon are not looking for truth, nor even an approximation of it; they are after a kind of amazement.'

I also believe that what I am looking for is truth, which by now I confidently expect to be more amazing than anything else.

These days it seems to me that when I look at the world I see many people, including politicians, television newsreaders, real estate agents and free market financiers, librarians too at times, dressing as sharks, eating leaves and drinking out of puddles, casually taking over the powerful and dangerous images that the imagination presents, eager to exploit the fictional forms that haunt us all, and sometimes becoming what, in the beginning, they only pretended to be. I once read that subatomic particles should not be seen as tiny bits of matter so much as mathematical singularities haunting space. I believe that inner space is haunted by other singularities, by stories, lines of power along which our lives align themselves like iron filings around a magnet defining the magnetic field by the patterns they form around it, and that we yearn for the structure stories confer, that we inhabit their patterns and, often but not always, know instinctively how to use them well.

World Without, World Within

Walter de la Mare has this to say:

> The mere cadence of six syllables *A Tale of Adventure* instantly conjures up in the mind a jumbled and motley host of memories. Memories not only personal but we may well suspect racial; and not only racial but primeval. Ages before history had learned its letters, there being no letters to learn, ages before the children of men builded the city and the tower called Babel and their language was confounded, the rudiments of this kind of oral narrative must have begun to flourish. Indeed the greater part of even the largest of dictionaries, with every page in the most comprehensive of atlases, consists of relic and records in the concisest shorthand from bygone chapters of the tale whereof we know neither the beginning nor the end—that of Man's supreme venture into the world without and into the world within.

Deeper Than You Think

Patricia Wrightson

In Australia in the last two decades the need for roots has been felt. There's been an outbreak of research and a sudden growth of family trees, a proud reclaiming of convict ancestors, and a number of eager gatherings called family reunions. These are really an establishment of family: all the descendants of some early settler, mostly strangers to each other, coming hundreds of miles to meet one another and celebrate the discovery of their common roots. We need the reassuring stability of roots.

I remember a hotel window high above the furious, noisy streets of Athens, and the Parthenon standing near: small in modern terms; dignified, gracious yet somehow homely; withdrawn but so immediately near. I remember my awed recognition: here it was, one of our visible, tangible roots; the Parthenon, still poised above the teeming, honking city. Yet for me this wasn't an emotional moment. It was one of warm, intellectual delight.

The emotional moment came in a different place and took me quite by surprise. It wasn't intellectual at all, or even reasonable; there were no familiar symbols, no known inheritance, no real understanding. Just a looming outcrop of rock in a flat, starved landscape, with a ledge polished to glass by naked feet and thighs; and above it a crowd of paintings in ochre and pipe clay and charcoal. The Obiri Rock, on the plains near Darwin, tells you that your roots are deeper than you think.

The Parthenon has stood over Athens for more than two thousand years; how long does it take for feet and thighs to polish rock into glass? It's five thousand years since two small kingdoms joined and the Egypt of the Pharaohs arose; the tales told at Obiri were already ancient then. Seven thousand years back, those strange Sumerians were about to invent the wheel; the people at Obiri were perfecting the boomerang.

Double that time to fourteen thousand years: you'll have to guess what tribes were roaming through the Old World, but we know who climbed the rock ledge at Obiri. Double the time again, make it thirty thousand years: you have not yet reached the early traditions of Obiri. For more than forty thousand years aboriginal Australians have lived there; and when you see those paintings, high and alone in a primitive landscape, your roots and not your mind will recognize them. We all inherit them.

The people came from Asia, an early stage in the great migration that peopled the Pacific. They walked most of the way, with a few short crossings by canoe. In time the seas rose; slowly the land bridges drowned, and the great migration swept on along new coasts. The Australians went on migrating, too, through a large and isolated land.

There they made migration a continuing way of life. On islands and coasts near at hand, their kin invented farming, towns, metallurgy, and navigation. The Australians knew it, but they were a people for whom the inward life was richer than the outward one—a people not pushed by competition or starvation. They chose to go on travelling light, kept to their tools of stone and wood, and instead of a technology invented a philosophy and a complex social system. For forty thousand years they preserved a stone-age, nomad culture.

They told stories of their coming and of what they found: mythic tales of giant animals and primitive Hairy Men, of active volcanoes, and of lush, green valleys where now there are deserts. Stories are more immutable than rivers or volcanoes, and now we see myth and history confirming each other: the giant bones and massive human skulls emerging, the volcanoes and vanished rivers mapped and dated. Even the ancient Sickness Country has given up its uranium. The mythic record is true.

'My country is out there,' says an old man gazing seaward from the beach, and he speaks with knowledge and pride of the rivers and hills and forests of his country, lost long ago under the rising sea. That bit of drowned Australian coast is another, an older, Atlantis; but this one is remembered.

These people are a branch from roots that encircled the Pacific, roots that perhaps struck west into Europe, and certainly east into America. There have been other long isolations, but nowhere else can we see our own nomadic past alive, its laws and its stories preserved. Surely this is a gift of strength and self-knowledge.

It has been a long migration. Over forty thousand years, a hundred countries and a whole great ocean have forced us apart; we have grown into widely different peoples. The differences are important and valuable, we know, but look around you at your family. We can trace common roots back, past the recent adventures of Greece and Egypt, Babylon and Sumeria, all the way back beyond Obiri.

And how could we celebrate better than through our stories? Their roots are deeper than you think. They've come with us out of the distant past and travelled with us through the long migration. They've changed with us, and changed again, reflecting our new lands and ways of living, our new selves. The changes are important and valuable; they've kept the stories true and alive and valid. In spite of the changes and because of them, our stories are more immutable than volcanoes and rivers.

In a story called *Moon-Dark* (McElderry), I borrowed from Australian folklore the figure of Keeting: the moon. This is his name in the place of my story; he has other names in other parts, sometimes a form of Uncle or Grandfather. But always, true to Australian tradition, he is a man of those first, heroic men who made or became everything in the world. Keeting became the moon in order to conquer death, and hundreds of stories must have grown out of this very old root.

All our ancestors must have wondered about the moon as they watched it waste away, and die, and be reborn. There must have been stories of it in the distant time before the Great Migration, and perhaps some of them survive—how can we know? Only if they come to us from a people who've continued as they were for all that time, isolated in the purity of their own traditions. In my story, Keeting claims seniority over all others in the world, the ancestor of Isis and Diana and all moon-figures. I think he can only be challenged out of Africa itself.

Even so, Keeting has many names and stories within Australia. He was wounded in a great ancestral war, and conquered death by becoming the moon. He was a greedy uncle, banished to the sky by angry nephews, always to die and be reborn. He's brother to the dugong and follows her into the sea when he grows old, to swim with her till his monthly death and rebirth. He's husband to the sun, or the evening star.

The story adapts to Australia's changing scenes: does the moon rise out of the sea, descend into it, or appear and disappear over land? Is there forest, or claypan, or rock? Is the staple meat, emu, or fish? Whatever the variations, all the versions are threaded on three unchanging strands: the moon is male, a man of the Dreamtime; he rejects and defeats death; he has powers over pregnancy and childbirth.

The stories of the rest of the Pacific are not a record of isolated purity but of dynamic change and interchange. Complex, forgotten irrigation systems in New Guinea, lost skills rediscovered in China, cities and temples lost in deserts or under the jungles of Asia and South America, outrigger canoes making voyages that Drake would have quailed at—they all tell of movement and change, of the forces of hunger and disaster, of people driven on and new waves sweeping over the old. But stories are immutable, as well as adaptive and reflective; somewhere the old strands might still be found.

This mutant immutability was the thing that first bound me to folklore when I began to examine and think about it: the powerful persistence of some themes, and their universal, on-going relevance. I wondered where they could have begun. In Hindu mythology, the experts suggested; but that's like the old suggestion that all our life began in the dust from other planets. It's no answer at all. Why did these stories spread so far and live so long? Probably because of trade routes, said the experts—another meaningless answer.

Stories, like trade routes, arise out of human need. They're rooted in the need to tell what is moving in the mind, to explain and pass on thought. They live and spread only if they succeed in doing it, if they articulate something we can recognize, something that needs the articulation of story. This is true of those that tumble in their thousands from the generous presses of the world, consuming forests; stories that can be kept on the shelf and easily passed from hand to hand. It is even more true of stories that must be spoken from mind to mind and remembered and retold as if they were newly written every time. The strong, universal themes, those that are always relevant, are only as universal as humanity; there are dreams that matter to us all.

The triumph of good and simple people over the proud and privileged: how important that is to all of us. From Cinderella, through a host of younger sons and virtuous stepdaughers, down to the written stories of today, there must be examples in every folklore, and in the literature of every period. It's the universal dream that supports the Australian lottery system. In aboriginal Australia, uncles are the privileged source of authority, and the cruel ones fall victim to nephews and nieces as regularly as if the society did not live by supporting authority.

The evils of personal power: witches and warlocks and wicked queens, all crushed at last by unselfish virtue; kings subdued by gentle fools. It happens in the ancient Australian stories, just as it does in the fiction of today. How could any literature exist without it? But where did the Little People come from, loved so long ago and still today? Not, as we used to be told, from the remnants of the ancient Britons living on in hiding; because there are Little People, both delightful and nasty, scattered all over the Australian continent. Some are hairy; some green or red; many tremendously strong. They're tricksters or wrestlers; they eat people or heal them, talk with animals, join in children's games at dusk, or are seen playing alone at the edge of the sea.

The Little People, magical and free, charming or evil but always a little secret and dangerous; unhampered by human rules and with more than human powers. They must have been a long time growing to have travelled so far and developed so wide a range. Could they possibly have begun as apes? It might tie in with another universal theme: the haunting sense of our nearness to, and estrangement from, the animals.

A hooked fish or a swarm of ants, the horse Faralda, cats and whales and monkeys and mice and deer: for a long time we've conversed with the animals and we're likely to go on doing it. It seems entirely natural, since the animals are so expressive, so responsive, and only vocally dumb. Once we did it with natural ease and respect; only lately have we imposed on the animals distorted human garb and false human sentiment, or patronized them with whimsical human smiles. If we manage to prove that there's any real strength left in the human race, maybe the fashion will pass.

Australian stories are full of talking animals, but only of animals who at the time of speaking were men. Maybe that's enough. The common ancestry is established, the relationships traced: you *know* the snake is your brother and the kangaroo only a distant cousin; you know what deeds they performed and what benefits they gave. They look at you with the eyes of your kin, and you treat them as the kinship demands. That may be what the rest of us are still looking for.

The only Australian animals I know who in stories speak as animals are dingoes; and these, interestingly, are not native but came with the people themselves in the Great Migration. If you hear them speak you will turn into stone, and one or two groups of people did; the stones are there to prove it. What the people heard the dogs say is also interesting: they complained of their unfair treatment by men. So these 'talking dogs', like the kinship myths, record the respect due from man to animal.

An even stronger sense of haunting comes to me from the stories of men turned into animals. People feathered and caged at the whim of a witch; princes made into frogs, struggling to achieve release through an improbable human kiss. Swan-brothers and little, human deer. I used to accept all these in the spirit of the modern nursery tale, where the shocking loss of identity is never realized, and only the happy ending counts. That was before I met, in Australian folklore, the story with all its horror preserved for adults. The nightmare darkened a whole book for me; our stone-age ancestors brooded more deeply and more darkly than you think.

There are dream ideals, too, that reach across the world; like the dream of the hero, the man fit to be followed. It permeates the story of every land including mine; and if the hero changes with the way of life, that only brings him striding forward through the centuries. When I wanted to work on a contemporary legend, I chose herohood for a main theme because it seemed so clearly relevant to our time. Everyone, it seemed, was searching for a hero—searching in universities and television studios and houses of parliament and among pop groups. It seemed the right time to ask, again, what makes a man fit to be followed.

Another dream, as timeless but more wistful and perhaps with more self-knowledge, is the dream of the ideal mate. In Australia she is one of the water-girls, beautiful creatures who can be caught by the right method and made into perfect wives. There are four or five kinds of them scattered across the land, and I call them water-girls because water is their habitat. It's also the habitat of the European varieties: the selkies and mermaids and swan-maidens who are sometimes trapped and married to human men.

It's not possible that these European stories could have reached Australia and spread so widely before white settlement; the Australian tales must be truly Australian. Yet in both, the fairy-wives are found in water and must be taken away from it by some special means; they all become loving and dutiful wives for a time; they all return to their own water-world at last, leaving behind their husbands and half-human children; and always because those bereft and suffering husbands have failed in some way.

'He cried, he cried for that Nyal worrai worrai. He cut and cut his head for that girl. He went away to another place, another country. I don't know where that man has travelled now.' But he'd sent her, alone, to draw water from the very spring where he'd first found her.

This astonishing story, so full of poetry and emotion, this reverie on the longings and failings of men, did not come from trade routes. If it came from Hindu mythology, that was only in passing. To span a world through forty thousand years, to speak truly and consistently for Celt and stone-age Australian, it had to come from deeper roots, our own roots. Stone-age man, groping to convey his awareness, is nearer, much nearer, than you think.

That should give us a comforting sense of family renewed. Perhaps we should abandon race altogether, now that the old estrangement of distance has been wiped out. Perhaps we could declare ourselves tribes. For if we don't yet feel strongly akin to each other, we are strongly kin to those migrating tribes. We stand where they stood, and feel the same pressures, and face the same unanswered questions. There are new and terrible diseases, too many people wanting homes and food. The earthquakes have come; the seas are restless again; and the coasts, uncertain. We must think in a new and global way, begin a new age not knowing how it will end. We know only that it has all been done before.

The stories have come down to us: stories of tyranny and greed defeated by heroes; of wanderers helped by ants and birds, or led by animals; wishful, hungry stories of the bowl that never empties and the cloth that is always laid and the generous coming of the rice; stories of islands emerging from the sea, and of powers let loose that must be caught and recaged. We might recognize those stories if only we'd never seen them in print; if we could feel how very far they have come, carried to us only on the breath of our forefathers.

Suppose you have to tell a story as they did, fumbling in clumsy words, reaching for an idea that can't be painted on rock or scratched on a bone. There'll be more than material limits: there'll be limits of time and memory, of philosophy and language. Your restless mind will be searching for words that don't yet exist, words to shape the idea for you as well as for your listeners. It's certain that you'll invent metaphor, to display what you can't explain, and then the extended metaphor of fantasy. You'll use humour as a memory-aid; repeat key phrases, first for emphasis and then for music and mood; find the descriptive power in simple nouns and verbs; give the words flow till the listening mind reaches for the next. You'll invent poetry.

You won't do these things for their own sake, or even knowingly. They'll be forced from you in the struggle to grasp the slippery, unseen thought, to shape it and reveal it and make it remembered; and perhaps it will be. Or perhaps the tribe will only chant the story for its sounds, or draw out of it some quite different thought; things haven't changed so much, and it doesn't matter. You'll discover, buried in you, the making of story. You'll learn in time that it's remembered by its telling and its truth, but that it lives by all the thoughts it generates.

The necessary, natural struggle to tell a story is always new, but the roots were there already: hiding in yourself, planted by your inheritance to be discovered through need. They were deep and strong even when you spoke to a glistening of eyes by a tiny fire, perhaps in the darkness of a rock called Obiri. The roots of writing are deeper than you think.

I wish people would remember this. It's not an exciting idea, I know; not new and glistening in its cellophane wrap, inviting you to spend your money. It's old and withered and mildewed and boring; truth gets like that by being true. But perhaps we've been buying enough new ideas for the present, all plastic-bright and biodegradable and designed for the purpose of filling up somebody's bubble-pack. Maybe this is a moment for hunting up old truths and giving them a polish.

We discarded this one in favour of a concept called inspiration. That did suggest the natural, deeply rooted process of story-telling, but also that it was mindless and involuntary and might happen to you in your sleep. A thousand writers, bruised and bleeding from their struggles to define and convey, cried out in protest; so, no doubt, did another thousand composers and painters, and the concept was dropped. But I often suspect that we're still looking for something as easy and effort-free to put in its place.

I prefer to know what I'm doing, or to find out quickly so that I can do it again. From very deep roots I draw a comprehension of the process of story: the ear and the eye for it, the involvement it demands, the tools if I can handle them, the flash of recognition when they work. Using them is up to me; nothing is dictated, every possible mistake often happens, the flash of recognition has to be fought for. But if the roots of writing won't dictate, neither will they allow any other dictation. They're stronger than you think.

They require me to write for people but not for any person; to test response but avoid the pressure of it; to look for criticism, weigh it, and, unless it brings the flash of recognition, ignore it. I'm afraid it's a test of friendship, but I can't help it. I didn't make the rules.

We, the faceless millions who make the books, have each a tiny share of authority. Each of us is a reader more often than a writer, with only the normal insights and creative responses of a reader. But as writers, we do have authority. We must accept our tiny share of it, for the shares add up to the whole. So let theorists argue about why we write as we do, and how, and for whom; we know. Let us listen when they tell us where we have failed and why; it matters. It's the glint of eyes by a fire in the shadow of Obiri. But let us trust only our purpose, our experience, our authority. The life of story is in our many hands, and without authority it will die.

That must never happen, for story is rooted in the need of every one of us: children and adults, readers and writers, Indonesians and Americans and Chinese and New Zealanders, the whole of the family.

PART III

FANTASY

Turtles All the Way Down

Jane Yolen

The famous philosopher Will James had just finished giving a lecture on the solar system in Cambridge, Massachusetts, when he was approached by an elderly admirer. She was shaking her head and her umbrella and looking very stern.

'Mr James,' she admonished him, 'I am shocked by your notion that we live on a ball rotating around the sun. That is patently absurd.'

Politely, James waited, inclining his head toward her.

'We live on a crust of earth on the back of a giant turtle,' the grande dame announced.

James, ever gentle, asked, 'If your . . . um . . . theory is correct, madame, what does this turtle stand upon?'

'The first turtle stands on the back of a second far larger turtle, of course,' the old woman replied.

James lifted his hand. 'Ah, madame, but what does this *second* turtle stand upon?'

The dowager's eyes were bright. She laughed triumphantly, 'It's no use, Mr James—it's turtles all the way down!'

And so it is with writing fantasy—whether books for adults or children, whether a plot revolving around elves or unicorns or travel through time or angels stalking the earth or Chinese dragons having tea with detectives. Each book stands on the back of story. And as the old lady in Cambridge would agree, it's no use—it's story all the way down.

The writing of fantasy relies on that relationship, thrives on the ironies of a modern intelligence at work on the old tales, is enhanced by the juxtaposition of what-we-know-now and what-we-once-believed. Making fantasy stories is *sciamachy*, or boxing with shadows. Old shadows. Devious shadows. Wily shadows. Weird shadows. Our own shadows.

Writer as the Careful Observer

Since the creating of fantasy worlds, which contains universes, is built on the sturdy crust of story, the first important rule is that one needs to be sure of one's roots. Socrates said about allegories and myths that:

He is not to be envied who has to invent them; much labor and inge-
nuity will be required of him; and when he has once begun, he must
go on and rehabilitate centaurs and chimeras dire. Gorgons and
winged steeds flow in space, and numberless other inconceivable and
portentous monsters. And if he is sceptical about them, and would
fain reduce them one after another to the rules of probability, this sort
of crude philosophy will take up all his time.

In other words, do your research and believe in your monstrosities—at
least as long as you are writing of them. Otherwise your scepticism will
translate into condescension on the page and alienate readers.

It is difficult enough to make believable what is not, in broad daylight,
believable: the seelie court alive and well in Minneapolis, water rats and
moles conversing and messing about in boats, a furry-footed manikin out
to save the world by tossing away a magic ring, a boy pulling a sword from
a stone and then becoming a king, a young man fighting his shadow self
for possession of power, a young woman calling her dark sister out of a
mirror, a world in which dragons can be ridden through time and alternate
space. The writer of such stories must know something, then, about the
seelie court, about the habits of water rats and moles, about his own furry-
footed manikin's genealogy, about all the things that will bolster belief.
Belief by the author, belief by the reader.

Background, then, is important. The landscape of the world must be
carefully limned. Sometimes, as in Emma Bull's *War for the Oaks*, the place
is real and the author lives there. Still, as well as Bull knows Minneapolis,
she had to research material on the seelie or elvin court. Sometimes the
author takes a trip to the place, as Ellen Kushner did for her novel *Thomas
the Rhymer*, striding across the Eildon Hills of Scotland, avoiding cowpats
and taking notes. As I did for *The Dragon's Boy*, scouting the Glastonbury
marshes for duckweed and frogbit and bright-yellow kingcup and the
white clusters of milk parsley, my wildflower book in hand. Sometimes the
research is done in libraries only, as Susan Shwartz did for her fantasy
novels about the Silk Roads. But in fantasy, outer landscape reflects inner
landscape. The hills and mountains must be true, whether they are based
on actual places like Minneapolis or Scotland or England or China—or are
made up analogue fashion, from places in the author's mind. All of the
fantasy authors I know own research volumes on wildlife, wildflowers,
insects, birds. *Peterson's Guides* have a use Roger Tory Peterson never
intended, perhaps, but they are useful all the same.

Analogue fashion. By that I mean if you are not using the city of Minneapolis or the actual Eildon Hills or the fenland around Glastonbury with the tor mounding up over the quaking land, but rather a construct of your own, it needs to have some sort of referent in real life. Writers need to be observers first.

If you have never seen a mountain, I mean really *looked* at one, don't put a mountain in your fantasy land. If you have not studied a wildflower and noted that certain types grow in marshy places, others in drier scrub, then don't pepper your fantastic landscape with red and blue *catch-me-nevers* or *beggar-my-neighbours* or whatever you decide to call them. You are sure to describe a hothouse variety where only a scraggle-rooted one will do. And don't send seabirds sailing over mountaintops, or water pippits stalking up rock slides. Look hard at the real world and then look slightly askance. That is how you make your fantasy analogue. As Emily Dickinson advised in one wise little poem, 'Tell all the truth/but tell it slant.' Fantasy looks at the world through slotted eyes.

So, too, the creatures of a fantastic world need careful observation. If you intend to use elves, for example, don't rely on Tolkien or any other modern writer's elves. Go back to source. You will find that elves are not the cute, pointy-eared, fur-loinclothed critters that modern comic books would have us believe. Rather, according to older lore gleaned from such books as Katherine Briggs's *The Fairies in English Tradition and Literature* or her *An Encyclopedia of Fairies*, they are amoral, they are lovers of tidyness, and they set high value on courtesy and respect, and yet 'honesty means nothing to (them). They consider they have right to whatever they need or fancy, including . . . human beings themselves.' Or if you want to put dragons in your story, find out as much about the difference between Western and Eastern dragons as a start, and then decide if your dragons *could exist.* (Would they, for example, need hollow bones like large birds?) If you wish Wotan or Coyote or Manannan MacLir to come striding into your fantasy, go back to source to get the descriptions of clothing, speech patterns, and the colour of mist that wraps around the god. If you decide to depart from source, at least *you will know what you are departing from.* The dilution of modern mythologies comes from writers who think that a Dungeons and Dragons manual is prime source material or that they can know all about Hercules from watching B movies and learning what the acronym SHAZAM stands for.

So the writer as careful observer comes first. If the writer creates what Eleanor Cameron calls 'the compelling power of place', building up the fantasy world or the real world in which the fantastic takes place with a wealth of corroborating details, the reader will *have* to believe in the place. If the place is real enough, then the fantasy creatures and characters—dragon or elf lord or one-eyed god or the devil himself—will stride across that landscape leaving footprints that sink down into the mud. And if those creatures are also compelling, having taken root in the old lore and been brought forward in literary time by the carefully observing author, those footprints in the mud can be taken out, dried, and mounted on the wall.

Writer as Vatic Voice

The vatic voice is the prophetic or inspired or oracular voice. Nowhere in writing is this voice used as narrative so well as in the literature of the fantastic. Fantasy is dreamer's history and often it is the dreamer's voice, the bard afire with the word of God, *vates*.

The voice of fantasy pipes through the writer down strange new-yet-old valleys wild. There is nothing tame in the world of faerie. Tendrils of green lianas crawl across the paths. Invisible beasts call from behind dark trees. The world is moonlit, a chiaroscuro world where light and dark are in constant play. But the calling is not one voice, the piping not one single tone. One might almost name three: the oracle, the schoolboy, and the fool.

The oracular voice speaks in a metaphoric mode, from hollow caves, out of swirling mists of perfumed, drugging smoke, in riddles and gnomic utterances. It sings with the bardic full chest tones. This is the sound of the high fantasy novel. Three who do it to perfection are J.R.R. Tolkien, Ursula Le Guin, and Patricia McKillip. Others include Robin McKinley, Meredith Ann Pierce, and Lloyd Alexander. It is no coincidence that riddles play an important role in their books.

There is the riddle of the ring poem in the beginning of *The Lord of Rings* that binds the three books (really four, counting *The Hobbit*) with as fierce a power as the rings bind the characters who dare put them on.

And in Le Guin's *The Wizard of Earthsea*, the riddles Ged, the young master wizard, must ask himself have to do with shadow and substance, good and evil, light and dark. He is told by the Master Wizard:

> This sorcery is not a game we play for pleasure or for praise. Think of this: that every word, every act of our Art is said and is done for good or for evil. Before you speak or do you must know the price that is to pay!

Ged answers, driven by shame: 'How am I to know these things when you teach me nothing?' His finding the right answers to the riddles of his master's teachings are, of course, the basic thrust of the book.

Patricia McKillip uses the riddle itself as the main metaphor for her entire trilogy. In *The Riddle Master of Hed*, the riddle is the key to Morgon's self-knowledge. As he says, 'The stricture according to the Riddle-Masters at Caithnard is this: "Answer the unanswered riddle!" So I do.' And he spends the rest of the three volumes trying to learn to temper his passion for unriddling with wisdom, compassion, and an understanding (inherent in all great fantasy novels) that *magic has consequences*.

The oracular tones are the full *basso profundo* of fantasy dialects, the ground bass on which the melodies of the others overswell. The words are sometimes archaic—elven, sorcery, stricture. Sometimes they are fanciful, Latinate, sonorous. There is frequent use of alliterations: 'a *ring* to *rule* them'; '*pleasure* or for *praise*'. And the sentences, like chants, often end on that full stop, the strong stress syllable that reminds one of a knell rung on a full set of bells. One can declaim high fantasy, sing out whole paragraphs, even chapters. I expect that if they were set to music, it would be Beethoven, full and echoing; melodic, resonant, touching deep into the most private places of the heart.

The schoolboy voice is more securely set in the here and now. While fantasy figures bend and bow around it, the voice remains childlike, innocent, a sensible commentary on the imaginary. Ray Bradbury, E. Nesbit, C.S. Lewis, Diana Wynne Jones, and Natalie Babbitt reign supreme here. The voice speaking in ordinary tones about the extraordinary recall us to our humanity in the midst of the fantastic.

Listen to the way a Nesbit child reacts when first coming upon a psammead, a creature that has 'eyes on long horns like a snail's eyes . . . a tubby body . . . shaped like a spider's and covered with thick soft fur . . . and . . . hands and feet like a monkey's.' She says: 'What on earth is it? . . . Shall we take it home?' which seems eminently childlike and sensible.

And while in C.S. Lewis's Narnia wars and witches are raging, the voice of a very real British schoolboy, Eustace, meeting the elegant and marvellous talking mouse Reepicheep, who has just bowed and kissed Lucy's hand, remonstrates:

'Ugh, take it away,' wailed Eustace. 'I hate mice. And I never could bear performing animals. They're silly and vulgar and—and sentimental.'

Two schoolchildren's reactions to marvels: opposite, apposite, and very real.

And when Winnie Foster in Babbitt's *Tuck Everlasting* first hears the strange story of the Tucks and their water of everlasting life, she thinks not about the unbelievability of their history but rather about the humanity that confronts her:

> It was the strangest story Winnie had ever heard. She soon suspected they had never told it before, except to each other—that she was their first real audience; for they gathered around her like children at their mother's knee, each trying to claim her attention, and sometimes they all talked at once, and interrupted each other in their eagerness.

There, quite simply, is the key to the schoolboy voice. The child in this kind of fantasy takes over the role of the adult, shepherding the fantastic creatures through their paces, guiding, guarding—even when frightfully afraid—for this world belongs *to* the child, this world in which magic has slipped through. And it is not the magic itself that is startling, because children expect that kind of magic to occur, but the vulnerability of the creatures of magic who are sad in their magnificence and, in Eustace's words, sometimes 'silly and vulgar and—and sentimental'. The child responds to this vulnerability by becoming both more childlike and yet adult, a paradox seen whenever a child plays house, giving advice and taking it at one and the same time.

These are the middle tones, carrying the tunes so familiar to us, dancing in and out of the fantastic as a Bach fugue does, using a simple tune made more complex by its interweaving; plain, unelaborated except where the fantastic itself is concerned, it is the everydayness of the language that reveals when set against the extraordinary. Natalie Babbitt does this brilliantly, eschewing the fanciful for the ordinary in the opening of *Tuck Everlasting*. She reports with a painter's eye, and that report becomes the metaphor for the book:

> The first week of August hangs at the very top of summer, the top of the live-long year, like the highest seat of a Ferris wheel when it pauses in its turning. The weeks that come before are only a climb from balmy spring, and those that follow a drop to the chill of autumn, but the first week of August is motionless, and hot. It is curiously silent, too, with blank white dawns and glaring noons, and sunsets smeared with too much color. Often at night there is lightning, but it quivers

all alone. There is no thunder, no relieving rain. These are strange and breathless days, the dog days, when people are led to do things they are sure to be sorry for after.

The third voice, high and piercing, full of ridiculous trills and anachronisms, ludicrous and punning, is the voice of the fool. But don't be guiled by it. Underneath the pratfalls and the bulbous-nose mask, behind the wild shrieks and the shaking of slapsticks, lie deep, serious thoughts. As Montaigne says in his *Essays*, attributing it to Cato the Elder, 'Wise men have more to learn of fools than fools of wise men.'

Examples of this voice are Lewis Carroll, Sid Fleischman, Norton Juster, Terry Pratchett, Esther Friesner, and Craig Shaw Gardner. Like a comic opera by Mozart, there are wild, sweet melodies hidden amid the silliness, and you would be a fool indeed to miss them.

When Lewis Carroll invented his Mad Teaparty, he little knew that it would serve generations of English teachers and writers as well as children. Listen:

'You should say what you mean,' the March Hare went on.

'I do,' Alice hastily replied, 'at least—at least I mean what I say—that's the same thing, you know.'

'Not the same thing a bit!' said the Hatter. 'Why, you might just as well say "I see what I eat" is the same thing as "I eat what I see"!'

'You might just as well say,' added the March Hare, 'that "I like what I get" is the same thing as "I get what I like"!'

'You might just as well say,' added the Dormouse, which seemed to be talking in its sleep, 'that "I breathe when I sleep" is the same thing as "I sleep when I breathe"!'

'It *is* the same thing with you,' said the Hatter. . . .

That is not just straight silliness. The applicability to everyday life is so fierce in *Alice in Wonderland* that I wish to remind you of the time of Watergate in this country when the following phrases—and more—were lifted from the *Alice* books by columnists, commentators, essayists, and editorialists and used to explain politics:

'I told you butter wouldn't suit the works'
'Believing six impossible things before breakfast'
'Sentence first, verdict after'
'Curiouser and curiouser'

Sid Fleischman's humour is regional, hyperbolic, and anything but casual. The silliness is unrelieved, or so it seems. But Fleischman is a traditionalist when it comes to humour, and he knows well how to disguise pain with the putty nose, to teach us wisdom with a wisecrack.

In *Chancy and the Grand Rascal*, my favourite of his many books, Chancy, who is so skinny he'd 'have to stand twice to throw a shadow,' goes through a series of picaresque adventures in order to find his family because 'kin belonged together, didn't they?' And when a wicked man is described as 'gander-necked . . . with a nose like a stick', the absurdity of it sets the tone and character with economy and grace. We laugh, but we are properly fearful, too.

Norton Juster's *The Phantom Tollbooth* is not just a book-long play on words, although at times it may seem so:

> 'If you please,' said Milo [speaking to King Azaz the Unabridged]
> '. . . your palace is beautiful.'
>   'Exquisite,' corrected the duke.
>   'Lovely,' counseled the minister.
>   'Handsome,' recommended the count.
>   'Pretty,' hinted the earl.
>   'Charming,' submitted the undersecretary.
>   'SILENCE,' suggested the king. 'Now young man, what can you do to entertain us? Sing songs? Tell stories? Compose sonnets? Juggle plates? Do tumbling tricks? Which is it?'
>   'I can't do any of those things,' admitted Milo.
>   'What an ordinary little boy,' commented the king. 'Why my cabinet members can do all sorts of things. The duke here can make mountains out of molehills. The minister splits hairs. The count makes hay while the sun shines. The earl leaves no stone unturned. And the undersecretary,' he finished ominously, 'hangs by a thread. Can't you do anything at all?'

That is a hymn to language, our use and misuse of it that William Safire, Russell Baker, and Edwin Newman would envy. But it is also story—not Sunday editorial polemic.

In the end, of course, the voice of fantasy is not a particular dialect at all—not the oracle, the schoolboy, the fool. There is a much older voice that lies in back of them all—the storyteller's voice—bridging the gap of history, singing to us out of the mists of time, telling truths.

As the Maori people say when beginning a tale:

The breath of life,
The spirit of life,
The word of life,
It flies to you and you and you,
Always the word.

If the fantasy story does not have that breath of life, whether it uses the words of the oracle, the schoolboy, or the fool, it does not deserve to live and will lie, stillborn, on the pages of a dust-covered book.

Writer as Visionary

It surprises no one that writers of realistic fiction write about the society in which they live, that their stories reflect current thinking, and that fictional accounts of child abuse or women's rights or nuclear issues are published in the decade of public awareness and social legislation. But fantasy authors are just as mired in society as authors of realistic work are, though their work is like the wicked queen's magic mirror that does not always give back the expected answer.

For example, Charles Kingsley's *Water Babies* is a picture of the under-belly of English society in the nineteenth century, but the plight of poor chimney sweeps is only the mirror's first casting. What Kingsley didn't realize was that later readings would judge his anti-black, anti-Jewish, and anti-Catholic attitudes, which are only slightly disguised in the book, rather more harshly than he ajudged the rich-poor dichotomy. Rudyard Kipling's otherwise brilliant *The Jungle Book* is marred by jingoism. *Mary Poppins* and *Dr Doolittle* share a culture bias against peoples of colour. *Charlie and the Chocolate Factory* in its first printing showed the Oompa-loompahs with skin 'almost black' because they are 'Pygmies . . . imported directly from Africa', as if they were so much yardgoods. In later printings of the book the little workers in Willy Wonka's factory have been transmogrified into a different colour and a different place of origin.

What is easy to see with these examples is that fantasy books deal with issues (consciously or unconsciously, in a good light or in a bad) as thoroughly as realistic fiction, but *one step removed*. For example, Randall Jarrell's book *The Bat-Poet* is about the artist in society, Le Guin's *Tehanu* about woman's power, Patricia Wrightson's *A Little Fear* about active old age, my *Sister Light, Sister Dark* about the integration of personality as well as the inaccuracies of history.

But it is the phrase *one step removed* that is the most important. Fantasy fiction, by its very nature, takes us out of the real world. Sometimes it takes us to another world altogether: Demar, Middle Earth, Narnia, Earthsea, Prydain, the Dales. Sometimes it changes the world we know in subtle ways, such as showing us the 'little people' who live behind the wall of our houses and 'borrow' things. Or that in a very real barn, but out of our hearing and sight, a pig and a spider hold long, special conversations. Sometimes a book of fantasy travels us between planets (*A Wrinkle in Time*), between worlds (the *Oz* books), or between times (*A Connecticut Yankee in King Arthur's Court*), or the traveller himself is from somewhere else, such as Nesbit's psammead or Bull's pucca or Diana Wynne Jones's goon.

By taking that one step away from the actual world, the writer of fantasy can allow the reader to pretend that the book is not talking about the everyday, the mundane, the real society when indeed it is. It is a convention all agree to. A mask. In eighteenth-century Venice, when masked balls were common, it became a convention that a person who wished to go about the street and be treated as if he were disguised needed only to wear a pin in the shape of a mask on his lapel. Thus accoutred, he was considered masked and could act out any part he wished without fear of shame or retribution or recognition.

So fantasy novels go capped and belled into literary society, saying in effect: this is not the real world we are talking of, this is of course faerie, make-believe, where bicoloured rock pythons speak, where little girls converse with packs of cards, where boys become kings by drawing swords from stones, and where caped counts can suck the blood of beautiful women in order to live forever.

Children who read fantasy *may* be beguiled, because they *may* not totally understand the conventions. They mistake the pin for the real. They write to Maurice Sendak and ask for directions to the place where the Wild Things live. They believe in Narnia and Middle Earth and Prydain and Demar, and for them these worlds *may* become even more real than the every day. After all, when we write about such places we must adhere to three very persuasive laws: first, that the fantasy world have identifiable and workable laws underpinning it. (Lloyd Alexander says that 'Underneath the gossamer is pre-stressed concrete.') Second, that there is a hero or heroine who often is lost, unlikely, powerless at first or second glance, or unrecognized and therefore easy for the reader to identify with. And third, that in a fantasy novel things always end justly—though not always happily. Come to think of it, adults are also beguiled—at least for the length of the book—that such things are so because of those three laws.

Therefore, it is important that writers of fantasy be aware of the moral underpinnings of their work. Lloyd Alexander wrote, 'Fantasy, by its power to move us so deeply, to dramatize, even melodramatize, morality, can be one of the most effective means of establishing a capacity for adult values.' Thus the writer of a fantasy novel must have a vision of the world, must be a visionary.

Of course, there is this to be understood about writing any kind of novel: the novelist knows very little about what she or he is doing at the start. We learn more as events, characters, and landscape take form. Every plunge into a new novel is a parallel adventure—for the hero and the novelist. Like our fictional counterparts, we take a journey into the unknown. We authors are Joseph Campbell's definition of the hero: 'A hero ventures forth from the world of common day into a region of supernatural wonder: fabulous forces are there encountered and a decisive victory is won; the hero comes back with the power to bestow boons on his fellow man.' We venture forth from our writing rooms—the *world of common day* into the *supernatural wonder* of the story. We encounter *supernatural forces* like slippery words, monstrous, unwieldy plots. *The decisive victory* won is the book completed. And after all, there is only one letter difference between the words *boon* and *book*, which we bestow on readers everywhere.

Once we understand the vision, it is our basic charge that we must write all stops out to make that vision sing. It is, after all, what fantasy does best, has done always. Turtles all the way down.

Some Presumptuous Generalizations About Fantasy

Perry Nodelman

Precise definitions of fantasy do not account for all the different things people do call fantasy. The best definition is the vaguest: fantasy depicts a world unlike the one we usually call real. All fiction creates its own world; the worlds of fantasy are clearly different from the world we live in.

Fantasies have four main elements: the world they describe; the things that happen in that world; the meaning of what happens; the way what happens is described.

Most criticism centres on the first element, and describes the cosmology of fantasy worlds. While such discussions do show the differences between fantasy worlds and the world we call real, they do not account for the particular effect of a particular novel. The invention of interesting worlds is not always accompanied by the ability to write about them well; our delight in fantasy is not merely our pleasure in the peculiarities of fantasy worlds.

Critics who emphasize what happens in fantasies usually confuse imagination with the unconscious, and assume that the plots of fantasies express archetypes, that fantasy is a symbolic representation of the patterns that underlie our usual reality. But if we believe that archetypes underlie reality, there is no reason to believe that fantasy is *more* archetypical than realistic fiction. Furthermore, the archetypes contained in any fiction are inevitably less interesting than the particular events that contain them.

But since fantasies do not describe ordinary reality, it may be assumed that the rules that govern them are metaphysical rather than physical. Critics who emphasize the meaning of fantasies assume that they are allegories, and that their essence is psychological or moral. The assumption is still that fantasy worlds are symbolic representations of our usual reality; and while in this case the meaning of a fantasy is personal to its creator and not a product of the generalized human unconscious, the same objection holds. Other fictional worlds may be approached in the same way, and with equally unproductive results. To understand what a book means is not likely to account for its uniqueness. And that is particularly true of fantasies; since by definition they do not describe ordinary reality, to assume that their significance is the meaning they give to ordinary reality is to miss the point of their extraordinary characteristics. We do not enjoy fantasies because of their psychological or moral meaning.

In fact, the meaning of fantasies may be different from the meaning of other novels. Writers of realistic fiction try to understand reality. Writers of fantasy, in coming to terms with their own apparently perverse act of writing about worlds that do not exist, often write about fantasy itself, and its effect on our lives in our usual reality (*Where the Wild Things Are, Earthfasts*). But not all fantasies explore the idea of fantasy; some merely take it for granted. And some non-fantasies are also about the implications of fantasy (*Harriet the Spy*).

But the way things are described in convincing fantasy does seem to be different from the way things are described in other good fiction, and for a good reason. The writer of ordinary fiction must persuade us that the events he describes could possibly happen in a world we live in and are already familiar with. The writer of a fantasy must persuade us that a world we are not familiar with is as he describes it to be.

That ought to be easy. Reading realistic fiction, we inevitably compare the writer's perception of the world with our own. Reading fantasy, we have nothing to compare the fictional world with; theoretically we have no choice but to accept what the writer tells us.

But we do not always accept it. If we do not, it is because the person who tells us about it has not established his own credibility. Realistic fiction convinces us by creating a world we can recognize; fantasy convinces us by establishing a believable narrator. We must trust the narrator before we can accept the world he describes.

That implies that the narrator is not the novelist, but a character the novelist creates—the person Aidan Chambers calls 'the author's second self'. Anyone who sets out to tell a story instinctively (and perhaps unconsciously) invents the right person to tell it, a narrator whose personality may or may not be like the storyteller's personality. So every story implies the imaginary person who tells it.

It also implies what Chambers calls 'the reader in the book', the ideal audience to hear it.

Consequently, there are two important questions: what is the character of the storyteller implied by good fantasy, and what is the character of the audience implied by good fantasy?

First, the ideal storyteller. If we are to believe the narrator, he must himself believe. He should be a citizen of the world he describes, so that he will not express uncertainty about its existence or be excited by its oddities. (In the case of many children's fantasies in which characters move from a normal reality to a fantastic one, the narrator's world should contain both; he should not be surprised by movement between them, even though his characters may.) His attention should be focused on the story, not on the world in which it occurs nor on its meaning. He should be neither a tour guide nor a moral philosopher, but a storyteller.

As a storyteller, he should trust his story *and* his audience. He should assume the audience knows the world he describes already, and that it is the particular story about that world he is telling that will interest them. He should not try to be charming, or call attention to his own wit or to his own interpretation of the story's meaning. He should be most interested in communicating the story in the best way possible, in finding the words to tell it that will make it have the effect he desires on his audience. He should act with the conviction that he can tell the story so well that its audience will both enjoy it and understand its implications.

As for the ideal implied audience: it should also live in the world the fantasy describes, and possess the knowledge citizens usually have of the place they inhabit. It should want to hear the story for its own sake, for the history it preserves or the enjoyment it contains. It should not want to be instructed either in morality or geography. For this reason, it should not consist of children, especially in a children's fantasy. If it does, the storyteller will talk down to the audience, and try to explain things to it. The implied audience should be people who want to hear real stories about real events in the real world they live in, or realistic stories about possible events in the real world they live in.

Only by ignoring the fact that it is fantastic, by pretending to be a true story about a real world shared by the characters in the story, the storyteller, and the people who hear the story, can a fantasy establish its credibility and work its magic on those who actually hear it.

In other words, the secret of good fantasy is the control of tone—the creation through the right choice of words of the right relationship between the writer and his audience. The right relationship in a fantasy is the audience's faith in the narrator; the right words create a tone of matter-of-fact acceptance that allows us to believe in what we know does not exist.

That implies a paradox. Fantasy does not really persuade us of the existence of the world it describes; it only allows us to *pretend* it exists. We pretend to be the ideal audience hearing the real truth about a real world only so that we can become conscious of the differences between that audience and ourselves, and that world and our own. We experience the pleasure of its otherness by pretending not to be different from it.

In fact, that pleasure is a consciousness of otherness, a revealing penetration of the limited vision imposed upon us by our own inevitably unique readings of reality—a freeing from solipsism. By experiencing something clearly and completely different from ourselves, we become acutely aware of who and what we actually are.

While much of what I suggest here about fantasy applies to other kinds of fiction, it is not always so important. The problem of credibility is less intense in fictional realities that purport to represent the world we usually call real, and in much good realistic fiction, the narrator's untrustworthiness is deliberate; the writer forces us to compare the narrator's faulty reading of events with our own knowledge of reality. In this kind of writing the narrator's tone is anything but matter-of-fact.

But children's literature, fantasy or not, is different. In fact, for grownups, all children's literature is much like fantasy. It is not so much literature *for* children as it is literature about childhood, literature describing the world as children might see it and understand it to be. In other words, it does not describe the world we as grownups consider real in a way we would consider realistic—*unless* we force ourselves to adopt a childlike attitude in order to determine whether or not the attitudes it contains are convincingly childlike.

Furthermore, children's literature is frequently about coming to terms with a world one does not understand—the world as defined and governed by grownups and not totally familiar or comprehensible to children. *All* fantasy is about worlds one could not possibly have understood before reading the novels that contain them. So both children's literature and fantasy place readers in a position of innocence about the reality they describe, and create the same peculiar relationship between the story and its audience. The ideal storyteller implied by children's fiction may be similar to the ideal storyteller of fantasy, with the significant difference that good writers for children seem to believe that the ideal audience their work implies is in fact exactly the same as their real audience—that the world they create in their stories is in fact the real world as children perceive it. And perhaps one of the main pleasures any fantasy offers us is its ability to let us, as newcomers to the worlds it describes, experience innocence again.

In any case, fantasy and children's literature have clear connections with each other. Understanding one may help in the understanding of the other. It may also explain why much of the best children's literature happens to be fantasy.

Fantasy: Why Kids Read It, Why Kids Need It

Tamora Pierce

I wonder why readers choose to read fantasy; rather, I wonder why more of them *don't*. Until they reach school age, children are offered little else on almost a continuous basis. The groundwork for a love of the fanciful is laid by children's literature, from A.A. Milne to Dr Seuss, and from Curious George to Max and his Wild Things.

Once children enter school, however, emphasis shifts from imaginative to reality-based writing, and many youngsters grow away from speculative fiction—but not all. Those who stay with it do so for many reasons, and it comes to fill a number of needs in their lives.

One of the things I have learned about YAs is that they respond to the idealism and imagination they find in everything they read. They haven't spent years butting their heads against brick walls; the edge of their enthusiasm, and of their minds, is still sharp. Some of the most perceptive social and political commentary I've heard in the last eight years or so has come from my readers. Young people have the time and emotional energy to devote to causes, unlike so many of us, losing our revolutionary (or evolutionary) drive as we spend ourselves on the details and chores that fill adult life. They take up causes, from the environment, to human disaster relief, to politics. We encourage them, and so we should: there is a tremendous need for those who feel passionately and are willing to work at what they care about, whatever their cause may be. YAs are also dreamers; this is expected and, to a degree, encouraged as they plan for the future. Their minds are flexible, recognizing few limits. Here the seeds are sown for the great visions, those that will change the future for us all. We give our charges goals, heroes whose feats they can emulate, and knowledge of the past, but they also need fuel to spark and refine ideas, the same kind of fuel that fires idealism.

That fuel can be found—according to the writings of Jung, Bettelheim, M. Ester Harding, and Joseph Campbell—in the mighty symbols of myth, fairy tales, dreams, legends—and fantasy. Haven't we felt their power? Remember that flush of energy and eagerness we felt as Arthur drew the sword from the stone? It's the same as that which bloomed the first time—or even the fifth or sixth time—we heard Dr King say, 'I have a dream.' An eyedropper's worth of that energy can feed days of activity, hard and sometimes dirty work, fund raising, letter writing. It can ease an idealist over small and big defeats.

Here is where fantasy, in its flesh and modern (i.e. post-1900) forms, using contemporary sensibilities and characters youngsters identify with, reigns supreme. Here the symbols of meaningful struggle and of truth as an inner constant exist in their most undiluted form outside myth and fairy tale: Tolkien's forces of Light fighting a mind-numbing Darkness; Elizabeth Moon's lone paladin facing pain and despair with only faith to sustain her (in *Oath of Gold*, Baen, 1989); Diane Duane's small choir of deep sea creatures holding off the power of death and entropy at the risk of the world's life and their own (*Deep Wizardry*, Delacorte, 1985). These stories appear to have little to do with reality, but they do provide readers with the impetus to challenge the way things are, something YAs respond to wholeheartedly. Young people are drawn to battles for a discernible higher good; the images of such battles evoke their passion. (I would like to note here that some of the writers mentioned herein normally are considered to be adult writers. Fantasy, even more than other genres, has a large crossover audience, with YAs raiding the adult shelves once they deplete their part of the store or library, and adults slipping into the youth sections.)

Fantasy, along with science fiction, is a literature of *possibilities*. It opens the door to the realm of 'What If', challenging readers to see beyond the concrete universe and to envision other ways of living and alternative mindsets. Everything in speculative universes, and by association the real world, is mutable. Intelligent readers will come to relate the questions raised in these books to their own lives. If a question nags at youngsters intensely enough, they will grow up to devise an answer—to move their world forward, because ardent souls can't stand an unanswered question.

The question of a place to belong is a burning issue in all YA literature, not just the speculative variety. Fantasy writers seem to have an affinity for it, particularly for the variation of outsiders who find, or rather *make*, a place that is their own. It is obvious in Mercedes Lackey's 'Arrows' series (DAW), in which the young heroine flees an abusive home to create a niche for a small, scared girl-child among the legendary Heralds. It is central to Barbara Hambly's books from her 'Darwath' trilogy (1982) to her recent *Dog Wizard* (1993, both Del Rey). A personal niche is the series-long quest of Lloyd Alexander's hero Taran ('Prydain Chronicles', Holt) and the drive that moves Schmendrick, the mage of Peter Beagle's *The Last Unicorn* (Del

Rey, 1987). Next to the normal, human flaws of my protagonists, the creation of a unique place in the world is the thing my readers mention most often in their letters. Some youngsters will always say, 'But that only happens in *books*,' but fantasy readers seem to know that what happens in books can be carried over, that the idea of change is universal, and that willpower and work are formidable forces, wherever they are applied.

Fantasy, more than any other genre, is a literature of empowerment. In the real world, kids have little say. This is a given; it is the nature of child-hood. In fantasy, however short, fat, unbeautiful, weak, dreamy, or unlearned individuals may be, they find a realm in which those things are negated by strength. The catch—there is *always* a catch—is that empower-ment brings trials. Good novels in this genre never revolve around heroes who, once they receive the 'Spatula of Power', call the rains to fill dry wells, end all war, and clear up all acne. Heroes and heroines contend as much with their granted wishes as readers do in normal life. Anne McCaffrey's Menolly, heroine of *Dragonsinger* (Atheneum, 1977), discovers life at Harper Hall isn't all music, as she'd dreamed, but hard work and entangle-ment in human problems and politics. In Edgar Eager's *Half Magic* (Harcourt, 1954), children receive a wishing coin that does things *only* by halves, a truly mixed blessing with which each of them has to cope. While Bruce Coville's 'Magic Shop' series (Harcourt) customers may not wish for a ring that changes the wearer to a werewolf, a dragon's egg that hatches, or a talking toad, they get them—and have to solve the many problems created by such possessions. Young readers seem to come away from the characters' mishaps not depressed but energized, as if the protagonist's struggle was something they survived as well.

One of the greatest legendary and imaginative symbols is that of the knight in shining armour. Paramedics, social workers, advocacy lawyers (and writers) keep it in some corner of their minds, while they work in settings that in no way resemble the feudal agrarian culture from which those symbols are drawn. Combat power holds allure for many fantasy readers, and the genre presents it in every form one could desire, starting with Arthurian legend. Strength isn't measured by modern world terms but usually in medieval ones, and such strength can change the fates of people and of nations. Here also, battles aren't always won by those who are big and strong, although such heroes are a popular aspect of this kind of fiction, from Little John and Lancelot to David Eddings's militant church knights.

Combat heroes who don't fit a traditionally heroic mould exist as well. Dwarves, for example. No one laughs at a dwarf as written by Tolkien or

Elizabeth Moon. They are short, squat, uncomely people who are also clever, tireless, formidable opponents. Sometimes they are heroines. Robin McKinley's Harry in *The Blue Sword* (1982) and Aerin in *The Hero and the Crown* (1984, both Greenwillow) start off as amateurs with little or no sword training. Both work hard to achieve their mastery. Harry is called to it by the powers that guard her new home and an awareness of disaster on its way; Aerin simply to make her own place in the world.

In fantasy, those normally perceived as unimportant are vital players. David Eddings's five-book 'Belgariad' series, beginning with *Pawn of Prophecy* (Del Rey), is the tale of a boy who is caught up in world-changing events whether he wants to be or not. He walks in the company of heroes as a very junior partner and, in spite of his errors, becomes one of them, a process with which any YA can identify. In Tolkien's 'Lord of the Rings' trilogy (Ballantine), plain, simple, everyday folk are taken into that same wider tapestry, where they affect the course of history simply by being who they are.

Most important of all in fantasy is that great equalizer between the powerful and the powerless: magic, the thing that keeps young children captivated by fairy tales and older ones enthralled by wizards, from Merlin to Zilpha Keatley Snyder's Mr Mazzeeck in *Black and Blue Magic* (Atheneum, 1972). Some get both in one, as more and more authors retell the ancient stories with a modern point of view. My favourite is Robin McKinley's *Beauty* (HarperCollins, 1978). The glitter of magic lures readers into a new universe in Diana Wynne Jones's *Charmed Life* (Knopf, 1989), and keeps them there when Cat's relationship with his rotten sister must feel all too painfully familiar. Even magic comes with complications: good fantasy won't let its readers off the hook. YAs live the inner conflict of Diane Duane's young mage Nita in *Deep Wizardry*, who rashly promises to do whatever is needed to help the marine wizards complete their magical ceremony, only to learn she has agreed to die, and that to default on that vow will undo their work, her own work, and that of her co-mage and friend, Christopher. Snyder's Harry Houdini Marco acquires truly horrific bruises and creates even more havoc as he tries to manage a pair of wings without getting found out.

Fantasy is also important to a group that I deeply hope is small: those whose lives are so grim that they cling to everything that takes them completely away for *any* length of time. I speak of readers like I was, from families that are now called dysfunctional. While the act of reading transported me out of reality for the time it took me to read, nothing carried over into my thoughts and dreams until I discovered fantasy. I visited

Tolkien's Mordor often for years, not because I *liked* what went on there, but because on the dead horizon, and then throughout the sky overhead, I could see the interplay and the lasting power of light and hope. It got me through.

Fantasy creates hope and optimism in readers. It is the pure stuff of wonder, the kind that carries over into everyday life and colours the way readers perceive things around them. I think everyone could use some extra hope and wonder as we rocket toward a new millennium. It can be found in the children's, young adult, and science fiction and fantasy sections of bookstores and libraries everywhere.

Dr Seuss and Dr Einstein: Children's Books and Scientific Imagination

Chet Raymo

A few years ago, when an insect called the thrips—singular and plural—was in the news for defoliating sugar maples in New England, I noted in my Boston *Globe* science column that thrips are very strange beasts. Some species of thrips give birth to live young, some lay eggs, and at least one species of switch-hitting thrips has it both ways. Not even the wildest product of Dr Seuss's imagination, I said—the Moth-Watching Sneth, for example, a bird that's so big it scares people to death, or the Grickily Gractus, a bird that lays eggs on a cactus—is stranger than creatures, such as the thrips, that actually exist.

As if to prove my point, a reader sent me a photograph of a real tropical bird that does indeed lay eggs on a cactus.

What about the Moth-Watching Sneth? Well, the extinct elephant bird of Madagascar stood eight feet tall and weighed a thousand pounds. In its heyday—only a century or so ago—the elephant bird, or Aepyornis, probably scared many a Madagascan half to death.

Pick any Seussian invention, and nature will equal it. In Dr Seuss's *McElligot's Pool* (Random) there's a fish with a kangaroo pouch. Could there possibly be such a fish in the real world? Not a fish, maybe, but in South America there is an animal called the Yapok—a wonderfully Seussian name—that takes its young for a swim in a waterproof pouch.

Dr Seuss, who died last year at age eighty-seven, was a botanist and zoologist of the first rank. Never mind that the flora and fauna he described were imaginary. Any kid headed for a career in science could do no better than to start with the plants and animals that populate the books of the madcap master of biology.

One thrips, two thrips, red thrips, blue thrips. The eggshell of an elephant bird, cut in half, would make a splendid salad bowl. Is it Seuss, or is it reality? You see, the boundary between the so-called 'real' world and the world of the imagination begins to blur. And that is just as it should be if a child is to grow up with a proper attitude toward science.

Do black holes, those strange products of the astronomer's imagination, really exist? What about electrons, invisibly small, fidgeting in their atomic shells? How about the dervish dance of DNA as it unzips down the middle to reproduce itself? No one has ever seen these things, at least not directly. Like the Gractus and the Sneth, they are wonderful inventions of the imagination.

Of course, we are convinced—for the time being at least—that black holes, electrons, and unzipping DNA are real, because of the way those things connect with other things we know about the world and because certain experiments turn out in certain ways. But it is important to remember that the world of science is a made-up world, a world of let's pretend, no less so than the strange flora and fauna of Dr Seuss. The physicist Michael Faraday once said, 'Nothing is too wonderful to be true.' To be a good scientist, or to have a scientific attitude toward the world, one must be able to imagine wonderful things—even things that seem too wonderful to be true.

Creative science depends crucially upon habits of mind that are most readily acquired by children: curiosity; voracious observation; sensitivity to rules and variations within the rules; and fantasy. Children's books that instil these habits of mind sustain science.

I am not talking about so-called 'science books for children'. I am not talking about 'fact' books. I would argue that many science books written especially for children may actually diminish the very habits of mind that make for good science.

I occasionally review children's science books for a splendid journal called *Appraisal*. Most of the offerings I have been sent for review are packed full of useful information. What most of these books do not convey is the extraordinary adventure story of how the information was obtained, why we understand it to be true, or how it might embellish the landscape of the mind. For many children—and adults, too—science is information, a mass of facts. But facts are not science any more than a table is carpentry. Science is an attitude toward the world—curious, sceptical, undogmatic, forward-looking. To be a scientist, or simply to share the scientific attitude, one must be like the kid in Dr Seuss's *On Beyond Zebra* (Random) who refused to be limited by the fact of the alphabet: 'In the places I go there are things that I see/That I *never* could spell if I stopped with the Z.'

We live in an age of information. We are inundated by it. Too much information can swamp the boat of wonder, especially for a child. Which is why it is important that information be conveyed to children in a way that enhances the wonder of the world. For example, there are several fine information books for children about bats. But how much richer is that information when it is presented this way:

> A bat is born
> Naked and blind and pale.
> His mother makes a pocket of her tail
> And catches him. He clings to her long fur
> By his thumbs and toes and teeth
> And then the mother dances through the night
> Doubling and looping, soaring, somersaulting—
> Her baby hangs on underneath.

There is every bit as much information in Randall Jarrell's *The Bat-Poet* (Macmillan) as in the typical information book. But, oh, what information!

If a child is led to believe that science is a bunch of facts, then science will not inform the child's life, nor will science enhance the child's cultural and imaginative landscape. Every September I meet a new crowd of students who have the dreariest impressions of science. For many of them, science is a dull, even painful, subject to be gotten out of the way as a general education requirement, then quickly replaced in life by astrology, parapsychology, or some other pseudoscience. By all means let's have books for kids that communicate what we know—or think we know—about the world; the more factual information we accumulate about the world, the more interesting the world becomes. But the scientific attitude—ah, that's something else. There is no better time to communicate the scientific attitude than during childhood, and no better way than with quality children's books. Consider these lines of Jarrell's *The Bat-Poet*:

> The mother eats the moths and gnats she catches
> In full flight; in full flight
> The mother drinks the water of the pond
> She skims across.

That wonderful line—'In full flight; in full flight'—conveys the single most important fact about bats: their extraordinary aviator skills. By repeating the phrase, Jarrell not only teaches us a bat fact but also helps us experience what it means to be a bat.

Curiosity, voracious seeing, sensitivity to rules and variations within the rules, and fantasy. These are habits of mind crucial for science that are best learned during childhood. Let us consider them one by one.

Curiosity. Albert Einstein wrote: 'The most beautiful experience we can have is the mysterious. It is the fundamental emotion which stands at the cradle of true art and true science.' At first, this might seem a strange thought as it applies to science. We are frequently asked to believe that science takes mystery out of the world. Nothing could be further from the truth. Mystery invites curiosity. Unless we perceive the world as mysterious, we shall never be curious about what makes the world tick.

My favourite books about curiosity are the children's books of Maurice Sendak, precisely because of their successful evocation of mystery. Sendak's illustrations convey the spooky sense of entwined order and chaos, good and menace that we find in nature. In *In the Night Kitchen* (Harper) Mickey hears a *thump* in the night. Down he falls, out of his pajamas, into the curious world of the night kitchen. The night kitchen is full of familiar things—the city skyline in the background consists of boxes and cans from the pantry—yet nothing is quite the same as in the daylight world. Mickey takes charge. He moulds; he shapes; he rearranges. He contrives clothes from bread dough, and a dough airplane, too. He takes a dip in a bottle of milk. The night kitchen is the awake world turned topsy-turvy.

Mickey's adventure is a dream, of course, but so what? The American social philosopher Lewis Mumford said: 'If man had not encountered dragons and hippogriffs in dreams, he might never have conceived of the atom.' It is an extraordinary thought, that science depends upon the dreaming mind. The dreamer, says Mumford, puts things together in ways never experienced in the awake world—joining the head, wings, and claws of a bird with the hind quarters of a horse—to make something fabulous and new: a hippogriff. In the dream world, space and time dissolve; near and far, past and future, familiar and monstrous merge in novel ways. In science, too, we invent unseen worlds by combining familiar things in an unfamiliar fashion. We imagine atoms, for example, as combining characteristics of billiard balls, musical instruments, and water waves, all on a scale that is invisibly small. According to Mumford, dreams taught us how to imagine the unseen world.

In science we talk about 'dreaming up' theories, and we move from the dreamed-up worlds of the night kitchen, Middle-Earth, Narnia, and Oz to dreamed-up worlds that challenge the adult imagination. An asteroid hurtles out of space and lays waste a monster race of reptiles that has ruled the earth for two hundred million years. A black hole at the centre of the Milky Way galaxy swallows ten million stars. A universe begins in a blinding flash from a pinprick of infinite energy. How did we learn to imagine such things? Mumford believed that dreams released human imagination from bondage to the immediate environment and to the present moment. He imagined early humans pestered and tantalized by dreams, sometimes confusing the images of darkness and sleep with those of waking life, subject to misleading hallucinations, disordered memories, unaccountable impulses, but also animated now and then by images of joyous possibility. These are exactly the characteristics I admire in Sendak's works. As long as children are reading such books, I have no fear for curiosity.

Voracious observation. I love books that stretch a child's powers of observation. Graeme Base's *Animalia* (Abrams). The books of Kit Williams. Richly textured books. Books hiding secrets. Of these, my favourites are the books in Mitsumasa Anno's Journey series—Bayeux tapestries that hide a hundred observational surprises. The more you look, the more you see, ad infinitum. Texture is everything.

The texture of a book can be too simple, or too complex. It can be uninteresting, or hopelessly cluttered. The nineteenth-century physicist James Clerk Maxwell said: 'It is a universal condition of the enjoyable that the mind must believe in the existence of a discoverable law, yet have a mystery to move in.' Anno's books have a rich textural complexity, but they are structured by discoverable laws. As often as I have perused these books, with children and alone, I have found new elements of law, subtly hidden, shaping the whole. With such books the child practises the very qualities of mind that led Maxwell to the laws of electromagnetism.

Rules and variations within the rules. If there is one thing that defines science, this is it. The Greeks called it the problem of the One and the Many. They observed that the world is capable of infinite variation yet somehow remains the same. And that's what science is—the discovery of things that stay the same in the midst of variation.

The human mind rebels from too much constancy and from too much chaos, preferring instead a balance of sameness and novelty. Endless variation within a simple set of rules is the recipe for the perfect game: patty-cake, ring-around-the-rosy, blackjack, chess, science. We learn this first in the nursery, with the rhyme on mother's or father's knee:

Jack and Jill
Went up the hill,
To fetch a pail of water;
Jack fell down,
And broke his crown,
And Jill came tumbling after.

Then up Jack got,
And home did trot,
As fast as he could caper;
To old Dame Dob,
Who patched his nob
With vinegar and brown paper.

The nursery song initiates the child into a kind of playful activity for which science is the natural culmination. Rhyme is a special activity marked off from ordinary experience by the parent's lap and the book. Presumably, the infant recognizes rhyme as a special use of language. The language of the rhyme is more highly structured than ordinary discourse, by rhyme, rhythm, and alliteration. In a chaos of unarticulated sound and dimly perceived meanings, the nursery song evokes a feeling of recognition and order. 'Ah, this is familiar,' is the emotion the child must feel. 'This makes sense.' The semantic aspect of the song is not the important thing. The rhyme creates order. Its perfection is limited and temporary, but it is enough to provide security and pleasure. The order of the rhyme is an end in itself, and the child will be quick to set even a minor deviation straight with, 'That's not the way it goes.' We do not begin to understand why the human mind responds this way, but in the nursery rhyme we are touching upon a quality of mind that drives science.

Tension between rules and the breaking of rules is a common theme of children's books. Chris Van Allsburg's award-winning *Jumanji* (Houghton) tells the story of a board game that two children find in the park. The game has three simple rules regarding the game pieces, rolling the dice to move through the jungle to the Golden City, and the object of the game. And a final rule: once the game is started, it will not be over until one player reaches the Golden City. And now comes the fun—and terror—as the children find themselves swept along by the rules of the game. Is it a dream? Is it life?

A side effect of those children's science books which stress factual information is a conviction on the part of the child that science is all rules, all order, all comprehensibility. Nothing could be further from the truth. The rules of science exist within a matrix of ignorance. The chaos and incomprehensibility of the natural world is not exhausted by science. As Thomas Huxley said, the point of science is to reduce the fundamentally incomprehensible things in nature to the smallest possible number. We haven't the foggiest notion what things such as electric charge, or gravity, or space, or time are. These are fundamentally incomprehensible. Why they exist we haven't a clue. We are content if we can describe a multitude of other things in terms of these fundamental incomprehensibilities. Science is an activity that takes place on the shore of an infinite sea of mystery.

Fantasy. The physicist Bruce Lindsay defined science this way: 'Science is a game in which we pretend that things are not wholly what they seem in order that we may make sense out of them in terms of mental processes peculiar to us as human beings. . . . Science strives to understand by the construction of theories, which are imaginative pictures of things as they might be, and, if they were, they would lead logically to that which we find in actual experience.' In other words, a scientific theory is a kind of fantasy which is required to match the world in a particularly strict sort of way. We have ample testimony from great scientists of the importance of fantasy to creative scientific thought. Einstein said: 'When I examine myself and my methods of thought, I come to the conclusion that the gift of fantasy has meant more to me than any talent for abstract, positive thinking.'

In the nineteenth century, educators often opposed encouraging a child's gift for fantasy. Knowledge imparted to children by Victorians was required to be 'useful', as opposed to 'frivolous'. Victorian children who wanted to read romances, or fairy tales, had to do so by candlelight in the night closet or in the privacy of the park. What a sad, sad notion of what it means to grow up! I would more quickly welcome into my science classes the child who has travelled in Middle-Earth and Narnia than the child who stayed home and read nothing but 'useful' information. In his most recent book of essays, *The Fragile Species*, Lewis Thomas says this of childhood: 'It is the time when the human brain can set to work on language, on taste, on poetry and music, with centers at its disposal that may not be available later on in life. If we did not have childhood, and were able to somehow jump catlike from infancy to adulthood, I doubt very much that we would turn out human.' And, he might have added, we would certainly not turn out to be scientists.

Let's not be too overly concerned about providing science facts to children. A child absorbs quite enough science facts from school and television, from computers and the other rich technologies at the child's disposal. If we want to raise children who will grow up to understand science, who will be citizens who are curious, sceptical, undogmatic, imaginative, optimistic, and forward-looking, then let's turn the Victorian rule on its head and put into the hands of children books that feed imagination and fantasy. There is no better time to acquire scientific habits of mind, and no better instigator than quality children's books.

In my Boston *Globe* science column I have had occasion over the years to make reference to Dr Seuss, Antoine de Saint-Exupéry's *The Little Prince* (Harcourt), Lewis Carroll's Alice books, Kenneth Grahame's *The Wind in the Willows*, Felix Salten's *Bambi*, and other children's books. In writing about science I have made reference to children's books far more frequently than to adult literary works. This is not an accident. In children's books we are at the roots of science—pure, childlike curiosity, eyes open with wonder to the fresh and new, and powers of invention still unfettered by convention and expectation.

PART IV

SCIENCE FICTION

SCIENCE FICTION AS MYTH AND METAPHOR

Monica Hughes

'I never read science fiction,' a group of Grande Prairie librarians confessed to me years ago. I still occasionally hear, 'I've always disliked science fiction,' but happily this is usually mitigated by, 'But I read *Keeper of the Isis Light*, and I loved it.'

Where does this prejudice spring from, and why is *Isis* okay? When I look back on my childhood reading, I can't remember even considering science fiction as any different from mainstream fiction. I do remember that my father's choices for Sunday afternoon reading aloud were most eclectic. After *Lorna Doone* he might give us Poe's *Tales of Mystery and Imagination*. After *Treasure Island* maybe the weird surrealism of G.K. Chesterton's *The Man Who was Thursday* or *The Napoleon of Notting Hill*. Or perhaps H.G. Wells' *The Invisible Man*. The touchstone was always a great story line; whether it took place in the past, the present or the future was immaterial to him.

My own taste was formed by good luck. In the classroom of the school I first attended was a shelf of books by E. Nesbit. For the first time I discovered magic. I discovered in *The Enchanted Castle* that:

> There is a curtain, thin as gossamer, clear as glass, strong as iron, that hangs forever between the world of magic and the world that seems to us to be real. And when once people have found one of the little weak spots in that curtain—which are marked by magic rings and amulets and the like—almost anything may happen.

Such enticing words: 'Almost anything can happen.' They have the same ring as 'What if?' which is the springboard for all science fiction. In fact some of E. Nesbit's work could as easily be defined as science fiction.

'What would happen if you discovered an ancient Egyptian amulet which enabled you to travel into the past?' There was a wonderfully spellbinding authenticity in Nesbit's description of Atlantis—not surprising, as I discovered years later when I read Plato's *Republic* and discovered where

Nesbit had got her material. When we lived in Edinburgh I used to search the jumbled trays of oddments in second-hand stores, hoping against hope that I too might find a magic amulet. After all, why not?

Before my lack of success blighted me entirely, my father gave me James Jeans' *The Mysterious Universe*, a very odd book to give a twelve-year-old. But it was the perfect gift for me, in that moment when I was beginning to suspect that I would never find that magic amulet. I reread James recently and was amazed at how far from today's understanding of the genesis of planets his writing was. Enlarging on the then popular theory that planets were formed as a result of the near collision of wandering stars, he postulated that this was a rare and almost miraculous event, as follows:

> The total number of stars in the universe is probably something like the total number of grains of sand on all the seashores of the world. Such is the littleness of our home in space when measured up against the total substance of the universe. This vast multitude of stars is wandering about in space. A few form solitary groups which journey in company, but the majority are solitary travellers. And they travel through a universe so spacious that it is an event of almost unimaginable rarity for a star to come anywhere near another star. For the most part each voyages in splendid isolation, like a ship upon an empty ocean.

Specifically false, maybe, but there is an underlying poetic truth in his words. I used to look up at the night sky and try to comprehend the magnitude of the distances of which Jeans spoke, and begin to ask myself: 'What if?'

In the old Carnegie Library close to our home in Edinburgh I discovered the nineteenth- and early twentieth-century writers of adventure stories, and among them was Jules Verne. His stories were to me no less real than the adventures of the Scarlet Pimpernel or the Three Musketeers or the Prisoner of Zenda. I had never been exposed to popular science fiction magazines or early 'space opera', and I thought of science fiction as a branch of literature as legitimate as historical fiction.

And why not? It has the honourable beginnings in the writing of Plato, whose *Republic* was a forerunner of More's *Utopia* and Butler's *Erewhon*, and in Lucian, who took an imaginative journey to the Moon in the second century AD, and whose satiric writings were to become an archetype of fantastic journeys such as Gulliver's.

But the prejudice still lurks. Perhaps it has something to do with the position of Science Fiction on the shelves of chain bookstores, squeezed in between Romance and Westerns. But, luckily for me, I was unaware of this prejudice, and I had not yet met the Grande Prairie librarians when I began writing, and I fell into the science fiction genre quite by chance.

Reading voraciously and longing to write like Rosemary Sutcliffe or Alan Garner does not, unfortunately, automatically produce a publishable book, and I was struggling with unconvincing adventure stories when I happened to see a TV program by Jacques Cousteau in which he talked about an undersea habitat, which he called Conshelf One, that he had designed and was testing on the continental shelf of the Red Sea, to find our human reactions to living beneath the sea at pressures of three to four atmospheres for a week or so.

As I watched, I thought that it was a waste that they would all go back to France at the end of the experiment, leaving the little house empty. What would it be like to live under the sea? What would it be like to be a *child* growing up under the sea?

As soon as these thoughts whizzed through my head I knew that I *had* to write about them and find out the answers to my questions. Almost at once I realized that I could turn to no 'expert' for advice, nor was I likely to find a book on 'living under the sea'. I was writing about the future! It took major research, but was a lot of fun as well as hard work, and it set me on the path I have followed since, that of juvenile Science Fiction writer, beginning with *Crisis on Conshelf Ten*.

It took me more questions, a few more books about possible futures, to realize the power of science fiction for the writer as for the reader and teacher. It can be a positive tool to help us think clearly and creatively in new modes. How will humans cope in a polluted world? How will we overcome the effects of global warming? Mythic stories can give us new hope for tomorrow and reflect, in a non-threatening way, on the social, economic and ecological problems of the late twentieth century.

Simple ideas can lead to fascinating conclusions. For instance, in 1974 I read a wire-service story in the Edmonton *Journal* about David, aged three, apparently condemned to spend the rest of his life isolated from true human contact, because of a fatal genetic flaw in his immune system. The story moved me deeply, and I cut it out and filed it in my 'Ideas' file, where I place every thought, chance news story, passing event or character that I feel may one day be a story. Each time I finished writing another book I would reread this story about David, but I didn't know how I wanted to handle it.

Five years later, having read this cutting and worried about it at least ten times, I realized that what I wanted was an answer to the question: 'David, are you lonely?' How to find the answer? Obviously not by researching the 'real' David, a horrible invasion of his privacy, but perhaps by finding a character in a situation *similar* to David's, putting this person in a story and then asking him this question.

First, I considered isolated places on Earth—such as lighthouses; only they are not so very isolated nowadays. It was than that I began to realize the strength of science fiction—that by taking my character to a planet far away from Earth, *alone*, I would achieve a real isolation.

Of course this had to be done *logically*, and the working out of this logic gave me my initial plot development, of Olwen, alone on Isis after the death of her parents, alone except for Guardian. It also led me to the character-driven, rather than the plot-driven story, and I began to realize that perhaps some of the 'bad press' about science fiction is due to the fact that much of it is plot-driven almost to the exclusion of believable and likeable characters. In order to answer my initial question: 'David, are you lonely?' I *had* to develop a character—the David paradigm—who could talk to me and tell me how she felt.

To my amazement and delight Olwen also developed physically into a woman different from anything I had anticipated when I began. Because of her physical difference from the colonists, I had Guardian design for her a body-suit, modelled on Guardian's memory of typical Earth beauty, that would hide her bizarre physical appearance from the colonists. As Olwen became aware of her difference, she asked Guardian to make a mirror so she could see herself. In an unexpectedly triumphant moment of personal growth, she looked at herself, liked what she saw and determined never to wear that concealing, lying, suit again. It wasn't until *Keeper of the Isis Light* was finished, much of it consisting of the words and actions that Olwen had dictated to me, that I realized that indeed the bodysuit was a metaphor for the Jungian masks which we all, at some time or another, wear and the discarding of which is one of the triumphs of 'growing up'.

The writing of science fiction is full of magic moments like this, when the writer discovers more in her work than she believed she had put into it. They happen at the subconscious level, perhaps more readily in science fiction and fantasy because the setting and situations therein are removed from the mundane to the more mythical, containing elements that echo the folk tales and legends of the past.

As Jane Yolen has pointed out in *Touch Magic*, many children today are illiterate in their own mythology and, like feral children unable to understand or communicate, have lost touch with the past, the knowledge of which is so necessary if we are to build a stable present and lay the foundations for a less precarious future. Lévi-Strauss tells us that the old mythologies were developed to explicate the terrors of an environment which seemed irrational and random in its actions to preliterate peoples. Despite—or perhaps in part because of—scientific advances, the world our young people have inherited is also a rather terrifying place. I believe that science fiction can at least fill the gap left by the loss of the old mythologies, that it can help explicate today's world and tomorrow's possibilities for young people.

Which all sounds pretty grandiose, but it is my defence to those librarians and teachers who still distrust Science Fiction as a genre. I do believe that all really good fiction for young people works at three levels, the top level being the story line, with a theme of universal application beneath and, somewhere lurking beneath that level, like mist, like the iridescent colour of bubbles, the mythic level. When one finds it, it enriches a story wonderfully, makes it resonate at many different levels, so that it can be read with pleasure over and over again. Natalie Babbitt's *Tuck Everlasting* and Ursula Le Guin's *The Tombs of Atuan* jump to the mind. I believe that, of their nature, Science Fiction and Fantasy are genres where one is especially likely to find this mythic level.

Having said that, I must say that I don't design a story with three levels and look for a suitable 'message' for my young reader. It would destroy my excitement in the discovery of story, and it certainly wouldn't work anyway. I write, with concentration and total selfishness, to try and answer for the child within me the myriad questions that come crowding into my head. From that first story, *Crisis on Conshelf Ten*, which answered to my satisfaction the question: What would it be like to be a young person growing up under the sea? through its sequel *Earthdark*, about life on the Moon, to all the others, such as two very different books in which I look at possible climate changes and their effect on society.

Back in 1980 the ecological question was: Is Earth heating up due to the greenhouse effect, or cooling down as a result of particulate pollution actually reflecting the sun's energy? Living on the prairies, I felt at that time that the Ice Age scenario had more drama—had I lived close to the sea, I'm sure I would have tackled the other possibility, with the threat of coastal city flooding.

The coming of another Ice Age would obviously take an enormously long time and require a story with generations of protagonists. Was there some possibility of 'speeding up' this disaster? I found the answer in an issue of *Nature*: the suggestion, now well known, that the 34-million-year event and the 56-million-year event, each of which appear to have wiped out whole species of fauna, were due to catastrophic collisions with either a very large meteor or a comet.

With the passage of Halley's Comet in mind, I developed this scenario. At first I intended the action to take place in and around the underground city where the scientists lived and worked. But, feeling that Nature as antagonist was not quite strong enough for a juvenile story, I thought of the Ekoes, imagined descendants of the Inuit people, living with Nature, rather than against her, as a metaphor antagonistic to the work of scientists. Once I had developed this idea, the story took on a life of its own. Liza met Namonnie, and at the end I found myself, to my surprise, facing the dilemma of the rights of technological society. At the time of writing the story I was involved in the church group, Project North, which was working with the findings of the Berger Commission on behalf of native peoples against the immediate development of the Norman Wells pipe line; out of my subconscious had come the ultimate reason for the story. Inadvertently, Science Fiction had become parable, and out of parable come questions. Whose rights should prevail? Is there another solution other than the weakest going to the wall? Questions of today, but presented as a parable of the future. Recognition of these elements in science fiction writing can make for challenging classroom discussion.

Much more consciously, I worked for a couple of years on a story to do with Global Warming, now considered the more likely future. Its immediacy was made clear to me in several years of frightening droughts in the southern regions of the Prairie provinces. The very clarity of the 'message' made this book extremely difficult to write. I did not want it to be a diatribe. It was only after a couple of events, one involving the folklore of the 'Dirty Thirties' and the other the opening of the UNESCO World Site at Head-Smashed-In Buffalo Jump in southern Alberta, that I was able to find a way of distancing my anger and frustration from the story I wanted to tell. This story, *The Crystal Drop*, is science fiction only in the sense that it is about the next century, for it is not a future of technological marvels, nor of space wars or laser guns. It is the story, on the one hand, of human greed in the face of diminishing water supplies, and on the other hand, of a transcendent hope that we can heal our damaged Earth.

Sometimes a passing conversation, such as the one I held with a librarian from Liverpool, northern England, is enough to start a story. The plight of young people there, leaving school with no hope of work, youths who have seen their jobless parents collecting their unemployment money for as many years as they can remember, was something that bothered her. It began to bother me too. What would become of a society, I wondered, in which there was absolutely no employment for the eager, imaginative young people leaving school? How could society contain all that wasted energy? What solutions would they come up with? Out of these questions, based on the reality of today's economic structures, came *Invitation to the Game*, which begins in a world not much different from ours, but then turns, at its conclusion, to a definitely science fiction solution.

The *what ifs* of science fiction can lead to stimulating classroom discussion, discussion that draws from the futuristic metaphor back home to rootlessness, loneliness, prejudice, anger, to the problems of broken homes or blended families, as well as, hopefully, keeping that magic I first discovered on my classroom shelf in the novels of E. Nesbit.

Let There Be Dragons

Terry Pratchett

I have still got the first book I ever read. It was *The Wind in the Willows*. Well, it was probably not the first book I *ever* read—that was no doubt called something like *Nursery Fun* or *Janet and John Book I*. But it was the first book I opened without chewing the covers or wishing I were somewhere else. It was the first book which, at the age of 10, I read because I was genuinely interested.

I know now, of course, that it is totally the wrong kind of book for children. There is only one female character and she's a washerwoman. No attempt is made to explain the social conditioning and lack of proper housing that makes stoats and weasels act the way they do. Mr Badger's house is an insult to all those children not fortunate enough to live in a Wild Wood. The Mole and the Rat's domestic arrangements are probably acceptable, but only if they come right out and talk frankly about them.

But it was pressed into my hand, and because it wasn't parents or teachers who were recommending the book I read it from end to end, all in one go. And then I started again from the beginning, because I had not realized that there were stories like this.

There's a feeling that I think is only possible to get when you are a child and discover books: it's a kind of fizz—you want to read everything that's in print before it evaporates before your eyes.

I had to draw my own map through this uncharted territory. The message from the management was that, yes, books were a good idea, but I don't recall anyone *advising* me in any way. I was left to my own devices.

I am now becoming perceived as a young people's writer. Teachers and librarians say, 'You know, your books are *really popular* among children who don't read.' I think this is a compliment; I just wish they would put it another way. In fact, genre authors get to know their reader profile quite intimately, and I know I have a large number of readers who are old enough to drive a car and possibly claim a pension. But the myth persists that all my readers are aged 14 and called Kevin, and so I have taken an interest in the dark underworld called children's literature.

Not many people do, it seems to me, apart from those brave souls who work with children and are interested in what they read. They're unsung resistance heroes in a war that is just possibly being won by Sonic Hedge-hogs and bionic plumbers. They don't have many allies, even where you would expect them. Despite the huge number of titles that pour out to shape the minds of the adults, my Sunday paper reviews a mismatched handful of children's books at infrequent intervals and, to show its readers that this is some kind of literary play street, generally puts a picture of a teddy bear on the page.

Perhaps the literary editor's decision is right. In my experience children don't read reviews of children's books. They live in a different kind of world.

The aforementioned school librarians tell me that what the children read for fun, what they will actually spend their money on, are fantasy, science fiction and horror and, while they offer up a prayer of thanks that the kids are reading anything in this electronic age, this worries them. It shouldn't.

I now know that almost all fiction is, at some level, fantasy. What Agatha Christie wrote was fantasy. What Tom Clancy writes is fantasy. What Jilly Cooper writes is fantasy—at least, I hope for her sake it is. But what people generally have in mind when they hear the word fantasy is swords, talking animals, vampires, rockets (science fiction is fantasy with bolts on), and around the edges it can indeed be pretty silly. Yet fantasy also speculates about the future, rewrites the past and reconsiders the present. It plays games with the universe.

Not all robots

Fantasy makes many adults uneasy. Children who like the stuff tend to call it 'brill' and 'megagood'. This always disturbs people. It worries them so much that when someone like P.D. James uses the mechanisms of science fiction helpful people redefine the field, thus avoiding bestowing on her the mark of Cain; the book isn't science fiction 'because it's not all about robots and other planets'. P.D. James writing science fiction? Impossible. But *Children of Men* is a science fiction book, as is *Time's Arrow* and *Father-land*. As was Brian Aldiss's *Methuselah's Children*, Kurt Vonnegut's *Slaughter-house Five* and Philip K. Dick's *Man in the High Castle*. Science fiction, the stuff that is seldom reviewed, is often *good*; it doesn't need robots, and earth is room enough.

Of course science fiction and fantasy are sometimes badly written. Many things are. But literary merit is an artificial thing and exists in the eye of the beholder. In a world where Ballard's *Empire of the Sun* cannot win the Booker, I'm not too in awe of judgements based on literary merit.

Not long ago I talked to a teacher who, having invited me to talk at her school, was having a bit of trouble with the head teacher who thought that fantasy was morally suspect and irrelevant to the world of the '90s.

Morally suspect? Shorn of its trappings, most fantasy would find approval in a Victorian household. The morality of fantasy and horror is, by and large, the strict morality of the fairy tale. The vampire is slain, the alien is blown out of the airlock, the Dark Lord is vanquished and, perhaps at some loss, the good triumph—not because they are better armed but because Providence is on their side.

Why does the third of the three brothers, who shares his food with the old woman in the wood, go on to become king of the country? Why does James Bond manage to disarm the nuclear bomb a few seconds before it goes off rather than, as it were, a few seconds afterwards? Because the universe where that did not happen would be a dark and hostile place. Let there be goblin hordes, let there be terrible environmental threats, let there be giant mutated slugs if you really must, but let there also be hope. It may be a grim, thin hope, an Arthurian sword at sunset, but let us know that we do not live in vain.

Good and evil

To stay sane, if I may gently paraphrase what Edward Pearce recently wrote in the *Guardian*, it is frequently necessary for someone to take short views, to look for comfort, to keep a piece of the world still genially ordered, if only for the duration of theatrical time or the length of a book. And this is harmless enough. Classical, written fantasy might introduce children to the occult, but in a healthier way than might otherwise be the case in our strange society. If you're told about vampires, it's a good thing to be told about stakes at the same time.

And fantasy's readers might also learn, in the words of Stephen Sondheim, that witches can be right and giants can be good. They learn that where people stand is perhaps not as important as which way they face. This is part of the dangerous process of growing up.

As for escapism, I'm quite happy about the word. There is nothing wrong with escapism. The key points of consideration, though, are what you are escaping from, and where you are escaping to.

As a suddenly thirsting reader I escaped first of all to what was then called Outer Space. I read a lot of science fiction, which as I have said is only a 20th century subset of fantasy. And a lot of it was, in strict literary terms, rubbish. But this was good rubbish. It was like an exercise bicycle for the mind—it doesn't take you anywhere, but it certainly tones up the muscles.

Irrelevant? I first came across any mention of ancient Greek civilization in a fantasy book—by Mary Renault. But in the '50s most schools taught history like this: there were the Romans who had a lot of baths and built some roads and left. Then there was a lot of undignified pushing and shoving until the Normans arrived, and history officially began.

Ways of seeing

We did Science, too, in a way. Yuri Gagarin was spinning around above our heads, but I don't recall anyone at school ever mentioning the fact. I don't even remember anyone telling us that science was not about messing around with chemicals and magnets, but rather a way of looking at the universe.

Science fiction looked at the universe all the time. I make no apology for having enjoyed it. We live in a science fiction world: two miles down there you'd fry and two miles up there you'd gasp for breath, and there is a small but significant chance that in the next thousand years a large comet or asteroid will smack into the planet. Finding this out when you're 13 or so is a bit of an eye-opener. It puts acne in its place, for a start.

Then other worlds out there in space got me interested in this one down here. It is a small mental step from time travel to palaeontology, from sword 'n' sorcery fantasy to mythology and ancient history. Truth is stranger than fiction; nothing in fantasy enthralled me as much as reading of the evolution of mankind from proto-blob to newt, tree shrew, Oxbridge arts graduate and eventually to tool-using mammal.

I first came across words like 'ecologist' and 'overpopulation' in science fiction books in the late '50s and early '60s, long before they had become fashionable. Yes, probably Malthus had said it first—but you don't read Malthus when you're 11, though you might read someone like John Brunner or Harry Harrison because their books have got an exciting space-ship on the cover.

I also came across the word 'neoteny', which means 'remaining young'. It's something which we as humans have developed into a survival trait. Other animals, when they are young, have a curiosity about the world, a flexibility of response, and an ability to play which they lose as they grow up. As a species we have retained it. As a species, we are forever sticking our fingers into the electric socket of the universe to see what will happen next. It is a trait that will either save us or kill us, but it is what makes us human beings. I would rather be in the company of people who look at Mars than people who contemplate humanity's navel—other worlds are better than fluff.

And I came across a lot of trash. But the human mind has a healthy natural tendency to winnow out the good stuff from the rubbish. It's like gold mining; you have to shift a ton of dirt to get the gold, if you don't shift the dirt, you won't find the nugget. As far as I am concerned, escapist literature let me escape to the real world.

Compost for the healthy mind

So let's not get frightened when the children read fantasy. It is the compost for a healthy mind. It stimulates the inquisitive nodes. It may not appear as 'relevant' as books set more firmly in the child's environment, or whatever hell the writer believes to be the child's environment, but there is some evidence that a rich internal fantasy life is as good and necessary for a child as healthy soil is for a plant, for much the same reasons.

Of course, some may read no other kind of fiction all their lives (although in my experience science fiction fans tend to be widely read outside the field). Adult SF fans may look a bit scary when they come into bookshops, some of them have been known to wear plastic pointy ears, but people like that are an unrepresentative minority, and are certainly no weirder than people who, say, play golf. At the very least they are helping to keep the industry alive, and providing one of the best routes to reading that there can be.

Here's to fantasy as the proper diet for the growing soul. All human life is there: a moral code, a sense of order and, sometimes, great big green things with teeth. There are other books to read, and I hope children who start with fantasy go on to read them. I did. But everyone has to start somewhere.

Please call it fantasy, by the way. Don't call it 'magical realism', that's just fantasy wearing a collar and tie, mark-of-Cain words, words used to mean 'fantasy written by someone I was at university with'. Like the fairy tales that were its forebears, fantasy needs no excuses.

Dragons can be killed

One of the great popular novelists of the early part of this century was G.K. Chesterton. Writing at a time when fairy stories were under attack, for pretty much the same reason as books can now be covertly banned in some schools because they have the word 'witch' in the title, he said: 'The objection to fairy stories is that they tell children there are dragons. But children have always known there are dragons. Fairy stories tell children that dragons can be killed.'

WHAT *IS* IT ABOUT SCIENCE FICTION?

William Sleator

Many adolescents tell me, in letters and in person, how much they enjoy science fiction. I believe them since, as we all know, one of the (sometimes charming) characteristics of adolescents is that their responses to books, as well as people, are pretty genuine. I also believe them because, judging from my royalty statements, a great many of them read my books. But what exactly is it about science fiction that appeals to them?

I will begin my very subjective treatment of this question with a few words about science fiction conventions, or 'cons,' as the participants refer to them. I have spoken at several of them. They are very different indeed from meetings of English teachers and librarians. I was apprehensive about the first one I attended because of the warning in the brochure: 'Weapons are absolutely not allowed. Costume weaponry ONLY may be worn at the masquerade party, and no swords may be unsheathed, no guns may be drawn.'

Obviously, I did survive the experience. I learned that the population of these conventions consists of two distinct groups, the pros and the fans. The pros are all the people involved in publishing—the writers, editors and artists. The fans are everybody else, many of them teenagers, and they consider themselves to be an élite. The fans refer to all other people in the world as 'mundanes', in such statements as, 'Did you see how we freaked out those mundanes in the elevator?' Many of the fans wear costumes and bizarre makeup throughout the entire convention, not just at the masquerade parties. Many of them are involved in role-playing strategy games of the 'Dungeons and Dragons' variety.

I suppose one could say that these fans are escaping reality. But, in most cases, I don't think there is anything wrong with a bit of an escape. On the contrary, Dr Jerome L. Singer has demonstrated, with rigorous scientific studies (*The Inner World of Daydreaming* and *The Child's World of Make Believe*), that the richer a person's fantasy life, the better s/he is able to deal with real life. I was really happy when I found out about these studies; they suddenly gave my own work validity. Imaginative literature is not only entertainment; it stimulates and exercises the reader's imagination and improves fantasy skills, making him/her better able to cope with frustrating situations in the real world. For example, it is a very useful and practical to put yourself mentally in another time and place when you are sitting in a traffic jam or waiting in line at the supermarket. And revenge fantasies, if you have the practised technique to construct really good ones, are a lot more satisfying in most ways than actually taking revenge on somebody, which can make you feel guilty or get you into trouble. In fact, it seems logical to me that kids who read science fiction are less likely to become criminals, but I can't really say that because, as far as I know, no one has demonstrated it—yet.

But what precisely is science fiction? My own definition is that science fiction is literature about something that hasn't happened yet, but might be possible some day. That it might be possible is the important part; that's what separates science fiction from fantasy. No one would ever think that the Tolkien books (which I love), with their animals, elves and magic swords, could ever really happen, and so they are considered to be fantasy. But, a book like *Rendezvous With Rama* (Arthur C. Clarke), which in certain ways is just as fantastic, is considered to be science fiction; we and the author assume that these things could actually happen in a universe like ours. It's not just unexplained magic that makes a large cylindrical body of water possible—it really *is* possible, because of the centrifugal force inside a rotating space ship.

One could argue that my definition breaks down when it comes to time travel, since time travel is always thought of as science fiction. Yet, time travel is totally out of the question scientifically. However, spinning black holes might make time travel possible after all. One of the things I love most about science is that the more we find out about the universe, the weirder and more bizarre it turns out to be.

The appeal of science fiction to adolescents, it seems to me, is that it is about things that might be possible. Of course, any writer of any kind of fiction tries to establish credibility. If the reader doesn't believe the story, if it doesn't have some connection with reality, s/he's not going to care about it, won't have an emotional response to it. So, why bother to read it? In fact, I think the reader's emotional response is directly proportional to how believable s/he finds the story. Which is more frightening, a book about vampires in nineteenth-century Transylvania, or a book about a homicidal maniac in a suburban neighbourhood?

I don't want to get into which kind of writing is harder to do, imaginative or realistic, but I will say that the writer of imaginative fiction has an added task. S/he has to do everything the realistic writer has to do, and also must convince the reader to believe in something that has never happened. This question of plausibility is especially vital when writing for sceptical, suspicious teenagers. Anything contrived or artificial in a book will scream at them; they'll spot it right away. And then they will be contemptuous of the book, they won't care about it, and they won't want to read it.

If you are writing a book about the fourth dimension, for instance, you have to be even more rigorous about establishing credibility than if you are writing a book about baseball. The baseball book by its very nature has a firm foundation of credibility. You don't have to go to a lot of trouble to convince the reader that a baseball game could really happen. But, the reader doesn't believe in the fourth dimension. So, if you are writing about the fourth dimension, your first and most fundamental objective is to make it seem real. But how do you do that? How do you get the reader to believe in something that has never happened?

One way is to begin the story in the real world, in a situation with which the reader can identify, and then unobtrusively sneak in the unreal elements. *The Boy Who Reversed Himself* begins with something extremely mundane with which all readers are familiar—a school locker. Laura opens her locker to find a note taped inside the door, in mirror writing, warning her of a surprise quiz the next day. These events are the first suggestions of science fiction in the story. Though odd, they can be rationally explained. There are ways of getting into other peoples' lockers and leaving notes; anyone can write in mirror writing with practice; it is not unheard of for a student to learn about a surprise quiz, in advance. No suspension of disbelief is necessary to accept any of it. But these incidents do, I hope, prepare the reader to accept the first truly unexplainable occurrence—the next day Laura takes her biology report out of her locker and finds that it is entirely in mirror writing, completely reversed from back to front. Once that is accepted, it is not a very big leap to believing in the next unlikely event— the mirror reversal of her neighbour Omar.

These three elements—getting into closed spaces, seeing the future and mirror reversal—at first have no apparent logical connection. They are unlikely juxtapositions which make sense only *after* learning the theory of the fourth spatial dimension. My intention in sneaking them in without explanation is to make the reader curious enough so that, when the explanation does come, s/he is willing and even eager to sit back and listen to it. In a textbook, one might give the equation first, and later give examples of its function. In fiction, you first toss the reader some intriguing examples, and only then, when s/he's begging for it, provide the equation.

Another important element in establishing credibility—and an area in which a lot of science fiction falls flat on its face—is characterization. The reader must know the characters are not fictional creations, but real people. When s/he can understand, and identify with, a character's motivation s/he is more likely to believe in that situation, even if it is quite improbable.

In *Interstellar Pig* I based the three aliens—as I do many of my characters—on people I know. I try to make them rather ordinary at the beginning, to avoid the predictable 'weirdness' of so many alien characters. I lift their likes and dislikes, their conversations and petty bickering from real life. If the reader comes to accept them as actual personalities, how much more frightening—and believable—it is when they become monstrous caricatures of themselves at the end.

When I was writing *Singularity*, a book about twins, I asked everyone I know who is a twin, or who has children who are twins, exactly what it is like, and especially what problems they have being twins. And they all said, 'Oh there are no problems at all, it is just wonderful, it is perfect.' So, cursing them under my breath, I invented the twins' problems based on my own interactions with siblings. And when these same people read the finished book, they said, 'That's exactly what it is like, we have the same problems.' And I said, 'Gee, thanks for telling me now.'

I always try to stay away from heroes and villains. No one is totally perfect, just as no one is totally rotten. And, I will do almost anything to avoid the ridiculous battle between the forces of good and evil that wages interminably in so many books. I don't believe in abstract good versus evil; I can't relate to it; it means nothing to me, and always detracts from credibility whenever it rears its ugly head.

Beginning a story in the real world and peopling it with believable characters are techniques used by fantasy, as well as science fiction, writers. But there is another element that is unique to science fiction, and the basis of its appeal to me, and I think for teenagers—science. Science is the ultimate down to earth reality. It's fact. I can truthfully tell my readers that gravity really does slow down time. Mathematicians make computer displays of four-dimensional objects. And, according to a new theory in physics, the Superstring theory, there actually are ten dimensions in this universe. Once you have a scientific principle going for you, you can then slyly stretch it beyond the limits of reality without the reader being aware of it. What science fiction does is to take scientific laws—which have built-in credibility—and use them to make nearly anything possible. Only in this genre can you really have your cake and eat it too. All sorts of wonderful, almost magical things can happen, and at the same time *you can really believe in them.*

In fantasy we are asked to believe in elves, ghosts and magic spells, which we all know do not exist. In science fiction we are asked to believe in aliens—and no one can tell me that aliens do not exist. I know I will not run into an elf tomorrow, but I can't say for sure I won't run into an alien. I tend to doubt that I will get to another world by walking into a wardrobe, but I don't doubt at all that I could get there in a space ship. Science fiction confronts teenage scepticism head on, and does away with it. It's imaginative literature that adolescents can really put themselves into, as exciting to the sceptics as to the romantics. And that's why science fiction is so effective at attracting teenagers to books.

Sometimes a science fiction writer can stumble upon a useful scientific principle almost accidentally. When I began writing *Singularity* I wasn't thinking at all about gravity or black holes. I was writing a story about a place where time moves at a different rate, an idea that had been in the back of my mind for years. Sixteen-year-old twin brothers are house-sitting at an isolated farm house. They discover a small playhouse that contains a time contraction field—time goes faster inside the playhouse. If you go inside and stay for an hour, when you come out, only one second has elapsed in the real world. One of the twins is frightened by the place, but the other sees its exciting possibilities. Let's say that it is 8 a.m. on Monday and you haven't done any of your homework. The school bus is coming down the street. If you have this playhouse, you can go inside, spend three hours doing your homework, and when you come out, only three seconds have gone by and the bus is only a little closer.

What I found out half way through the book is that it is a scientific fact that gravity slows down time. People living in earth gravity age a bit more slowly than people in orbit. However, the effect is so infinitesimal that under most conditions it is essentially non-existent. It only becomes noticeable in extreme conditions, such as in the vicinity of a black hole.

It's well known that black holes are collapsed stars with tremendous mass and relatively little volume, and that their gravity is so extreme that not even light, the fastest thing in the universe, can escape them. But, what most people don't know is that because of gravitational tidal forces there is a radius around a black hole, known as the event horizon, in which time almost completely stops. (I love the scientific term, 'event horizon'. I came across it in *Gateway*, a science fiction book by Frederick Pohl. I then went to my little brother Tycho, a physicist, and got all the accurate details from him.)

Those are the facts. But scientists who wonder what happens to all the matter pulled into black holes speculate that they may be tunnels to other universes where all the matter goes. I learned all this when I was halfway through the first draft of *Singularity*. And I took it one step further, saying that if time slows down on one side of a black hole, then maybe it speeds up on the other in order to preserve the conservation of momentum. That could be the reason why time speeds up in the playhouse. It's also true that 'singularity' is the scientific term for the core of a black hole. I shouted out loud when I realized this. Now I had the perfect title with an ironic double meaning: *Singularity* meaning black hole, and *Singularity* referring to twins who are not twins at the end of the book.

Though science fiction writers have to stretch scientific laws, we also must respect their limitations as much as possible. Once the rules for a particular story are established, they must be struck to rigorously. Thus, in *Singularity*, though alien objects are pulled into our universe by the black hole, nothing can travel by that route from our universe into the other one. Everyone knows black holes only work in one direction; if they are tunnels, they must be one-way tunnels.

And, here I cannot resist mentioning my favourite example of an author respecting limitations. It's not science fiction, it's an uncategorizable novel called *His Monkey Wife* (John Collier) about a man who inadvertently gets married to a chimpanzee. The chimpanzee, Emily, is the hero of the story. She is brilliantly intelligent, is passionately in love with her school teacher husband, and by the end of the book has achieved wealth and status as a Spanish dancer, the toast of the London stage, riding in Hispano-Suizas and dining at the Ritz. However, one thing Emily *can't* do is talk—everyone knows chimpanzees can't talk. Limitations like this do more than provide credibility. Working within them also makes for all sorts of interesting plot twists, peculiar ideas the author might never have thought of if he had ignored the limitations and just did anything he wanted. Emily's inability to speak causes many complications until she learns to type at the end of the book and then can explain herself.

The lure of science fiction is that it is imaginative literature in which teenagers can believe. It allows them to explore exciting, often dreamlike situations in which they might conceivably find themselves. And the tremendous advantage that science fiction literature has over the visual media is that it is not limited to special effects. The story takes place in the reader's mind; it is an active, rather than passive, experience.

For this reason, I always end my books on a note of ambiguity. I try to provide a satisfying conclusion, but at the same time I don't tell absolutely *everything*. When readers ask me what happens when the parents come home, or whether or not the earth is going to blow up the next day, I tell them I don't know. I remind them that stories do not end neatly in real life; they go on and on through the years. My hope is that after finishing the book the readers will be stimulated, even compelled, to use their own imaginations to continue the story. I have spent many pleasant hours in traffic jams and supermarket lines doing exactly the same thing myself.

PART V

POETRY

THE POEM
ON PAGE 81

Myra Cohn Livingston

Pulling apart a poem is an act, I have usually found, better reserved for private moments, or those spent with older children seeking the means to answers in a creative-writing group. Nevertheless, in this act of experiencing one poem—in asking, as does John Ciardi, 'how does a poem mean?'—are implicit a number of rather important matters.

The poem is Robert Frost's 'The Pasture'.

I'm going out to clean the pasture spring;
I'll only stop to rake the leaves away
(And wait to watch the water clear, I may):
I sha'n't be gone long—You come too.

I'm going out to fetch the little calf
That's standing by the mother. It's so young
It totters when she licks it with her tongue.
I sha'n't be gone long—You come too.

A first look at this poem (just as we might see a painting) shows us a boy (illustrators are inclined to dress him in overalls with a rake over his shoulder) going off to perform a few chores. He tells us that he must clean the pasture spring and fetch a calf.

But almost in the same second our auditory sense becomes involved (music might certainly play a part here), for we hear him talking to someone. Not only is he relating what he is going to do, but he is mentioning to an invisible someone that he 'sha'n't be long—You come too.' He is extending an invitation, therefore, to join him.

Sharpening our vision and our hearing further, we become aware that the boy is more deeply involved than in simply doing two chores. For in the first stanza he tells the unseen someone that he *may wait* to watch the water clear—in other words, it is not mandatory he do so as part of his job; he does not *have* to do so; he *may*. In the second stanza the chore is simply to fetch the calf; that is all that is expected of him. But he tells us more: it is a little calf standing by its mother; it totters when she licks it with her tongue.

We hear, therefore, if we listen, that the boy is not merely concerned with responsibilities and work, but that he is seeking something more: watching the water clear, watching the calf and its mother—acts of wonder and interest. These are the extras—the joys, the emotional involvement—far beyond duty.

Remember too that he is issuing an invitation to another; not to join and help with the work, but to share with him what follows. Perhaps he is not only seeking companionship, so as not to go it alone, but holding out to another a promise of something exciting and wonderful.

The invitation, you will note, is earnestly meant—for it is repeated in both stanzas of the poem, and is prefaced with man's eternal plea when he asks another to join him: it won't take much time. The gentle persuasion is there, repeated twice. Join me when I clean the pasture spring and rake the leaves away; perhaps I'll even stay on to watch the water clear. Join me while I fetch the calf; you'll have a chance to see how young it is, how little, how its mother licks it with her tongue, how it totters. The piece of description serves a twofold purpose, for it not only holds out the promise of seeing something special, but adds appeal to the invitation.

But now the poem becomes something more. It is no longer simply a boy on his chores; it beckons as the poet's invitation to all of us (you, me, the unseen invisible someones and everyones) to fulfil our chores and responsibilities, but also to take a few moments to experience the serendipity of it all! To watch, to perceive, to marvel, to enjoy and observe matters as well as tend to them. And the twice-repeated invitation—'You come too.' We must, in our lives, do our work as expected, but must we not also take a few moments to pause and reflect, to enjoy the wonders about us, to become emotionally involved?

Is Robert Frost speaking of a boy going out to do his chores, or is he saying much, much more?

It is most interesting that in an article titled 'Where are we going with poetry for children?' Patrick J. Groff, a professor of education at San Diego State College, defines very neatly something no one else I have ever read has been able to do—what poetry for children is. The very term 'Poetry for Children' seems moot, for I have come to think in terms of poetry children enjoy, or poetry to which children respond. In any case, Groff rejects any definition based on an emotional approach and chides Eleanor Farjeon for not being able to define poetry, remarking that her question in the poem 'What is Poetry? Who Knows?' expresses false bewilderment. Groff writes:

The definition is apprehensible and to the point: poetry for children is writing that (in addition to using, in most cases, the mechanics of poetry) transcends the literal meaning of expository writing. . . . It is writing that goes beyond the immediately obvious . . . [it] consists of those aspects of writing that cannot be readily explained, unless one has some knowledge of what is going on. In contrast to that which is readily and completely understandable to all, poetry is often ambiguous.

One may or may not agree with this definition. The point is that, even should it be acceptable, what follows in the article is a source of amazement to me. For the writer now speaks of Frost's 'The Pasture.' I quote:

'The Pasture' tested against this definition is revealed as a poem only in the mechanical sense. True, it has some poetic features: a certain cadence, rhyme, and some slight inversion of sentence pattern—'And wait to watch the water clear, I may.' The word order seems used largely to satisfy a rhyme scheme, away-may.) The poem does have a refrain, and even a colloquial word, 'sha'n't' (if colloquialisms are poetic). But these are all a part of the mechanics of poetry. To identify a poem on the basis of such elements is too easy . . . Obviously to define poetry merely in terms of its mechanical features does not take much perception or maturity.

The article continues:

In another sense, 'The Pasture' is not exceptional poetry because with startlingly few changes the poem could be made into a paragraph of prose. To show this, drop the first refrain in the poem and put the third line into a regular pattern.

(What he says here, of course, is that the first invitation might just as well be omitted!)

And later on, his concluding remarks about the poem are: '. . . in "The Pasture" the emphasis on subject denies the poem much status as poetry.'

Now, I would not be nearly so concerned with Groff's indictment of 'The Pasture' if I felt that he was a stupid man, an uninformed man, a man unaware of what goes into the making of a poem, instead of a man whose opinions I have read and enjoyed in the past. But he has obviously given poetry much thought, for earlier in the article he pointedly rejects one definition of a poem as 'merely a reconstruction of an experience'. With this, I agree. He has, moreover, very clearly stated his understanding of the fact that words in poetry have more meaning than they do in prose.

Groff understands intellectually very well the use of words and language, the tone. He recognizes that a poet must use a certain means to express his meaning. Yet he utterly fails to look beyond the technical features of 'The Pasture'; indeed, he has separated the 'means' from the meaning. In poetry this cannot be done. Both are inexorably entwined, part of each other.

Enough of technicalities; what I am interested in pointing out is that the writer seems not to allow himself to experience poetry, to feel it, to (in his own words) 'plumb' the words. He is so obsessed with technicalities and definitions that he fails to allow himself to respond or react. He may look, but he does not see. He may listen, but he does not hear. Somewhat earlier in the article he has even dismissed among many others a claim that poetry allow children to experience life in a deeper sense. It may happen, he admits, if a poem and a child hit it off, but prose does this just as well, if not better. To Groff, therefore, poetry may be embarrassing when one has to involve his emotions. Poetry in his terms, at least to me, can never be a meaningful experience.

The crime of our civilization, Archibald MacLeish has said, is that we do not feel: 'To feel emotion is at least to feel. . . . If poetry can call our numbed emotions to life, its plain human usefulness needs no further demonstration.' How beautifully he points out that while the mind alone cannot logically make sense out of images (the stuff of poetry), emotion can, feeling can.

The intellect tells us, reason tells us, of course, that there is a time and a place to smother emotions. Many adults stood aghast at the arrival of *Harriet the Spy, Dorp Dead, Durango Street*. Is it necessary, they asked, that children should know of violence, of spying, of plotted murder, of cruelty, of the baser emotions? A few even doubted that young children should see the place where the wild things are—fear, terror, death, nontruths. But what can we know of peace, truth, the Ten Commandments, if we know not their opposites?

Those who would attempt to smother the ogres of fairy tales, water down the witches, have risen again and again only to be quelled, for, as Lewis Mumford so aptly commented in speaking of the anti-fantasy pro-here-and-now movement, 'We did not get rid of the dragon, we only banished St George.' Television commercials, with their varying monsters, doves that fly in the window to magically soothe dishpan hands, translucent cages that conveniently fly stuffy sinuses to Arizona—these will always be with us in one form or another because they fulfil a need. What we all seek, of course, is a more meaningful sort of fantasy, one that does not only embody escape, but enriches. How unbelievably encouraging it is that Frodo, Bilbo, and J.R.R. Tolkien have been welcomed by people of all ages, including our thinking young college students.

For Sartre, even Jean Paul Sartre, recognized the value of his early boyhood escape reading: 'The return to order was always accompanied by progress: the heroes were rewarded; they received honours, tokens of admiration, money; thank to their dauntlessness, a territory had been conquered, a work of art had been protected . . . From those books I derived my most deep-seated phantasmagoria: optimism.'

Optimism! I am optimistic. I feel that when emotions come out into the open, whether in the form of what seems to me rather peculiar, but certainly emotional, dancing such as our teenagers do; when marches and even strikes and riots break a heretofore passive populace (although I would prefer protest to be in another form), when the mode of dress changes (although I myself prefer a neater and more kempt look)—when emotions come out into the open, it is a healthy sign. What is more fearful is that they be strangled and smothered. 'To feel emotion is at least to feel.'

When we do not question the neat definition, when we fail to feel and experience the meaning behind the words, relating it to our own emotions, then, and only then, are we lost.

And what has all this to do with the poetry we share with children?

Poetry, however else it may be defined, carries with it appeal to the emotions . . . 'a more than usual state of emotion', in the words of Samuel Coleridge; what Louise Bogan and William Jay Smith in their introduction to *The Golden Journey* call 'many kinds of emotion which prose cannot convey'. Whether it be the gay, singsong, simple rhymes of Mother Goose that amuse the very young, or the recognition of the world about him that a young child will find captured by rhyme and music, a certain reinforcement of experience, most easily communicated and understood in brief word form; or whether it touch the older child by its insistence upon, as Wallace Stevens has written, 'a tune beyond us, yet ourselves'—still, it must touch the emotions. It would seem to follow, therefore, that when we are thinking of poetry to share with children, we take into account the subject, but far more pertinent, those emotions that are within the range of childhood. Since all poetry is made of words caught up in a pattern of music, it is doubtful that we need to dwell on the mechanics, the feet, the rhyme or nonrhyme (note the popularity of haiku). We need rather to probe what lies behind what the poet is saying. Does it relate to the emotions and experiences of the younger ages? Do we need to stick to the poets of childhood, or should we rather choose from all poetry with an eye and ear to what a poet is saying in a particular poem that might have meaning, value, and enrichment through an essential enjoyment for children, or a particular child?

There is, of course, no easy guide, no formula for finding such poems. They are met in anthologies, in collections, in magazines, in odd and assorted places. What one does learn is that surprise is at every turn—a poem that appeals to one seven-year-old will pass his neighbour by; subjects that delight girls may bore boys and vice versa. Words that set one child to laughing will leave others in silence. One learns, too, that it is not always at the nursery-school level that Mother Goose is best received. Levels of achievement, socioeconomic factors may also play a big part in the sort of response a poem may meet.

Nor will the poems one generation enjoys necessarily be meaningful to the next. It struck me as interesting, during a recent rereading of Vachel Lindsay's *The Congo and Other Poems*, published in 1914, that I have seen and heard dozens of times his 'Explanation of the Grasshopper':

The Grasshopper, the grasshopper,
I will explain to you—
He is the Brownies' racehorse,
The fairies' Kangaroo.

Brownies today are better known as little Girl Scouts, and fairies go in and out of vogue. Perhaps, then, it would be wise to use instead an earlier poem called 'The Lion':

The Lion is a kingly beast
He likes the Hindu for a feast
And if no Hindu he can get,
The lion family is upset.

He cuffs his wife and bites her ears
Till she is nearly moved to tears
Then some explorer finds the den
And all is family peace again.

Not a great poem, but certainly more in tune with our times!

Pink, sugary-smiling fairies dressed in gossamer are, for the most part, vanishing. In their stead are creatures of the imagination with more blood, bone, and downright character. No longer passive and goody-goody, they display astoundingly realistic emotions!

The dwarfs in *The Hobbit*:

> Chip the glasses and crack the plates!
> Blunt the knives and bend the forks!
> That's what Bilbo Baggins hates—
> Smash the bottles and burn the corks!

Children are not to be deceived. The subject matter we share with them may delight, but try to place it in a false landscape, in false emotions, and they will, as Paul Hazard tells us, rightfully reject it. Why else have we lost the didactic turn-of-the-century verse?

> Oh Mary this will never do.
> Your work is sadly done, I fear.
> And such a little of it too;
> You have not taken pains, my dear . . .

Children not only shun didactic and moral verse (that so-called poetry in which the writer sermonizes directly) but almost insist on what Marianne Moore has called in poetry 'imaginary gardens with real toads'. Children love imaginary gardens, even as we ourselves do, but they insist the toads be real!

Even in Edward Lear, where there is undisguised fun in an imaginary world, silly things happen in spite of and because of very human emotions. The table complains to the chair of chilblains on her feet; the kangaroo cautions the duck to sit quite steady on the way to the Dee and Jelly-Bo-Lee; the owl charms the pussycat with words of romantic endearment; the Jumblies reject the plea of those who fear they will drown in their sieve. And who but children (or the children in us) would but doubt that a woman's chin might grow sharp enough for playing a harp, or that a man's beard might well house owls, wren, larks, and a hen.

Even in the most realistic of poems, the realm of the imagination has play in the poet's world, his garden, as it were. But it must be peopled with those who bear some resemblance to what the child knows is genuine, deeply and honestly felt.

And this, I think, is precisely where the difficulty lies in our attempts to work with poetry. For so often we feel a gross inadequacy in ourselves, we feel shy, embarrassed, afraid. And this is the result of not living fully enough in the poet's garden, of not letting our emotions, just for a little time, rule our heads!

Poets, after all, are human beings. They just happen to be sensitive to their world; they have something to say about their experiences in and relationships to this world, so strongly that they must share it with others in the hope that others, too, will feel what they are saying as it applies to their experiences and relationships. And they capture it in what they believe to be the most suitable and appealing means—words, the eternal and intuitive sense of and need for rhythm, music.

What distinguishes the poem from mere verse or rhyme (for the form seems similar enough) are the voices of the poets; their courage, if you will, to seize hold of the experience, the object, and turn it into meaningful shape. This, of course, demands that poets deeply involve themselves, laying their emotions bare. To search out poetry, therefore, we must listen to the poets, hear what they are saying. If we shy away from this, we end up with only a meaningless analysis, a ripping apart of words and feet, and except for some extraneous rhymes something just as well said in prose.

For poets need readers, just as they need the world around them. Frost has talked of the 'right reader'.

I am not suggesting that many of us have the time to pull apart poems and view them in perspective. But I do believe that we should allow ourselves the time to stop, occasionally, and become 'right readers', not through analysis of metrics and inverted sentences, not through rhyme, but in the giving of our feelings and sensitivities to what lies behind the words.

A piece of advice I have often heard given is to only read a poem that one, oneself, likes. The enthusiasm of the reader is carried over to others. I think this is good counsel, but I would hope that those who share poetry would go one step further, not just digging into a neat little storehouse, but searching out more poems, new poems. It is a commitment, but a rewarding one.

Giving back poetry to children as an emotional experience means stepping on toes. The 'purposeful' method of the classroom, where poems are given as exercises in finding verbs, descriptive words, capital letters, must inevitably be encountered and quashed. It is important, before reading poetry with a group, to explain that no person in the group will like, or be expected to like, all of the poems. To admit that each of us has a different makeup, with varying sensitivities and reactions, takes the onus out of that elusive 'beauty' with which poetry supposedly abounds.

How much more realistic, how much more honest, to allow a child room for emotions, room to respond to that poem or that within the poem that touches the child.

Here is a poem I found on page 81 of the anthology *Up the Line to Death*:

Up and down, up and down
They go, the grey rat, and the brown.
The telegraph lines are tangled hair,
Motionless on the sullen air;
An engine has fallen on its back,
With crazy wheels on a twisted track;
All ground to dust is the little town;

Up and down, up and down
They go, the grey rat and the brown.
A skull, torn out of the graves nearby,
Gapes in the grass. A butterfly,
In azure iridescence new,
Floats into the world, across the dew;
Between the flow'rs. Have we lost our way,
Or are we toys of a god at play,
Who do these things on a young Spring day?

Where the salvo fell, on a splintered ledge
Of ruin, at the crater's edge,
A poppy lives: and young, and fair,
The dewdrops hang on the spider's stair,
With every rainbow still unhurt
From leaflet unto leaflet girt.
Man's house is crushed, the spider lives:
Inscrutably He takes, and gives,
Who guards not any temple here,
Save the temple of the gossamer.

Up and down, up and down
They go, the grey rat, and the brown:
A pistol cracks: they too are dead.

The nightwind rustles overhead.

This poem 'After the Salvo' by Herbert Asquith is unique for its widely varying imagery, even apart from its sobering meaning. You will hear it differently, feel it differently from the nine-, ten-, and eleven-year-olds whose expression and emotional response go into clay, ink, collage, and paint at the Los Angeles County Museum of Art.

This was their response. One girl pictured the rats as symbols of evil, each with its shadow. To another the rats were only toy mice, climbing up a hickory-dickory clock. A boy turned the engine upright and drew it with mechanical precision; several other children depicted it upside down on twisted track. A skull emerged in one picture. A graveyard with tombstones dominated another. A huge black spider was drawn over and over again, on three pieces of paper, by a seemingly placid nine-year-old girl who later confided that a horror-science fiction film depicting giant spiders that she had seen on television at the age of four had bothered her ever since. Hitler dominated one picture. Another girl spattered paint at random on a piece of paper and labelled it 'Destruction'. Someone took wood and wire to make a sculpture of the twisted track. One boy put into a glorious pastel drawing all of the images plus buildings and trappings of a town. Butterflies were flying across one paper. Flowers were the subject of another. All but butterflies, flowers, and grass were done in deep reds, browns, black, and gold paint.

Unlike many other class sessions during which poems were read, in this one not one child failed to respond.

What definition is there to encompass all the poems that have meaning and appeal to children? Do not definitions belong, rather, to science, to the laboratory? Our varying emotions, our needs as human beings, are not so easily stuffed into formulas and test tubes. The language of experience, of feeling, is not, as Ciardi so well points out, the language of classification, and the point of poetry is not to arrive at a definition but to arrive at an experience—to feel, to bring our emotions and sensitivities into play.

In a poem, says MacLeish, the poet gives us a 'means to meaning'—the meaning of our human experience. If we refuse to involve ourselves in more than its technical appearance, if we ask 'What does it mean?' rather than 'How does it mean?' we have only cheated ourselves.

You may remember the Philosopher in James Stephens's *The Crock of Gold*; the philosopher who lived only by reason, fact, and intellect until his interview with Angus Ogg. 'He had stamped up the hill with vigour' for the encounter. 'He strode down it in ecstasy.' 'I have learned,' said the Philosopher, 'that the head does not hear anything until the heart has listened, and that what the heart knows today, the head will understand tomorrow.'

I believe that science occupies an important place in our world, as does its very basis of being, fact. I believe that responsibility and work are important, but so, also, is the pause for reflection, for searching into the meanings of emotions, the creativity they unleash into and through art, music, dance, and poetry. And I believe in discovering imaginary gardens with real toads, in searching for the means with which to bring delight and enjoyment back into poetry; in extending an invitation to children through poetry to not merely look and listen, but see—and hear.

You come too.

Strict and Loose Nonsense: Two Worlds of Children's Verse

X.J. Kennedy

Often in discussions of children's literature, the term *nonsense* is slung around haphazardly. Without much worrying about it, writers and publishers casually pin the name of nonsense on things not nonsensical at all, but merely funny or silly. As far as I know, this situation has yet to cause librarians to organize protests, nor to inspire a Society for the Rightful Nomenclature of Nonsense; and this reckless and irresponsible lack of concern strikes me as justified. After all, you can't worry about everything.

As a sometime nonsense writer, I remain happy with the present confused and indulgent state of affairs. I'm grateful that the name of nonsense is bestowed so freely. I wouldn't want my product denied the label just for making too much sense. It would be a shame to withhold the cheerful and appetizing designation of nonsense from works not clearly descended from Lewis Carroll, yet manifesting zaniness, such as Nikki Giovanni's engaging poem:

> Yolandé the Panda
> sat with Amanda
> eating a bar-be-cue rib
> They drank a beer
> and gave a big cheer
> 'Hooray! for women's lib'

(That last line may date this work a little, but somehow it remains young and sprightly.)

Labelled as nonsense, too, are all of Edward Lear's limericks, even though some of them might easily happen in reality, if public lunacy were tolerated.

Let me propose a working definition: Nonsense in a children's book is an account of anything that isn't likely to happen, whether or not it conceivably could. In the hope of being useful to anyone wishing to plumb this bottomless subject, let me propose two labels for two leading varieties of nonsense: *strict* and *loose*.

Strict Nonsense

Strict nonsense is a highly specialized game: clear-cut, distinct, and easy to recognize. In its best-known and most elaborate form, we find it in the classics: in Lear's verse and in some of Lewis Carroll's, in the Alice books, in certain Mother Goose rhymes. 'There is nothing more inexorable than a game,' remarks the English poet and novelist Elizabeth Sewell, author of *The Field of Nonsense* (London, 1952)—the most brilliant critical book I know, one that deserves rediscovery. Sewell confines herself to the kind of nonsense I'd call strict, and she cuts through a great deal of critical clutter.

Pioneering critics of Lear and Carroll had thought their nonsense merely lunatic and disorderly; Sewell instead finds the worlds of both writers fearsomely reasonable. Lear and Carroll think like those children observed by Jean Piaget who imagine a strictly logical universe controlled at all times by cause and effect. In asking 'Why?' questions (Why do robins have red breasts? Why is snow cold?), the child sensibly expects everything to occur for a reason—never simply by chance or for the heck of it.

In the world of *Through the Looking Glass*, every event has a cause, with few exceptions. The looking glass world is planned with a ferocious thoroughness, with the logic of a game of chess—the inverted logic of a chess game played in a mirror. *Looking Glass* is, I think, the strictest work of strict nonsense ever made. Yet in both Alice books, Alice keeps bumping against arbitrary rules, as in the Mad Tea Party that obliges guests to change their seats in frequent rotation. The Red Queen and the Queen of Hearts are reasonable persons whose reason has gone to insane excess, and it remains for the sensible Alice—without whose saving presence these nonsense worlds might seem monstrous and oppressive—to give them their final come-uppance: 'You're nothing but a pack of cards!'

Sensibly, Elizabeth Sewell refuses to stretch Lewis Carroll upon the couch of psychoanalysis, despite her sensitive understanding of what went wrong with him. Evidently the Reverend Mr Dodgson fell prey to a growing temptation to play God, even Supergod, striving to design universes neater and better ordered than the Almighty's own. Because he came more and more to violate his own unstated rules for the game of strict nonsense, he produced at last that disappointing work *Sylvie and Bruno*—in which, as Dr Sewell remarks, 'the game dies, and instead the reader is left with a dreary, odious, and pretentious mixture of false sentiment, preaching, and whimsy.' About all that can be said in defence of *Sylvie and Bruno*, I think, is that it includes a few imperishable bits of self-contained nonsense verse.

Suspending the Laws of Nature

What then are the rules behind the game of strict nonsense? First of all, in strict nonsense, the laws of nature must be suspended, replaced by new laws which the author decrees. The result is a new world extremely systematic and, in its goofy way, eminently reasonable. Such a new world comes with its own animals, birds, insects, and plants; and in this department the inventiveness of nonsense poets is wonderful to behold.

Lear gave us a whole zooful of imagined beasts and even invented a 'Nonsense botany'. Often a nonsense writer seems to parody the natural world, as does that fecund designer of new birds, William Jay Smith. In 'The Baybreasted Barge Bird', Smith invents a creature who lines her nest with labels from old tin cans and feeds her young on rusty cooking utensils. In 'Gooloo', Shel Silverstein invents a bird which, because it has no feet, is unable to land, and so has to lay eggs in midair. Thus one nonsensical fact will lead to another.

As such madcap ornithology demonstrates, it is characteristic of strict nonsense to monkey around with the natural world and combine it with unnatural and artificial ingredients. Thus Christina Rossetti in 'Sing-Song Verses' gives us fish who carry umbrellas to protect themselves from the rain and lizards who shade themselves with parasols. Another living animal made partly artificial is Hilaire Belloc's bison:

> The Bison is vain, and (I write it with pain)
> The Door-mat you see on his head
> Is not, as some learned professors maintain,
> The opulent growth of a genius' brain,
> But is sewn on with needle and thread.

Carrying on this great tradition, the interesting new children's poet J. Patrick Lewis in his 1990 collection, *A Hippopotamusn't*, crosses pelicans and canaries to produce 'Pelicanaries', who live among the nomadic Kurds:

> They fill their bills with pitted dates
> and Kurdled cheese from paper plates,
> then sit beside the Kurds and weigh
> the heated issues of the day.

Those 'paper plates' seem to me a touch of truly Learian strictness. The reverse of artificializing nature, I suppose, is to personify a manufactured object, as Lear does in 'The Broom, The Shovel, The Poker, and The Tongs'—characters who all take a drive in the park. Theodore Roethke, too, observes this custom in my favourite among his nonsense poems, 'The Ceiling':

> Suppose the Ceiling went Outside
> And then caught Cold and Up and Died?
> The only Thing we'd have for Proof
> That he was Gone, would be the Roof;
> I think it would be Most Revealing
> To find out how the Ceiling's Feeling.

In a strict nonsense world, then, a writer invents new scientific laws; but usually we can recognize this world without even needing to figure out which laws its author has revised. Right away, we will know it by certain familiar signs. One indication of its fierce rage for order is the author's love of numbers and systems and alphabets. Myra Cohn Livingston has shown her devotion to Lear in her own *A Lollygag of Limericks*, notably in these lines:

> Cried a man on the Salisbury Plain,
> 'Don't disturb me—I'm counting the rain;
> Should you cause me to stop
> I might miss half-a-drop
> And would have to start over again.'

John Ciardi, too, in his late work *Doodle Soup*, observes the tradition of carefully numbering things:

> There was an old lady in Bumbletown.
> She had three black cats and five were brown.

She had two red cows and three were blue.
Which is rather strange, but so are you.

That final surprise, incidently, is characteristic of Ciardi, who loves to keep a reader from feeling smug.

Power of Repetition

Fond of things in sequences, strict nonsense is marked by repetitions, refrains, and rigmaroles. Carroll's song with the chorus 'Sing Beans, sing Bones, sing Butterflies!' seems a typical nonsense refrain, and who can forget Lear's alphabetically-minded Mrs Discobbolos, who keeps crying 'Oh, W, X, Y, Z!' over and over? Rigmaroles, a form widely found in folk verse, develop in an orderly fashion, making amazing leaps over bridges of association. Recall the jump-rope jingle, 'My mother gave me a nickel / To buy a pickle, / The pickle was sour / So I bought a flower,' and so on for as long as the jumper desires.

Some of the stricter nonsense verse I know is the work of Canadian poet Dennis Lee, whose debt to the classics is evident in his tribute to the Lesser Glunk:

Alas, he is a Tearful Thing
And sobs at almost anything,
Such as the root of πr^2 . . .

There is a classical Learish or Carrollian ring to these lines, not only in Lee's allusion to mathematics but in the creature's tearfulness. Notice that the Glunk cries, but the poet doesn't.

A further rule of strict nonsense is that the writer has to maintain a tone of emotional detachment. Although Lear's characters are sometimes given to blubbering and Lear himself is said to have wept over his pen as he chronicled their miseries and frustrations, no matter. On the page, no teardrops must show. The writer may not directly express personal feelings, and can betray neither affection nor kindness.

Because Lear plays the game, some find an apparent cruelty and indifference in those limericks wherein poor old characters are humiliated, publicly ridiculed, beaten, and even put to death like the 'Old Person from Tartary / Who divided his jugular artery.' Why don't we hold Lear accountable for the violent, psychotic behaviour of his characters? Is the following limerick to be blamed, as we might blame a televised police show, for portraying and even glorifying violent destruction?

> There was an old person of Newry
> Whose manners were tinctured with fury;
> He tore all the rugs
> And broke all the jugs
> Within twenty miles distance of Newry.

Now the more you think about that, the more unlikely it gets. Imagine this old person conducting a search of every house and flat within exactly 20 (the number is in itself nonsensical) miles of Newry and confiscating and destroying people's rugs and jugs—nothing else!—while the homeowners look on, appalled.

One difference between Lear and a violent TV show may be that, while the TV show strives for reality, Lear strives for total unreality. He banishes his characters to a nutty world all their own, and he stakes out the boundaries of that world by writing in bouncing metre and jog-trot rhyme. Besides, each poem comes with a loony drawing. The pictures are meant to be one with the poems, for Lear depended on them (so he told a friend) to show that he wrote of unreal things.

Like Lear, incidentally, Shel Silverstein also has insisted that his poems and his pictures form units not to be put asunder. As editors compiling an illustrated anthology, Dorothy M. Kennedy and I recently had to omit Silverstein because of his insistence that anyone who reprints one of his poems must reprint the illustration too, for we couldn't have worked his pictures into our book.

Verse as a Game

Verse form to Edward Lear, and indeed, to any writer of strict nonsense, advertises the fact that a poem is a game. (I don't know of any strict nonsense written in free verse.) Write in rhymed stanzas with a romping rhythm and you say, 'I'm kidding; don't believe a word of this.' I suspect that it may be those elements of rhyme and metre that allow us to tolerate, even enjoy, those turn-of-the-century 'Little Willie' rhymes originated by Harry Graham in *Ruthless Rhymes for Heartless Homes* (1899), with their blithe hard-heartedness. The old masterpiece of the genre must be this poem by Anonymous:

> Little Willie from the mirror
> Licked the mercury all off,
> Thinking in his childish error

> It would cure the whooping cough.
> At the funeral, weeping Mother
> Sadly said to Mrs Brown,
> "Twas a chilly day for Willie
> When the mercury went down.'

Imagine how terrible, how revolting, those lines would be if they didn't rhyme. If they didn't end in a pun, if they didn't bounce along so cheerily to a rambunctious beat. The form, at odds with what is said in it, produces an effect of irony. Such a nonsense poem is like an animated cartoon: its very medium prevents us from taking it seriously.

Certain features of language in a strict nonsense poem also can proclaim its unreality. This proclamation is loud and clear when a writer makes up a whole new vocabulary, as Carroll does in 'Jabberwocky' or as Lear does in his many playful coinages: the wondrous new adjectives *mucilaginous* (a 'mucilaginous monkey', 'I have pretty well made up my mucilaginous mind'); and *scroobious* ('the Scroobious Snake', 'scroobious dubious doubtfulness').

In recent America, no doubt the most conspicuous practitioner of strict nonsense is Dr Seuss, who (like Lear) writes in swinging measures, tells stories, draws pictures, and coins new words galore. *On Beyond Zebra* even invents a new alphabet. I hold Seuss in higher regard than many do: his cartoons may look drawn with his foot, but he is a brisk and brilliant versifier, and I stand in awe before his powers of invention.

For reasons of ignorance, I have confined my examples of contemporary nonsense to those written on this side of the Atlantic. But it strikes me that one intriguing difference between classic English nonsense and the North American product is the latter's debt to our tradition of the tall tale. Dennis Lee's 'The Big Blue Frog and the Dirty Flannel Dog' may start out like the story of an ocean trip by the Jumblies or the Owl and the Pussycat, but it is shaped by the poet's native Canadian geography. After Frog and Dog go to sea on the good ship *Hollow Log*—

> First they sailed to Saskatoon,
> Where they stole the harvest moon
> And they strung it as a headlight on the log.

Compare Mark Twain's account (in *Life on the Mississippi*) of the bragging keelboatman who claims, 'Smoked glass, here, for all! Don't attempt to look at me with the naked eye, gentlemen! . . . I put my hand on the sun's face and make it night in the earth; I bite a piece out of the moon and hurry the seasons.' Dennis Lee's grandiose moon-stealing seems the kind of thing that might happen in a tall tale about Mike Pink or Paul Bunyan. Coincidentally, it seems echoed by Shel Silverstein in 'Moon-Catchin' Net', in which a child vows to hunt for the moon, with butterfly net in hand, with Bunyan-like aspirations.

Like a tall tale is that American folksong for children, 'The Frisco Whale', another revision of nature. Here is a composite version, roughly singable to the tune of 'Dixie':

In Frisco town there lives a whale
And she eats porkchops by the pail,
By the pill-box, by the bathtub,
By the washtub, by the schooner.
Her name is Sarah, and she's a peach,
But you can't leave food within her reach
Nor nursemaids, nor babies,
Nor chocolate ice cream sodas.
She eats a lot, and when she smiles
You can see her teeth for miles and miles,
And her adenoids, and her tonsils,
And things too fierce to mention.
Now what can you do in a case like that,
What can you do but step on your hat,
Or your grandfather, or your toothbrush,
Or anything else that's helpless?

Loose Nonsense

Well, what about loose nonsense, the kind that declines to play such an elaborate, strictly rule-bound game? Defined loosely, it is any old nonsense that isn't strict. Loose nonsense is the kind most of us writers settle for, but let me not imply that just because it is freer than the classic game of *Through the Looking Glass*, it is inferior and no-account. It too can offer satisfactions.

Most loose nonsense is comic writing about a single unlikely event. It surprises us by defying convention and routine. It may not give us a whole systematic world, but it can make much out of a square foot of nuttiness. Where strict nonsense suspends all scientific laws, permitting a cat to fiddle and a dish and a spoon to elope, loose nonsense settles for a single defiance of nature—permitting only, say, the cow to jump over the moon. Or if the cow merely jumps over a barn, that is enough for loose nonsense. A single exception to nature takes place in Shel Silverstein's 'Stop Thief!'

> Policeman, policeman,
> Help me please.
> Someone went and stole my knees.
> I'd chase him down but I suspect
> My feet and legs just won't connect.

In any nonsense world, by the way, the human body endures all sorts of harmless if unnerving change—as Alice finds in Wonderland, shrinking and growing and having her neck stretched long as a giraffe's.

Sometimes loose nonsense verse will crack a single joke, as in Jack Prelutsky's portraits of children with monstrous appetites, like 'Pumperly Pott's Unpredictable Niece', who devours a whole automobile, steel-belted radials and all, or 'Herbert Glerbett', who ingests 50 pounds of lemon sherbet and turns into a puddle of green goo. The relative simplicity of this kind of thing may be seen by comparing it with stricter and more complicated nonsense such as Eve Merriam's 'I Scream', in which a boy, before eating the one dish of ice cream he's allowed, gets his mother to let him choose the dish. This wonderful dish is large enough to hold a dolphin and a kangaroo, ten tall ships, and more besides. Merriam goes into a whole classical rigmarole in detailing its possible contents.

Not all the verse I write for children is nonsense—only some of it turns out that way. And I don't ever set out to write loose or strict nonsense deliberately and methodically. Writers, I suspect, do best to work unselfconsciously, not too fully aware of what they're up to. If they cogitate too much beforehand, or while they work, they risk becoming like the centipede in the anonymous jingle, who was going along, doing fine, until a malicious toad asked her, 'Pray, which leg comes after which?'; whereupon 'This raised her mind to such a pitch / She lay distracted in a ditch / Considering how to run.'

While my stuff is taking shape on the page, I don't stop to analyse it, I'm too busy trying to get the lines to rhyme and the rhythm to keep moving and to get a story told. It seems that in regard to nonsense I have vacillated between loose and strict, more often loose. Sometimes a poem will start out as a loose, joking kind of thing, then grow into stricter nonsense. This happens in an item called 'Family Genius'—mainly just a catalogue of somebody's uncle's odd inventions. It begins with frozen spinach on a stick: unlikely enough, but possible to make in your freezer if you want to. But as the catalogue goes on, it becomes more wildly implausible: Uncle constructs a paper airplane nine miles long, designs a pair of wooden shoes for a one-legged stork and a gadget for removing King Kongs from Empire State Buildings. In this fashion, a small unlikeliness will sometimes lead to larger ones.

Sometimes a poem—looser nonsense, I suppose—repeals a single law of nature. Such, I reckon, is an item called 'Backyard Volcano' in which a smoking crater, belching lava, crops up in a suburban neighbourhood. Uncle cheerfully goes swimming in it, shouting before he dives, 'Last one in is a old molten stone!' At least one usual law of nature is set aside, I think: the law that hot things can burn you.

I believe that the hippity-hop rhythm and tinkly rhymes of those lines may help tell the child, 'This is only kidding—don't go jump in any volcanoes like that.' But while no child I know of has yet had this problem, I have found that some adults have trouble distinguishing between nonsense and reality. Here is my only nonsense item to have been banned by censors, 'Mother's Nerves':

> My mother said, 'If just once more
> I hear you slam that old screen door,
> I'll tear out my hair! I'll dive in the stove!'—
> So I gave it a bang, and in she dove.

Now most children do not need to be told that any mother who behaves that way is loony. The rhyme and metre, too, brand the piece as a work of artifice, not faithful reporting. But the school board of North Kansas City did not see it that way when they removed an anthology containing it, William Cole's *I'm Mad at You!*, from their school library shelves, charging this and other innocuous works with 'subversion of parental authority'. (A protest mounted by some North Kansas City librarians, bless them, succeeded in getting the book out of jail.)

Whenever a piece of verse turns out to be strict nonsense, I'll have to admit, I develop a soft spot in my heart for it. Such is an item called 'What We Might Be, What We Are', in which two geographically distant and ill-matched things fall in love:

> If you were a scoop of vanilla
> And I were the cone where you sat,
> If you were a slowly pitched baseball

And I were the swing of a bat,
If you were a shiny new fishhook
And I were a bucket of worms,
If we were a pin and a pincushion,
We might be on intimate terms.
If you were a plate of spaghetti
And I were your piping-hot sauce,
We'd not even need to write letters
To put our affection across.
But you're just a piece of red ribbon
In the beard of a Balinese goat
And I'm a New Jersey mosquito,
I guess we'll stay slightly remote.

I'd be thankful if anyone were to find in that plaintive lament a little echo of the sadness in Lear's tales of poor thwarted old characters with long noses, whom nobody loves.

In conclusion, I have an awful hunch that, like the Teutonic scholar who wrote a dissertation on poems beginning with the word 'and', I have dwelt more earnestly on my subject than was necessary. Let me claim, though, that both varieties of nonsense can have valuable and salutary effects. Loose nonsense challenges our sense of what is real and proper, the better to define reality and propriety. Strict nonsense builds a whole new and different world, thus refreshing and illuminating our notions of the world we know. Once in a while, with any luck, both can cast new light on old reality. Like Andrew Jackson in the traditional rhyme, I may be full of beans—

Old Andy Jackson
Was part Anglo-Saxon,
He was so full of beans
That he took New Orleans.

Still, let me trust that, like a caramel pillow, some of this mucilaginous rigmarole may stick to your head.

PART VI

PICTURE BOOKS AND ILLUSTRATION

WHAT IS A PICTURE BOOK?

Uri Shulevitz

Glancing at the shelves of children's books in a library or bookstore, you'll find many of them labelled 'picture books'. They are profusely illustrated—a picture or more per double-spread—usually contain less text than a juvenile novel, are written in simple language, and are set in a large typeface. They're often smaller or larger than a standard-size book as well. The classification as a picture book is based on the book's appearance, its format.

I believe this way of classifying picture books is confusing, however. It doesn't differentiate, for example, between *Hector Protector*, a true picture book, and *The Fool of the World and the Flying Ship*, a profusely illustrated folktale in picture book format. This classification ignores the difference between a picture book *format* and a picture book *concept*.

What is the difference between the two? The first is a *picture book*, the second a *storybook*. A storybook, as the word implies, puts the emphasis on the story. The words carry the story (which can be fully understood without the pictures), the pictures enhance it. The storybook's reliance on words is part of a literary tradition dating back to at least the 18th and 19th centuries. Narration, as crystallized in the 19th-century novel, extensively utilizes descriptions consisting to a great extent of what is seen and heard:

> 'Ah!' said the old man, turning to me with a sigh, as if I had spoken to him but that moment, 'you don't know what you say when you tell me that I don't consider her.' (Charles Dickens, *Master Humphrey's Clock*)

This description (or representation by words), consists essentially in sight—'turning to me'—and sound—'Ah! . . . you don't know. . . .' The seen and the heard are both expressed in words.

> 'There are two of us now; and as you serve him, you serve me,' he cried, turning fiercely round. (Herman Melville, *Omoo*)

> 'No thank you,' replied Anxious (Squirrel) in a very dramatic tone, wringing his paws together till tufts of fur flew forth.' (Jan Wahl, *Pleasant Fieldmouse*)

Mr McGregor was on his hands and knees planting out young cabbages, but he jumped up and ran after Peter, waving a rake and calling out, 'Stop thief!' (Beatrix Potter, *The Tale of Peter Rabbit*)

These quotations are examples of the same descriptive approach. Beatrix Potter's *Tale of Peter Rabbit* and Jan Wahl's *Pleasant Fieldmouse*, although shorter and simpler, are in the same literary tradition as the excepts from Dickens and Melville. Potter's pictures enhance the story, but *Peter Rabbit* can be fully understood without them. The complete story is contained in the words, which not only provide the necessary information, but contain the picture as well: 'Mr McGregor was on his hands and knees. . . .' The same is true of Wahl's *Pleasant Fieldmouse*: 'wringing his paws together till tufts of fur flew forth.' *Pleasant Fieldmouse* and *Peter Rabbit*, although varying in length and degree of complexity, use the same verbal approach and are therefore both storybooks.

In a true picture book, words cannot stand on their own; without pictures, the meaning of the story will be unclear. The pictures provide information not contained in the words. Furthermore, picture books not only rely on pictures to supplement but to clarify or take the place of words. In a picture book both the words and the pictures are read. Naturally, such an approach leads to using fewer words or none at all.

Without the pictures, the information in Randolph Caldecott's *Hey Diddle Diddle* would be incomplete. The words, 'Hey, diddle diddle,' meaningless except as sound, provide a kind of soundtrack to the pictures, which carry the story. Caldecott's picture books, created between 1878 and his death in 1886, are possibly the first to realize the picture book concept and utilize it to the fullest.

In Maurice Sendak's *Hector Protector*, the pictures, not the words, tell the story. This is indeed an entirely different approach from a storybook. This is equally true of Sendak's *Where the Wild Things Are*. The words alone, without the picture, don't tell us which mischief is 'of one kind'. Without the picture, our information is incomplete. The book's climax, 'the wild rumpus', is wholly conveyed through pictures—using no words at all.

The words, 'One Monday morning' (in my book by the same title), could refer to a sunny day in the country. The picture completes our information by showing that it is a rainy day over dreary tenement houses in New York City. The description, which would have been represented by words in a storybook, is here contained in the picture. The words 'One Monday morning' are a general statement, a headline, if you will, while the picture provides the specific details. Furthermore, the words don't repeat what is in the picture and vice versa; their relationship is contrapuntal, they complement and complete each other.

When the words serve as a soundtrack to the pictures, that too is a contrapuntal quality. Such is the case in *One Monday Morning*, based on a folk song, *Hey Diddle Diddle*, a nursery rhyme, or in *Where the Wild Things Are*, with its rhythmic prose.

When in *Where the Wild Things Are*, 'they roared their terrible roars and gnashed their terrible teeth and rolled their terrible eyes and showed their terrible claws,' it would be misleading to take these words as mere description. Neither do they repeat what can be seen in the picture. In addition to serving as soundtrack, the words tell what the picture cannot show: the rolling of the eyes and the showing of the claws.

Limited in the number of pages, a picture book often cannot afford the additional space necessary in order to focus on a detail for emphasis. Unlike film, a picture book with its still pictures cannot show movement itself. That is when the words can help to emphasize a detail, clarify an action, or link two pictures together. Unlike a storybook, which expresses sight and sound through words, a picture book separates the two, representing the sight by a picture and the sound by words. But since a picture book is read to the very young child, who doesn't know yet how to read, he will *see* the pictures and *hear* the words.

In other words, the picture book is a return to an original premise: to see and to hear directly, without the intermediary of the printed word. By representing visibly, instead of representing by words (describing), a picture book becomes naturally a *dramatic* experience: direct, immediate, vivid, moving. One can see the importance of reading the words aloud from a picture book: it is more important how the words will sound when heard, than seen when read. The kinship between picture books and theatre or film, the silent film in particular, becomes evident. The words in a picture book at times approach the quality of folk ballads or nursery rhymes, such as Caldecott's picture books. It is no mere coincidence that the picture book concept has been used to a greater extent by artists than by writers.

Judging by the full bookshelves labelled as such, there aren't as many true picture books as we are led to believe. Some children's books unknowingly mix the picture book and storybook concept. The ultimate test is, of course, whether the book works or does not. Storybooks and picture books are different, but one is not necessarily better than the other. Understanding the difference between the two and applying it intelligently, however, can be of considerable help in creating better picture books or storybooks.

In summary, the meaning of words in a picture book is unclear or incomplete without the pictures. A true picture book cannot be read to children over the radio, for example, because it wouldn't be understood. The difference between a storybook and a picture book is not a matter of degree or of the amount of words or pictures; it is a difference in *essence*. A picture book uses a unique concept, and it is a unique book genre.

'He pulled ribbons out of his mouth and turkeys out of his boots.' *The Magician*, adapted from I.L. Peretz's *Der Kunzen-Macher* and illustrated by Uri Shulevitz (New York: Macmillan, 1973).

How Picture Books Work

Perry Nodelman

Pictures in children's books should be clear and simple and colourful. They should not be abstract. The figures in them should be large, and they should not blend into the background.

These opinions, shared by many of the students in my children's literature classes, say more of their ideas about children than their understanding of art. They think that pictures in children's books should be simple because children, being inexperienced, are simple-minded; clear, because children's untrained eyes cannot perceive subtleties; colourful, because children themselves are bright spirits with no capacity for gloom.

My students also think that while words are always hard to understand, the right sort of pictures—ones that are simple and clear and non-abstract—require no effort at all. In fact, they believe that is *why* children's books contain pictures; the pictures contain information that allows children to understand the words. They think that children can make no sense of an idea like 'a woman sat at a window' until a picture shows them what a woman is and what a window is: and they are sure that a complex depiction of an unactual woman sitting by an abstracted window does not do the job.

But of course children are not simple-minded, nor always cheerful. Their pictures are rarely simple, and need not be colourful or non-abstract. Words are no harder to understand than pictures; even though knowing how to *read* words is hard, infants understand spoken ones before they understand pictures. Above all, children's books do not contain pictures merely to convey factual information.

In fact, pictures by themselves convey little. Just as our understanding of language depends on our knowledge of the grammar that gives it shape, our understanding of pictures depends on our knowledge of the conventions they operate by. Even understanding a photograph requires a knowledge of conventions; we must understand that the one-inch person we see in a three-by-five-inch photograph is not really one inch high; that that person is probably not as flat as his image, nor surrounded by a white frame; that the place the photograph depicts is probably more colourful than a black and white photograph of it; and that even though the subject's hand will be raised in the photograph for as long as the photograph exists, he has probably lowered it by now in the world outside the picture.

As well as the usual pictorial conventions, picture books have conventions of their own. When my three-year-old son looks at Wanda Gàg's *Millions of Cats*, he cannot understand why the pond the cats have emptied on the right-hand page that first caught his eye has become full again on the left-hand page. He has not yet learned that time conventionally passes from left to right in picture books. He also does not understand that the ten cats on one double-page spread in the same book are all actually the same cat, depicted at different moments in a chronological sequence that moves from left to right.

But conventions aside, there are many things pictures simply cannot communicate. A picture of a woman sitting at a window does not tell us if she has been there a long time or has just sat down; if the significance of the picture is her beauty, or her dress, or the things she does while she sits; if she is remembering, or planning, or just waiting for someone. We need words to make sense of the picture.

In some instances, pictures may actually hinder communication. A student once conducted an experiment to prove to me that young children do not respond to a story without pictures. She divided her nursery school children into two groups. She read one group a story without pictures, the other the same story accompanied by the pictures meant to go with it. She did her best to make the experiment come out right; the book she chose was intended for beginning readers, and its pictures were more subtle and more interesting than its unrhythmic, repetitious, and simplistic text. To her horror, the children who saw the pictures wandered about during the storytelling, and remembered little afterward; the ones who heard the story without pictures paid careful attention and remembered the story in detail.

These children may have been trained by television, with its many short sequences, to have short attention spans for visual experiences. A filmmaker recently suggested in a newspaper interview that the repetitious way television processes information into segments of equal length has become a new language, 'a tautly organized system of conveying what are presumed to be messages . . . it is applying the same manner of delivery, the same fragmentation, to all subjects.' On the other hand, we all tend to look at pictures in a disorganized way that hinders their ability to communicate; most of us browse erratically through magazines and picture books when we first look at them. We rarely treat words that way.

Obviously the pictures in picture books do not convey information more readily than words; but they do tell us some things that words can covey only inexactly—in particular, the way things look. The ability of pictures to give us exact knowledge of appearances is especially important in children's books, in which the limited linguistic experience of the intended audience controls the complexity of language. Children unfamiliar with the technical words that describe clothing can still perceive the wimples and fichus and raglan sleeves shown in a picture. In fact, contemporary picture books characteristically have simple and often graceless texts, and very sophisticated and highly accomplished pictures.

But in addition to facts of appearance, pictures show things no words could ever convey—as we see if we compare two different renderings of the same subject. It would take someone exceedingly fluent to even begin to describe how Snow White as drawn by Trina Schart Hyman differs from Snow White as drawn by Nancy Eckholm Burkert. Their features are surprisingly similar; they even wear their hair in the same style. Yet they are quite different from each other, and we know that even after a quick glance.

As in most fairy tales, the words that tell the story of 'Snow White' are almost toneless; they imply a surprisingly matter-of-fact objectivity toward the strange events they describe. Consequently, we may respond quite neutrally to the words, 'she had a daughter as red as blood and as white as snow'—at least when those words appear in their original context. But we cannot respond neutrally to either of the two pictures; in fact, *any* picture of that red and white daughter will demand our involvement, ask us to feel something—something about the daughter, and also, something about the depiction of her. E.H. Gombrich says that 'the visual image is supreme in its capacity for arousal.' But in addition to exciting our attention, pictures almost always demand an emotional response, simply because artists cannot easily avoid interpreting the things they depict. By depicting Snow White in different ways, as they inevitably must, Hyman and Burkert inevitably convey different attitudes toward her, and ask us to feel differently about her. While both their Snow Whites have flowing locks, Hyman's flow tempestuously like the branches in the wind they seem to mingle tempestuously with; Burkert's merely wander enough to announce their wearer's human difference from the decorative motionless and meticulously detailed branches behind them.

The different ways these pictures make us feel about the same information is a matter of style—not what is depicted, but *how* it is depicted. Style is interpretation. The basic information contained in a picture of a woman sitting at a window is simply that a woman is sitting at a window. But Trina Schart Hyman shows us Snow White's mother from behind; we are in the room with her, looking out the window. We see what she sees; we also see the servant who pours her tea, the candles she keeps lit in front of a small triptych, the comforting darkness that surrounds her. We are involved in her life. Nancy Eckholm Burkert shows us the sitting woman from outside the window; we look *at* her, not with her. We do not see what she sees; and we see *her* as part of a larger picture which also includes other parts of the castle. Furthermore, the room she inhabits is depicted as a series of ornate patterns, all shown in the same light; there is no depth of perspective to tell us what objects contain which patterns. This woman is an object among other objects, to be admired for its beauty. She is not a human being to become involved with and care about, and Burkert does not even show us the drop of blood that falls on the snow. Hyman's picture takes us inside, and tells us that this is a story about people; Burkert takes us outside, and tells us to keep our distance and put things in perspective—like the small woman engulfed by the huge castle. In other words, the way these pictures communicate the same information changes the information; the style changes the substance enough to become the substance.

The information that a woman sits at a window, or that a child is as red as blood and as white as snow, is open to many interpretations. The woman could be driving a bus; the child could have red skin and white lips, or she may have an overall checkerboard complexion. But we can imagine such possibilities only until pictures like those by Hyman and Burkert control our response. Paradoxically, the specific image these pictures offer limits the information contained in the words by amplifying it.

In fact, since the words in picture books are often simple enough to be vague, the pictures in these books often have the express purpose of limiting the range of possible meanings. After hearing the story in Sendak's *Where the Wild Things Are* without seeing the pictures, my students say it is too frightening for young children; when they see the pictures, they change their minds. The wild things they imagine on their own are far more frightening than the ones Sendak actually provided. Sendak's comparatively gentle pictures allow his scary words.

Furthermore, my students tell me that Sendak's wild things are more interesting than the ones they imagined themselves. Some people claim that pictures limit imagination. But while Sendak's wild things and Burkert's Snow White do limit my response to the words, they expand the realm of my experience. I could never have imagined Sendak's unusual wild things on my own, and my own image of Snow White was not much less vague than the words of the story. If pictures limit our imaginations, then so do words, and the only safe alternative is utterly blank pages. In fact, both words and pictures exercise our imaginations by giving us something definite and new to think about.

Pat Hutchins's *Rosie's Walk* contains only thirty-two simple words: 'Rosie the hen went for a walk/ across the yard/ around the pond/ over the haystack/ past the mill/ through the fence/ under the beehives/ and got back in time for dinner.' This is too vague to be interesting, and not much more complex than blank pages; Hutchins' pictures make it a story (and engage our imaginations) by making it more specific. They show us that Rosie is blithely ignorant of the fox who is following her, and that every move Rosie takes leads the fox into another slapstick disaster. But they do more than that. In a way far less subtle than the Snow White illustrations, they change our response to the text. Considered along with the pictures, it is not just an objective description of boring events; the person who speaks these words in this situation is either as blind as Rosie, or else deliberately leaving the fox out in order to tease. In either case, the pictures force us to be conscious of the inadequacies of the text, and in fact, to enjoy them; it is the distance between the story the words tell and the story the pictures tell that makes the book interesting.

That distance is inevitable. Pictures always change the meanings of words by interpreting them in a specific way; they always tell a different story. Like Hutchins, many illustrators turn that into a game, in which our pleasure derives from our consciousness of the distance. One version of this game is the expansion of simple rhymes into complex stories, a tradition begun by Caldecott and continued by, among others, Wallace Tripp and Maurice Sendak. In *Hector Protector*, Sendak amplifies a simple four-line verse about how Hector was sent to the Queen and then sent back again into a complex story involving a snake, a cake, and a lion, all of Sendak's invention; our delight here is in finding out that the story those vague words implied was quite different from and far more specific than we had imagined.

We should not forget that Sendak's story of Hector would be less fun if the words were not there at all; the pictures make a joke about the vagueness of the words that demands their presence. But books like this do make us sensitive to the ability of pictures to tell us something different from words. We pore over them looking for interesting details, in the knowledge that these details will be clues to a more interesting story than the one the words tell. Many picture books demand this sort of attention. Artists like Richard Scarry and Mitsumasa Anno have built careers on it. Their crowded pages demand and repay close attention, and while there is a great difference in style, the pleasure in finding either Scarry's Gold Bug or Anno's Red Riding Hood in a welter of other details is the same. There are also many books in which various animals are hidden in foliage, among them Burkert's *Snow White*, Susan Jeffers's *Three Jovial Huntsmen*, and Anno's *Animals*. In fact, this sort of visual puzzle has become something of a cliché; it even appears in a recent advertisement for the Sierra Club, which says that Earth is 'the only paradise we ever need—if only we had the eyes to see.' Making us use our eyes and take delight in what they discover is the whole point of such pictures.

In *Nothing Ever Happens on My Block*, Ellen Raskin takes this game to its logical conclusion, and uses it to involve readers actively in the meaning of her story. Chester Filbert insists that nothing happens on his block; but we are too busy discovering the interesting things going on behind him to pay much attention to him. We see and enjoy more than he is able to tell us; so we know he is wrong. Raskin cleverly uses the distance between pictures and words to comment ironically on her narrator.

In all of these books the ironic relationship of pictures and words is deliberate; but a less extreme tension between the two is inevitable, simply because they communicate different things in different ways. *Where the Wild Things Are*, in which Sendak does not seem to have intended any particular distance between pictures and words, begins this way: 'The night Max wore his wolf suit and made mischief of one kind and another his mother called him "WILD THING"!' No one reading this for the first time would be content to pause in the middle of the sentence, before the meaning is complete; but Sendak spreads these words over three pages, and provides three different illustrations for them. And we do want to look at these pictures, if only because they are there. So the words drive us forward, to find out their complete meaning, while the pictures pull us back, to explore the specific scenes they depict in more detail. There is automatically a tension between the two.

In picture books that tell stories that tension is strong. Stories inevitably describe the passing of time; good ones tie a series of events together in a smooth flow that keeps us turning pages to find out what happens next. But except for artificial conventions like the one Wanda Gàg used to show a cat's weight gain, pictures cannot depict time passing. Rather than show how one moment is related to the next, they make us consider in detail how a specific place looks at one moment removed from time. Even a series of pictures can show us only a sequence of isolated moments—not the connections between those moments. Stories describe both space and time, pictures only space. And if we stop to look carefully at Max's mischief or Burkert's forest full of animals, as the pictures ask us to do, we may lose sight of the story's movement through time.

Obviously pictures can be a distraction, a pretty way of ruining good stories. But intelligent illustrators understand and make use of the contradictory pull of words and pictures, so that the two together tell a story that depends on their differences from each other.

The beginning of *Where the Wild Things Are* shows how that happens. The words alone say little and seem clumsy; the rhythm of the sentence depends on the pauses Sendak creates by placing the pictures where they are. By interfering with the forward thrust of the words, the pictures both create small moments of suspense and turn undistinguished prose into good prose—and they do it without any consideration of what they depict or how they depict it.

What they depict is a series of moments which, we assume, form a sequence; but the story they tell is fragmentary. A boy in a wolf suit pounds a nail into a wall to make a tent. The same boy chases a dog with a fork. The same boy stands in a room at night and looks at the door. While Sendak's words join these moments together so that we understand their relationship, the pictures still focus our attention on specific moments removed from the flow of time. We see one moment clearly and in great detail—in much greater detail than the vague text implies; then we jump to another moment seen clearly and in great detail.

In this way, picture books are like fairy tales. Max Lüthi says that the fairy tale style 'isolates the episodes. Each is complete within itself; the relation to the earlier episodes need not be established.' For instance, the story of 'Snow White' tells about the old Queen sitting at the window in some detail; then it moves years in a few sentences before it settles down to a description of the new Queen at her mirror. Good picture books move in much the same way; they concentrate our attention on a series of carefully perceived moments of stopped time, like the stages of Max's mischief.

But Lüthi goes on to add that '. . . fairy tale episodes are not completely sealed off from each other, after all. Tendencies . . . toward self-sufficiency of the individual scene and integrated structure . . . stand in opposition to each other.' In fact, the plots of fairy tales always show the connections between apparently disconnected moments. The beauty of the young Snow White quickly establishes the previously mysterious connection between one woman at a window and another at a mirror—and also the significant differences between windows and mirrors, between a healthful looking-outward and a dangerous self-regard. Much the same thing happens in good picture books. The text establishes the relationships between disconnected moments that pictures cannot show; we understand how the boy chasing the dog became the boy standing in the room. The suspense created by words alone is a constant thrust forward that builds to a climax; but the excitement of a good picture book is the constant tension between the moments isolated by the pictures and the flow of words that join those moments together. The jumpy rhythm of picture books is quite different from the gradually intensifying flow of stories told by words themselves.

How different illustrators deal with that rhythm becomes apparent if we compare two different renderings of the same story. Appropriately enough, the story illustrated by both Trina Schart Hyman and Nancy Eckholm Burkert is a fairy tale: 'Snow White' was a collection of isolated and then united movements even before Hyman and Burkert illustrated it, so their versions of it suggest much about relationships between words and pictures.

Even including the picture on the dust jacket, the ornaments on the title page, and the decorated letter that begins the text, Burkert's version has only ten illustrations. Hyman's has twenty-five, all but two of them double-page spreads. As a result, two quite different rhythms are established. Hyman clearly considers more moments worthy of isolation; but the mere fact there are so many of them makes them seem less isolated. The effect is something like a movie, which is a collection of still pictures arranged to create the effect of motion; the pictures flow together in a way that downplays the inevitably jumpy rhythm of picture book storytelling. In fact, Hyman's many pictures dominate the words; they even physically surround the small white blocks in which the words are printed.

Burkert's pictures appear on double-page spreads with no words on them, interspersed between double-page spreads of words alone. Rather than conceal the inevitable thrust forward of words and backwards of pictures, the physical distance between Burkert's pictures and the words amplifies it. The rhythm created by our movement between pictures and words is pronounced in Burkert, diluted in Hyman.

Furthermore, the mere fact that Hyman's version contains so many pictures governs our response to any one picture. Seeing more or less the same rooms and objects in more or less the same way on page after page, we do not pay close attention to them. We let them affect us unconsciously, the way we register the backgrounds in movies. In fact, Hyman seems to use objects primarily to create atmosphere. The many candles by the Queen's mirror, or the vaguely troll-like carvings on the dwarfs' furniture, blend into the rest of the scene and draw little attention to themselves; but taken together, they create the melodramatic feeling of the book as a whole.

Burkert's pictures are fewer, and more unlike each other both in subject and in composition. So we look at each of them more closely. Not surprisingly, they become meaningful in a different way. The mere fact that we spend more time away from the story when we look at these pictures makes us less involved in the events it describes; but our close attention to visual details is repaid by a deeper and more objective *understanding* of the events. In fact, these pictures work in much the same way as the medieval illuminations they are modelled on; the details in them are symbolic representations of the meaning of events or characters.

Our search for the animals hidden in the forest makes us aware of many things: despite the apparent beauty of the forest, Snow White is in danger; she is too innocent to perceive that danger; and we, who perceive it, are distanced from her. Burkert's pictures all demand this sort of response. The Queen's workroom is filled with so many traditional symbols of death that we perceive the specific significance of the deadly but tempting apple she holds aloft. The dark stairway topped by a figure of Justice which the Queen appears to have descended at the end of the story is symbolically balanced by the light-filled stairway which Snow White and her Prince ascend; and they move past a tapestry of a symbolic lush garden. The depiction of the apparently dead Snow White is even more carefully balanced; set up like a page from a Book of Hours, it places the Queen's action in perspective by surrounding it with a symbolic depiction of the entire kingdom and the effect of her action on it. Snow White and the Queen on the left are explained by the dragon holding a defenceless rabbit on the right, while the landscape behind these two pictures contains a grim reaper, a sun descending, and clouds dropping rain on the Queen's castle; not surprisingly, the dwarfs are going downhill.

The story of Snow White does not need illustrations; it has been told for centuries without them. But once illustrations exist, they inevitably change the story. It seems worth considering which of these new stories works best—the one by Hyman or the one by Burkert.

Like the original story, Burkert's illustrations do not draw attention to the emotions, the thinking, or even the individual personalities of the characters. Burkert's picture of Snow White is like a portrait photograph; while it is explicit about her appearance, it says nothing specific about her character. It only tells us she is young, innocent, and beautiful—which is all we know about Snow White in the fairy tale. Furthermore, we look at her the way we look at a photograph of a stranger; as detached observers, we admire rather than empathize. As a result, we find ourselves aligned with the values of the original story. Instead of emotional rapport with the characters, we are asked to feel moral approval; and the story shows us that trusting one's emotions, as the Queen does, is actually a matter of self-indulgence.

The atmospheric gloom of Hyman's pictures emphasizes the emotions felt by the characters; her depictions of the rooms people live in give us insight into their characters. In fact, Hyman's pictures oppose the spirit of fairy tales, which were created long before individuality became the all-consuming interest of mankind. By making us see things in emotional terms, Hyman aligns us with the one person in the story who gives in to her emotions—the Queen.

In fact, the mood of Hyman's pictures makes us see the Queen as a kind of Byronic anti-heroine, a liberated woman who feels deeply, tries to shape her own destiny according to her feelings, and is doomed by repressive circumstances to a tragic end. She obviously does not deserve the punishment the story insists she receive; not surprisingly, that punishment is the only important event in the story that Hyman chooses *not* to depict. She does not show Snow White's reward either; but the mood of her picture makes it clear that Snow White is a dull, passive girl who deserves no reward. She does nothing but look blandly pretty, cook and clean, and fall asleep again and again and again. Hyman's emotionally charged pictures are at great odds with the values of the story they are meant to illustrate; Burkert's cool, detached pictures support those values.

Beyond that, there is a matter of rhythm. The isolated moments characteristic of fairy tales that Lüthi talks about are easy to pick out in 'Snow White':

1. The Old Queen sits at the window and pricks her finger.
2. The new Queen sits at her mirror and learns of Snow White's beauty.
3. The hunter tries to kill Snow White, and cannot.
4. The dwarfs find Snow White in their house.
5, 6, 7. The Queen offers Snow White the lace, the comb, and the apple.
8. The dwarfs place Snow White in her glass coffin.
9. The Prince sees Snow White and falls in love.
10. Snow White awakes.

I made this list before I looked at Hyman's and Burkert's pictures; these are the moments that the story itself isolates and etches on our memories, the ones that recur in every retelling in the midst of a variety of other details.

Each of them is something like a picture itself, a clearly perceived moment removed from the flow of events.

Hyman depicts all of these moments, with the interesting exception of the last one. She is not alone in doing so; Wanda Gàg depicted six of them in her version, Jack Kent seven, and both Fritz Wegner and Otto Svend S. nine. But this emphasis on moments the story itself already emphasizes seems wrong. We do not really need to see the moments the story has already carefully and characteristically isolated for us; the result is overemphatic and inappropriately melodramatic.

Furthermore, the moments Hyman depicts between the key ones only emphasize emotions more. She shows us the Queen brooding on Snow White's beauty, the Queen standing jealously at her mirror, the Queen alone and desperate in her room. Gàg, Kent, Wegner, and Otto Svend S. all distort their versions with an unhealthy interest in the cuteness of dwarfs; but Hyman loses the key moments of the story in a welter of deep feelings. Yet again our attention moves from the story's essential meaning to the overemphasized and overpowering atmosphere Hyman provides for it.

Burkert shows only *one* of the key moments, and the one she shows is the least interesting one—Snow White in her coffin as the Prince looks at her, and not, significantly, the more intense moments in which she enters the coffin and leaves it. Burkert depicts the old Queen at her window *before* she pricks her finger; at least there is no blood. And while we see Snow White in the forest, it is *after* the huntsman has left her but *before* she sees the dwarfs' house. Instead of the exciting moment of discovery, Burkert's picture of Snow White with the dwarfs depicts a typical domestic scene, one of the many times that the dwarfs sit down to a meal Snow White has prepared for them. Her next picture shows Snow White in a faint *after* being laced up, not the exciting, triumphant moment of lacing. Finally, the last picture depicts a moment *after* the Queen has danced herself to death but *before* the Prince and Snow White marry. In fact, Burkert does not illustrate the story of Snow White at all; nothing much happens in her pictures, let alone the main events of the story.

In deliberately contradicting the original emphasis of the story, Burkert accomplishes two things. First, she insures that her pictures are not superfluous; she shows us things the story itself does not bother with, so her story is quite different from the original. Second, she takes the paradoxical way in which fairy tales isolate and unite events one step further. The story itself establishes a tension between its key moments and the plot that ties them together; Burkert creates an additional tension between the moments she isolates for our attention and the moments the story isolates for our attention.

Furthermore, the moments Burkert depicts are both relatively unimportant and curiously inactive—people sitting, people in a faint, people standing around at a party waiting for something to happen—moments before or after something important happens. They are both emotionless and motionless; and they are made more motionless by their tightly balanced construction, meticulous attention to detail, and unvaried light, which causes us to regard all things equally and carefully, rather than to notice the flowing lines that move out of darkness toward brightly lit centres of attention in Hyman's pictures. Burkert's pictures not only stop the action, as all pictures must; they also make us concentrate carefully in a way that retards action further. Paradoxically, the static quality of these pictures is what makes them exciting in relation to the fast-moving story they accompany. On the other hand, Hyman's pictures try so hard to mirror the energy of the story that they make either themselves or the story superfluous; looking at them while reading the story is like eating chocolate mousse with a side order of chocolate pudding.

Chocolate pudding is not much like chocolate mousse; and pictures cannot actually depict action or energy. When they attempt to create the effect of action they seem silly, as in the case of the POWs and BAMs and giant fists of comic books, or overripe and melodramatic, as in the case of Hyman's illustrations for 'Snow White'. But when illustrators accept the static quality of pictures and use it in an interplay with the forward thrust of stories, they create exciting, worthwhile books—books like McDermot's *Arrow to the Sun* or Leo and Diane Dillion's *Why Mosquitoes Buzz in People's Ears* (both of which stop action in order to depict it): like *Rosie's Walk* and *Where the Wild Things Are*; and like Burkert's *Snow White*. All these books tell stories about strenuous activity in highly unenergetic pictures that stop time and encourage us to explore the details of space, of texture and shape and colour. They all have spare, undetailed texts and sumptuously rich pictures. And they all create an exciting rhythm that takes advantage of the inevitable differences between two different means of communication.

BLACK AND WHITE
SET THE TONE

Tessa Rose Chester

Children's bookshops today, particularly around Christmas, are Aladdin's caves of unreality, overflowing with picture books full of jewel-like images, or fantastic constructions of technical wizardry. This assault on visual senses that are already saturated by constant exposure to advertising and the media is confusing for both parent and child. Furthermore, the elaborate use of colour found in many children's books is not necessarily an indication of quality, and is more often a superficial device calculated temporarily to seduce, but not sustain, the eye.

One can re-appreciate the attractions of the art of black and white illustration by looking again at some of the classic names from childhood days. Names such as Brock, Shepard, Ardizzone, conjure up nostalgic memories, and their work in the first half of this century is a refreshing antidote to the present glut of polychrome.

Charles Edmund Brock (1870–1938) and his younger brother Harry (Henry Matthew, 1875–1960) belonged to a family of four artist-brothers who lived and worked in Cambridge for more than 50 years. Both Charles and Harry had become established book illustrators by their mid 20s and the standard of their work remained consistently high, unaffected by current artistic trends, despite the output that encompassed huge amounts of magazine and book illustrations.

The most obvious influence on them was Hugh Thomson, who founded the so-called 'costume' school of illustration with his drawings for the Cranford series published by Macmillan in the 1890s, and to which Charles also contributed. The world the Brocks so frequently portrayed was that of a pre-industrial, pastoral haven, less robust perhaps than that of Randolph Caldecott, but no less idyllic. Costumes, furnishings and architectural details were always correct for the period, and their elegant ladies and portly, gaitered gentlemen were instantly recognizable, precisely drawn with a lively, humorous touch.

Charles's illustration to E. Nesbit's *The Railway Children* is typical of the Brock approach. No unnecessary detail is included. There is a suggestion of movement in the angle of the horse's head, of concern in the doctor's

"Now, then, what's the trouble?"

Charles Edmund Brock's illustration of 1906 for Edith Nesbit's *The Railway Children*. Metropolitan Toronto Reference Library

face. The landscape is merely a hint, yet sufficient to set the scene. A charming study from a confident and sure hand.

The Brocks were prolific *Punch* contributors. So, too, was Ernest Shepard (1879–1976), who shared with them a preference for romantic settings peopled by pretty maids and handsome young beaux. Shepard, of course, is best known for his illustrations to A.A. Milne's *Pooh* stories and two verse collections. The partnership was so popular that Milne once commented: 'Anybody who has heard of me has certainly heard of Shepard. Indeed, our names have been associated on so many title pages that I am beginning to wonder which of us is which.'

Shepard's graceful decorations for *When We Were Very Young* (1924) well matched Milne's light, whimsical verse with its mixture of sentiment and irony, while his drawings for *Winnie-the-Pooh* (1926) and its sequel helped create a permanent place for Pooh and his friends in the nation's heart. In the original pen and ink drawing for the frontispiece to *The House at Pooh Corner* (1928) the affection between Christopher Robin and his bear is beautifully expressed with deliberate economy of line and the delicacy characteristic of all Shepard's work.

Both Shepard and the Brocks produced comfortable visions of a rose-tinted past. Edward Ardizzone (1900–79) also depicted an England seen through a haze of half-memory, half-myth, but added other dimensions that make him one of the greatest illustrators of this century. From years of observation, he was able to transfer a deep understanding of people and situations onto the page, and had a special eye for all corners of life, however shabby and cramped. He was as happy drawing the bustle of a London street as he was depicting children picking acorns in a Welsh field.

His work is full of movement, humour, character, and a paradoxical combination of realism and fantasy. One peers into this vanished world that is unmistakably Ardizzone, only to find it is familiar, and that his blowzy ladies, elderly gents, newspaper boys and village girls are all around us still, in the park, on the bus, at the corner of the street. He has a narrator's skill with the pen, subtly expanding the text, catching the author's mood and recreating it in his own special way. And when he applies colour, it is restrained, and never dominates the drawing, which, as he said himself, is always of paramount importance.

In 1961, Ardizzone wrote that illustrating other people's books was never quite as easy or pleasant as illustrating one's own, though the work of a fine and poetic writer was a different matter. For example, he found the illustration of Walter de la Mare's *Peacock Pie* 'sheer delight', and though his own excellent Little Tim series showed just what could be achieved by

Ernest Shepard's frontispiece to *The House at Pooh Corner*, 1928. Metropolitan Toronto Reference Library

the author/artist, his best work for children can be seen in his response to the rhythm and song and childhood memories in both *Peacock Pie* and Eleanor Farjeon's *The Little Bookroom*.

How well he captures the spirit of the three jolly farmers, clicking their fingers as they leap round and round, 'footing a lightsome' through Watchet, Week and Wye—and how well, too, he conveys a quite different atmosphere in the chapter heading to Farjeon's 'The Glass Peacock'. There he depicts a grimy courtyard in an old London alley, where children skip and dance to the organ-grinder, or peer longingly into the bow windows of the sweet-shop. A sense of yearning and pathos pervades this little scene, setting the tone for the following tale.

Ardizzone's timeless evocations of rural and urban life, safe harbours from present cruel seas, are evidence of a genius at work, one who never underestimated the emotional power of line drawing. This is the secret of successful book illustration. When energy and sensations are allied to a proper sympathy and respect for the accompanying poetry or prose, then the illustrations will give a child a uniquely satisfying and lasting visual experience.

THE CONSTRUCTEDNESS OF TEXTS: PICTURE BOOKS AND THE METAFICTIVE

David Lewis

Imagine a conversation around the dinner table. The subject is books. You overhear someone enthusiastically describing what they have recently read, but you miss the titles and authors. You hear of a story where the main character is a compulsive tale-teller misleading the other characters and redescribing insignificant events in outrageous detail. Someone else recounts the astonishing exploits of a character who, when threatened by adversaries, can step out of his role as a fictional character and re-create his circumstances in authorial fashion so that his enemies are foiled. Staggering! A third voice chips in with the outline of a book where a young girl appears to be simultaneously a character within two stories and then goes on to describe another book by the same author where the reader is given so much repetitive, trivial detail that the narrative seems submerged in a welter of information.

This sounds pretty avant-garde stuff, and being a bookish sort yourself you are keen to get involved. But who and what on earth are they talking about? You are deciding you really must find out more when you hear praised to the skies a book whose richness and humour arises from diverse fragments of text which must be physically lifted out from the fabric of the book itself and unfolded in order to be read. Suddenly you catch the words 'picture book', and all is made plain. We are not dealing with the sophisticated avant-garde at all but with good old favourites like Jill Murphy, Anthony Browne, John Burningham and the Ahlbergs.

Could such a misunderstanding come about? Admittedly I have stacked the cards somewhat by suggesting a wholly imaginary set of circumstances. This has given me the opportunity to summarize some well-known picture books in a slightly unusual fashion, but I don't think I have distorted them too much. I think that *On the Way Home, Bear Hunt, Come Away from the Water, Shirley, Where's Julius?* and *The Jolly Postman* are discernible through my sketchy outlines. We just don't usually think about them in that way. I believe that the kind of misunderstanding I have tried to suggest in my own little fiction is not beyond possibility because, although many popular and successful contemporary picture books for the young do lend themselves quite naturally to the kinds of summary description attempted above, our familiar ways of thinking and talking and writing about picture books tend to limit what we can say about them (something that is true of all ways of thinking and talking). In other words, there is a tendency for us not to perceive picture books as unconventional and exceptional creations despite the fact that they frequently possess a playful and subversive quality.

In what follows I want to explore the distinctive and quite remarkable features of some of the most popular contemporary picture books and, in addition, consider the reasons why we remain largely blind to these features. I also wish to suggest some ways to see more of what we may hitherto have been missing. A good place to begin might be with my parallel between picture books and 'experimental' fiction.

Postmodernism and the picture book

The kind of experimental or avant-garde writing I have in mind is that written in the last thirty years or so and variously associated with terms like 'fabulation', 'metafiction', or 'postmodernism'. The labels are not particularly important. Metafiction catches the quality of this kind of writing best, emphasizing its refusal to take for granted how stories should be told and thus implicitly commenting upon the nature of fiction itself. However, postmodernism is the name we hear most often. In America writers like John Barth, Donald Barthelme, Richard Brautigan, Thomas Pynchon, Leonard Michaels and William Gass, and in Europe Italo Calvino, Alain Robbe-Grillet, Samuel Beckett, Milan Kundera, B.S. Johnson and John Fowles have explored, in their novels and short stories, the codes and conventions of storytelling that usually remain implicit—and thereby invisible—in works of realist fiction. Their books are to varying degrees explorations of what it means to create, and by implication to interpret, the illusory world of a story.

Such writers were, and still are, considered to be experimental and unorthodox though, increasingly, metafictional elements may be found in mainstream contemporary fiction. The recent bestsellers *Foucault's Pendulum* by Umberto Eco and *A History of the World in 10½ Chapters* by Julian Barnes are good examples of how the postmodern impulse may be assimilated into traditional fictional modes.

To illustrate the parallels between postmodernism in adult literature and the contemporary picture book, let us briefly consider three metafictional devices that can readily be found in each. John Barth, Kurt Vonnegut and Milan Kundera among others quite frequently interrupt the flow of narrative in their books to allow the 'author' to address readers directly or, alternatively, a character from one level of narration may appear in another. In *Narrative Discourse* Gérard Genette calls such slippages 'metalepses' and cites the example of a book by the Latin American writer Julio Cortazar, in which there is a tale of a reader murdered by a character in the book he is reading. Similar examples of narrative 'boundary-breaking' are relatively common in picture books too. *Bear Hunt* by Anthony Browne has already been referred to, and further examples may be found in Monique Felix's *Story of a Little Mouse Trapped in a Book*, Alan Baker's *Benjamin's Book*, Henrik Drescher's *Simon's Book*, and *Monsters* by Russell Hoban and Quentin Blake. All these books expose and subvert levels of narrative which, in realistic fiction, are normally quite stable.

A second parallel might be found in the way both categories of book (adult and children's) frequently delight in displays of sheer excess. Donald Barthelme, Thomas Pynchon, Richard Brautigan and Alain Robbe-Grillet, for example, resort to various forms of verbal or narrative gigantism, an accumulation of detail beyond the norm for literary effects. This might compare with, say, the tall tales of *On the Way Home* by Jill Murphy, the exploded universe of Satoshi Kitamura's *Angry Arthur* or the minutely detailed menu-like lists in John Burningham's *Where's Julius?* Here we see how real-seeming stories rely for their effects upon a learned but otherwise unnoticed codification of information—an 'economy of significance', as Susan Stewart puts it in *On Longing*. Thus when we have too much information to deal with, our settled perceptions of a recognizable secondary world are tested and we have difficulty constructing an intelligible story.

Finally, when we have too *little* information, we often find that issues within a story which we would normally expect to have resolved are in fact undecidable. Picture books like *Granpa* and *Come Away from the Water, Shirley* by John Burningham and *How Tom Beat Captain Najork and His Hired Sportsmen* by Russell Hoban and Quentin Blake contain high levels of indeterminacy not wholly unlike that found in John Fowles's *The French Lieutenant's Woman*, Pynchon's *The Crying of Lot 49*, Philip Roth's *The Counterlife* and Calvino's *If on a Winter's Night a Traveller*, where outcomes are left unresolved or relationships remain permanently unclear.

It is, I believe, far from accidental that these three features—narrative *boundary-breaking* or 'slippage', *excess*, and *indeterminacy*—are common to both children's picture books and postmodern literature. They suggest ways of studying, describing and evaluating picture books, and we shall return to

In *The Baby* Burningham's illustrations hint at a pre-school child's drawings of a new sibling.

consider them later. Before that, I need to make explicit what has until this point been implicit: the nature of the fictional mode being undermined and subverted by the metafictive. We must leave picture books aside temporarily and make a lengthy but necessary digression into literary realism.

Realism and rules

Implicit in my comparison of certain kinds of contemporary picture book with postmodern literature is the belief that the picture books cited, and

COURTNEY

John Burningham

In both style and story Burningham's tale of a family factotum appeals to early school-age children.

many more like them, deviate in significant ways from some kind of fictional norm. Clearly there are many types, modes and genres within the broad category of fiction, and equally clearly picture books could be subdivided in the same way that we habitually distinguish romances from horror stories. But I see picture books deviating from the norm not so much because they occupy different slots within a genre typology (fairy tales and animal fantasies, say, rather than thrillers and murder mysteries) but because they regularly refuse to conform to the conventions that apply generally to *all* fiction.

In reviewing the nature of literary realism I want to lift the bonnet, so to speak, just a crack on the motor that drives the kinds of stories we are most familiar with. We need to get a grip on how such stories work so that we can see more clearly what it is that we normally take for granted and thus what it is that metafictional techniques and devices—whether in picture books or adult fiction—expose.

1. *Illusionism*

When we read a story, we rarely reflect upon the rules and the literary conventions that have been followed in its creation and that we, in our readerly, symmetrical fashion, are following as we read. Withdrawing attention from the fictional events to attend to how they were put together interrupts the flow of the narrative and breaks the involvement with the secondary world of the tale—and usually happens only when books are being studied systematically rather than read unreflectively. We take the illusion of the story world pretty much for granted, and we expect the reading experience to provide, in Susanne Langer's words, 'the illusion of a life in the mode of a virtual past'. In other words, the reading of fiction seems to require that we lose our normal, everyday consciousness of self and submerge it in the virtual, illusory lives of others.

So used are we to reading stories in this mode (and viewing them, for that matter, as the same holds true for the vast majority of film and TV fiction) that we tend to accept it as natural and normal, and there seems to be little to say about it. In its most extreme forms, where we become 'lost' in a book, the medium itself—language—becomes invisible as we read or listen. If such an account of reading and books seems a little too prescriptive, think of how, as a culture, we laud books that 'grip', 'move' and 'engage' us most. Think of how a good writer for children can weave a spell that leaves the reader transfixed, deaf to all voices save those in the head.

Clearly there is a good deal of variety in the extent to which fictional texts aim, or are able, to create 'the illusion of a life . . .' and, significantly, much depends on the reader. After all, we do not have to succumb to the spell. Literary study itself would be impossible if the invitation to become involved were an offer we could not refuse! Indeed, it is a characteristic of experienced readers that they freely move in and out of fictional texts savouring not only the ebb and flow of the tale but also the skill and artistry of the writer.

The most important point here, however, is that this absorption in fictional worlds would be impossible without the reader's knowledge of the rules and codes and conventions that go into the construction of different kinds of text. (See, for example, Todorov on 'Reading as Construction'.) Fictional texts can be 'activated' only to the extent that the reader possesses what Jonathan Culler calls 'literary competence'. An important part of such a competence would be interpreting and synthesizing the information being parcelled out to us by the author in order to construct a self-consistent secondary world.

2. Narrative closure

In *Critical Practice* Catherine Belsey surveys and summarizes much of the theoretical work that has been carried out in this field, and to the illusionism discussed above she adds two further key features of the realist mode. One is the sense of closure that we have when we approach the end of a realist text. As we read, we sense that the story is 'going somewhere' and that all will be satisfactorily resolved in the end. Loose ends will be tied up, and we will retrospectively come to understand much that has gone before.

Once again, there will be some variation in the extent to which closure can be effected but, generally speaking, the vast majority of printed narratives proceed from the establishment or assumption of some kind of order, through a disturbance or disruption of that order—an adventure, a mystery, a murder, a love affair—towards an inevitable resolution wherein the original order is reinstated or developed. Our implicit and naturalized understanding of narrative closure ensures that we are no more aware of it as a feature of the *constructedness* of texts than we are aware of what produces the phenomenon of illusionism.

This 'sense of an ending', to use Frank Kermode's phrase, is very easily disturbed, however. In normal circumstances, even if the plot of a story is densely tangled, we would expect some kind of resolution, but if the resolution were endlessly deferred—say, to a point well beyond the end of the narrative and thus inaccessible to the reader—we would feel that some crucial part of the reading experience was missing. I have suggested already that some postmodernist writers exploit this expectation to create their effects of dislocation and disorientation. In Thomas Pynchon's *The Crying of Lot 49*, for example, the one essential clue that will resolve the dilemmas and puzzles that lie at the heart of the story—the 'lot 49' of the title—remains beyond the reader's reach. The story finishes as the main character settles down at an auction where the lot in question, the nature of which neither we nor the central character are privy to, is to be sold.

3. Discourses and narrative

Belsey's third key feature of realist text is what she terms the 'hierarchy of discourses'. She draws attention to the fact that stories aiming for realistic effects usually comprise a number of different discourses, languages or voices. Sometimes this will simply mean the weaving together of the strands of a dialogue, in which the author creates a form of writing that is as convincing as speech. In a complex novel the forms of language an author might employ could include different kinds of written text—letters, diaries, various technical vocabularies—as well as a great variety of spoken forms. What we habitually refer to as an author's style is actually determined by the distinctive ways he or she orchestrates these different forms of language.

In his important collection of essays *The Dialogic Imagination* Mikhail Bakhtin argues that it is this multiform quality that marks out the novelistic impulse. In the hands of the most creative novelists it leads to a polyphony, the interweaving of voices, manners and modes that is the hallmark of the great novel.

Writers working squarely in the traditions of realism manage to convince us of the naturalism of their tales by ordering the disparate voices and languages of the story into a *hierarchy*. Belsey writes:

> The hierarchy works above all by means of a privileged discourse which places as subordinate all the discourses that are literally or figuratively between inverted commas.

Most often this 'privileged discourse' takes the form of an authorial, narrating voice which guides the reader into interpreting the other voices out of which the story is woven. As we read, we seem naturally and effortlessly to understand motives, thoughts, emotions, consequences. Though we are not usually aware of it, we are taken by the hand and led through the maze and shown how to make sense of everything.

When this embedding discourse is ruptured or is missing altogether, the embedded discourses become free floating and can be very difficult to locate within the scheme of things. Consider this extract from Donald Barthelme's short story 'Great Days':

> —Friendship's the best thing.
> —One of the best things. One of the very best.
> —I performed in a hall. Alone under the burning lights.
> —The hall ganged with admiring faces. Except for a few.
> —Julia was there. Rotten Julia.
> —But I mean you really like her don't you?
> —Well I mean who doesn't like violet eyes?

—Got to make the effort, scratch where it itches, plans, schemes, directives, guidelines.

—Well I mean who doesn't like frisky knees?

—Yes she's lost her glow. Gone utterly.

—The strains of the city working upon an essentially non-urban sensibility.

—But I love the city and will not hear it traduced.

—Well, me too. But after all. But still.

Composed of fragmentary utterances, a story like this can leave the reader with a sense of dislocation, wondering who is speaking to whom and what the significance of some of the remarks might be. It is not even clear how many voices are entwined in this rambling discourse. A more traditionally ordered tale would indicate how all these loose threads were to be woven into a pattern. The simple device of 'he said . . . she said . . .' would go a long way towards clearing up what is going on. The important point to be made here is that, when it is present in conventional realist text, we assume the *authority* of the voice that says 'he said . . . she said . . .' at the very same time that we assume its *absence*. We are usually simply not aware, inasmuch as the flow of the story is concerned, of these linking, ordering devices. Postmodern fictions often foreground our reliance upon such devices and bring to consciousness our need for the self-effacing, narrating voice.

Let me try to sum up the point and the significance of this digression into literary realism. The stories we are most familiar with, the ones we take to be 'natural' and 'straightforward', are in fact sophisticated textual artefacts that work to create within us the illusion of a real world that we share with the characters. Such stories are shaped and ordered in such a way that they make a strong, and in many cases irresistible, appeal to us. Thus we savour the resolutions and the dénouements without being aware of the constructedness of these movements. Similarly, we are unaware of what might be called the connective tissue of realist text, the way the textual bone and muscle is articulated to create a moving, convincing whole.

For all of us, realism is the commonest coin in the literary economy and is, therefore, most easily overlooked and misunderstood—it is for all of us naturalized and made commonsensical from the moment we begin to hear stories and share books with parents and caregivers. From the beginning we take realism for granted, and its techniques become invisible to us. It is, of course, no more natural than any other type of text, and whether we realize it or not, we learn its techniques and its conventions as children, for most of us at the same time as we learn to read.

What we are inescapably led to is the realization that there are always two participants in the making of a story at the point of reading: the text and the reader. Writers write books in the way they do because they share with their readers a set of understandings about how texts work. In *Structuralist Poetics* Jonathan Culler puts it like this:

> To be an experienced reader of literature is . . . to have gained a sense of what can be done with literary works and thus to have assimilated a system which is largely interpersonal.

It is this relatively stable interpersonal system (writers and readers sharing assumptions about textuality) that is disturbed and subverted by the metafictive. We are brought to see, in an exaggerated way, the gaps that exists between text, story and reader. There is a distinct pleasure to be had from confronting such disturbances to the settled decorum of literature—a pleasure we might call *interstitial*—and we are now quite used to the idea of sophisticated writers stretching Culler's sense of 'what can be done' to the very limit for the delectation of their sophisticated readers. Each Booker Prize shortlist, for example, contains new frissons for the educated reading public, and the boundaries of what can count as a work of fiction are constantly being eroded. What we are perhaps less familiar with is the idea of sophisticated writers and illustrators doing precisely the same thing for the least experienced readers—the beginners and the very young.

Constituting the picture book

If it is true that many picture books seem to be fashioned in a nonrealist mode, if they persistently and habitually cut across the realist grain, we might ask why this feature is so seldom remarked upon. The reason is, as I suggested at the outset, that we are limited in what we can say about picture books by our familiar ways of thinking and talking and writing about them. This is an important point, and one that arises from a crucial feature of language and its use: its constitutive function.

When we name things, we call them into being. We permit them to enter our consciousness but only in the garb in which we have dressed them. We see this process in operation particularly clearly when we *rename* things. All teachers, for example, will be familiar with the way mothers and fathers of children attending school are now described, in the official jargon, not simply as *parents* with specific interests and concerns (the care, welfare and well-being of their children) but *consumers* of education with a consumer's attendant interests and concerns (value for money, a high standard of product, and so on). Similarly, there is more than one way to describe or analyse picture books, but each time we attempt analysis or description we are constrained by the particular vocabulary we have at our disposal. There is only so much that is sayable or thinkable within each discourse. If we review briefly some of the main ways picture books are written about and discussed, we may see how certain features become highlighted and others obscured or suppressed.

Let us consider then three ways in which picture books are often described and analysed. We might call these descriptive vocabularies or discourses the *pedagogic*, the *aesthetic* and the *literary*. The *pedagogic* constitutes the picture book as text for the beginner reader. This form of discourse is founded upon educational assumptions about the paramount importance of the long-term attainment of reading competence. It tends to generate a privileging of the printed word and a gravitating of attention away from the pictorial aspects of the form. Important though it is, this order of description often relegates the pictures to the lowly role of prop for the beginner reader who is tackling print for the first time. The pictures thus become one of several cue systems that new readers might exploit to sustain their construction of a meaning that is assumed to be generated primarily, if not solely, from the printed word. Much reviewing of picture books draws upon this approach.

In contrast the *aesthetic* constitutes the picture book as a book of pictures. The discourse here draws on art criticism or art history and, not surprisingly, it usually causes the written text to drop below the horizon while pictorial or illustrative matters are dealt with. There may well be acknowledgement of the importance of the written text to the over-all success of a particular book, or to picture books generally, but this usually takes the form of little more than a gesture towards the 'balance' of pictures and words or towards the way they 'enhance' each other. But there can be no sustained analysis of the diverse ways in which words and pictures might interact, for the discourse itself does not admit the verbal elements as an object of attention. However, such an approach does have the great value of making us pause and look more closely at pictures we might otherwise simply glance at. At its best this approach helps us see more acutely.

Finally, the *literary*. What happens to the picture book when it is absorbed into the broader category of children's literature? Often it is submerged without trace. Just as children's literature is frequently considered to be little more than capital-L Literature writ small, so picture books are taken to be 'just stories' writ even smaller. Statements about the current state of children's books, or about their future or their past, often fail to consider picture books at all or, at best, treat them as a marginal genre, or a larval stage of literature proper.

Jacqueline Rose, for example, in her recent study of the discourses of childhood and the children's book, has claimed that the language of literary realism is 'gravitating down to the nursery'. 'Realism,' she claims, 'is being asserted with increasing urgency in relation to fiction for the child.' While I feel this to be most certainly true for the kinds of developed narrative text she quotes and examines, I think the claim that such an unambiguous aesthetic dominates books in 'the nursery' cannot withstand examination. Indeed, if 'nursery' is taken to extend roughly across the early years of schooling, there are altogether different concerns being urged upon the reader. Either Rose is simply not interested in the picture book—in which case we are entitled to ask why she lumps the youngest children in with the rest—or she simply fails to perceive any difference between picture books and other forms of children's literature.

My point in briefly surveying these varied perspectives is not to carp about their failings but to demonstrate, first, that working within any form of analytic or critical discourse restricts the writer to a particular vocabulary that will construe the object of study in certain ways and, second, that our more familiar ways of writing and speaking about picture books have obscured some of their distinctive, interesting features. I do not suggest that the pedagogic, the aesthetic or the literary should—or even could—be replaced, but I would like to offer the outline of another view that may allow us to see the picture book afresh.

Reconstituting the picture book

So far I have urged that many of our most popular and acclaimed picture books possess highly distinctive features that are seldom fully and specifically acknowledged. I have suggested that these features might be best characterized by the way they deviate from, or cut across, the ubiquitous conventions of realist fiction, and I have also suggested that we have failed to recognize the metafictive features because we are bound by forms of discourse that only provide a partial view of what is in fact a compound and complex whole. An adequate theory of the picture book must directly address the bifurcated nature of the form (words *and* pictures) and must account for the whole range of types and kinds, including the metafictive. While elaborating such theory is beyond the scope of one short article,

I will try to suggest the direction from which such a theory might come.

Picture books of all kinds are inescapably plural. They always require a command of two different forms of signification: the verbal or textual and the pictorial or iconic. Meaning is always generated in at least two different ways. It is simply not possible to read a picture-book story as you would illustrated prose. Attention always has to be withdrawn from one aspect (the pictorial, say) for it to be directed to the other. The gap between the two may be smoothed over, and this is most commonly done by assuming the pictures to be in the service of the words, there being but one story parcelled out rather unequally between the two. Such a view forces upon sequences of words and pictures a greater degree of homogeneity than they warrant and blurs the distinction between what the words tell us and what the pictures show us. Many metafictive picture books prise open the gap between the words and the pictures, pushing them apart and forcing the reader/viewer to work hard to forge the relationship between them. Sometimes the gap is wide enough for the relationship to remain wholly indeterminate.

When we look at a picture book, we attend to and 'read' both pictures and words. They act upon each other so that, to a greater or lesser degree, we read the pictures through the words and the words through the pictures. To put this another way, the two 'languages', or systems of notation, *relativize* each other. Picture-book makers have always attended to this feature of the form, and are sensitive to the many ways in which words and pictures may be played off against each other. Randolph Caldecott's work is exemplary in this respect, as in much else.

This unceasing interplay and interaction of word and image in the picture book is one of two main reasons for the form's extraordinary openness and flexibility. It appears to be able to absorb and ingest other, more closed and 'finished' forms. It is itself very much a motley, a ragbag of different genres, types, manners and modes, many of them non-narrative in kind and all bringing with them their different forms and registers of language. All are easily accommodated within the flexible category of 'picture book'.

Once pictorialized (a better term than 'illustrated', I feel, despite its clumsiness) no one type or genre remains immune to the relativizing influence of the visual image. Consider, for example, how the complete and timeless form of the traditional fairy tale bends and stretches under the influence of Tony Ross, or how it becomes intertwined with a host of other discourses and language registers in the hands of the Ahlbergs. Consider also how the alphabet book and the counting book, both of which are inherently tightly constrained forms, become interpenetrated with elements from other forms when treated by, say, Shirley Hughes or Satoshi Kitamura. Not only do we have words and images rubbing shoulders, but different kinds of words, even in some instances different kinds of images.

Viewed like this, the picture book begins to emerge as a kind of super-genre, always developing and open-ended. In this respect the picture book strongly resembles the novel as characterized by Bakhtin in *The Dialogic Imagination*. For Bakhtin the novel is a polyphony of 'voices' and 'languages' skilfully woven into a whole; it develops perpetually by devouring other genres, both literary and nonliterary, and thus continually shapes and reshapes itself. According to Bakhtin the novel possesses this singular characteristic because it is the only form of verbal art that is in constant close contact with the unfinished and incomplete nature of contemporary life. This feature of Bakhtin's analysis suggests to me the second main reason for the picture book's openness and flexibility.

The picture book too is in close communion with the still-evolving and the incomplete, and its open-ended quality arises from contact with the developing world of the young child. Many picture books have the air of refusing to take anything for granted; they seem to assume an audience for whom the shape and nature of much in the world, especially the activity called reading, is still in flux. Culler speaks of readers who have developed a sense of 'what can be done with literary works', but beginning readers are precisely those for whom the issue of 'what can be done' is *not yet settled*. What counts as 'reading' and what counts as 'a book' and what counts as 'a story' are still open questions. The way we normally speak of 'learning to read' disguises from us the fact that as children learn *how* to read they are also learning *what* reading is. Picture-book makers are clearly alert to this fact—that for their primary audience little need be taken for granted—and respond with displays of fluid invention that writers of prose narrative for older, more experienced readers find hard to match.

Viewed in this light we see that the two basic, and crucial, features of the picture-book form are, first, its ineradicably bifurcated nature, a duality that causes us to read any individual element of a particular book through, or in the light of, the other elements that surround or embed it. Thus we read the pictures through the words and the words through the pictures. In Bakhtin's terminology, each one becomes 'dialogized'. Second, picture books tend to be produced for an audience for whom the world in general (and the portion of it we adults call literacy) is in a perpetual state of becoming. What counts as a book and what counts as reading are, at this stage, not set in concrete.

Both these features tend to push the picture-book form towards a state of flexibility and fluidity where other, already existing forms can be appropriated and ingested, each one coming into contact with the dialogizing influence of the visual image and often into contact with other, similarly ingested forms.

The metafictive in picture books can now be seen as an extreme and exaggerated manifestation of a tendency already deeply rooted in the form itself. By its nature, the picture book tends towards openness, the playful, the parodic—fertile ground in which the metafictive can flourish.

The metafictive in the picture book

I began by discussing parallels between some well-known contemporary picture books and the movement in adult fiction known as postmodernism. I now conclude by returning briefly to the three metafictional features mentioned there and consider their emergence in the picture book. The three features were: *excess*, *indeterminacy* and *boundary-breaking*.

1. *Excess*

Going too far, or 'over the top', is commonplace in the culture of childhood. When boundaries are unclear and limits unknown, to paraphrase William Blake, you cannot know what is enough until you know what is more than enough. We find this concern with testing limits—linguistic, literary, social, conceptual, ethical, narrative—reflected time and again in picture books for the young. The traditional cumulative tale, for example, is exploited and subjected to endless variations in books like *Mr Grumpy's Outing* by John Burningham, *Mrs Armitage on Wheels* by Quentin Blake, and *On the Way Home* by Jill Murphy. In this last book there is an accumulation of preposterous, contradictory tales that puts to the test not only the reader's sense of narrative logic and consistency but also the ethical sense of what is appropriate for little children to tell others.

The unthinkable and the unmentionable appear with startling regularity in picture books. Alarming, disturbing or embarrassing possibilities are tested in John Burningham's *Would You Rather . . .* , a piling up of extravagant images that the reader is invited to contemplate. Many of the options on display are grotesquely comic, others put social norms under strain. *Angry Arthur* by Hiawyn Oram and Satoshi Kitamura portrays the astonishing results of one little boy's temper tantrum—the destruction of the universe, no less. Again, in an accumulation of increasingly extravagant imagery that goes well beyond the bounds of the 'normal', John

Burningham's *Where's Julius?* heaps up textual detail in the form of endless mealtime menus that far exceeds what is necessary for the realistic depiction of a domestic milieu. These books exhibit what Susan Stewart calls 'a festive display of accumulation over balance', which resists a too rapid and easy entry into the decorum of the storybook.

2. Indeterminacy

All stories are built upon gaps, upon absence. We know how to read the cinematic 'cut' when we jump from one scene to another in a film, and we have no problems building a tale from partial information. Indeed metafictive excess teaches us how ridiculous it would be for a writer to try to say absolutely everything. Some picture books expose the gaps for us and reveal the comic absurdity of the situation we are left in when textual props are missing. Two examples show the possibilities open to the picture-book maker.

How Tom Beat Captain Najork . . . by Russell Hoban and Quentin Blake has at its heart a series of three testing 'games' that are conspicuous by their absence. Womble, Muck and Sneedball are named (and thus brought into being as actualities within the tale) but the reader is never allowed to learn the precise nature of these ludicrous pursuits, though Blake's illustrations give some inkling of their complexity, and we are teased with some hints and suggestions about scoring and so on.

Come Away from the Water, Shirley and its companion piece, *Time to Get Out of the Bath, Shirley*, by John Burningham also rely upon an absence, but here it is a deliberate withholding of information about how two sequences of images are related. The pictures and words on the left-hand pages clearly relate to the images on the right-hand pages in some way (the figure of the little girl appears at the beginning and the end of the book with her parents on the beach) but we are left to make up our own minds about the precise nature of the relationship. Of course, an alternative way of reading the Shirley books is to accept and savour the indeterminacy itself.

3. Boundary-breaking

As I have suggested, all metafictive devices involve the transgressing of boundaries since, by definition, the metafictive draws attention to conventions by breaking them. We can give boundary-breaking a more specific meaning by linking it to the kind of slippage (Genette's *metalepsis*) mentioned earlier. Browne's bear draws his way out of difficulty in a light-hearted act of parody. Drawing is the artist's province, not the fictional character's. Similarly, Shirley Hughes's *Chips and Jessie* address the reader directly at the beginning of the book in which they appear as eponymous figures, for all the world as though they were really existing people. The fact that they speak of Shirley Hughes as a friend adds extra dimensions to the play. The creature at the heart of Monique Felix's *Story of a Little Mouse Trapped in a Book* finds a way out of her prison by tearing out a 'page', fashioning it into a paper aeroplane and gliding down to safety in the landscape revealed by the torn-out paper. Thus the very fabric of the book is fictionalized.

These three metafictive devices exemplify the freedom from literary constraint that makers of picture books for the young frequently appropriate. They are not mutually exclusive categories but ways in which the invention of the picture-book maker, liberated by the freedom and flexibility of the form, can manifest itself. I have suggested that an examination of the metafictive in the picture book can lead to a way of framing the subject so that we see the picture book grounded in the inseparability of texts and readers and constituted as a compound and flexible form. By acknowledging and addressing these features we may find ways of examining and studying the articulation of word and image in what is without question one of the most extraordinary and innovative of literary/artistic forms.

References

Bakhtin, Mikhail, *The Dialogic Imagination: Four Essays*, University of Texas Press, 1981

Belsey, Catherine, *Critical Practice*, Methuen, 1980

Culler, Jonathan, 'Prolegomena to a Theory of Reading' in Susan

Suleiman and Inge Crossman, *The Reader in the Text: Essays on Audience and Interpretation*, Princeton University Press, 1980

Culler, Jonathan, *Structuralist Poetics: Structuralism, Linguistics and the Study of Literature*, Routledge & Kegan Paul, 1975

Genette, Gérard, *Narrative Discourse: An Essay in Method*, Basil Blackwell, 1980

Kermode, Frank, *The Sense of an Ending: Studies in the Theory of Fiction*, Oxford University Press, 1966

Rose, Jacqueline, *The Case of Peter Pan, or The Impossibility of Children's Fiction*, Macmillan, 1984

Stewart, Susan, *On Longing: Narratives of the Miniature, the Gigantic, the Souvenir and the Collection*, Johns Hopkins University Press, 1984

Todorov, Tzvetan, 'Reading as Construction' in Susan Suleiman and Inge Crossman, *The Reader in the Text: Essays on Audience and Interpretation*, Princeton University Press, 1980

PART VII

GENDER RELATIONS

THE ABSENT MOTHER: WOMEN AGAINST WOMEN IN OLD WIVES' TALES

Marina Warner

Plato defined fairytales, in the oldest theory about them, as tales told by nurses. Possibly the earliest story extant that recognisably anticipates the classic fairytales—*Cinderella* and *Beauty and the Beast*—is Apuleius's *Cupid and Psyche*, interpolated in his metaphysical comedy, *The Golden Ass*, written in the second century AD. In the novel, a young bride is captured by bandits and separated from her husband and thrown into a cave; there, a disreputable old woman chooses to tell her the story of Psyche's troubles before she reaches happiness and marriage with Cupid. It is 'an old wives' tale', she says, (*anilis fabula*) and will distract her from her troubles.

Charles Perrault, in his preface to the fourth edition of his classic collection of fairytales, first published in 1695, under the title *Contes du Temps Passé* or *Contes de ma Mère l'Oye*, issued an apologia on their behalf, linking them explicitly to the comic tradition of Milesian tales to which Apuleius belongs, and comparing his own directly with *Cupid and Psyche*: It is 'une fiction toute pure et un conte de vieille comme celuy de Peau-d'Ane (Donkey-skin)', which was also told, he went on, by old women, grandmothers and governesses to the children in their charge. However, the moral of *Cupid and Psyche* is impenetrable, he wrote, while his own is patently clear.

The femaleness of fairytale as a genre manifests itself historically, through attested storytellers, literary interpreters, and their audiences. The *veillées*, as storytelling gatherings were called in France, offered women an opportunity to talk—to preach—which was forbidden them in other situations, the pulpit, the forum, and frowned upon and feared in the spinning rooms and by the wellside. Though male collectors have dominated the publication of popular wondertales, from the Venetian, Giovan Francesco Straparola, who published the rumbunctious *Le piace voli notti* in 1550, to indefatigable nineteenth-century folklorists like the Scotsman, Andrew Lang, who created the Blue, Green, Red, et al. Fairy Books at the turn of the century and after, women have not been laggards in the related fields of folklore and children's literature. Female talespinners outnumber males by ten to one in the forty-one-volume *Cabinet des fées*, an anthology of seventeenth- and eighteenth-century stories.

It reveals the durable affinity of the female sex with fairytale that Straparola's talespinners (like Boccaccio's before him) figure as so many Sheherazades using narrative to bring about a resolution of mercy and justice. Andrew Lang relied on his wife Leonora Alleyne, as well as a team of women editors, transcribers, and paraphrasers to produce the many volumes of fairystories and folktales from around the world. Oscar Wilde's father, a doctor in Merrion Square, Dublin in the mid-nineteenth century, used to ask for stories as his fee from his poorer patients; he then wrote them down. Many of these were told to him by women. The sources used by Calvino for his classic anthology of Italian folktales were chiefly women and mostly illiterate.

The matter of fairytales reflects lived experience, with a slant towards the tribulations of women, and especially young women of marriageable age: the telling of the stories (assuming the presence of a Mother Goose either as an historical source, or a fantasy of origin) gains credibility as a fatalistic record of lives lived, of characters known, and shapes the expectations of the young in a certain direction.

The orality of the genre remains central even in the most artificial and elaborate literary versions or inventions of the Victorians. It is often carried in the texts through an imagined narrator, (a grandmotherly or nanny type, called Gammer Gurton or Mother Hubbard, as well as Mother Goose or some such cosy name); the consequent style imitates speech, with chatty asides, plentiful exclamations, direct appeals to the imaginary circle round the hearth, rambling descriptions, gossipy parentheses, and other bedside or lap-like mannerisms create an illusion of collusive intimacies, of home, of the bedtime story, the winter's tale.

Yet, while fairytales tend to shore up traditional views, and circulate the lessons of the *status quo*, they can also act as fifth columnists, burrowing from within; utopian yearnings beat strongly in the heart of fairytale. Many writers, Salman Rushdie included, hide under its guileless and apparently childish façade, wrap its cloak of unreality around them, and adopting its traditional formal simplicities, attempt to challenge received ideas, many of them to do with the expectations of the sexes. Feminism and the fairytale have been strongly associated, in the saints' lives which are entangled in many stories, in the writings of the French *précieuses* and their disciples, like Marie-Jeanne Lheritier, Marie-Catherine d'Aulnoy, Gabrielle-Suzanne de Villeneuve, and Jeanne-Marie Leprince de Beaumont, who all campaigned through their fairytales for women's greater independence, and against arranged marriages.

Nineteenth- and early twentieth-century writers of both sexes also struggled to shape an egalitarian, communal, anti-materialist ethic, like John Ruskin with *The King of the Golden Mountain*, and Frank L. Baum, in *The Wizard of Oz* books, where he fantasised a feminine realm of justice and kindness. The contrary directions of the genre, towards acquiescence on the one hand, and rebellion on the other, are linked to its fabulism, intrinsic to its role of moral arbitration and soothsaying: the teller matters less than the audience whom he or she addresses, and so the teller struggles to locate and find that audience who will receive the stories' message with favour.

Children emerge as hearers because they are less likely to be committed already to a certain way of thought, and can be moulded; when adults want to mark their difference from their peers they take refuge in make-believe that they have become childlike again, fantastical, receptive, irrational, unconstrained by convention.

The extraordinary fad for fairytale that the court and the salons fostered in the years 1694–99 in France coincided with the growing aristo-cratic enthusiasm for the Child Jesus and for Christ's demonstrative affec-tion for children ('Suffer the little children to come unto me'; 'Be ye as little children'). At the same time, Louis XIV's capricious policies, his wars and depredations, were plunging the country—and even the nobles—into ruin.

The fairytale offered a coded way to dissent at a time of tough censor-ship and monarchical control, it created a picture of a possible escape from tyranny, and it used the naïve setting of childish beliefs in magic, the simple structure of the marvellous tale with its binary oppositions and neat resolutions. They could adduce the unimpeachable claim of the genre to time-honoured, authentic, native tradition in order to mount a critique of the times. When writers want to speak their minds, they can step up onto a rostrum and put the matter openly, and risk that rostrum changing to a scaffold. Or they can pretend to be little old grannies telling wellworn homespun stories filled with the nonsense of dyed-in-the-wool wisdom.

Fairytale offers a case where the very contempt for women opened an opportunity for them to exercise their wit and communicate their ideas: women's care for children, the prevailing disregard for groups, and their presumed identity with the simple folk, the common people, handed them fairytales as a nursery indeed, where they might seed their own gardens and foster their own flowers.

Fairytales told by women contain vivid examples of female evil: wicked stepmothers, ogresses, bad fairies abound, while virtuous figures like Cinderella's mother are dead from the start.

Early 16th-century woodcut of Cinderella weeping over the task of sorting peas in the ashes. The British Library; Metropolitan Toronto Reference Library

In many famous stories, like *Beauty and the Beast*, the absence of the mother from the tale is often declared in the start, without explanation, as if none were required. Thus Beauty appears before us, in the opening paragraph of the first, elaborate version by Madame de Villeneuve in 1740, as a daughter to her father, and a sister to her six elders, a Biblical seventh child, the *cadette*, the favourite: nothing is spoken about her father's wife.

One reason for this is historical, for the wondertale, however far-fetched the incidents it includes, or fantastic the enchantments it relates, takes on the colour of the actual circumstances in which it was told: while the elements remain familiar and the tales' structure dependably dialectical, the variant versions of the same story often reveal the particular conditions of the society which told it and retold it in this form: the absent mother can be read literally as exactly that: a feature of the family before our modern era, when death in childbirth was the most common cause of female mortality.

Children whose fathers had died often stayed in the paternal house to be raised by their grandparents or uncles and their wives, while their mothers were made to return to the homes of their youth and forge another, advantageous alliance for her native family. However widows remarried less frequently than widowers, who, in almost all cases under the age of sixty in Tuscany in the fifteen century, for instance, took another wife and started another family. In France, in the seventeenth and eighteenth centuries, 80 per cent of widowers remarried within the year.

The antipathy of stepmothers to children of earlier unions marks stories from all over the world, from the ancient world to the present day, and exhibits the strains and knots in different types of households, from patrilineage in conflict with dotal rights, to the tensions of polygamy. One tale from Dahomey, written down in 1958, tells how a dead mother manages to kill a wicked stepmother from beyond the grave with a handful of palm nuts.

Both the psychoanalytical and the historical interpreters of fairytale enter stories like *Cinderella*, *Snow White*, or *Beauty and the Beast* from the point of view of the protagonist, the orphaned daughter who has lost her real mother and is tormented by her stepmother, or her sisters, sometimes her stepsisters; the interpreters assume that the reader or listener naturally identifies with the heroine—which is of course commonly the case. But that perception sometimes also assumes that because the narrator makes common cause with the protagonist, she identifies with her too. This may be an error. Fairytales are not told in the first person of the protagonist, and though she engages our first attention as well as the narrator's, the voice of the latter is located elsewhere.

If we imagine the characteristic scene, children listening to an older person telling this story, we may find the absent mother present in the narrator herself. When the mother disappears, she has been conjured away by the storyteller, who dispatches the child listeners' natural parent, replaces her with a monster, and then often produces herself within the pages of the story, as a good old fairy, working wonders on their behalf. Thus the older generation speaks to the younger in the fairytale; pruning out the middle branch on the family tree as rotten or irrelevant, and thereby lays claim to the devotion, loyalty and obedience of the young over their mothers' heads: this is the classic Cinderella story.

Such an old woman storyteller may be a grandmother, or a mother-in-law. A woman in this situation had good reason to feel intense rivalry with her son's wife, when she often had to strive to maintain her position and assert her continuing rights to a livelihood in the household. If she was widowed, her vulnerability became more acute. Christiane Klapisch-Zuber uses the chilly phrase 'passing guests' when she describes the condition of wives in the house, both symbolic and geographic, into which they have married, in fifteenth-century Florence.

The conflicting claims on women of their paternal and marital homes continued throughout their lives and exacerbated their insecurity and stirred up much misery and misogyny in consequence, and Italian fairy-tales reflect this turbulence, filled as they are with wicked stepmothers and other female tyrants. English wills of the seventeenth century show that widowed parents were customarily cared for in the household of their eldest child: the right to shelter, the family hearth, bed and board, was granted and observed. However, as *King Lear* reveals, in the case of a widower, the exercise of such a right could meet ferocious resistance and reprisals. Just as Cordelia is a fairytale heroine, a wronged youngest child, a forerunner of Cinderella, so Goneril and Regan are the wicked witches, ugly sisters: the unnatural daughters whom fairytales indict. In Florence, some widows who wished to return to the family of their birth, as they had a right to do, were forced to bring suits against their children in the marital household in order to wrest back the dowry which was also theirs by right and necessary to their survival outside.

Women lived longer than men, then as now, and there were more old female dependents (like the old nurse, Anfisa, in *The Three Sisters*), than King Lears. Olga, who takes in the old woman when her brother's wife Natasha has brutally assaulted her as a good-for-nothing parasite, and thrown her out of the house where she has worked her whole life, shows a Cordelia-like spirit of gentleness and courage.

In France, after the revolution, a widow did not retain her keys to the household or to the family's business. Thus dispossessed by her husband's death, she was often only grudgingly provided for by his legatees; destitute and homeless old women were a feature of nineteenth-century society. Yet at the same time, the rights of grandparents began to be considered: in 1867, for instance, an important law was passed allowing the mother's parents to visit children who had remained in their father's custody after a divorce. This sign that grandparents' role in a child's upbringing was being recognised and valued coincides exactly with the publication of many editions of *Contes* in which an old woman is telling children tales by a fireside, began in France and England.

But the woman who threatens society by her singleness and her dependency was not always a widow; she could be a spinster, an unmarried mother, an old nurse or servant in a household. In the centuries when the image of Mother Goose was being disseminated through numerous editions of fairytale collections, 'there was,' writes Michelle Perrot, 'in a radical sense, no place for female solitude in the conceptual framework of the time.' She quoted Michelet: 'The woman who has neither home nor protection dies.' Yet there were many such and they had to survive, however precariously. The census of 1851 in France showed that 12 per cent of women over fifty had never married, and 34 per cent were single; this ratio remained the same nearly fifty years later.

The old wives who spin their tales are almost always represented unattached: spinster, or widows. Mother Goose is the anomalous crone, the unhusbanded female cut loose from her moorings of the patriarchal hearth: kin to the witch and the bawd. It is not difficult to see that the storyteller may be speaking from a position of acute vulnerability, the kind that makes enemies in the heart of the family.

The storyteller's mirror image is the ragged old woman whom the heroine meets by chance, who turns out to be a powerful fairy in disguise: she rewards virtuous sweet-talking girls who perform acts of kindness to her, like giving her food and drink, while their wicked mother, and the unkind daughter who resembles her, scorn the old woman as useless and will not provide for her. Again, paying attention to the structure of the story, one can assemble a picture of strain across three generations, in which the old struggle to survive and plead for the mercy of the young.

The wicked stepmother who has become the stock figure of fairytale first appears as a mother-in-law, in Apuleius's *Cupid and Psyche*. In *The Golden Ass* fairytale Cupid's mother, the goddess Venus, orders her son to destroy Psyche, her rival in beauty, but instead Cupid falls in love with her: he then visits her only at night, making love to her invisibly in an enchanted place. Eventually, her spiteful and jealous sisters goad her into spying on him while he sleeps, telling Psyche that he must be 'a savage wild beast'. Her fatal female curiosity—the familiar lesson—overcomes her and a drop of oil from the lamp spurts up with the flame on to the sleeping god's shoulder: he wakes, reproaches her furiously, and then everything—her fairy surroundings, as well as her divine groom—disappears.

In the fifteenth century, before the first extant variations on the tale were written down as fairy stories, *Cupid and Psyche* was chosen by *cassone* painters as a fitting theme for the trousseau chests brides took to their new home: alongside other tales of wronged daughters and aberrant marriages, like Patient Griselda, Potiphar's wife, and Helen of Troy, Psyche's troubles and eventual triumph could suitably furnish the room of a bride and help her keep in mind the pitfalls and the vindication of her predecessors in wedlock. Francesco di Giorgio (on a *cassone* panel in the Berenson Collection at I Tatti) chose the scene where Venus's vicious sidekick is dragging Psyche by her hair into the goddess's presence.

The stories of *Cinderella, Beauty and the Beast, Snow White* have directly inherited features from the plot of Apuleius's romance, like Psyche's wicked sisters, the enchanted bounty in her mysterious husband's palace, and the prohibitions that hedge about her knowledge of his true nature. At a deeper level, they have also inherited the stories' function, to tell the bride the worst, and shore her up in her marriage. The more one knows fairytales the less fantastical they appear: they are the vehicles of the most grim realism, expressing hope against all the odds with gritted teeth. As Angela Carter has written, they are marked by a mood of 'heroic optimism'.

The Wicked Stepmother makes another savage appearance as a mother-in-law in the *Vita* of Saint Godelive, patron saint of Bruges, an historical figure who was born around 1050 and married to Berthulphe de Ghistelles. According to the contemporary account of the priest, Drogo, she gave away food and goods to the poor behind his back, but was saved from detection by angels who replaced what she had taken. Hagiography and fairytale are often intertwined, and Godelive's story then takes a familiar turn and relates how Berthulphe's mother was furious at the match, how Berthulphe himself neglected his wife by his frequent absences and maltreated her when they were together, until finally, mother and son conspired to murder her. She was held head down in a pond and throttled by the servants. She was then put back to bed to make out she had died in her sleep. Berthulphe remarried but he later repented, made the pilgrimage to Jerusalem, and returned to become a monk. Godelive was canonised in 1084, very soon after her death, for miraculous cures had taken place: the blindness of one of her successor's children was suddenly lifted, and this was attributed to Godelive's intercession—a kind stepmother working wonders beyond the grave and making amends for the wickedness of the other mother in the story.

The proliferation of mother figures in the most conventional literary fairytale does not only reflect wishful thinking on the part of children, though I would not deny that fantasies of gratification and power over parents play their part: the aleatory mothers of Madame de Villeneuve's *Beauty and the Beast* reflect the conditions of aristocratic and less than aristocratic life in early modern France. Beauty, the heroine, was brought up in a foster home, discarded by her biological mother, like many other protagonists, when the fairies cast her out (the fairies figure as thinly disguised Versailles mignons and schemers) and compelled her to give up her child. For his part, the Beast has been cared for by his mother's closest friend. When he grows up she attempts to seduce him and then does him violence when he rejects her.

It is not hard to glimpse personal histories in these seemingly farfetched schemata: Mme de Villeneuve herself lived with Crébillon *père* as her patron and protector, though not her lover. His son, the playwright, Crébillon *fils*, took up writing fairytales in the satirical, semi-licentious tone that became *à la mode* in the 1720s. Improvised families of this sort were not uncommon in the *ancien régime*.

In Mlle Lheritier's even more complicated and apparently far-fetched tale, *La Robe de Sincérité* of 1695, the relations of wet nurse, foster parents, guardians, court patrons and godparents can be glimpsed as family networks interpenetrating and combining with the natural, biological family. It is significant that in English, French, and Italian, for instance, the very word 'mother' designated many women who were not natural mothers, nor women acting directly in lieu of her, like a foster parent, but occupied in some way with the care of other, often younger women—and sometimes men: Mère Arnault at the convent of Port Royal, *la mère maque-relle*—the notorious Madame of a brothel in colloquial speech (like Hogarth's notorious Ma Needham in *The Progress of a Harlot*), or the *mères* of the *compagnons* who take part in the *Tour de France*, and still meet their chosen champions at different stations on the route.

In England, midwives and other female carers as well as wise women and witches were granted the status of Mother in common parlance: the *Oxford Dictionary* declares it was 'a term of address for an elderly woman of the lower class'. In usage, it also implies something subtly marginal, with a whiff of the comic, to do with taboo mysteries of the body and the associated matters of life and death. Mother Trot, for instance, as in *Tell-troth's New Year Gift* of 1593, would be related to Old Dame Trot, of nursery rhyme witchery, and both are popular descendants of Trotula, the author of the midwifery manual of the Middle Ages, who may or may not be an historical figure, but certainly gave her name to venereal and obstetric lore of all kinds.

In the borough where I live in London there were, until recently, two pubs whose names recalled two such characters, *Mother Red Cap* and *Mother Shipton*, the last a byword in witchcraft and prophecy who was first mentioned in a pamphlet of 1641. Both have changed their names: one to *The World's End*, the other to *The Fiddler's Elbow*. The old names no longer held any meaning for their customers, and this is a symptom, in my view, of a larger alteration in consciousness: the meanings of the word 'mother' becoming more and more restricted to the biological mother in the nuclear family. The implications of the story villain in fairytale, the wicked stepmother, have been dangerously attenuated as a result.

The experiences fairy stories recount are remembered, lived experiences of women, not fairytale concoctions from the depths of the psyche;

they are rooted in the social, legal and economic history of marriage and the family, and they have all the stark actuality of the real, and the power real-life has to bite into the psyche and etch its design: if you accept Mother Goose tales as the testimony of women as old wives' tales, you can hear vibrating in them the tensions, the insecurity, jealousy and rage of both mothers-in-law against their daughters-in-law and vice versa, as well as the vulnerability of children from different marriages. Certainly, women strove against women because they wished to promote their own children's interests over those of another union's offspring: the economic dependence of wives and mothers on the male breadwinner exacerbated—and still does—the divisions that may first spring from preferences for a child of one's flesh, a child to whom the mother has been bonded physically. But another set of conditions set women against women, and the misogyny of fairytales reflects them from a woman's point of view: rivalry for the prince's love.

The effect of these stories is to flatter the male hero; the position of the man as saviour and provider in these testimonies of female conflict is assumed, repeated and reinforced—which may be the reason why such 'old wives' tales' found success with audiences of mixed men and women, boys and girls, and have continued to flourish in the most conservative media, like Disney cartoons.

For Further Reading:

See Angela Carter's introduction to *The Virago Book of Fairy Tales* (Virago, 1990); Jack Zipes, ed. and trans. *Beauties and Enchantment: Classic French Fairy Tales* (New York, 1989); Mary Elisabeth Storer, *La Mode des contes de fées* (Lausanne, 1928): Michelle Perrot, editor; *A History of Private Life, vol. IV: From the Fires of the Revolution to the Great War*, trans. Arthur Goldhammer (Cambridge, MA and London, 1990); Christiane Klapisch-Zuber, *Women, Family and Ritual in Renaissance Italy* (Chicago and London 1985); Robert Darnton, 'Peasant Tell Tales', in *The Great Cat Massacre* (New York, 1984).

Women's Coming of Age in Fantasy

Brian Attebery

A strength and a weakness of fantasy is its reliance on traditional story-telling forms and motifs. By making its conventional basis explicit and primary, rather than submerging traditional tale types or character functions beneath a surface of apparent reported reality, fantasy is empowered to reimagine both character and story. But a willingness to return to the narrative structures of the past can entail as well an unquestioning acceptance of its social structures.

This danger is particularly evident when the inherited story focuses on the process of coming of age, the transition from immature individual to mature member of society. In the societies from which we derive our legacy of myths and fairy tales, coming of age was a process of accommodating oneself to a strictly defined social role: hunter, chieftain, farmer, king. The passage from childhood to adult status was generally marked by the enactment of rituals which not only marked the individual's transition but also at the same time reaffirmed the hierarchical order in which the newly adult member was to find a place. Sometimes accompanying the rituals and sometimes serving in their place were spoken narratives.

We see this pattern reproduced in some form in virtually every modern fantasy. For example, in Lloyd Alexander's *Chronicles of Prydain* (1964–68) an orphaned young man discovers a destiny, true love, and his identity. T.H. White's *The Sword in the Stone* (1938) describes the transformation of the child Wart into King Arthur. The title character of Le Guin's *A Wizard of Earthsea* (1968) matures by testing his powers and learning his own limits. Tolkien describes the way an amiable young hobbit grows into a heroic and sober figure. George MacDonald's *Phantastes* (1858) concerns a youth who wakes up in a room transformed into woodland and undergoes a series of tests and adventures that lead him to self-knowledge. Each of these coming-of-age stories reflects traditional sources, such as the tale-type known as the 'sorcerer's apprentice', on which the second example is partially modelled. From the earliest traditional fairy tales to the most recent fantasy novels, protagonists have moved from the end of child-hood (or at least a condition of unformedness) to adulthood as the story unfolds. The magical adventures are tied together and the story given shape by the hero's gradual assumption of his proper powers and his place in society.

Each of the protagonists referred to above—Taran Wanderer, Wart, Ged, Frodo, and Anodos—is male. That's not surprising; a majority of the central figures in fiction are male, reflecting cultural biases and the prevalence of men in the ranks of writers. But the creator of one of those characters is a woman. The treatment of the coming-of-age story by women writers such as Ursula K. Le Guin demonstrates how a tradition may be made to reflect contemporary concerns, and how inherited story structures may be used to question the practices and beliefs that gave rise to them.

Le Guin chose the young man Ged as the hero of her first major fantasy *A Wizard of Earthsea*. Not until the second book of her trilogy, *The Tombs of Atuan* (1971), did she explore directly the coming of age of a young woman. The experience of that character, Arha, is significantly different from that of Ged, whom we may take as typical of the male hero. Ged begins in obscurity but soon attracts attention for his native gifts in sorcery, leaves the domestic world of his aunt's house, undergoes an apprenticeship under a (male) master who gives him a new name, attends a school for wizards (all male), disobeys an injunction, wanders the world looking for a cure for the evil he has unleashed, is tempted by a (female) witch, bests a dragon in a test of wits, and finally overcomes the evil. Ambitious, proud, and impulsive, he must learn the limits of his powers. His only real adversary is himself, and his chief accomplishment is self-mastery.

For Arha, however, the problem is unleashing rather than mastering herself, and outside rather than within the institutional constraints of her culture. Accordingly, for Le Guin the problem is to find a way of adapting the conventions of fantasy to reflect this other kind of coming of age. Her solution, drawing upon her knowledge of earlier narratives and of anthropological studies of rites of passage, is to create a new assemblage, with new meanings, out of existing materials. Other women writers in turn have learned from her techniques. Like the women's art of quilting, fantasy writing is a cooperative enterprise, in which individual vision is expressed within prescribed forms, and innovation is an outgrowth of the process of continuity.

A large proportion of contemporary fantasy fiction is written by women. Patricia McKillip, Diana Wynne Jones, Susan Cooper, R.A. MacAvoy, and dozens of other writers have found fantasy—with its conventions derived from fairy tale, romance, supernatural legend, and myth—to be an appropriate vehicle for conveying the ideas and experiences they have found significant enough to work into narrative form. These writers and the women who explored the mode of fantasy before them constitute a tradition of a new sort. Thelma Shinn's *Worlds within Women* (1986) and Charlotte Spivack's *Merlin's Daughters* (1987) both describe the thematic consistency within contemporary fantastic literature by women: drawing on common experience and knowledge of one another's work, women fantasists are engaged in such joint enterprises as refurbishing the archetypal images of the goddess, redefining the qualities of heroism to include female experience, and reaffirming women's access to the narrative storehouse of the past.

Coming of age is central in any mythology. Like all rites of passage or of initiation, it marks the passage of an individual from one state to another: from one tribe to another, from the laity to the priesthood, from life to death, or, in this case, from childhood to adulthood and full participation in society. Arnold van Gennep, whose 1908 study of *Les rites de passage* stands behind most popular treatments of the subject and thus shapes the way we continue to think of it, treats these rites as essentially concerned with changes of status in males:

> Transitions from group to group and from one social situation to the next are looked on as implicit in the very fact of existence, so that a man's life comes to be made up of a succession of stages with similar ends and beginnings: birth, social puberty, marriage, fatherhood, advancement to a higher class, occupational specialization, and death.[1]

This one-sided emphasis on 'a man's life', ignoring a woman's, probably reflects both van Gennep's own bias and that of the cultures he is examining. Until recently, few ethnologists would have thought to look for women's rituals, and unless fieldworkers were themselves women, much of women's culture was inaccessible to them. Van Gennep's study primarily documents male activities from birth to grave, discussing women only in conjunction with pregnancy, childbirth, and marriage, and the last with respect to the man's acquisition of a wife.

Do women come of age? In van Gennep's view perhaps not, for he considers women and children to form a single social group. Boys require a drastic break from this group to that of adult men; girls merely work their way through it. The further implication is that women never do become fully adult, that they are like those salamanders that stay underwater all their lives, able to reproduce but otherwise still in the gill-breathing, immature stage.

Carolyn Heilbrun reflects the general view when she suggests that women even in our own culture have no coming-of-age ritual and that they pay a psychological penalty for the lack:

> All societies, from the earliest and most primitive to today's, have ceremoniously taken the boy from the female domain and urged his identity as a male, as a responsible unfeminine individual, upon him. The girl undergoes no such ceremony, but she pays for serenity of passage with a lack of selfhood and of the will to autonomy that only the struggle for identity can confer.[2]

A fantasy writer can invent a ritual for herself, holding her own imaginative initiation ceremony. But she faces limitations not faced by her male counterparts. If she is aware of the female rites of passage that do exist, she may not be content to induct her characters into the female roles to which those rites lead. The challenge she faces is to retain the values of the female initiation—its bestowal of identity and mystery upon the initiand—without turning her characters into tribal mothers and drudges. To do so, she must turn to other models from life and literature.

However, such models have long been difficult to find, especially in print. Copying the male initiation story with a female protagonist is one solution, but an inadequate one if the writer wishes to connect with women's actual experience in our culture. Few women even today can find in their own lives any analogue of the male hero's freedom of movement or his expectation of power and rank at the end of his quest. An effective female initiation fantasy should be, at least at the beginning, more recognizably grounded in the biological and social reality of a woman's life, but in the course of events it should somehow transcend that reality.

The mainstream novel of the eighteenth and nineteenth centuries mirrors social realities, but it has no mechanism for transcending them. For this reason, it has little to offer women in the way of successful transitions to maturity. Beginning with Samuel Richardson's influential creations, youthful women in such novels are generally confined to two fates. They marry, like Pamela, or die, like Clarissa. Either fate ends the heroine's development.

One should note that this limitation applies only to stories of young women: there is a large class of fiction that 'shows women developing later in life, after conventional expectations of marriage and motherhood have been fulfilled and found insufficient'.[3] In fantasies, such middle-age emergence has been well treated by Nancy Kress in *The Prince of Morning Bells*

(1981) and by Le Guin in *Tehanu* (1990). Yet a coming-of-age story requires an adolescent hero, of the sort so prevalent in fiction by men. Patricia Meyer Spacks asks rhetorically where one can find female equivalents for Stephen Dedalus or Holden Caulfield and answers that one cannot, because of restrictions placed on independent young women:

> Female rebellion may be perfectly justified, but there's no good universe next door, no way out, young potential revolutionaries can't find their revolution. So they marry in defeat or go mad in a complicated form of triumph, their meaning the inevitability of failure.[4]

Realistic fiction is limited in two ways. First, it can find no 'good universe next door'. It is limited to the circumstances of the recognizable world, in which women have, or have had, little outlet for revolutionary or artistic impulses. Second, it is surprisingly limited in available plot lines. Marriage and madness or suicide correspond to the dramatic formulas of the comic and the tragic. These formulaic constraints exerted such control over nineteenth-century novelists that Jane Austen, who herself never married, ended every novel with multiple marriages, while George Eliot, Kate Chopin, and Edith Wharton, who all reached artistic success and a measure of economic independence, wrote of women unable to forge new social roles and driven thereby to untimely deaths.

Both formulas can, of course, result in profound and original fiction. The heroine's selection of a proper husband may be overlaid with wit and social commentary, as in *Pride and Prejudice*, or laden with ethical implication, as in *Middlemarch*. Nonetheless, it does not show how a woman can become a self, independent of her choice of mate. It is still the story of Cinderella, waiting for the fulfilment that comes only with the right man. In a way, the realist marriage plot is worse than 'Cinderella', for without the markers of fictionality—most notably magic—that are built into the fairy tale, we are encouraged to take these equally arbitrary story structures as reality.

Cinderella, along with her sisters Snow White and the Sleeping Beauty, has given fairy tales the reputation of being, for women, indoctrinations in passivity. These most familiar of fairy tale heroines all undergo intervals of confinement, metamorphosis, and reemergence as prospective wives to the more active male figures. Their rites of passage are striking echoes of those described by anthropologists, and arrive at the same ends, limiting their usefulness as models for fantasy.

Yet not all fairy tales involve heroines like Sleeping Beauty. A sizable minority of traditional tales describe a courageous, independent heroine winning her own way and reaching adulthood in the process. In Joseph Jacob's collection *English Folk and Fairy Tales*, for instance, the following tales have young female protagonists: 'Tom Tit Tot', 'Nix Nought Nothing', 'Cap o'Rushes', 'Mollie Whuppie', 'Mr Fox', 'Earl Mar's Daughter', 'The Fish and the Ring', 'Kate Crackernuts', 'The Well of the World's End', and 'The Three Heads of the Well'. The heroines of these tales outwit devils, kill giants, work enchantments, work for a living, unmask false suitors, and rescue siblings. The princess in 'The Three Heads of the Well' does not wait around to be rescued from an evil stepmother; instead, 'The young princess having lost her father's love, grew weary of the Court, and one day, meeting with her father in the garden, she begged him, with tears in her eyes, to let her go and seek her fortune. . .'[5]

The unfamiliarity of tales like these is the result of a process of selection by fairy tale collectors, retellers, and editors that amounts to suppression of the independent female hero.

In the brothers Grimm's collection, which already represents a considerable editorial bias in favour of bourgeois domesticity for female characters, there remain nonetheless a handful of active heroines—which later popularizations have proceeded to weed out. Whatever conception of female coming of age may once have been conveyed in the folktales of Europe can therefore only be imaginatively reconstructed. The evidence is hopelessly skewed, and much of it irrecoverable.

Nevertheless, the power of the folktale as narrative pattern is such that women readers and writers have devised strategies to regain it as a tool for the exploration of their own experience. Carolyn Heilbrun suggests one such strategy in the reader's refusal to limit her identification to the passive heroine, her discovery 'that she is not confined to the role of the princess; that the hero, who wakens Sleeping Beauty with a kiss, is that part of herself that awakens conventional girlhood to the possibility of life and action.'[6]

Heilbrun's approach is an effective one for some readers but may not be workable for all, especially young girls untrained in the art of reading subversively. Another tack is the sort of reverse discrimination practised by editors like Ethel Johnston Phelps, whose *Tatterhood and Other Tales* (1978) assembles stories from many cultures, all featuring 'heroic women distinguished by extraordinary courage and achievements, who hold the center of interest in the tales'.[7] It may be that these two approaches reinforce one another: as readers become more familiar with nonpassive heroines, they find it easier to identify with active characters of either sex.

A third strategy is the invention of original stories drawing on the motifs and structures of the traditional tale but introducing reversals of expected character roles. One of the first such stories is Jean Ingelow's largely forgotten but haunting *Mopsa the Fairy* (1869).

Ingelow was best known in her day as a poet. A friend of Browning, Ruskin, and Christina Rossetti, she seems to have shared their interest in the fairy tale as an alternative form of symbolic expression. Her only novel-length fairy tale, *Mopsa the Fairy*, reveals in its plot and symbolism some of the tensions between cultural expectations for women in the Victorian era and the aspirations of a woman writer. Many of these narrative and symbolic patterns continue to appear in fantasies by women a century later.

The story begins with Jack, but Mopsa and her fate are far more interesting. Jack seems to serve primarily as an avenue into the realm of the fairy tale, a conventional fairy-tale hero with a conventional name. Since more people seem to be aware of male-oriented tales than of the 'Mollie Whuppie' sort of fairy tale, perhaps Ingelow thought the form required someone like Jack. Hers is not the only fantasy by a woman to begin from a male point of view. As mentioned earlier, Le Guin wrote one book about a male wizard before looking at the coming-of-age process from a female viewpoint. Patricia Wrightson's *The Ice Is Coming* (1977) and Patricia McKillip's *The Riddle-Master of Hed* (1976) also have male heroes, with female counterparts not appearing until the sequels.

What all these writers seem to be doing is reinforcing a reading like that suggested by Heilbrun for fairy tales: the male who acts as catalyst for the female's transformation is also, in a sense, herself. He represents those impulses toward independent action and self-definition which society insists the young girl suppress. Since those qualities are culturally defined as masculine, they must enter the story in male guise, but the outcome is the redefinition of the female. By the end, the heroine has grown to encompass his qualities as well as her own 'masculine' initiative and 'feminine' wisdom.

Andre Norton, whose Witch World series waited until its third volume, *Year of the Unicorn* (1965), for a full-fledged female hero, explains why the unexamined choice of protagonist, even for a woman writer, might be male-audience expectations:

> To write a full book from the feminine point of view was a departure.
> I found it fascinating to write, but the reception was oddly mixed. In

the years now since [*Year of the Unicorn*] was published I have had many letters from women readers who accepted Gillian with open arms, and I have had masculine readers who hotly resented her.[8]

Only when the coming of age includes sexuality does it become absolutely necessary to split the androgynous hero into male and female. Le Guin, speaking of the second book in the Earthsea trilogy, associates femininity with the sort of physical changes that were mostly left out of *A Wizard of Earthsea*:

> The subject of *The Tombs of Atuan* is, if I had to put it in one word, sex. There's a lot of symbolism in the book, most of which I did not, of course, analyse consciously while writing; the symbols can all be read as sexual. More exactly, you could call it a feminine coming of age. Birth, rebirth, destruction, freedom are the themes.[9]

For the same reasons, Ingelow begins with Jack and moves to Mopsa when things get interesting. His kiss calls Mopsa to her fate, which then becomes the real subject of the book. The same pattern reappears in the work of more recent fantasists. In *The Tombs of Atuan*, published just about a century after Ingelow's novel, the protagonist Arha is raised as priestess of the Nameless Ones, dark, inhuman forces worshipped by her society. Her education is designed to suppress or destroy her individual personality and make her an empty vehicle for the gods she serves. When the wizard Ged arrives, he restores her humanity and individuality by giving her back the name she was born with, Tenar. That is the beginning of her rebellion and maturation. Again the male character initiates a transformation in the female, from alien to human.

Another meaning for the male catalyst emerges in Patricia Wrightson's *The Dark Bright Water* (1979). In that book, the hero from *The Ice Is Coming*, a young Aborigine named Wirrun, meets many of the creatures from his people's folklore, among them the Yunggamurra. This is a sort of fresh-water siren, a beautiful woman-shaped singer that lures men to their deaths. The Yunggamurra is not evil; her main interest is not killing men but playing in the water with her sisters. The siren song is a game she plays. After she drowns Wirrun's friend Ularra, Wirrun finds out the other rule of the game: he catches her in the smoke of a grass-fire and she is transformed from silvery water spirit to golden mortal woman: trapped, tamed, humanized.

Wrightson is making use of a traditional motif here: the swan-maiden, seal-maiden, or similar spirit creature caught by the human male, thereupon becoming his bride. But Wrightson's perspective on the story gives it a different significance. The transformed Yunggamurra, now named Murra, loves Wirrun, but she regrets her lost life: 'to flow with the water and ride it; to be one strand among weeds, one voice in the singing. To rise to the sun or sink from the wind as the others do. To be no one but to be many, and to play.'[10] She has given up a wild, anonymous freedom for a name and a lover.

It is an exchange Murra makes against her will, but she is willing to abide by it. However, she warns Wirrun that he must keep her away from water, where her sisters might find her: 'They will call and call and I will hear and hear; and one day they will find me in water. They will catch Murra more surely than ever you caught Yunggamurra. They will take me back to the rivers and the games and I will be Yunggamurra again. You should keep me always from the water.'[11]

Read as metaphor, Murra's transformation is from child to woman. Children are wild and free. They are anonymous insofar as adults fail to distinguish among them, and their identities are not fixed but fluid, responding to everything around them. A girl-child looking at her mother sees someone bounded by convention and tied to the needs of husband and children. Girl and woman might as well be different species. If the mother was once a girl, she must have been trapped and transformed. The magic spell that will do the same to her, society informs the girl, is called love.

That is one possible meaning for all these stories of witch, fairy, or animal turned into woman. In many of the traditional tales, the woman is mistreated and goes back to her old life. The man has caught her, but he does not have her soul. In a patriarchal society, that is as free as a woman can be. She accepts the bargain, lives a circumscribed life, bears her children, and becomes an adult according to her culture's dictates, but she retains an escape clause.

In *The Dark Bright Water*, Wirrun admirably refuses to play the game. He won't keep Murra locked up away from water; she is now human and must stay with him or go by her own choice. He has not sought a subservient wife but an equal companion. Much of the third volume of the trilogy concerns Murra's coming to terms with a relationship not covered by the magical game.

Jean Ingelow's fantasy does not take up such adult dilemmas, but Jack's kiss of Mopsa carries some of the same implications. Jack himself is unaware of the effect of his attentions, since men are not caught in the same way women are. By the end of the book, Mopsa has outgrown Jack (though Ingelow describes her as looking only ten years old—she has more growing to do). She has moved on to a new realm of knowledge and responsibility. Her last act in the story is to give Jack back his kiss and send him on his way home. She has accepted womanhood, but she does not tie herself to the one who triggered her transformation.

Mopsa had no older woman to guide her to maturity. The image of older woman as threatening rival rather than as mentor is familiar to us from 'Hansel and Gretel' and 'Snow White'. This image may derive from the fact that mother and daughter must compete for favours from a dominant male. It also reflects the daughter's awareness that the mother is 'in on it'—she is one of the forces pushing the girl into the constricting mould of female adulthood. In *The Tombs of Atuan*, Le Guin shows older women in the latter role. The priestess Kossil is as fearsome as any fairytale stepmother. She is ambitious, cruel, and hypocritical, and she resents the young priestess of the Nameless Ones, her only peer. Arha must reach adulthood literally over Kossil's dead body, when the latter is trapped in the caverns of the Nameless Ones.

In a few very recent works, women characters come of age in ways different from that mapped out in *Mopsa the Fairy*. No male characters are required to initiate the plots of Diana Wynne Jones's *The Spell-coats* (1979), Virginia Hamilton's *Justice and Her Brothers* (1978), Michaela Roessner's *Walkabout Woman* (1988), and Suzette Haden Elgin's Ozark trilogy (1981). Nor are their women characters portrayed as something other than human to begin with, though they may grow into something greater than human.

Responsible of Brightwater, the heroine of Elgin's trilogy, is on centre stage from the beginning. She needs no man to teach her independence. Fourteen years old at the beginning of the series, she possesses an adolescent self-assurance not always short of arrogance. She has her magical power well in hand and is fully supplied with female mentors in the persons of the Grannys [sic] who run households on the planet Ozark. Ozark society is organized in a fashion derived from its earthly namesake: men and women inhabit largely separate spheres, with the men handling politics, feuds, food-raising, and major magical spells, and the women concerned with household maintenance, child rearing, the preservation of knowledge, and small bits of 'Granny Magic'. What the men do not know is that there is always one woman, always named Responsible, who is the 'meta-magician' of Ozark. She can do anything the male Magicians of Rank can do and more. She is the channel through which magical powers reach the magicians.

No earlier fantasy that I know of is told so squarely from a woman's perspective. The world of Ozark incorporates the rituals, institutions, and insights that early anthropologists thought women lacked. Having shown that women do indeed come of age, Elgin next points out the necessity of adapting society to accommodate the resulting adult woman. Responsible of Brightwater deserves the company of a man who will not confuse communion with invasion or courtesy with capitulation.

It is possible to go beyond Elgin's formulation of the female coming-of-age story, but only by positing a vastly different world from even our comparatively feminized one. This is a step that fantasy has been reluctant to take, but science fiction provides many examples of all-women, androgynous, or nonsexist societies and the development of young heroines within them. Science fiction readily proposes changes in economic systems, family structures, political relationships, even language (such as David Gerrold's unnerving use of single pronoun *she* for characters of either sex in his 1977 novel *Moonstar Odyssey*). Fantasy's reliance on traditional motifs makes it less adaptable to such wholesale transformations of society; it usually focuses on the development of the exceptional individual rather than the reformation of culture. It is probably not accidental that Elgin's Ozark trilogy, unlike the other stories discussed in this chapter, is really science fantasy, combining the magic of fantasy with the future setting and technological underpinnings of science fiction. Science fantasy can do many things that traditional fantasy cannot.

But even without remaking every cultural institution, fantasy can call certain assumptions into question. It can begin with inherited story structures and direct them toward unexpected ends, turning Cinderellas into Princesses Charming and waking sleeping strengths in Sleeping Beauties. Its very avoidance of the details of contemporary society gives it flexibility, for its heroines need not carry such cultural burdens as women's economic dependency, religious rationales for the suppression of women, and the commercial exploitation of women as sex objects. Freed of these, heroines have a chance of coping with personal relationships and with their own limitations.

Individually composed narratives like these are not an exact analogue of culturally sanctioned rites of passage, but they serve to remind us of the ritual process and its value to the individual. Though lacking the authority of ritual, narratives are in some ways better suited to the needs of an evolving society. Because a reader undergoes only a vicarious induction into a new identity, that identity remains provisional and subject to further testing and growth. As such narratives proliferate, they serve to complement and comment upon one another.

When we follow Mopsa's path from toy-like creature to queen, we see how the extraordinary individual may defy societal expectations to achieve self-determination. When we follow Responsible as she comes to terms with her own power and authority, we see how the hidden operations of a culture may oppose its own official institutions to offer support to the emerging self. Each of the narratives considered here describes a different route to maturity and defines it in different terms: physical, emotional, metaphysical, political. Some of the heroes do, like their fairy tale predecessors, mark their passage by marriage, but in no case does marriage constitute or justify their achievements.

None of them fails in their quests for expanded knowledge and scope of action. Because the conventions of fantasy require that a task undertaken be completed within the narrative, the outcome may, especially in formula fantasy, seem forced or inadequate to the problems posed. It will not, however, be the madness, suicide, or despair that seem the lot of the realistic heroine. In the works considered here, there is no forcing: maturity is hard-won but worth the winning, and the female heroes represent an unprecedented range of models for development. Their success in emerging as women of power and self-knowledge makes them more universal, as well: the male reader (like myself) can adopt Carolyn Heilbrun's strategy and, by identifying with Tenar or Raederle or Responsible, learn more truly what it means to come of age.

Notes

[1] Arnold van Gennep, *The Rites of Passage*. Trans. Monika B. Vizedom and Gabrielle L. Caffee. Chicago, University of Chicago Press, 1960: 3.

[2] Carolyn G. Heilbrun, *Reinventing Womanhood*. New York, Norton, 1979: 104.

[3] Elizabeth Abel, Marianne Hirsch and Elizabeth Langlands, eds, *The Voyage In: Fictions of Female Development*. Hanover, University Press of New England: 7.

[4] Patricia Meyer Spacks, *The Female Imagination*. New York, Knopf, 1975: 158.

[5] Joseph Jacobs, *English Folk and Fairy Tales*, 3rd ed. revised. New York, Putnam's, n.d.: 232–3.

[6] Heilbrun, *Reinventing Womanhood*: 150.

[7] Ethel Johnston Phelps, *Tatterhood and Other Tales*. Old Westbury, The Feminist Press, 1978: xv.

[8] Andre Norton, 'On Writing Fantasy' in *The Book of Andre Norton*. New York,

DAW, 1975. Rpt. in *Fantasists on Fantasy: A Collection of Critical Reflections*, eds Robert Boyer and Kenneth J. Zahorski. New York, Avon, 1984: 161.

[9]Ursula K. Le Guin, 'The Language of the Night' in *Essays on Fantasy and Science Fiction*, ed. Susan Wood. New York, Putnam's, 1979: 55.

[10]Patricia Wrightson, *The Dark Bright Water*. New York, Atheneum, 1979: 216.

[11]Ibid.: 220.

Fathers Fare Poorly in Children's Books

Michael Valpy

Sexism is sexism. My 2½-year-old son gets equal time from his parents. We have here child-rearing's progressive notion of the day, plus the modern statistic of two parents with jobs outside the home.

This boy, in consequence, is as familiar with daddy at the stove and the working end of a diaper as he is with mummy.

He knows no gender differences between who takes him to the doctor, who buys him his clothes, who loses sleep with him when he has a fever, who tells him not to bat the cat, who plays soccer with him in the park or boats with him in the bathtub or who focuses on the fascinating task of his toilet training.

This is contemporary urban Canada (minus—which I agree is significant but let's set it aside for now because, for one thing, they're still not the norm—the growth of women-led, single-parent families). It has been blossoming for, what, the past 20 years?

Why, then, has children's literature not marched in step?

I may be looking in the wrong places, but I scour the local library and the best of the children's bookstores for stories that do not appallingly stereotype parental roles. It is, as fathers across the country undoubtedly have found, a hard job.

In almost every major theatre of life, mothers are shown as the main actors with children.

Books on visits to the doctor have mothers marshalling the event. When children debate with a parent whether monsters are really under the bed or tigers in the garden, it is their mothers who are the protagonists.

It is mothers who are shown making lunch, attending to scraped knees, ordering the wearing of mittens; mothers, in general, who are depicted as commanders of the household.

The stereotyping extends into what most parents would agree are stories of quality.

Margaret Laurence's *Six Darn Cows* has mother coming out with a flashlight to find her children when darkness falls and they're still looking for the escaped cows. (Where's father? Comfortably in his armchair reading *Report on Business*?)

The much-admired Robert Munsch's *Love You Forever* tells the story of a son's powerful love for his mother—father is nonexistent—from his infancy to her old age. If you want to think about this, it's just a little bit emasculating.

When my son was younger, I got away with sometimes changing 'mummy' to 'daddy' when I read to him. That stopped working when he recognized the difference between drawings of men and women.

One book came into the house promisingly titled *Just Me and My Dad*. Its stereotyping began on the first page, with mother (in apron) waving goodbye to son and husband as they head off on—wait for it—a camping trip.

Father, wearing lumberjack shirt and boots, is shown throughout the book as master of the wilderness, teaching junior (and he probably is called Junior) the skills of campfire-making, canoeing and fishing—skills which I and (at a guess) 95 per cent of my fellow urban Canadian fathers are without.

I am a modestly competent cook. Where can you find fathers who do this except in nerd comic strips? Or in books so earnestly and painfully anti-stereotyped that most fathers want to hide them under the sofa?

The books that do have fathers still too frequently present them as stern, remote, judgemental figures, frowning critically at their children's mistakes. Only occasionally is there a find. Jill Murphy's *Peace At Last*, for example—the story of a lovable father who can't sleep because the son is playing airplanes in his bed, and the mother is snoring. Good. Some women—although none I've known—snore.

The point to all this is obvious. The road to gender role-equality remains a muzzy path. With perhaps too few men writing children's books.

PART VIII

YOUNG ADULT LITERATURE

Innocence and Experience in the Young Adult Romance

Sarah Ellis

Teenagers constitute a market, a market for fashion, video, food, music, and books. The young adult romance in particular has become a highly marketable commodity. *Pace* the 'print is dead' pundits, books are doing rather well with the new generation. But in our concerns for young adults as a market, for packaging and format, we may be losing sight of what gave the literature its strength in the first place. We may be forgetting the literary potential of adolescence as a subject.

The exhilarating and painful period of adolescence can be seen as the movement from innocence to experience. Even the bland formula romance recognizes this theme: personifying innocence, perhaps in the form of a pretty blonde sophomore, submitting to the siren call of experience, generally in the person of a dark and dangerous heavy metal fancier.

But in real life with all its lumps and grit and fraying edges the two states are not mutually exclusive, and the movement from one to the other is neither straightforward nor conclusive. William Blake recognized this complexity in his *Songs of Innocence* and *Songs of Experience*. So do perceptive and challenging writers for young adults.

Blake's *Songs of Innocence* are filled with images of small, enclosed, comforting places: children on mothers' laps, in cradles and angel-guarded beds, birds in nests. He presents a world of closeness, of views of the small and the near, where the quest is played out on the scale of an ant and a glowworm. He even infuses dark shades with the potential for joy; sooty chimneys and a vision of the coffin are mere stages on the journey to freedom and the green plain.

In *Songs of Experience* these enclosing images still figure, but their flavour is one of bondage, frustration, and imprisonment. The nest has become a cage:

How can the bird that is born for joy
Sit in a cage and sing?

And a new dimension has entered the poetic world, that of the far horizon:

> In what distant deeps or skies
> Burnt the fire of thine eyes?

From a verdant pastoral world where nature is tamed to the village green or the cultivated meadow, we have entered an expanded world of majesty and terror.

These two prospects, the near and the far, form the basis of some of Blake's most powerful images. And these images are pervasive in novels dealing with the growth from innocence through experience. The infant sorrow of Blake's swaddling bands finds its echoes in Creep's closet under the stairs in Jill Paton Walsh's *A Chance Child*, in Aremis Slake's one-hundred-and-twenty-one-day New York subway sojourn in Felice Holman's *Slake's Limbo*, and in the school janitor's cubbyhole in Virginia Hamilton's *The Planet of Junior Brown*.

Likewise, Blake's distant deeps and skies recur in some of the most moving passages in young adult literature. One remembers Madge's view of the distant Godrevy in Jill Paton Walsh's *Unleaving* and Olwen's view of her planet from her mountain home in *Keeper of the Isis Light* by Monica Hughes.

As innocence and experience are, in Blake's terms, contrary states co-existing within the human soul, so these images of the near and the far can be juxtaposed in the creative tension of a single, unified vision. And such a vision is not achieved without strength and wisdom. As Blake says:

> And what shoulder and what art,
> Could twist the sinews of thy heart?

The story of this struggle of shoulder and art is one of the strands that weaves into each of three novels popular with young adults today.

Written well before the advent of the young adult novel, and indeed before the invention of adolescence itself, Charlotte Brontë's *Jane Eyre* is such an accurate and emotionally valid portrayal of this passage from innocence through experience that it finds its way rightly and inevitably onto the shelves of young adult collections. In many ways Sheila Greenwald, in her delightful 1980 spoof of the young adult novel (*It All Began with Jane Eyre*) is right.

The first time we see young Jane she is sitting in a window seat, enclosed and isolated. To her right is a scarlet curtain, cutting her off from human contact. To her left is a vision, through the window, of a landscape that has no distance:

> I studied the aspect of that winter afternoon. Afar it offered a pale
> blank mist and cloud; near, a scene of wet lawn and storm-beat
> shrub, with ceaseless rain sweeping away wildly before a long and
> lamentable blast.

On Jane's lap is Bewick's *History of British Birds*, a book whose delight for
her lies in its descriptions of exotic and faraway places. Jane's only experience of distance is at the remove of art. Thus we have, in this opening
scene, two sets of images that will resonate through the novel, in conflict,
and finally, through Jane's struggles, in harmony.

The initial image of an enclosed space is echoed soon after in the terrifying scene in the red room. The significant pieces of furniture in the room
are a wardrobe and a curtained bed, the imprisoning implications of which
lead Jane to thoughts of the late Mr Reed lying in the church vault. This
combination of images produces Jane's mental agony and unconsciousness.
Her horizons could not be closer. But this incident leads, in turn, to the
first expansion of these horizons.

The first few scenes at the school at Lowood are full of the same
isolated suffocating images that enclosed Jane at Gateshead:

> The garden was a wide enclosure, surrounded with walls so high as to
> exclude every glimpse of prospect . . . it was an inclement day for
> outdoor exercise—not positively rainy but darkened with a drizzling
> yellow fog. . . . As yet I had spoken to no one, nor did anybody seem
> to take notice of me. . . .

But there is hope for Jane when she finds Helen Burns and the teacher,
Miss Temple, friends. The expanded horizons of the intellect that these
allies introduce to Jane are echoed in the imagery of distance that is associated with them. Helen is described in terms of a distant planet, and Miss
Temple approaches in moonlight:

> Some heavy clouds, swept from the sky by a rising wind, had left the
> moon bare; and her light, streaming in through a window near, shone
> on both of us and on the approaching figure, which we at once recog-
> nized as Miss Temple.

It is at this point in the novel that we are introduced to Jane's drawings. As an artist she is concerned with space and distance. The style and
subject of her visualized world are described in some detail, and these
descriptions illuminate Jane's development:

I feasted instead on the spectacle of my ideal drawings, which I saw in the dark—all the work of my own hands, freely pencilled houses and trees, picturesque rocks and ruins, Cuyp-like groups of cattle, sweet paintings of butterflies hovering over unblown roses, of birds picking at ripe cherries, or wrens' nests enclosing pearl-like eggs, wreathed about with young ivy sprays.

Here are both innocence and experience, both the enclosed safety of the bird's nest and the hint of Gothic distance, of rocks and ruins. We see how Jane has taken her limited experience of art and the experience of her own expanding horizons and integrated them into artistic expression. Here is presented a pattern that will recur throughout the novel.

And again, the view of the landscape changes accordingly. Up to this point we have only had fog and mist, but now:

I discovered, too, that a great pleasure, an enjoyment which the horizon only bounded, lay all outside the high and spike-guarded walls of our garden: this pleasure consisted in prospect of noble summits girdling a great hill-hollow, rich in verdure and shadow; in a bright beck, full of dark stones and sparkling edges.

Such growth is painful for Jane, and this brief period of comparative happiness is followed by the outbreak of typhus and the death of Helen. Again images of the near and far occur. Helen represents the distance of infinity, of the spirit. She dies of consumption, and, as Susan Sontag points out in *Illness as Metaphor*, consumption represents a kind of rarefaction. Yet when Jane sees Helen for the last time, it is in a curtained bed, the terror-ridden image from Jane's past. Thus far there is no middle distance for Jane, only the painfully near and the impossibly remote.

Jane's decision to leave Lowood is prompted by a vision of the landscape and a desire to enter that distance:

. . . there was the garden, there were the skirts of Lowood; there was the hilly horizon. My eye passed all other objects to rest on those most remote, the blue peaks. It was those I longed to surmount; all within their boundary of rock and heath seemed prison-ground, exile limits. I traced the white road winding round the base of one mountain, and vanishing in a gorge between two. How I longed to follow it further.

Her arrival at Thornfield is followed by the first description of a view in which Jane seems to integrate all distances in one cohesive vision:

> . . . I surveyed the ground laid out like a map; the bright and velvet
> lawn closely girdling the grey base of the mansion; the field, wide as a
> park, dotted with its ancient timber; the wood, dun and sere,
> divided by a path visibly overgrown, greener with moss than the trees
> with foliage, the church at the gates, the road, the tranquil hills, all
> reposing in the autumn day's sun; the horizon bounded by a propi-
> tious sky, azure, marbled with pearly white.

This heightening of perspective sets the stage for the entry of Rochester.
Again a significant turning point is expressed in terms of the landscape.
Rochester is seen as a bold foreground which effaces the distance of the
picture.

Jane's struggle to reconcile these distances forms one thread of the rest
of the novel. This struggle is symbolized in the fullest descriptions we have
of Jane's paintings. The three pictures that she shows Rochester, the first of
a drowned corpse, the second of a woman emerging from evening cloud,
and the third of a giant head against an iceberg, contain a multitude of
strange, macabre images. One can trace their style to that of John Martin, a
painter admired by the Brontë children.

In terms of the novel itself the pictures suggest that Jane has certainly
viewed the distant deeps and skies. She is an enclosed, isolated child no
more. The far, as well as the near, has entered her experience and she has
externalized her inner torment. There is no suggestion, however, that the
elements in the picture are related, there is no sense of perspective or unity.
There is description of foreground and background in sharp contrast. Total
vision is still to come for Jane. It is significant that human characters have
entered Jane's pictures for it is to be through people that Jane finally
achieves integration.

In the early stages of Jane's love for Rochester he is as exotic and
remote as the turbaned character he plays in the charade. He is unreach-
ably distant:

> . . . I was tossed on a buoyant but unquiet sea, where billows of
> trouble rolled under surges of joy. I thought sometimes I saw beyond
> its wild waters a shore, sweet as the hills of Beulah; and now and then
> a freshening gale, wakened by hope, bore my spirit triumphantly
> toward the bourne, but I could not reach it, even in fancy. . . .

He has entered Jane's consciousness, however, and the portrait she
sketches of him on her return trip to Gateshead is described in great detail.

One senses that, finally, Jane's art has achieved focus and unity as Rochester has entered the foreground.

In the proposal scene in the garden a neat link is made to Jane's earlier view of the world. She encounters Rochester as he is closely examining a butterfly, a symbol that we recall from Jane's schoolgirl drawings of things small and close. But he has not lost his heady flavour of distance for Jane as she describes him as 'more than the world, almost my hope of heaven'. Rochester is foreground and background, but where is the linking middle distance? Ominous too is the dream that Jane confides to Rochester in which she is fettered and cannot move as he rides away, his horse a disappearing speck.

During the interval following the revelation of Jane's wedding day, she seems to enter a catatonic state reminiscent of her childhood fit. There is no closeness, no distance, no art. It is ironic that St John Rivers, who offers so much in terms of physical distance, the trip to India, should offer neither the distance of true vision—his religion is described in the most cold, closed terms—nor the closeness of genuine love.

In the end it is Rochester who must change. When Jane first sees him after the accident, she uses an image of imprisonment: 'the fettered wild beast or bird . . . the caged eagle'. It is now Rochester who, imprisoned in his blindness, has a vision only as far as his hand reaches, and it is Jane who, independent and mature, can come to him from a distance. Both have now had the experience of the near and the far and can, in the combination of their love, create the full resonant picture:

> . . . never did I weary of gazing for his behalf, and of putting into words the effect of field, tree, town, river, cloud, sunbeam—of the landscape before us; of the weather around us—and impressing by sound on his ear what light could no longer stamp on his eye.

A hemisphere and more than a century away, a young New Zealand girl, Laura Chant, struggles as Jane does with innocence and experience, with distance and closeness and with the question of identity. Margaret Mahy's *The Changeover* is a remarkable fusion of classic demon-possession horror story with contemporary suburban young adult fiction.

On the naturalistic level it is the story of Laura's pain at her father's desertion of the family, jealousy of her mother's new boyfriend, and attraction to Sorry Carlisle, an older boy at her school. On the supernatural level the plot concerns the invasion of Laura's toddler brother Jacko by the life-sucking spirit of the evil Carmody Braque. Sorry, who is a witch, and

Laura, who must become one, intervene to save Jacko's life. The interplay between these two sets of conventions creates a startling coming-of-age novel.

In Blake's *Songs of Innocence* there is more than a hint of the dark and cruel side of the innocent state. In *The Changeover* this darkness is at the heart of the novel. At the beginning of the story three-year-old Jacko has the energy, charm, and integration of the totally self-absorbed child. He sees the world as an entertainment staged for his pleasure. He is innocence, the least ambiguously portrayed character in the novel.

But such self-absorption is given another face entirely in the character of Carmody Braque, a spirit of such solipsistic power that he can suck the life from others. The imagery Mahy uses when he enters the book is of containment, not the containment of an integrated personality but of decay:

> . . . the man leaned forward as he spoke and his dreadful smell struck her like a blow—a smell that brought to mind mildew, wet mattresses, unopened rooms, stale sweat, dreary books full of damp pages and pathetic mis-information, the very smell—she thought she had it now—of rotting time.

In this initial scene Braque puts his mark on Jacko, seducing innocence with the prospect of experience in explicitly Blakean terms:

> . . . and I'll make it up to the little brother, poor, wee lambie. Do I see a stamp on the right paw? How about another on the left? Hold it out, you little tiger, tiger burning bright, and you shall enter the forests of the night.

The images surrounding Jacko as he tucks his toys into his basket and as he himself is tucked into bed have been of cosy containment. As he lies comatose in his hospital bed, suffering from what Sorry ironically calls 'consumption', these cosy images transform into those of horror, Blake's hints of the prison and the grave that the nest can become.

Sorry Carlisle presents yet more images of containment. In initial scenes he presents the sophisticated, poised exterior of the typical adolescent male as he appears god-like in the young adult romance. But Sorry is no cardboard heartthrob. In him containment goes beyond poise. He lives in a house surrounded by a walled garden. When Laura enters his study she has a flashing vision of entering Bluebeard's chamber. Sorry has, in his own words, 'sealed off' his emotions.

In contrast to these characters, Laura contains a maelstrom of self-doubt and conflicting emotions. On a bus ride she muses:

> Often she felt a little of herself running out into houses and telegraph poles along the way, as if she were a blob of bright paint put down on wet paper, spreading out and dyeing the world with faint traces of her own color, even as she took color back from the world.

The images of leaking and absorbing punctuate her thoughts of herself throughout the book. Leaking and absorbing, giving of yourself and incorporating the outside world into your own being, this is the stuff of experience, of growing up. And through the complex and suspenseful plot runs the simple story of Laura and Sorry growing up.

Laura's route to maturity is expressed in mythical terms. During the 'changeover', when she becomes a witch in order to save Jacko, she takes the quest journey to distant deeps and skies, down into the darkness of a prison tomb, through the fairy tale 'forest of the night', under water, and up to the hills to look out over the distance to the 'beginning land' and finally back home.

Sorry too must journey. As Laura, the realistic character, takes a mythic journey, so he, the supernatural character, goes on a realistic psychological quest. He must confront the memory of the abuse he suffered at the hands of his foster father, the beatings and the final imprisonment in a small cupboard. In his childhood the nest did literally become the prison. Having been pushed into the world of experience too soon, he must unseal himself in order to forgive and heal.

Having completed their respective journeys, Laura and Sorry are powerful. Laura can recognize the true horror of Braque, the horror of misplaced innocence. She sees Braque:

> . . . in the angle of his head, mirroring the more innocent, but none the less terrible, attitude of a hawk about to tear a live mouse in two, and all she had to combat it was an old ritual of possession which her hard-won new nature enabled her to use.

In supernatural terms her 'new nature' is that she is a witch. In psychological terms it is the power of an integrated personality. Laura becomes a convincing witch while never ceasing to be a recognizable and fully-realized adolescent. That Mahy can combine the supernatural and the naturalistic so seamlessly is a narrative *tour de force*.

Like Jane Eyre, Laura will find that her destiny lies with the romantic hero. Sorry does represent a threshold:

> Something is going to happen, Laura thought. She was going to be kissed. On one side of a kiss was childhood, sunshine, innocence, toys and, on the other, people embracing, darkness, passion, and the admittance of a person who, no matter how loved, must always have the quality of otherness, not only to her confidence, but somehow inside her sealing skin.

But the point of the romance convention is not that it holds out some easy solution to life's ambiguities and frustrations, but that it symbolizes the integration of innocence and experience.

In *Shadow in Hawthorn Bay*, Janet Lunn takes the romance and rings yet another change upon it. She embeds the conventions of the young adult novel in the archetypal Canadian narrative of the immigrant experience.

Mary Urquhart, a Highland Scots girl at the age of fifteen, in 1815, travels alone to Upper Canada. She takes this bold and dangerous step because she hears the voice of her cousin Duncan Cameron, her childhood companion, summoning her over the thousands of miles. Duncan had emigrated with his family four years previously. Mary finally makes her way to the Cameron home only to discover that Duncan is dead and his family has returned to Scotland. The agonized voice of Duncan continues to haunt her. She finally discovers the truth about Duncan, lays his spirit to rest, and finds a reason to stay in the new land.

As children, Mary and Duncan are innocents in the true Blakean tradition, at one with each other and with the natural world, filled with joy and energy. Together they are self-contained:

> Born in the same week, they had understood one another from the first with hardly a word having to be spoken. Almost as soon as they could walk, the two had gone racing over the hills together until the rocks, the deep corries, and the swift-flowing burns had become more home to them than the hearth in either of their houses. They were so in tune that Mary's mother called them reflections of one another. 'And who is to say which is the child and which the shade?' Aunt Jean would ask—and there seemed to be no answer.

Even death will not be able to separate them:

'When I am old, I will lie myself down on the hill and my roots will push themselves into the earth and I will sleep. The grass will come to cover me then, and I will be part of the hill forever.'

'And I will be there, too!'

Here are Blake's green plains and the voices of children heard on the hill.

But distance intervenes when the Camerons emigrate. And, separated by three thousand miles, both Mary and Duncan feel constrained. Duncan hates the dark, forested land of his new home; Mary feels smothered by the closeness of her family cottage. Both behave with the cruelty of self-absorbed innocence. Duncan beckons Mary across the distance until she cannot resist and abandons her family to go to him.

The convention of the immigrant novel is that the new land represents freedom. 'The settlers in America and the Canadas had written home to say that it was fine to have no landlords.' But Mary's journal leads to tighter and tighter constrictions. She arrives in Montreal to find it a 'hot, stinking, crowded place'. Her feeling of claustrophobia deepens as she travels by coach to Upper Canada:

Before the coach had driven very far into the forest, Mary had to restrain herself from pushing open the door, jumping out, and running back to the river, back to the city, to where those gigantic trees would not close in on her so relentlessly.

The ever-narrowing road leads to the community where the Camerons had settled. When Mary learns of Duncan's death she retreats into herself, in a coma-like sleep.

The kindly community offers Mary work and assistance, but the new world presents to her not liberation and reunification with Duncan, her other self, but imprisonment and servitude. She hates the domestic work, and the landscape of thick forests appalls her. The woods of Upper Canada are, for her, truly 'the forests of the night'. Death punctuates her story, the death of a young wife on shipboard, Duncan's death, the death of a baby and a young woman in her new community.

In Scotland Mary could climb the hills and look out over the lochs and valleys to the hills beyond. But here her only distance is inside her. Explaining her gift of second sight to the sceptical Loyalists, she says, 'Sometimes I see the distance'. And in a landscape with no hills she wonders where the fairies, the 'old ones', live. Deeply disturbed by

Duncan's continued calling, she begins to walk in her sleep but is surrounded by the prison of the encircling forest.

The community, and particularly Luke Anderson, make friendly overtures, but Mary is in no state to respond. Her misery is relieved somewhat by her relationship with Henry, a small abused boy that she befriends and eventually takes into her care. At their first meeting Mary shares with Henry memories of her childhood with Duncan, stories of birds in their nests. Like Jacko, Henry is innocence, a state that Mary cannot now recover. Nor can she move ahead. She is trapped.

Further relief is promised by her discovery of the cottage on the bay where the Camerons had lived. At least here she is able to look into the distance over the water. When the bay freezes over, Duncan's voice is stilled. But with the thaw he calls her more persuasively than ever from the dark waters. When Luke proposes marriage, Mary expresses clearly her feelings of claustrophobia:

> 'I am not meant for living in houses all closed and full of smoke. I am not meant for a life of spinning and weaving. I am not meant for living in a forest that shadows the world with its great dark and swallows what is most precious.'

Her relationship with the community deteriorates as they come to distrust her gift of second sight. Even Henry begins to fear her. In despair Mary walks into Hawthorn Bay, following the image of Duncan.

But she comes to herself. In a cathartic moment she realizes that Duncan represents not freedom but servitude, not distance but the confinement of the grave. 'Duncan, *dubh*, in death as in life you would have bound me to you.' She is finally able to see that in her work, in her courage, and in her love for Henry and for Luke, she has grown.

When she says at the end of the book, 'We are the old ones here', she is in one sense expressing the role of all newcomers who must make their own history and mythology. Yet in another more personal sense she is acknowledging that she is an old one, an experienced one, an adult.

Jane and Laura and Mary travel far from the checkered shades of their childhood innocence. They stand at the threshold of the adult world, empowered by their experiences, ready for, as Mahy puts it, 'a labyrinth in which one could, after all, find a firebird's feather, or a glass slipper or the footprints of the minotaur. . . '. We should be offering our young adult readers no less rich a vision.

THE ADOLESCENT NOVEL OF IDEAS

Peter Hollindale

Nineteen seventy, and a year or two either side that date, can be seen as a 'great leap forward' in the study of children's literature. Both *Children's Literature in Education* and *Signal* were founded in 1970, followed soon afterward by the annual of the Children's Literature Association, titled simply *Children's Literature*. In both the United States and Britain there was suddenly a more ample forum for intelligent discussion of the children's book. As college courses were established and book-length studies of increasing sophistication started to appear, the genre gained respectability and status. Cinderella was invited to the academic ball.

This was not before time. From the mid-1950s to 1970 there had been what became conventionally known as a second golden age of children's books, matching the decades just before and after the turn of the century in its production of exceptional works and a richly diverse supporting cast of accomplished novels, especially in the subgenre of children's fantasy. But 1970, the year when specialized criticism came of age, can also be seen in retrospect as a turning point in the literature itself. As with criticism, the calendar year is central and pivotal rather than exclusive; the changes that matter took place within a year or two on either side.

What happened at this time was that the torrent of good new books for younger children slowed down to a modest stream, and simultaneously an alternative watercourse opened up for the older preadult reader. The category variously known as *teenage*, *adolescent*, or *young adult* fiction suddenly came into prominence. Ten years earlier it had scarcely existed. With the publication of such influential books as Josephine Kamm's *Young Mother* (1965) and S.E. Hinton's *The Outsiders* (1967), a new kind of fiction was born in both Britain and America, marked by taboo-breaking realism in the depiction of teenage social experience and conflict, and by documentary explicitness in the presentation of emotional and sexual development. In 1970 came Judy Blume's *Are You There, God? It's Me, Margaret* and, with it, a well-defined form of writing which has ever since enjoyed commercial success and caused critical dispute. Variously characterized by street-wise deflationary humour, physical candour, cultural insulation from the adult community, and a kind of disabusing gospel of wariness, the 'realistic' novel which purports to offer teenage readers a mirror image of their lives has come to represent for many readers what the 'adolescent' novel is. We continue to overlook the fact that these 'teenage novels' are enthusiastically read by *preteen* readers. They answer in part to a social phenomenon which has won plenty of attention in this quarter century: the foreshortening of childhood, earlier physical maturity, and the virtual coming to be of a two-phase adolescence, where the 'preadult' (roughly from ten to thirteen) precedes the 'young adult' (fourteen or so until the age of leaving school).

Perhaps we need to look at these twenty-five years of writing and subdivide our thinking about the adolescent novel, recognizing not only that it addresses a multitude of themes from the everyday-realistic to the abstract, theoretical, and conjectural, or uses a range of modes from parochial urban naturalism to cosmic fantasy, or enlists narrative procedures from simple linear story to complex multi-voiced, multitemporal, intertextual strategies, but that its implied readership embraces a wide range of predicted maturity, education, and intellectual competence. To put the critical problem crudely: How can we discuss the adolescent novel when at one extreme it is a simpler children's book with added sex, violence, and family collapse, while at the other it asks questions about *Homo sapiens* which most adult readers are too frightened or too stuck in their ways to face up to?

In popular belief, and also for many professional teachers, librarians, critics, and 'adult' novelists, the 'adolescent novel' has come to be identified with the first of these two extremes. For some commentators adolescent fiction is an unnecessary commercial invention, impeding progress to adult reading and pandering to teenage immaturity and emotional narcissism. Typical of a widespread hostility is this observation in a recent article by the novelist Alice Thomas Ellis:

> Until my daughter was 11, I had never read any fiction written specifically for teenagers. I read children's books by Richmal Crompton, Violet Needham, L.M. Montgomery, Kenneth Grahame, as well as the comics *Dandy*, *Beano*, *Girl's Crystal* and anything else I could get my hand on. By 13, I was reading Baroness Orczy, Edgar Allen Poe, Dorothy L. Sayers—and anything else. It had not then occurred to anyone that those between the ages of 12 and 20 were so alien or possibly so unintelligent that they needed a branch of literature all to themselves.

The examples she quotes, however, show that her adverse judgement is based on series books, on Judy Blume and her imitators, and on works which 'are intended to reassure . . . but as they are devoid of any hint of real passion or emotion they fail to hold the interest,' and which 'give the impression of having been written by members of the ubiquitous counselling profession'. We all know what she means. The comment is nevertheless intemperate, generalized, and unfair: there are books in this documentary mode which do not tranquillize emotional complexities and which have true imaginative power. But undoubtedly there is also lots of rubbish.

Rubbish has its honourable place in children's reading, as Peter Dickinson pointed out in *Children's Literature in Education* many years ago. The life of reality is unlivable without rubbish, and so is the life of fiction. Even so, adolescent fiction is distinguished by much that is not rubbish, and that far excels the 'adult' fiction which Alice Thomas Ellis enjoyed in her teens. It includes Peter Dickinson's own novels, to which I shall come later. Only a brief condescending reference to Margaret Mahy ('whose books for children can be read with pleasure by grown-ups') shows Thomas Ellis's awareness that such literature exists. In this article I hope to illustrate its best achievement to date, which I would term the *adolescent novel of ideas*.

The authors and particular books I have in mind can often be read with pleasure by the age group I call *preadult*, as soon as the reader is mature and literate enough, and they can certainly be 'read with pleasure by grown-ups'. In this sense Thomas Ellis is right when she says that 'writing specifically for teenagers is a waste of time'. Yet the fact remains that over the years since 1970 a highly intelligent and demanding literature has emerged which speaks with particular directness to the young adult mind—the mind which is freshly mature and intellectually confident, mentally supple and relatively free of ideological harness. Although we can find frequent overlaps of interest in these books such as character types (a young adult is usually the protagonist) or relationship (variants of parent or mentor or leader and child or apprentice are frequent) or theme (such as biological self-definition and maturational rites of passage), these novels are best defined in terms of their preferred and most appropriate readership.

Writing in *Twentieth Century Children's Writers* about Virginia Hamilton, Betsy Hearne observes:

Hamilton has crossed boundaries of time, space, style and genre. Inventive minds cannot be confined. . . . She has taken artistic integrity as far as it will go, beyond thought or popular reading, but with much thought to communicating. This is a tradition which is accepted in adult literature and which must be accepted in children's literature if it is to be considered a true art form. With plenty of books that fit easily, there must be that occasional book that grows the mind a size larger.

The 'adolescent novel of ideas' embraces those books which 'grow the mind a size larger'. Hamilton could well exemplify its achievement, but my chosen examples are Ursula Le Guin, Robert Cormier and, in particular, Peter Dickinson. Le Guin's first children's book, *A Wizard of Earthsea*, and Dickinson's *The Weathermonger* were both published in 1968. They are writers of great imaginative gifts and also of high political and philosophical intelligence, delighting in patterns, analogies, and concepts, a combination which is not unduly common in novelists at any level. In rather different ways they have progressed from writing fairly straightforward children's books just before 1970 to writing adolescent novels of ideas in recent times. Cormier's case is different again. His first young adult novel, *The Chocolate War*, was published in 1974; before that, he had written only for adults.

Discussing the genesis of *The Chocolate War*, which was not originally conceived as a young adult novel, Cormier in an interview described a similar event to the story's chocolate sale which happened at his own son's school, and that passed off without incident: 'But then I began to think—using the two words that I think all writers use—"what if"?' The adolescent novel of ideas is marked at its best by the logic, spaciousness, and lack of compromise of its 'what if's?'. Cormier, who is not a particularly intellectual novelist, does not explore or generate ideas with the profusion of Le Guin and Dickinson, but he pursues a narrative concept with such tenacity and rigour that a relatively simple central idea acquires resonances and reverberates far beyond itself. In all his first three young adult novels (which stand somewhat apart from his later books, including the unsatisfactory sequel *Beyond the Chocolate War*), Cormier hunts down a narrative 'what if?' to the point where it becomes a political hypothesis, in each case surgically examining the soft tissue joining public and private behaviour, and questioning the survival power of individual autonomy and selfless personal action.

The central pessimistic thesis of *The Chocolate War, I Am the Cheese*, and *After the First Death* is that power is invested in a mechanistic abstraction—the school, the state, the cause—which exacts fanatical devotion from its servants and reduces their humanness to mere instrumentality. Cormier seems to test the thesis with increasing rigour. In *The Chocolate War* Archie and Brother Leon are personally vile, not merely functionaries of an abstract institution tyranny, but in *I Am the Cheese* the empowered official is nameless, faceless, and *decadently selfless*, and humans are the creatures of bureaucratic expediency. Worse still, in *After the First Death* a fanatical patriotism, mindlessly intelligent in dedication to its cause, makes General Marchand betray his son. This relationship epitomizes Cormier's recurrent thesis. Ben Marchand is sent by his father to a terrorist location, unknowingly equipped with bogus secret information which he is intended to reveal under torture. Later, his father tells him that this was all planned, and the knowledge that he was programmed to fail drives Ben to suicide. The ultimate in supine imbecility is General Marchand's asinine reassurance to the guilt-ridden boy that he has been *instrumentally* successful, by failing as intended: words which the father sees as comforting are deadly. Humanity is the creature of its machine; it serves a political god without form, and void.

As a novel of ideas, however, much the best of Cormier's books is *I Am the Cheese*, because its complex narrative procedure accords with its reading of the political world. The book is technically demanding, requiring a sophisticated reader. However, *sophisticated* is not synonymous with *adult*, as Cormier himself notes:

> I get a lot of letters from readers about . . . what happens in the book and about who is the narrator—and these come from adults as well as young adults. In the same mailing I got a letter from a woman studying for a doctorate in adolescent psychology and she asked a series of questions about the book—and I received a letter from a thirteen-year-old boy who asked much the same questions—though in different language.[1]

As that event suggests, the adolescent novel of ideas requires (and finds) not less but more intelligence in its young readers than previous generations would have expected. That writers should envisage such a readership reflects the fact of earlier maturity and two-phase adolescence that I noted earlier. That writers should write for this audience as they do, with challenging, disturbing, and often pessimistic visions of the modern human plight, reflects a prevalent sense of political and biological emergency, in which the minds and imaginations of educated late-twentieth-century adolescents may have a vital part to play. Early childhood, which is shorter in any case, is no longer the dominant phase for new human beings which inspired the children's masterpieces of the innocent 1950s and 1960s.

In their different ways, both Le Guin and Dickinson have noticeably raised the age group and the intellectual maturity of their target readership. Cormier as a young people's writer wrote for adolescents from the outset. His narrative technique in *I Am the Cheese*, however, invites comparison with another novel of postwar America, about childhood but emphatically 'for' adults. This is John Hersey's *The Child Buyer*. Its theme is the attempt by a powerful company to buy exceptionally gifted children from their parents and artificially upgrade their brains at the cost of their bodily normality to serve as the ultimate computers, with resources of intelligence that no machine could replicate. This bizarre conspiracy to purchase brain slaves is examined in hearings before a state senate committee, and the novel takes the form of a transcript of these proceedings. They include extensive testimony from the intended merchandise, ten-year-old Barry Rudd, so that we live for much of the novel inside his mind.

The parallels with *I Am the Cheese* are evident. These features are common to both books: There is a power (the company, the state) which is somehow beyond the grasp of those who serve or control or even ostensibly own it; there is a sympathetic, individualized, juvenile human victim; and the narrative is structured to provide a double perspective—the intimate revelation of a child's intelligence and point of view is set against the impersonal and dehumanizing voices of exterior power. And in both cases the novelist uses extra-literary methods (the transcript of hearings in *The Child Buyer* and the tape-recorded interviews in *I Am the Cheese*) to embody in narrative procedure the mechanistic process which the novel is indicting. The theme which these books share is common to all three of Cormier's earliest adolescent novels. They all concern the existence of an institutional organism which acquires independent if amorphous life and enslaves the human beings who invented it.

The difference is that *The Child Buyer* is a satire, serious but also funny, while *I Am the Cheese* repudiates comedy and deploys greater psychological realism. The relation between the two books is analogous to that between Orwell's *Animal Farm* and Golding's *Lord of the Flies*. However, as Golding himself pointed out in a famous lecture, both Orwell's novel and his own are *fables*, and the fable is by definition a didactic form. *The Child Buyer* and *I Am the Cheese* can likewise be seen as fables. As Golding's example suggests, the fable can marry successfully with diverse other narrative modes, such as fantasy, science fiction, political thriller, and adventure story. Despite their outward differences, the adolescent novels of Cormier,

Le Guin, and Dickinson (and the adolescent novel of ideas in general) have the common property that they are variants of modern fable.

The years since 1970 have been the years of feminist influence and radical rethinking of gender, and these, too, have profoundly influenced the adolescent novel. Although there has inevitably been a steady delivery of formulaic sociopolitical treatises disguised as novels, commercially produced to exploit the mood, there has also been work of manifest distinction. Nowhere has the change been more vividly apparent than in the publication in 1990 of Ursula Le Guin's *Tehanu*, a sequel to the *Earthsea* trilogy which was published between 1968 and 1973. Much has been written about Le Guin, and here I do not attempt to do justice to *Tehanu* or the tetralogy as a whole, but simply to relate the work to the novel of ideas.

The first three books are, in the main, intensely conservative. Their key words are *equilibrium* and *balance*. The world of these books is masculine and heroic, and the purpose of significant action is to protect a benign stasis. The female is unimportant and more-or-less invisible in the initial trilogy, and correction of the gender imbalance is seen by most readers, and by the author herself, as the most important innovation in *Tehanu*. In fact it is only one of many, important though it is.

The first three books are wonderfully precise and strict in their imaginative arguments for Earthsea. Just as in *King Lear* interlocking crises affect the order and balance of the individual man, the nation-state, and the whole order of nature, so the Earthsea books explore the balance of the individual (*A Wizard of Earthsea*), the secular or religious commonwealth (*The Tombs of Atuan*), and the laws of life itself (*The Farthest Shore*). Of course this is too schematic, but it illustrates the trilogy's lucid intellectual design. Fundamental human concepts are in play, yet readily approachable by preadult as well as young adult readers.

Tehanu is something else. In *Earthsea Revisioned*, Le Guin writes:

The late sixties ended a long period during which artists were supposed to dismiss gender, to ignore it, to be ignorant of what sex they were. . . . By the early seventies, when I finished the third book of Earthsea, traditional definitions and values of masculinity and femininity were all in question. . . . I couldn't continue my hero-tale until I had, as woman and artist, wrestled with the angels of the feminist consciousness. It took me a long time to get their blessing. From 1972 on I knew there should be a fourth book of Earthsea, but it was sixteen years before I could write it.

Tehanu is certainly a feminist revisioning of Earthsea, giving pride of place to Tenar, the priestess-heroine of *The Tombs of Atuan*, who is now a farmer's widow on Ged's home Island, Gont, and to Therru, a mutilated girl whom Tenar adopts after she has been raped, beaten, and burnt. These two apart, the key figure in the novel is the genderless dragon Kalessin.

The regendering of Earthsea is crucially significant in *Tehanu*, and this theme alone introduces a complex set of ideas. Yet this is only one of several intermeshing changes in the 'revisioning' of Earthsea. The world itself has changed:

> What Lark had said about gangs and thieves was not just the complaint each generation makes that things aren't what they used to be and the world's going to the dogs. In the last several years there had been a loss of peace and trust in the towns and countryside of Gont.

There is a prevalent sense that 'things fall apart; the centre cannot hold.' When Tenar speaks with the gifted young king, Lebannen, about the acts of the sacrilegious wizard, Cob, she suggests:

> 'I wonder if there might be more to be done than repairing and healing. . . . But I wonder, could it be that . . . one such as Cob could have such power because things were already altering . . . and that a change, a great change, has been taking place, has taken place? And that it's because of that change that we have a king again in Earthsea—perhaps a king rather then an archmage?'

The traditional power of the wizards on Roke has weakened, and responsibility for order in an increasingly anarchic world has shifted to the secular authority of Lebannen. Along with this, traditional power and status vested in the male is under question, and the female is newly empowered. Nor is this all. The significant empowered female is the desecrated child, Therru, and she is the child who can call the dragon to her aid. In *Earthsea Revisioned* it is noticeable that Le Guin, who is usually so clear about her mythology, is strangely tentative about the meaning of her dragon, but she ends with this clear statement:

> I understand the mythology of *Tehanu* in this way:
> The child irreparably wronged, whose human inheritance has been taken from her—so many children in our world, all over our world now—that child is our guide.

The dragon is the stranger, the other, the not-human: a wild spirit, dangerous, winged, which escapes and destroys the artificial order of oppression.

In *Tehanu* there is a paradox: a prevalent threat and fear of anarchic licence (which I suspect reflects Le Guin's reading of contemporary society), which can be answered not by a renovated equilibrium but only by true freedom, and a decadent wildness in humanity, which can be subdued only by the redemptive wildness of the dragon, the not-human. The intermediaries and guardians of such fundamental change are the females, and especially the no-longer-innocent, prematurely scarred, endangered child, who stands perhaps for the preferred reader. Guided by such complex and radical rather than simple and conservative ideas, *Tehanu* is a splendid completion of the series, but it is an adolescent novel, not a children's book.

Le Guin's writing for the young has been occasional and discontinuous over the quarter century (including several picture books), but Peter Dickinson's has been regular and quite prolific. His work displays with exceptional clarity the steady evolution of the adolescent novel of ideas. The formidable intellectual and imaginative challenge of his recent novels could not easily have been predicted from his earliest experiments in children's fiction around 1970.

Dickinson has consistently argued that private imaginative experience matters most in children's reading, that character is relatively unimportant at this level, and that narrative is paramount. Certainly his earliest books are chiefly adventure stories. The 'Changes' trilogy, beginning with *The Weathermonger*, is a kind of sci-fi fantasy about an England gripped by medieval superstition and violent fear of machines; *Emma Tupper's Diary* is an unconvincing comedy adventure based on the Loch Ness Monster; *The Gift* is a mystery story about the foiling of a wages snatch; *Annerton Pit* concerns the thwarting of planned 'green' terrorism; and so on.

Yet even in these early books there is repeatedly a book-behind-the-book, a hinting at the context of political, cultural, and biological realities which surround all human behaviour and prompt us to ask just where the human animal fits in the scheme of things. Because of the youthful (child rather than preadult) readership, however, the hidden agenda surfaces only sporadically above the adventure narrative. In the later adolescent novels, this context of ideas is central to the books.

A much more prominent foreshadowing of Dickinson's later work is the strategy of displacement by which the reader is dislodged from conventional human angles of perception. Dickinson encourages the reader to engage with changed and heightened possibilities of human self-awareness. For example, in *The Devil's Children*, Nicola not only becomes infected by the endemic hatred of machines but finds refuge in an uninfected Sikh community, so that she undergoes a *double* cultural dislocation and learns a great deal from it, seeing humanity afresh. In subsequent early books, Dickinson similarly changes the rules and opens new doors of perception, by either giving his child characters exceptional new powers or denying them faculties we take for granted. Davy in *The Gift* is cursed by telepathic access to other people's minds; Pinkie in *Healer* can alleviate suffering through her gifts of psychological telepathy; Jake, the boy hero of *Annerton Pit*, is blind but has gained enhanced nonvisual perception. Living with these and other characters, young readers (and adult readers, too) experience the world differently.

It is a logical development, not only in fictive technique but in continuous and deepening ideas and interests, from these early books to the series of major adolescent novels that Dickinson has published in recent years. They fall approximately into three categories. There is a concern with human cultural displacement, bringing revelatory encounters with the *other* (*Tulku*); and with the politics of war and terror, the friction between idealism and reality, the meanings and limits of freedom (*The Seventh Raven* and *AK*); and above all with the relativity of human biological status, explored through profound imaginative interchanges between humanity and other species, or humankind's own distant evolutionary past (*Eva* and *A Bone from a Dry Sea*). I personally believe that these, especially the last two, are the finest achievements to date of the adolescent novel of ideas.

Writing in *Children's Literature in Education* in 1986, Dickinson observed:

> I get bored with reading books by ecobiologists and such specialists, which contain some glib remark that Homo Sapiens is the only species which is self-aware. I don't see how they can know. Gorillas do a lot of sitting around, frowning—perhaps they're beginning to think it out. Dolphins, for all we know, thought it out sixty million years ago and don't let it bug them the way we do. But for all that, we do know that we are self-aware. There must have been a moment, thousands of years of gradually extending moments perhaps, when our almost-monkey ancestor made that imaginative move, stepped in thought outside its own body.[2]

Dickinson's work can be seen as a continuous attempt, through increasingly complex ideas and exacting levels of narrative demand, to get the reader to step in thought outside her or his own body, to see these various components of the human plight anew. And increasingly he has sought to embody that process of evolving perception, and the very act of conceiving new ideas, within the narratives themselves.

Theodore in *Tulku*, the Christian boy in a Buddhist Tibetan culture, is an advanced version of Nicola in *The Devil's Children*. Paul Kagomi, the marvellous boy hero of *AK*, *thinks* his politics and loyalties through his rifle, as Ian in *The Gift* had sketchily done; Eva, the human brain in a chimpanzee body, and Li, our human ancestor, in *A Bone from a Dry Sea* are reconceptualizing the human creature from square one. Many years ago Dickinson said in an interview, 'I am a very cerebral writer. I think that I distance, I transmute things very much in my books.' These recent masterpieces of distancing and transmutation are possible only because the emergent readership for the adolescent novel of ideas has produced an appropriate audience; they testify to the quarter century's change in adolescence itself.

'Fantasy,' wrote Dickinson, 'is the poetry of ideas,' and he said of science-fiction writers: 'What stimulates them to write is not character but ideas.'[3] Ideas are not incompatible with works of profound imagination, such as Cormier, Le Guin, and Dickinson have brought to this new subgenre. Elsewhere similar ideas and questions have been raised in relatively more conventional ways, for instance, in the abundant, pessimistic postholocaust narratives and more complex time-travel fantasies of recent years.

I suggested earlier that these books have the common underlying property of fable. In his lecture on *Lord of the Flies*, William Golding observed:

> There are fables from other centuries, *Gulliver's Travels*, *Pilgrim's Progress*, perhaps *Robinson Crusoe*. Children love them since by a God-given urgency of pleasure, they duck the morals and enjoy the story. But children do not like *Animal Farm*. Why should the poor animals suffer so? Why should animal life be without point or hope? Perhaps in the twentieth century, the sort of fables we must construct are not for children on any level.[4]

Perhaps not. But this is the kind of question which the adolescent novel has been unafraid to ask for the preadult and young adult reader. Such books, at their best, can 'grow the mind a size larger', and none more so than the splendid and original novels considered here.

References

[1]Robert Cormier, 'An Interview', *The English Magazine*, 1980: 33.

[2]Peter Dickinson, 'Fantasy, the Need for Realism', *Children's Literature in Education*, 1986, 17 (1): 44–5.

[3]Ibid.: 48.

[4]William Golding, 'Fable', in *The Hot Gates*, London, Faber & Faber, 1965: 86.

PART IX

RECENT TRENDS AND OVERVIEW

THE TURBULENT YEARS

John Rowe Townsend

The half-century that followed the end of World War II in 1945 was a time of turbulence rather than tranquillity. For most of those fifty years the world faced, above all, the threat of the Bomb. For the first time, humanity was in a position to exterminate itself, and to do so in a singularly horrible manner. The balance of terror held, however, and at the end of the 1980s came developments of breathtaking size and speed which appeared to break down the rigidities of the Cold War and make early nuclear catastrophe unlikely. It was impossible, as the nineties got under way, to predict what was going to happen next. But the Bomb had not gone away; the danger that sooner or later nuclear weapons would fall into extreme or irresponsible hands had not diminished. Other threats to the future were perceived: among them growing populations, dwindling energy resources, damage to the environment, the rapid spread of AIDS.

There was no major war, but conflicts seethed all over the world, and the electronic media brought them instantly and vividly into people's homes. Terrorism became commonplace. The gap between rich and poor nations showed no sign of closing. In the advanced western countries, poverty remained, though on a far less desperate scale than in the Third World. The United States lived through the Korean and Vietnam wars, through racial turmoil and political scandals. Britain ceased to be a Great Power and suffered relative economic decline; the British Empire was dismembered, though its ghost lingered on in the form of the Commonwealth. Old certainties broke down; the bulwarks of religion and family life were weakened. Groups that had been denied their place in the sun began to assert themselves.

For individuals in the West who had earning power there was growing prosperity; the 'haves' were beginning to outnumber the 'have-nots'. Ownership of cars, refrigerators and washing-machines became the norm rather than the exception. It was the age of consumerism, of the computer, of television. TV became the dominant cultural medium, and American culture the dominant influence. New movements, new ideas, new fads tended to cross the Atlantic from west to east, though there was a modest continuing counter-flow both of 'high' and 'pop' culture.

On its smaller scale, children's literature reflected changes in the wider world. The Bomb itself did not feature to a great extent, but its shadow was there. Writers and editors of children's books came to accept that the world is a perilous place in which nobody can lead a protected life. Although for younger children the winds must still be tempered, older children's fiction moved away from the secure worlds of tradition; 'tell it like it is' became the motto.

This development did not begin at once. After the recovery from wartime shortages, the 1950s were a peaceful era in children's books. America had what Ann Durell, a distinguished editor, has described as 'the Indian summer of the Eisenhower years', when 'society was dominated by a sort of mid-Atlantic bourgeoisie that felt it had saved the world for democracy and had thus earned the right to perpetuate forever the sociological and cultural values of Edwardian England'. The children's book world in the United States was solidly Anglophile, and, Miss Durell added, 'it seemed that almost any book published in London would have an American edition sooner or later'.[1] Protectiveness extended to an unwritten ban on lying or stealing—unless punished—on drinking or smoking, sexual suggestiveness and bad language. Drugs were not even over the horizon.

In Britain, the decade was a hopeful one. Publishing houses were at last appointing children's editors with standing and ambition, and building up 'quality' lists. Oxford University Press, for instance, before and during the Second World War, had published the much-execrated books about the intrepid airman Biggles by Captain W.E. Johns. Now Biggles was dropped, and under the successive editorships of Frank Eyre, John Bell and Mabel George the Oxford children's list achieved extraordinary prestige. Other major publishers also raised their standards. Puffin Books had been established by Penguin during the war, and with Eleanor Graham as editor became the world's first major children's paperback imprint. Conditions were right for a renaissance, and it came with the emergence of a new wave of writers headed by Rosemary Sutcliff, Philippa Pearce and William Mayne, and such artists as Brian Wildsmith and Charles Keeping.

The 1960s seemed at first to be continuing the reign of peace and prosperity. Institutional support for children's books was increasing on both sides of the Atlantic. American publishers had the boost of Title II (of President Johnson's Elementary and Secondary Education Act, 1965) which made huge funds available for book purchase. The books themselves still tended to preserve the traditional values. Family life was exemplified in the reassuring pages of Eleanor Estes, Elizabeth Enright, the early Madeleine L'Engle (as in *Meet the Austins*) and many others. As late as 1964, the then-new edition of May Hill Arbuthnot's *Children and Books*, the Bible of American children's literature teachers, observed:

> It is in the family that the child learns his first lessons in the laws of affectionate relationships. . . . The status of the mother and the father in the family circle provides a child with his first concepts of the woman's role and the man's role in life, and often determines his consequent willingness or unwillingness to accept his own sex. Books such as *Caddie Woodlawn* can help in this necessary process of growing up, for tomboy Caddie, despite her love of boys' games and adventures, gradually learns to appreciate her woman's role.[2]

This pronouncement was greatly modified in the succeeding (1972) edition, revised by Zena Sutherland after Mrs Arbuthnot's death.

In Britain, the rise of the 'quality' children's book in the 1950s and early 1960s had several consequences. One, an excellent one, was that many talented authors, some of them already established as writers for adults, were attracted into the field. Another was that people, notably educators, who had previously shown little interest in children's literature began to take notice of it. They were not always delighted with what they found. A long-running controversy brewed up in the late fifties and continued through the sixties over the so-called reluctant reader. There were complaints, not unfounded, that children's books and their authors were 'too middle class' and that there were not enough books about life as it was known to less privileged children. This deficiency was to a great extent remedied as the sixties went on and writers themselves began to come from a wider social spectrum; but the complaint was succeeded by a new and more political one: that children's books were reinforcing the existing social structure rather than working towards a new one.

The sixties were the years when everything happened. The key phrase of the decade was coined in February 1960 by the British Prime Minister of the day, Harold Macmillan, when he referred in a speech in South Africa to a 'wind of change' that was blowing through the African continent. The context of the phrase 'wind of change' was rapidly broadened to extend to any powerful movement for radical change; and in the sixties many winds were beginning to blow. In August 1963 the Rev. Martin Luther King led a march to Washington and spoke the famous words: 'I have a dream that one day this nation will rise up and live out the true meaning of its creed: we hold these truths to be self-evident, that all men are created equal.' In 1967 the first Black Power conference was held. Black Americans were on the move.

In 1965, in a seminal article in *Saturday Review* on the 'All-White World of Children's Books', Nancy Larrick complained of 'the almost complete omission of Negroes' (she did not use the word 'black') 'from books for children'. Integration, she went on, 'may be the law of the land, but most of the books children see are all white'.[3] There had in fact already been a good many American children's books about racial minorities, but they were by white writers and they tended to imply that a black or brown child was a white child under the skin. This was well-meant but not what was needed. A search by editors for black writers, and a great deal of soul-searching by white ones, were positive outcomes of the new consciousness; a less welcome outcome over the succeeding years was a determined sniffing-out of alleged racism in what often amounted to a witch-hunt.

An article with almost as great an impact as Nancy Larrick's appeared in *School Library Journal* for January 1971: 'A Feminist Look at Children's Books' by the 'Feminists on Children's Media', an anonymous collective of women. The authors studied award-winning and recommended books, which, they found, 'fell or were pushed by our merciless analysis' into various, mainly undesirable categories: the plain Sexist Book, the Cop-out Book, in which after a show of independence the girl character adjusts to the stereotyped role of women, and so on.[4] The campaign against sexism in children's books was now in full swing in the United States, though it was slow to take off in Britain. I commented on it in a column in the *Guardian* in January 1972 and got no response at all, whereas a column at that time attacking or defending Enid Blyton would have brought shoals of letters. A year or two later I was to receive inquiries almost daily from anxious mothers who wondered whether I could recommend *any* non-sexist books for their daughters to read.

Yet in many ways the most significant phenomenon of the sixties and early seventies was a less spectacular one: the accelerating loss of confidence on the part of the parental generation. Traditionally, as was assumed by May Hill Arbuthnot in the passage previously quoted, the parental role was to guide and set an example to the children; parents were the repositories of society's wisdom and experience, the benefits of which they would hand on to the succeeding generation. But in the turbulent world of the 1960s, parents were no longer sure that they embodied the wisdom of the ages. They had not, after all, built a safe, ordered world for their children to come into.

Along with wars, racial and sexual tensions and fear of the Bomb came recognition of a great deal of hypocrisy on the part of the middle generation. High divorce rates, the sometimes almost casual break-up of marriages, cynicism and self-seeking in business and professional life—these were adult, not childish or teenage phenomena. Adults did what they liked, and it was up to children to face the consequences. In the past there had been—among the white middle classes, at least—an unwritten social contract between children and parents. The children gave, if not total obedience, at least a willing allegiance, respect and cooperation; the adults provided a stable home and emotional security. This contract was increasingly breached on one side and was beginning to be breached on the other. A teenage culture was growing up, of which the basis was in part positive—the recognition of adolescence as a springtime in which one has boundless energy, growing independence and a great capacity for enjoyment—and in part negative: a rejection of adult values. And younger children were growing not directly towards adulthood but towards this new intervening status.

Authors were now writing into, and about, a world which had changed since their own younger days. One result, in the late sixties and early seventies, was a spate of teenage novels by writers whom I described as 'aunts in miniskirts', tackling with determined understanding the fashionable problems of the day. Farther down the age range, children were expected to face in fiction the harsh realities of divorce, illness and death, as well as war and holocaust.

The happy two-parent white family ceased to be the fictional norm. Not only were there one-parent families and broken homes; parents slid rapidly down the moral slope. In young-adult books particularly, parents were more and more likely to be useless or positively vicious, reaching bottom probably with the collection of no-good and alcoholic parents populating the novels of Paul Zindel.

The social and political pendulum, having swung a long way in one direction between the mid-fifties and the late-sixties, had to swing back. The backward swing was impelled by the ten-year recession that struck much of the world in the early seventies. Unemployment rose; it was no longer easy to drop out of society and drop back in again. The result, in the English-speaking countries, was not revolutionary fervour but a drift towards conservatism and orthodoxy. This did not immediately affect the content of children's books, though it did encourage a conservative backlash against anti-racist and anti-sexist groups, and there were attempts at book-banning from the Right and complaints of the subversion of traditional values and of law and order.

The recession did, however, sharply affect the economics of children's book publishing on both sides of the Atlantic. Hardcover books, still the bedrock, are sold mainly to school and public libraries. In the seventies, library budgets were cut, yet book production costs rose remorselessly. Obviously fewer books could be bought. Libraries did their best to keep on buying new books, but tended not to replace their stocks of old ones. Publishers cut down the length of their initial printing runs, thereby increasing unit costs still further. At the same time, high interest rates and warehousing charges meant that a rate of sale that would formerly have justified a reprint was now insufficient.

These trends have continued, at least in Britain. A report published by the Book Trust in 1989 showed a ten-year decline in the purchasing power of public libraries, and noted that librarians struggling to preserve their book funds had 'a near impossible task when faced with the requirements for capital expenditure and for the maintenance of opening hours and access to libraries'.[5]

A drastic effect of recession was thus the crumbling of backlists. Traditionally, children's books were published for the long term, and, if they were any good, could be expected to stay in print for years; but the new pattern of publishing meant early death for those that were not generating sufficient profit. Inevitably, this made it more difficult for writers to establish themselves in the children's field, since in order to prosper it is necessary to build up a list of titles in print and achieve steady sales over a long period. A further effect of the decline in the library market was that publishers became more dependent on sales in the bookshops—and also in supermarkets and any other outlet they could find—with the result that they were on the whole selling to less informed purchasers than the librarians. There was more demand for shelf appeal and less for literary quality. The concentration of publishing into fewer hands, and the build-up of big conglomerates, frequently operating on both sides of the Atlantic, has meant growing emphasis on 'the bottom line', and has intensified these effects. At the time of writing, fiction for older children and teenagers seems to be suffering most as a result of the swing from library to bookshop sales: in part perhaps because parents and relatives will buy books for younger children but hesitate to guess what older ones will like. And the price of a new book, especially in hardback, bears little relation to the pocket money of the potential reader himself or herself. The library—if it has funds—can offer a choice for all tastes and keep young people reading.

In Britain especially, the flow of new writers in the late fifties and the sixties was followed as the seventies went on by a relative dearth. By the mid-1980s new talent had become so scarce that the appearance of one exceptionally gifted young writer—Janni Howker—put the children's book world into a state of excitement. Too high a proportion of the worthwhile children's books of the eighties came from writers whose reputations were already made. Later in the decade there were signs of an upturn, but it was precarious. The world recession had lifted, but Britain's economic outlook was once again in doubt, and the general atmosphere was somewhat gloomy.

Happily, the other major English-speaking and book-producing countries were in a more cheerful state. The United States, where children's literature has stronger institutional support, avoided many of Britain's ups and downs, and the emergence and recognition of talent proceeded more steadily. At the end of the decade, children's publishing and bookselling were doing well—specialist children's bookstores were said to be the fastest-growing sector of the American retail market—and there was an air of optimism. Canadian writing and publishing for children were now setting an example to other English-speaking countries. Since the late 1970s there had been an upsurge in both the numbers and quality of books coming out. Much was owed to generous Government support, but the vitality and excitement surrounding all aspects of writing, publishing and selling books for children were remarkable and have continued. Australia had already for many years produced large numbers of good children's books and writers, and continues to do so, while high levels of interest and support and excellent bookstores help to sustain an enthusiastic atmosphere.

Writers and publishers outside the United States and Britain still have difficulty however in getting their books onto the international circuit. Children's book publishing still revolves largely round a New York-London axis. In present circumstances one has to hope that books of sufficiently high quality will make their way eventually to the lists of major American or British publishers, or both; but at the time of writing books from other English-speaking countries are not getting the exposure or recognition they deserve.

Among the genres of children's literature, historical fiction unfortunately seems to have lost ground. It suffers in some quarters from a self-fulfilling belief: 'children don't like historical fiction, so we will not offer it to them'. Fantasy has held its place, though it is no longer true—if it ever was true—that it is the realm of all the highest talents. Realism, for long the dominant mode in the United States, has come increasingly to the fore in Britain. As between Britain and the United States, I have the impression that the balance has shifted; that more American books for children and young people have been successfully published and sold in Britain than previously, while in contrast the going has become much harder for British writers in the United States. I regret the latter development but not, on the whole, the former. Twenty years ago, even interested adults in Britain were often unaware of 'quality' American children's literature; it would be hard for them to be unaware today. In both countries however alarmed voices are being raised over the amount of horror fiction being produced for and consumed by older children and adolescents.

The effects of television and the video-cassette on children's reading are uncertain. Studies have produced conflicting results. There is no doubt that more child-hours are spent on watching than on reading, but it is of course fallacious to suppose that the child who sits in front of the television set for thirty hours a week would otherwise spend the time reading good books. The head of BBC children's television, Anna Home, has pointed out more than once that the adaptation of a book for TV results in an instant increase in demand for the book. But this is of course demand directed at a small number of books, not at books in general. Computer games and multimedia products have also arrived on the scene to occupy children's time.

In Britain especially, the status of the children's writer remains low, and, whether as a cause or a consequence, writers lack the stimulus of informed critical attention. Children's book reviewing in newspapers and magazines is starved of space and is often of poor quality; and little appears in the general press that displays much knowledge or percipience.

Pressures to stamp out alleged racism and sexism have abated, partly perhaps because they have served the useful part of their purpose in increasing the necessary sensitivities of writers and publishers, and partly because the public has grown bored with the wilder absurdities of the pressure groups. In the late 1980s and early 1990s new subjects of concern were finding their way into children's fiction and even into picture-books, prominent among them being conservation of the environment and homelessness. The Green cause is one with which we all profess agreement—nobody is going around demanding more pollution or the indiscriminate slaughter of wildlife—and, worthy as it is, it has produced some rather boringly didactic books. Homelessness, especially the homelessness of children and young people, is a more stirring and dynamic topic, lending itself readily to fiction. Shanty towns and cardboard cities have inspired some good novels, as well as, in America, Maurice Sendak's most challenging picture-book so far.

The present scene in Britain, though probably not elsewhere in the English-speaking world, is less inspiring than it was a generation ago, when it seemed to some commentators, including myself, that we were living in a golden age of children's literature. But I do not wish to sound too pessimistic. There are still a few British publishers who will bring out books because they are good, even while knowing they are not going to make much money. Interest in children's literature in universities and colleges has increased greatly, and several degree or diploma courses are now on offer. School bookshops thrive; so do the children's book groups formed by parents. 'Treasure Islands', a BBC radio program devoted to children's books, has built up a keen and sizeable audience. Paperback publishing for children—spearheaded for much of the period by the dynamism of Kaye Webb at Puffin—has expanded greatly, and whereas 'quality' books in hardback are sometimes alleged to sit unread on the library shelves, these same books in soft covers are read, and frequently read to pieces. And there is strong demand for 'babylit', as concerned young parents seek to set the newest generation on the reading track. That is hugely encouraging. Mother's or father's knee is where it all begins.

Notes

[1] Ann Durell, 'If There is No Happy Ending: Children's Book Publishing—Past, Present and Future', *Horn Book Magazine*, February 1982: 23–30 and April 1982: 145–50.

[2] May Hill Arbuthnot, *Children and Books*, 3rd ed., Chicago: Scott Foresman, 1964: 5.

[3] Nancy Larrick, 'The All-White World of Children's Books', *Saturday Review*, 11 September 1965: 63–5 and 84–5.

[4] 'A Feminist Look at Children's Books', *School Library Journal*, January 1971: 19–24.

[5] *Public Libraries and their book funds*: report from the National Book Committee, Book Trust, 1989.

Trends in Children's Books Today

James Cross Giblin

As we move into the 90s, the children's book field is sending out mixed signals.

I'd like to offer a broad overview of some trends I see in the field. It will necessarily be a personal perspective, and somewhat limited, as all such overviews are. But I hope it may provide insights that will be helpful to both beginning and established children's book authors.

The boom in children's books in the last few years has affected every aspect of the field. What caused it?

- First, a new generation of enlightened parents wanted their children to be good readers.
- Bookstores specializing in children's books were established to meet these parents' and children's needs, and the major bookstore chains such as B. Dalton and Waldenbooks began to show a new interest in books for children.
- Beginning in California in the mid-1980s, educators proposed a much wider use of children's trade books in the teaching of reading. Instead of getting snippets of children's literature in textbook anthologies, students from preschool through high school were introduced to outstanding examples of picture books, novels, and nonfiction titles. This innovative method—part of what became known as 'the whole language approach'—has since been adopted by educators in many other states and has resulted in greatly increased sales of children's books to schools in both hardcover and paperback editions.
- Children's book publishers responded to this growth in bookstore and school markets by expanding their lists, and many new publishers entered the field in order to get a slice of the pie the boom created. As a result, authors with established reputations have been able to command better contract terms than ever before, and talented new writers have found a more receptive market for their efforts.

However, all is not rosy. Recently, there have been signs that the boom in children's books has peaked. Certainly the recession and the cutbacks in library and school budgets don't bode well for children's book sales in the immediate future.

But still, more and more children's books continue to be published. How can authors make the most of this situation? What steps can they take to insure that their manuscripts will attract first the attention of editors, and then the attention of bookstore customers? What values can authors instil in their projects so that librarians and teachers will feel they're essential purchases even with tight budgets?

Some answers to these questions can be found by looking into each of the key areas in children's book publishing. Let's start with *picture books*.

1. There's a need for fresh material for children of one to three, but the texts can't be just another introduction to colours and shapes and familiar everyday objects. Editors are looking for more authors who can tell simple but strong stories for this age group, as Cathryn Falwell has done in her books about a little boy named Nicky.

2. Folk and fairy tales attract many writers who retell traditional tales or try to write a new story that follows the classic pattern. But this type of picture book has become more and more the province of illustrators, many of whom write the texts as well as illustrating them. A good example is the 1990 Caldecott Medal winner Ed Young, who translated and also illustrated his own version of the Chinese Red Riding Hood story, *Lon Po Po*.

Of course, an illustrator who writes his own text receives the entire royalty and doesn't have to share it with a writer.

3. Instead of retelling an old tale, why not think of a fresh variation on a common family or preschool situation? Careful observation of your own children or incidents that occur in your neighbourhood can yield appealing new approaches to such themes as sibling rivalry, parent-child relations, and adjusting to the routines of kindergarten and first grade. Editors are always on the lookout for such stories, especially if told with charm and insight.

4. What other sorts of picture book stories would editors like to see more of?

- Stories with real plots and lots of action that suggests exciting illustrations, all presented in a manuscript of not more than four or five double-spaced, typewritten pages. Anything longer won't allow room for the illustrations.
- Genuinely funny stories, like Harry Allard's picture books about Miss Nelson and John Scieszka's *The True Story of the Three Little Pigs by A. Wolf*.

- Stories with strong endings. Too many picture book manuscripts start off well but end flat or just stop in a very unsatisfying way for young children. To avoid this, you should have your ending in mind before you begin. Eve Bunting, author of *Scary, Scary Halloween* and *The Wednesday Surprise*, uses this approach. She never begins a picture book story until she knows what the last line—the final twist—will be.

5. Another type of picture book in demand today is the story that will lend itself to what I call 'beautiful' illustrations. With the bookstores' market for children's books growing in importance, especially for picture books, buyers gravitate toward large, strikingly illustrated books that will catch the eye of their customers. Stories set in exotic locales, or in the remote past, or that record dramatic events like a blizzard or a forest fire, all lend themselves to this kind of sweeping editorial treatment. But they must *first* of all be strong stories in their own right. No picture book has ever been an enduring success on the strength of its illustrations alone.

6. Editors generally prefer stories, written in lyrical prose rather than verse. Far too many authors—especially beginners—make the mistake of thinking they'll have a better chance of placing their picture book manuscripts if they're written in verse. They're wrong. Too often the authors get so involved in maintaining the rhyme scheme that they lose the thread of the stories they're trying to tell. They'd stand a much better chance with editors if they wrote their stories in prose instead.

7. Now for some picture book themes that editors definitely *don't* want to see more of because they've been done to death:

- The story that ends with the protagonist waking up and discovering it was all just a dream.
- The text that personifies an inanimate object or substance—'How Gerald Germ Travelled Through Billy's Body', or some such. In most instances, personification should be limited to human beings.
- The story in which the protagonist wants to be something else and imagines a long list of alternatives. Just once, at the end of one of these stories, I wish the hero *wouldn't* decide he'd rather be himself after all.

What about *nonfiction*? How has the boom affected it and its authors?

1. There's been a proliferation of nonfiction series. Running the gamut from biographies, to sports books, to explorations of topical issues, they are being offered by such relatively new publishers as Chelsea House and Crestwood House, as well as by such established firms as Franklin Watts.

Some of these books are well edited and produced; some aren't. They give many authors the opportunity to be published, some for the first time. But it's difficult for any one title in a series to rise above the rest and get individual critical attention. So if you want your nonfiction book to be noticed, you'll be better off doing it with a house that publishes each title as a separate entity.

2. The boom has also affected the individual book in a positive way. Never has children's nonfiction received as many prestigious prizes and awards as in the past few years. Newbery Honours have gone to Rhoda Blumberg's *Commodore Perry in the Land of the Shōgun* and Patricia Lauber's *Volcano: The Eruption and Healing of Mt St Helens*, and the Newbery Medal itself to Russell Freedman's *Lincoln: A Photobiography*.

3. Why have these and similar nonfiction titles received so much acclaim? It seems to me there are several reasons:

- The texts are not only accurate, but are carefully written with moments of humour and drama, and attention to literary style. They tell true stories that are entertaining as well as informative.

- They find a fresh angle on sometimes familiar subject matter, like Freedman's *Lincoln* with its extensive use of archival photographs that hadn't appeared in other biographies of Lincoln for children. Or else they centre on offbeat topics that, for one reason or another, haven't been treated before, like my book *Chimney Sweeps*.

- Where appropriate, they include the contributions of non-Western peoples and cultures. For example, in my book *From Hand to Mouth*, which is a history of eating utensils and table manners, there's a chapter on chopsticks and how to use them. Such multicultural information is much sought after by teachers and librarians.

- Unlike many children's nonfiction titles of the past, books in this category today focus closely on a single topic instead of surveying an entire subject area. They may broaden out to make general points, but they don't attempt to be encyclopedic. For example, Lauber's *Volcano* is about a single volcano, Mt St Helens, not volcanoes in general. Such a close focus stands a better chance of getting a reader's attention and making a lasting impression.

- Most important of all, today's nonfiction books are visually inviting. The pages and type are laid out with as much care as a picture book, the paper is of high quality, and the books are elaborately illustrated, with photographs. When appropriate to the subject, many of the photographs are being reproduced in full colour. But sometimes black-and-white photographs are more effective, like the archival pictures that appear in *Lincoln*.

After most nonfiction writers have finished the texts of their books, they have to do illustration research for them. Finding just the right photos is a time-consuming job, but it is also enjoyable—and it's essential these days if you want your book to be eye-catching and satisfying to readers.

Finally, let's take a look at what's happening in the *fiction* field today.

1. Editors continue to call for chapter books for the 7- to 10-year-old audience. These are short novels divided into six or so chapters, each of which runs to about five or six manuscript pages. They can be any type of story— mystery, adventure, home-and-school—but they all should have appealing characters and fresh dramatic situations at the core. And they don't have to conform to any limited vocabulary lists. Examples of successful chapter books include Jane Resh Thomas's dramatic story, *The Comeback Dog*, Stephen Manes's wacky comedy, *Be a Perfect Person in Just Three Days*, and Sue Alexander's tender story of a lonely girl, *Lila on the Landing*.

A word of warning: Don't make the mistake of thinking a slight, uninvolving story will pass muster with an editor looking for chapter books just because it's short. If anything, a chapter book has to be more compelling than other types of fiction if you want it to catch and hold the attention of beginning readers.

2. Editors are also seeking middle-grade fiction for 8- to 12-year-olds. Contemporary stories featuring characters with whom readers can easily identify dominate this area, but there's room for other types of material including fantasies. However, these must be written with today's young readers in mind and move along at a faster pace than many middle-grade novels of the past. If you're interested in writing for this audience, the novels of Katherine Paterson, Lois Lowry, Betsy Byars, Mary Downing Hahn, and Marion Dane Bauer are excellent models to study.

3. For several reasons, fiction for young adults is a more problematical category today than it was a few years ago. In the paperback area, the fad for teenage romances seems to have run its course, and it isn't clear what new type of story will inspire the same sort of enthusiasm in readers.

Whether published in paperback or hardcover, the 'problem novel' has lost its power to shock since virtually every topic, from drugs to incest to AIDS, has been explored in numerous stories aimed at teenagers. Most damaging of all for the young adult field, library studies show that serious young readers are turning to adult books at earlier ages than ever.

Even so, there continues to be a market, although a limited one, for the hardcover novel for older teens. But to convince an editor to buy your manuscript, you'll need to people it with strong characters, treated in depth, and put them into an unusual dramatic situation. Your writing style will have to be rich and distinctive, too, if it is to win the kind of praise from reviewers that will result in sales to libraries—still the key market for hardcover young adult books. Authors whose novels have earned this kind of critical acceptance, and whose titles merit study in terms of craft, include Richard Peck, Pam Conrad, Bruce Brooks, and M.E. Kerr.

4. Now for two suggestions that can apply to stories for any of the age groups we've discussed:

- Give historical fiction a chance, especially historical novels set during the last forty or so years. The drug scene today may be too unclear and confusing for you to treat in a novel, but what about the choices kids made back in the 1960s, when drugs first became a national concern? You might be able to approach that historical material with the necessary perspective, and use it as the basis of a convincing story.

  It's interesting to note that two popular Newbery Medal winners in the last few years—Patricia MacLachlan's *Sarah, Plain and Tall* and Lois Lowry's *Number the Stars*—are both historical novels. And *Number the Stars* takes place in a fairly recent period, the Nazi occupation of Denmark during World War II.

- Don't feel you always have to be serious. Fiction can appeal to a wide range of emotions, and children, like their elders, love to laugh at something funny, or feel a chill run down their spines when something scary happens. In light of this, editors wish more children's fiction writers would turn their attention to humorous stories, to clever mysteries, to ghost stories and stories of suspense—in other words, to escape literature. But, of course, it must be done well.

Though the children's book boom may be easing off, and children's book authors, faced with stiffer competition in the marketplace, may have a harder time placing their manuscripts, I'm sure the majority will rise to the challenge. Is this a really fresh idea? they'll ask themselves. Will it result in a truly special book manuscript, one that no editor—or young reader—will be able to resist?

If authors achieve these goals, children everywhere will be the beneficiaries. And the children's book field will continue to grow and thrive, even without a boom.

CULTURAL POLITICS FROM A WRITER'S POINT OF VIEW

Katherine Paterson

Recently, I got one of those letters that makes a writer's heart sink. A thirteen-year-old who had loved *Bridge to Terabithia* (1977) when she was younger wrote to tell me how offended she was by *Park's Quest* (1988). The girl explained that she was Korean and therefore was embarrassed and hurt by Park's calling Thanh, the Vietnamese-American girl he meets on his grandfather's farm, a 'geek'.

My heart sank because I really do not want to offend any of my readers, young or old, but I was also saddened that this young reader had not understood what was happening in the book.

'You *should* be offended by Park's attitude toward Thanh,' I said in my reply to her. I expect, indeed, I hope that any sensitive reader will be. But in order for the writer to show how Park changes in his attitude toward Thanh—how he realizes in the end that she is not only his true sister but the one person who can give both him and his grandfather the symbolic Holy Grail—the writer must first show how far away from this understanding he is initially. In the scene where he is mentally calling Thanh names, he is furious. She can do everything, except speak English, better than he can. And I've always suspected her brand of English is a pose. Anyone as clever as she could have mastered English months before had she chosen. She has a contempt for everything American which shows in the way she handles the language. Park senses her superiority and is humiliated and so acts badly.

I am aware that many real people, not just characters in books, are racially prejudiced. I have lived in both China and Japan, and my two daughters are Chinese and Native American, so I realize, perhaps better than many white Americans, what it is like to live in a culture dominated by one race as a person of a different race. I would never deliberately choose to offend another human being for any reason. However, when depicting imperfect people in a novel, I will constantly run the risk of offending. I hope you can understand the difference.

The example I have just cited is, as I see it, the problem for the writer who cares about the feelings of her readers, but who must write as honestly, as truthfully, as she knows how. *Bridge to Terabithia*, the book my young Korean correspondent loved, has from time to time over the years, succeeded in offending feminists, Jews, Christians, adoptive parents, and parents and teachers in general.

I can't define 'political correctness'. It seems a very slippery term, and frankly I have more pressing concerns. But I can express the anguish of the writer who wants to write with integrity but who is truly grieved when the reader sees that attempt as a personal attack.

Although I am better known as a writer of contemporary realism, and this is where most of the complaints against my books have centred, my first three novels were historical fiction set in Japan. When I began to write the first one, I wasn't even conscious of genre. I just wanted to write a good book which I hoped wistfully that someone might be willing to publish. They weren't willing to publish anything else I was writing. At the time, I was a bit homesick for Japan, which in four years had been a challenging and nurturing homeland for me. I was fascinated by swordmakers and intrigued by the Gempei Wars. I thought writing a story set in the 12th century would give me an excuse to visit ancient Japan in my imagination.

I was too naïve to realize during those two years that the book was travelling about collecting rejection slips that historical fiction for young people set in 12th century Japan was not your typical publisher's over-the-transom dream manuscript. I didn't realize there was practically no market for such a book. I just thought the book was being rejected because everything I wrote was destined to be rejected.

Ann Beneduce, the daring Editor-in-chief at Thomas Y. Crowell back in 1971, took a chance on *The Sign of the Chrysanthemum* (1973). I was so grateful that I sent Crowell two more books set in feudal Japan. And we wonder why T.Y. Crowell no longer exists today.

Well, naïveté can serve as an excuse only so long. I have known now for some time that historical fiction written for the young and set in Asia has an extremely limited market. Yet in 1981, I went back and wrote another one, set in 19th century China.

Now why would I do that? I can't truly claim a lofty intent. I write historical fiction because I love to. I'm fascinated by a time or a place or an event, or, in the case of *Lyddie* (1991), by a group of people, and I want to explore this initial fascination by means of a story.

Still, when I look back at the now five books of historical fiction—which means that half of the novels I have published to date are historical fiction—I can see that I have chosen to tell stories set in times however ancient, and places however exotic, that in some way shed light for me on what is occurring in my own time.

Jill Paton Walsh said to me once, and I've quoted her often, 'If you want to understand a period of history, don't read the contemporary fiction written during that period, but the historical fiction.'

Shakespeare wrote the rousing historical drama *Henry the Fifth*, for example, not when Elizabeth was at the height of her powers but in her declining years. The Queen had no husband, no heir. What would become of the land? So the playwright takes us back to another troubled era when the crown was perched on the head of a young, untried youth with a troubling past. Could Shakespeare be assuring his audience or himself that everything would turn out well even if young James of Scotland came to the throne?

Two novels for young people set in our own Revolutionary War period come to mind. *Johnny Tremain* (1946), a stirring patriotic look at that war, was written at the time of World War II when to fight and die for our country was to live valiantly and to die nobly. At the other end of the spectrum is the sober anti-war stance of *My Brother Sam Is Dead* (1974) which comes, not surprisingly, out of the anguished reexamination of patriotism which went on during the Vietnam era.

So I look back at my three novels set in Japan and realize that they, too, were written between 1968 and 1974. From 1966 to 1979, we were living one block outside of Washington, DC. If you are old enough to remember those difficult days, especially the protests against the war in Vietnam and the riots which occurred after the death of Martin Luther King, Jr in April of 1968, you may guess why I chose to write of the civil wars of 12th century Japan and of the extreme misery of the poor in the 18th century which exploded into violence in the streets.

Rebels of the Heavenly Kingdom (1983) takes place in 19th century China. Since I was born in China and lived most of my first eight years there, it might seem natural that I would want to set a book in that country. For years I had no such desire. When I tried to ask myself why not, the one thing that seemed to stop me was the practice of foot-binding. If I wrote a story set in China in the past, I would have to deal with the fact that most women of pre-revolutionary China lived out their lives with bound feet. I remembered as a child watching the old women of Hwaian hobbling along the street on their crippled stumps. I imagined that pain of the tiny girls. It seemed too awful to me. How could I write about it?

Yet, finally, in the early 1980s I did. I wrote about a nationalistic religious movement that arose in 19th century China called the Great Peace

Heavenly Kingdom—Taiping Tenkuo. The Taiping were, in 1850, talking about the equality of men and women before God. They opposed any sort of oppression—footbinding, prostitution, multiple marriages, the buying and selling of other human beings for any purpose. They forbade killing, stealing, the use of enslaving drugs. Moreover, they believed (all this back in the 1850s mind you) that every child had a right to an education regardless of gender and economic or social station.

I was thrilled reading about these wonderful people. Where had they gotten their exemplary ideals, and what had become of them? And as I read further, I uncovered the tragic story of what happens to a group of people with high ideals when they decide that they have been given a mandate from God to destroy anyone who opposes their beliefs.

The year I began this book was 1981. It was published in 1983. We were celebrating Morning in America in those days. We were sending troops and arms to governments and guerrilla movements all over the world. Under the banner of freedom we were set to kill and destroy all the foes of democracy. And anyone who opposed us was not only our enemy but the enemy of God.

No, in answer to a question that I have been asked about this book, I didn't write *Rebels of the Heavenly Kingdom* because I'd lost my faith. I wrote it in the chilling knowledge that, as the Bible tells us, judgement begins with the household of God—that, in other words, those of us who claim to be chosen by God in a special way must answer to God for our actions. How can we justify killing in the name of the one who has commanded us to love our enemies?

Sometimes you think you are writing historical fiction quite apart from current political and social concerns. I chose to write *Lyddie*, a story about a Vermont farm girl of the 1840s who goes to work in a cotton mill in Lowell, Massachusetts, to help celebrate the place of women in Vermont's two hundred years as a state. When I began the book, I had never heard of Anita Hill or chicken factory fires or modern sweatshops for illegal aliens. A lot of relevant history simply occurred or was exposed while I was trying faithfully to recreate the period 1843–1846 in New England—a time when small farms were failing and industrialists were growing more and more greedy, replacing skilled American labour with starving immigrants who could be more easily exploited.

There's no need to try to make historical fiction relevant, I thought; it becomes so behind your back. Or maybe history is repeating itself for those who didn't learn from it the first several times around. We didn't learn after the riots of Watts in the sixties, so in the nineties Los Angeles was back in the headlines. Sadly, nothing seems to have changed this time around either. Perhaps historical fiction can help readers think about injustice and feel with those who suffer its effects. At any rate, the writer has to think and feel, so that's one person who will have to come face to face with the evil human beings inflict on one another throughout history.

The historical novelist's responsibility begins with choice of setting, which, as I've suggested, is likely to be influenced by her contemporary setting. Having chosen a setting, the responsibility of the writer, it seems to me, is to be as true to the period and the events and sensibilities of that place and period as she can possibly be. It is my job, as I see it, to create living characters and tell a story about them that really might have happened to people who lived in that world—who experienced those events.

There is a danger for the writer who sees the relevance of a particular period in history for her own day. The danger is that she will go to the blank page with an agenda already in her mind. This is the way to write propaganda, and there is certainly a place in this world for propaganda. But good fiction does not result from a fixed agenda. A novelist has to come more humbly to the page. She must seek to approach the materials of history without preconceived notions, but rather with a childlike eagerness to hear what the materials are saying to her. I try always to remember that when I write historical fiction I am learning, not teaching. I must be constantly open to the unexpected truths. the surprises which the story will give me if I am willing to receive. I cannot, I dare not impose my personal agenda on the story.

Thus there will be plenty of brothels in Kyoto in the 12th century but no churches. The Japanese puppet theatre in the 1700s will not practise equal opportunity employment. And Lyddie is more likely to be interested in saving the farm than in joining the movement.

Of course, I cannot rid myself of all bias. As carefully as I research, as sensitively as I try to write, as hard as I try not to impose my own beliefs on the story, there is no way I can eliminate myself entirely—the over middle-aged, middle-class, somewhat liberal, white, American, Presbyterian female who has lived in China, Japan, Virgina, West Virginia, North Carolina, Tennessee, New York, New Jersey, Maryland and now lives in Vermont. I will be present not only in the original choice of subject but in all the choices which flow from it. That can't be helped. I am the author. The reader is warned. My name and bio are on the book.

In the case of historical fiction, I ask at least one expert in the field to read the book and check it for accuracy of fact and atmosphere. The book must past muster with my husband, please my editor and satisfy the company's picky copy editors, or it won't be published. But there it stops.

Those, basically, are the only people who are invited to give me suggestions for this book. A writer cannot write with a chorus standing over her shoulder, urging her this way or that.

Ray Bradbury makes this point better than I. He takes the occasion to speak out against would-be censors from the left and the right in a coda written in 1979 for a new edition of his 1950 classic *Fahrenheit 451*. In this coda, Bradbury relates all the well-intentioned suggestions which he has received over the years from critics who wish he would make his various works more acceptable for today's readers. Anyone who has read this particular book will immediately see the irony here. *Fahrenheit 451* is the temperature required to burn a book, and Bradbury's book is the definitive fictional treatment of censorship. It escapes being labelled propaganda through powerful characterization and a point of view that manages to offend everybody who is against censorship but thinks a little tinkering with somebody else's books is justified if the cause is good enough. And one's own cause always is.

Bradbury laments all the chopping and changing that earnest but misguided editors inflict on books in order to prevent them from offending anyone. And he concludes with this exhortation:

> All you umpires, back to the bleachers. Referees, hit the showers. It's my game. I pitch, I hit, I catch, I run the bases. At sunset I've won or lost. At sunrise, I'm out again, giving it the old try.
>
> And no one can help me. Not even you.

I am very fortunate that I have had the same editor for all my novels. Virginia Buckley is truly a writer's dream of an editor. She has never asked me to chop, change, or soften for the sake of the audience. Others certainly have, but never Virginia. The book has my name on it. The contents are my responsibility for better or for worse. I have tried to be sensitive to the feelings of others, but my first responsibility is to the story I am writing. I want it to be as close to the truth as I can make it.

I learned that early on. I began writing *Of Nightingales that Weep* (1974) because a friend asked me to write a book about a strong female character that would be a model for her daughter. At the time, I'd only written one novel, so I didn't realize that you couldn't write a book to order. As I got to know my strong young heroine, I found that I could not write both fiction and propaganda, no matter how worthy the aim. Takiko was not going to be a good role model for anybody's modern American daughter. And more than one teacher and parent has since said to me wistfully that she wishes I'd done this or that to make Takiko a more fitting example for the girls in their schools or homes.

No. Takiko is not a role model. But maybe she can be a companion—a comfort—a friend. Perhaps she can bridge a gap of culture and history so that a child of my own day and my own country may know something of Takiko's times and care about her life. And if, in so doing, the reader chooses to see some cautionary parallel between Takiko's world and her own, I would be delighted, but that is an extra. It would mean that the reader got a glimpse of what I learned in the process of writing the book, rather than an abstract moral or social value that I intended to lay upon any reader who stayed with me to the last page.

If you ask me what I want the reader to carry away from this book, it is this: I want the reader to love Takiko herself, and the reader can't do that if Takiko is something less than a real person living in a time and place which rings true because I have managed to paint it vividly and accurately.

So, no, my books will never be politically correct—that is, they will always run the risk of offending someone. My characters will never be blameless role models for today's children and youth. They and their stories will invite disappointment or even disapproval from left, right, and centre—in short, from any reader who looks to fiction to support a point of view rather than to mirror human experience.

But these books which have my name on the cover will be as true to history and human experience as I, within my own limitations of time and cultural bias, can make them.

THERE WAS
ONCE

Margaret Atwood

—There was once a poor girl, a beautiful as she was good, who lived with her wicked stepmother in a house in the forest.

—Forest? *Forest* is passé, I mean, I've had it with all this wilderness stuff. It's not a right image of our society, today. Let's have some *urban* for a change.

—There was once a poor girl, as beautiful as she was good, who lived with her wicked stepmother in a house in the suburbs.

—That's better. But I have to seriously query this word *poor*.

—But she *was* poor!

—Poor is relative. She lived in a house, didn't she?

—Yes.

—Then socio-economically speaking, she was not poor.

—But none of the money was *hers*! The whole point of the story is that the wicked stepmother makes her wear old clothes and sleep in the fire-place—

—Aha! They had a *fireplace*! With *poor*, let me tell you, there's no fireplace. Come down to the park, come to the subway stations after dark, come down to where they sleep in cardboard boxes, and I'll show you *poor*!

—There was once a middle-class girl, as beautiful as she was good—

—Stop right there. I think we can cut the *beautiful*, don't you? Women these days have to deal with too many intimidating physical role models as it is, what with those bimbos in the ads. Can't you make her, well, more average?

—There was once a girl who was a little overweight and whose front teeth stuck out, who—

—I don't think it's nice to make fun of people's appearances. Plus, you're encouraging anorexia.

—I wasn't making fun! I was just describing—

—Skip the description. Description oppresses. But you can say what colour she was.

—What colour?

—You know. Black, white, red, brown, yellow. Those are the choices. And I'm telling you right now, I've had enough of white. Dominant culture this, dominant culture that—

—I don't know what colour.

—Well, it would probably be *your* colour, wouldn't it?

—But this isn't *about* me! It's about this girl—

—Everything is about you.

—Sounds to me like you don't want to hear this story at all.

—Oh well, go on. You could make her ethnic. That might help.

—There was once a girl of indeterminate descent, as average-looking as she was good, who lived with her wicked—

—Another thing. *Good* and *wicked*. Don't you think you should transcend those puritanical judgemental moralistic epithets? I mean, so much of that is conditioning, isn't it?

—There was once a girl, as average-looking as she was well-adjusted, who lived with her stepmother, who was not a very open and loving person because she herself had been abused in childhood.

—Better. But I am so *tired* of negative female images! And stepmothers—

they always get it in the neck! Change it to step*father*, why don't you? That would make more sense anyway, considering the bad behaviour you're about to describe. And throw in some whips and chains. We all know what those twisted, repressed, middle-aged men are like—

—*Hey, just a minute? I'm a middle-aged*—

—Stuff it, Mister Nosy Parker. Nobody asked you to stick in your oar, or whatever you want to call that thing. This is between the two of us. Go on.

—There was once a girl—

—How old was she?

—I don't know. She was young.

—This ends with a marriage, right?

—Well, not to blow the plot, but—yes.

—Then you can scratch the condescending paternalistic terminology. It's *woman*, pal. *Woman.*

—There was once—

—What's this *was once*? Enough of the dead past. Tell me about *now*.

—There—

—So?

—So, what?

—So, why not *here*?

The Lion, the Witch, and the Drug Addict

Susan Smith

Everyone knows that children love stories, love to be read to, and need to experience the imaginative world of fiction as part of the process of growing up and maintaining psychological health. Children who are discouraged from reading or belief in fantasy and who are encouraged to seek only 'reality' often grown up without the ability to empathize or sympathize with others. They may also lack the ability to cope with the fears and problems of childhood.

In *The Uses of Enchantment*, psychologist Bruno Bettelheim argues that classic fairy tales are necessary to a child's understanding of the world and to coping with fear of adults, often represented as giants. In this magical world, the child can confront fears of growing up, with the aid of enchanted animals and supernatural happenings. In *The Wind in the Willows*, and C.S. Lewis's Narnia stories, for example, animals have adventures, adults are merely marginal characters, and the perennial battle of good versus evil is shown in a comforting and cozy manner.

Sadly, this isn't the case in one of publishing's recent trends: bibliotherapy. As the children's publishing market continues to expand and prosper, there is an alarming increase in self-help titles for children. However good the intentions, is it really necessary for children to encounter this dismal territory of alcoholism, AIDS, divorce and homosexuality? Practically every current family or social crisis is included in this new category of blatant candour.

In *Heather Has Two Mommies*, an illustrated book for preschoolers, the three-year-old child of lesbian parents learns about her mother's love affair and the mechanics of artificial insemination. Another picture book, *Daddy's Roommate*, explains his father's homosexuality to a young boy. Many of these books, such as *Dinosaurs Don't Do Drugs* and *Dinosaurs Get Divorced*, use graphics and one-dimensional text to outline major issues. Others, such as *Children and the AIDS Virus*, contain photographs of children with AIDS. For older children, such books as *Living With a Parent Who Takes Drugs* give advice on recognizing the signs of addiction in their parents, where to go to get help, and the child's legal rights.

The idea is, I suppose, to advise children and to give parents a back-up for dealing with real-life issues. The danger is that the books will be used in place of adult guidance and care.

Parents are under great stress and are finding it increasingly difficult to balance the demands of growing children with a career. If they find it difficult to cook proper meals and give their children help with their homework (and this happens at all strata of society, not just in deprived or single-parent households), how much more tempting will it be, then, to deal with draining and enervating emotional issues by handing a child a book (assuming the child isn't just plunked down in front of a TV set)? Unfortunately, for an anxious child, a book simply cannot replace an experienced and caring adult.

Some might argue that children's books have always contained a heavy dose of reality. It is true that children's literature deals with such themes as loss, betrayal, trust and cruelty. What is different with the new flux of stories is their paucity of metaphor and imagination. These issues, and more current ones such as the AIDS virus, are handled with an unyielding realism that makes them read more like textbooks. Add to this the average child's diet of *Beavis and Butthead* and *Married . . . with Children*, whose rationale, like most of television programming, is to sell, not to improve relationships or make people happy, and you are courting disaster.

Sometimes the best way to deal with a crisis is through fantasy and the imagination. Fairy tales, with their stories of human relationships and families, go a long way toward helping children learn about human nature, and at the same time the child's imagination is enriched with the beauty of the images and metaphors. That is not to say there is no place for self-help books for children, but they should have limited use and only as an adjunct to discussion with those closest to them.

By their status, children are often helpless. As childhood becomes more complex and short in its life span—because of the problems of modern family life—it's more important than ever to give children heroes, someone to look up to. If a large number of children are coping with exhausted and absent parents, and many are coping with hunger, perhaps it's asking too much to dish up reality in all its harshness as bedtime reading.

GREENING THE CHILD

Rosalind Coward

Authors of 'green' books are given to dedicating them, in rather fulsome terms, to children. David Icke's new book is for 'Kerry and Gareth and their future'. Virago's *The Young Person's Guide to Saving the Planet* addresses its targeted readers as 'the only people who can get us out of this mess'.

Children and ecology are two terms that seem to go naturally together. Much green rhetoric is about our children's future. As Jonathan Porritt puts it, 'Green parenting is not an optional extra; it is a precondition for creating any kind of compassionate and sustainable future for our children.'

But there is also a sort of common sense belief that children, or at least young people, are way ahead of adults on environmental issues. Anita Roddick, for example, insists it is the young who shame their elders into action. 'Everyone of my kids' age group believes that they are put on this planet to save it.'

The market has been quick to respond. Books, guides, toys, T-shirts and TV programs aimed at young greens all confidently assume that the link between youth and environmentalism is so strong that these products will be perceived as speaking *for* youth, rather than *at* them.

Whether the currently high level of awareness of environmental issues comes from the young is debatable. But environmentalism is indisputably youthful in its appeal, making sense in a way that traditional political thinking around race, class and sex just doesn't. In fact, environmentalism is youthful now in the way that feminism was in the late sixties. It may not have originated among the very young—in fact most of the spokespeople for green politics seem to come from the *thirtysomething* generation. But it is the dominant political concern among the young, the main place where perceived discontents are articulated.

In a recent article, R.W. Johnson described how the new generation of Oxford students no longer find feminism appealing. He reiterated what some feminists themselves have been saying—that the rhetoric of 'personal oppression as the index of political opinion' left no room for the expression of collective discontent by people who considered themselves 'ordinary'.

Environmentalism, on the contrary, appears to offer a much less con-flict-ridden, more altruistic and caring politics. Guilt is certainly central, but it is not guilt about being more privileged and therefore less entitled to speak than contemporaries; instead it is a collective human guilt.

This absence of conflict is probably another reason why there has been far more approval for spreading the environmentalist message to children than there ever was for spreading the anti-racist and anti-sexist message. Teaching tolerance for different domestic arrangements is obviously considered far more dangerous than pressurizing schools into creating wildlife gardens or introducing recycling schemes.

Many environmental children's books even promulgate a social morality, made quite explicit in what the *Blue Peter Green Book* has to say about 'graffiti as vandalism'. 'Most graffiti is done by people who are more interested in selfishly defacing our cities than improving them.' It advises children: 'Tell people it's illegal and selfish to do graffiti on public property without permission,' and encourages them to 'join an organisation like the Tidy Britain group that campaigns to clean up and stop ugly graffiti such as "tags".'

Positions like this could easily convince us that environmentalism for children has been appropriated to fill a vacuum left by the slow decline of a confident middle class morality since the war. It uses a language of public responsibility and caring—attitudes which have had no hegemonic appeal in the last few decades.

One might have expected that such moralism would produce instant resistance, but the fact is that 'green morality' has taken deep root in children's culture. This can be seen clearly in the way environmentalism has been grafted onto the older morality of adventure cartoons. In many contemporary American cartoons, the plot is provided by some threat to the earth—no longer coming from megalomaniac conquerors but from polluters or destroyers of nature.

In children's television cartoons there are growing numbers of heroes or heroines who are forest dwellers: like David the Gnome dispensing herbal medicine in the Channel 4 cartoon, or the furry Ewoks, who live in the tops of trees in harmony with their environment.

Even where the basic militaristic structure of children's cartoons is held intact, bizarre compromises are made with the idea that 'environmental sensitivity' is the hallmark of goodness. The BBC cartoon *Brave Star* is symptomatic here: the hero is a cross between the Lone Ranger and Tonto, and has a partner who is a horse. These ethnic and environmental credentials are then used to endorse a traditional militaristic fantasy.

In children's literature, too, protecting animals or the environment often provides the moral backdrop against which adventures can unfold.

Judy Allen's story *Awaiting Developments* is typical. The enemy (and the outcome) are realistic, with the young heroine resisting property developers rather than an alien force determined to destroy the forests. But the structure has distinct similarities with the 'fight' between the protector and destroyer of the earth.

The fact that environmentalism for children can be incorporated into a moral or ethical scheme probably explains why many adults consider it far less threatening than other political messages directed at children. Aspects of children's advice books reinforce the impression that environmentalism is largely a question of personal ethics or consumer choice. In *The Young Green Consumer*, John Elkington and Julia Hailes encourage a market-led politics often at the expense of party political understanding. After discussing fish farming, they remark, 'There's very little you can do about the problems of fish farming. But there's another fishy problem you *can* do something about. . .' This turns out to be dolphins caught in tuna nets, a problem susceptible to pressure from consumers if they boycott certain types of tuna.

It would be very easy for children to be put off by the patronising moralism which is often directed at them, were it not for the fact that almost all these products, books and programs encourage children to 'shame' adults, to pressurize adults about their consumerist lifestyle. What is clearly being recognised or offered here is the child's right to be not only represented but *powerful* within the family, even if largely in terms of consumer choices. It is a strange reversal, because it is being supported by those people who are most critical of advertisers' use of 'pester power' to get children to buy such ecologically unsound products as chocolate.

But even if the decisions are mainly about recycling or changing the car to lead-free petrol, there is an important sense in which children are being encouraged to feel effective within their immediate environment. More significantly, they are being encouraged to be knowledgeable, with television promoting an interest in understanding ecology and conservation. In some ways this is merely a continuation of a trend in British television since the 1950s. *Owl TV, The Really Wild Show* and *Wildtracks* are in a direct line of descent from Johnny Morris in 'having fun' with animals while informing viewers about them.

Animals and natural history have always been areas where children's knowledge has been encouraged, with the result that it is one of the few areas where there are large numbers of skilled amateurs. But what is different now is that animals, natural history and conservation have come together with wider issues about the environment and global resources which require more political and scientific understanding. It remains to be seen whether adults will be able to resist using children as a moral dumping ground and equip them with this broader knowledge that the situation requires.

Abandonment:
The New Realism
of the Eighties

Marilyn Fain Apseloff

Children's literature has a long tradition of unorthodox families, departures from the norm of parents and children. Orphans are plentiful, and Huck Finn's Pap was notorious for being absent more often than present. In the eighties, however, there has been a noticeable increase in the number of books involving abandonment. Often in the past the deserter was the father, but that is no longer the case; now the person who wants to do her own thing is the mother. This is a reflection on contemporary life, where more importance has been placed upon the individual's needs and less upon the family's, perhaps inevitable with the increasing focus on the women's movement and the right of women to be their own persons in equality with men. The result, more women going back to school and getting jobs, even leaving the family to 'find themselves', is now beginning to appear more and more frequently in books for older children. The earlier books of alienation focused more often on the teens' lack of communication with their parents, as in *The Pigman*. Now, more often than not, it is the parent who removes himself or herself from the child and family, and increasingly, that parent is the mother.

One of the most notable books of the beginning of the last decade was Cynthia Voigt's *Homecoming* (1981), in which four children are abandoned by their only parent, their emotionally disturbed mother, at a shopping mall. Dicey takes charge with a strength of character reminiscent of Mary Call Luther in the Cleavers' *Where the Lilies Bloom* (1974). Although their problems and situations are completely different, both girls strive to keep the family together despite almost overwhelming difficulties at times and the resentment of their siblings. These children must grow up quickly and assume responsibilities far beyond their years, yet they are still children with a child's hopes and fears. Dicey and her siblings manage to survive and reach their grandmother, but even there, the welcome they receive is less than cordial. Their grandmother does not want to have anything to do with them, but under the circumstances, she reluctantly takes them in.

The fate of the mother is revealed in *Dicey's Song* (1982): she dies in a Boston hospital after Dicey and her grandmother go to see her. In a later book, *Sons from Afar* (1987), Dicey's brother James becomes obsessed with finding his father, who abandoned them years earlier, because James hopes to discover and understand why he is different from his siblings and other children. He wants to be able to come to terms with himself, to learn what forces handed down to him might be motivating and controlling him. His younger brother, Sammy, reluctantly agrees to help. Through their search James realizes that he will be what he makes of himself, but Sammy still aches from the way his mother, in particular, treated them: 'it wasn't normal to just abandon your kids, even though you loved them, and then go die in a hospital for crazy people.' Yet abandonment in the eighties is a fact of life.

A sadder commentary on contemporary life and priorities is reflected in novels showing a more selfish abandonment of children than that of the emotionally disturbed mother in *Homecoming*. Newer books portray mothers so intent upon finding themselves and doing their own thing that they are willing to leave their families in the process. In Gayle Pearson's *Fish Friday* (1986), the mother has been gone a year. She has left her family and their small-town life to go to New York to pursue art studies, but her husband keeps telling Jamie, fourteen, and Inky, her younger brother, that she will return. Jamie becomes a surrogate mother, assuming the duties of the missing parent, yet she is a disgruntled teenager, too, dissatisfied with the small town of Sensaby. Her father, aware of Jamie's feelings, contemplates sending her to live with her mother, where he feels that she might be happier. A near tragedy opens the lines of communication at last between father and daughter, and they realize how much they mean to each other. The resolution does not include the mother's return, although all of them still love her. This novel, rich in characterization and plot, gives insight not only into the children's feelings but into the father's as well.

In other novels the abandonment is temporary. In Kristi D. Holl's *Patchwork Summer* (1987), the mother has also been gone a year, but unlike the mother in *Fish Friday*, Marilyn does return, bringing new problems with her. Randi, thirteen, seethes with resentment over her mother's desertion, which is compounded by her coming home to the family as if nothing had happened. In her absence Randi has shouldered the burden of taking care of the house and of her younger sister, Meggie. Randi's anger at her mother is fuelled by Meggie's quick acceptance of her truant mom, and Randi tries to win Meggie away from Marilyn. When mother and daughter finally have a talk, both realize that they have misunderstood each other:

'you had nothing to do with my leaving last year. I thought you knew that. . . . It was *my* problem, and I had to work it out.' Marilyn adds, 'I knew my leaving would be a shock at first, but I didn't think it would hurt that much.' The book ends on a hopeful note as the two reconcile. Despite the reconciliation, the book does not satisfy as much as *Fish Friday* does because the characterization does not ring as true. The mother's last comment above is an example.

Still another kind of abandonment occurs in books for older readers: the desertion of the mother when the child is still an infant. Colby Rodowsky's *Julie's Daughter* (1985) deals with that problem and its ramifications. Slug October was abandoned by her mother, Julie, when Slug was three weeks old; she was raised by her grandmother, Gussie. She does not meet her mother until Gussie's funeral seventeen years later. Through chapters alternating among three points of view—Slug's, Julie's, and that of an irascible neighbour artist, Harper—the reader gains access to motives and emotions from a variety of perspectives. Slug has gone to live with Julie after the funeral, and there she meets Harper Tegges who has an accident and then learns that she is dying. Near the end Harper mistakes Slug for the daughter, Suzanne, she has never seen; she left *her* baby when Suzanne was only a year old: 'I left you. Left you with your father, because there wasn't any other way I could stay all in one piece. There wasn't anything else I could do.' Harper tells Slug that 'I stayed for a year and we played pat-a-cake and blew at dandelions and lay on our backs watching clouds, and all the time I was shattering like glass.' Slug is horrified at the disclosure (the reader has a feeling of overkill). She comes to terms with it, though, and at the same time gains a new understanding of her mother and how Julie felt seventeen years earlier.

A similar novel in terms of abandonment in infancy is Bruce Brooks's *Midnight Hour Encores* (1986). The protagonist, Sibilance T. Spooner, now sixteen and a master cellist, finally decides that she would like to meet her mother (Taxi, her father, has given her that option each year) when she goes out to San Francisco to audition for the prestigious Phrygian Institute. Taxi, afraid that Sib will not understand her mother, a flower child of the sixties when she left Taxi and her baby, makes the cross-country drive (Taxi and Sib live in New York) a learning experience for Sib as he tries to show her what life was like seventeen years earlier. Sib's mother turns out to be a wealthy businesswoman. She and Sib have the ubiquitous mother-daughter revelatory talk common to these books, and she explains why she left Sib with Taxi:

I was afraid I didn't love you. At all. I stayed up all night with you the
first night. So did your father. I hated it. He didn't. Hell, he took care
of *both* of us, and for that I hated *him*. I hated the thought of ever
doing it again, much less doing it every night for a year. I didn't want
to give you milk from my body; I wanted my body back for myself,
after you had had it from inside for nine months.

Sib says that she can understand how her mother felt, but when she must
choose between staying with her mother and working at the institute with
a superb teacher or returning to New York with her father and going to
Juilliard, the reader is not surprised by her choice.

Most of the books mentioned here have a revelatory scene between
mother and child. In Robbie Branscum's *The Girl* (1986) however, no such
scene occurs. When their father dies, five children are taken by their
mother to their grandparents' poor sharecropper's farm in Arkansas. Years
pass, and the oldest three children are forced to do most of the work on
the farm (Grandpa says that he has a bad heart). Grandma is abusive, especially toward the girl, never named. The girl's brother Gene

had known for a long time that Grandma whipped the girl too much,
but didn't yet know what to do about it. . . . Grandma whipped,
slapped, and pinched when ever she felt like it, and that was most of
the time.

Uncle Les is another threat. Married, his wife pregnant and badly treated,
he spends most of his time at his parents' farm because his mother dotes
on him. He also abuses the girl: 'when the girl passed, he reached out a
hand, squeezing her breast and saying, "Well a-looky here, Ma. The
dummy's a-growin' up".' Only Granny, almost a hundred and bed-ridden,
loves and is loved by the girl in addition to her siblings, but she must keep
that love secret 'because if Grandma found out how much she loved
Granny, Grandma would take the caring for Granny away from her'.

The situation becomes more critical as Granny dies and Les makes
bolder advances on the girl, who knows that she cannot tell Grandma
because the woman will believe no ill of Les. Gene finally takes control,
standing up to the grandparents and reminding them that if the children
leave, the welfare checks will go with them. The situation looks even
brighter when a letter comes from their mother: she is coming with a
surprise for them. 'All of them knew without a doubt the surprise was
Mother taking them home with her.' When she arrives, she does not hug or

touch her children. Her son Lee finally asks about the surprise, and she tells them, 'I have married again, and you have a new half sister two years old and a brother four.' She spends the day and evening talking to her parents as the children still wait and hope she will take them with her, but her parting words as she heads for her car are 'Be good and mind Grandpa and Grandma.' The girl cannot believe it: 'She broke from the others running, running after the car. If she could talk to Mother, Mother would take them. . . . She ran, but Mother never looked back.' The book ends as she is comforted by her siblings.

Here is unsoftened realism, an indictment of contemporary society, where adults no longer want to assume the traditional roles of protectors and nurturers of children. Such people have always existed, of course, but their numbers seem to be increasing, more adults being concerned with their own welfare and well-being first, before those of the rest of the family. Sheila Egoff, in her essay 'The Problem Novel' (1980), observed that 'most realistic fiction being written today for young people features some kind of shocking "rite of passage".' The children in Branscum's novel, especially the girl, have to undergo several as the book unfolds. Egoff notes that 'children's literature has always responded to changes in social attitudes and values,' and she wonders 'what new trend will manifest itself for children of today'. That question seems to be answered—in part, at least—by this paper. Adults are being portrayed with more weaknesses than ever.

The message of the eighties for children appears to be that adults are human, too, with faults and weaknesses and with a need, almost a basic right, to consider their own psyches and well-being before those of other members of the family. Being a wife and mother no longer suffices; one must be true to oneself first. That leaves this reader with the uneasy feeling that responsibility to others has taken a back seat to selfishness. There is no element of compromise, of trying to be your own person *within* the family unit. These books do not even offer the reader the consolation of divorce where the breakup is because the adults cannot get along with each other. Abandonment is far more shocking and unnerving to children because of its suddenness and the implication that the missing parent did not care enough about the child to stay. Such novels, even when they end with reunions, must leave the reader with an uneasy feeling: 'Could it happen to me?'

The eighties have already been a decade of social issues such as incest and other child abuse, apartheid, and AIDS that have found their way into fiction for children.[1] One can only wonder what the nineties will have to offer. Will the current be-true-to-yourself trend continue, or will the slight downward trend in the divorce rate signal a return to an emphasis on the values of the family unit? Certainly writers of today feel what Mary Q. Steele expressed, that

> the world has not spared children hunger, cold, sorrow, pain, fear, loneliness, disease, death, war, famine, or madness. Why should we hesitate to make use of this knowledge when writing for them?[2]

We can only hope that the subject matter is handled with consummate skill and that there will always be more novels of hope than of despair.

Notes

[1] For an overview of some of the issues in current novels for young adults, see Marilyn Apseloff, 'Current Trends in Literature for Young Adults', *Papers on Language and Literature* 23, 3 (Summer 1987): 397–411.

[2] Mary Q. Steele, 'Realism, Truth, and Honesty' in *Children and Literature: Views and Reviews*, Virginia Haviland, ed. Glenview, IL: Scott, Foresman, 1973: 190.

TAKING POLITICAL STOCK: NEW THEORETICAL AND CRITICAL APPROACHES TO ANGLO-AMERICAN CHILDREN'S LITERATURE IN THE 1980s

Jack Zipes

Ever since the formation of the Children's Literature Association in 1971 and the foundation of such journals as *Children's Literature, Children's Literature in Education, The Children's Literature Association Quarterly, The Lion and the Unicorn*, and *Signal* during the 1970s, there has been a marked change in the quality of the literary criticism of children's literature in North America and England: whereas the majority of the academic books on children's literature written before 1972 tended to be bland literary histories that celebrated the good nature and intentions of children's literature with positivist methods and a paternalizing ideology to match,[1] the more recent studies have probed the ulterior motives of children's literature and explored its socio-political and psychological ramifications.

This 'revolution' of criticism in the domain of children's literature did not happen overnight, and there is still a good deal of academic gibberish published about children's literature. However, there can be no doubt that the new journals concerned with children's literature and culture, along with various organizations, like the Children's Literature Association and the Children's Book Council, that have pushed for the expansion of teaching children's literature (especially in the United States), prepared the way for an ideological shift in the criticism of children's literature, one that is not unified, but one that represents a break from the benign conservatism of the postwar period, 1945–70.[2]

Ironically, while America and England turned politically to the Right during the periods of Reaganism and Thatcherism in the 1980s, the criticism of children's literature began harvesting the fruit of the radical efforts of different critical schools, marked by liberal and left-wing politics, that emanated in the late 1960s and 1970s. In fact, there has been such a plethora of interesting studies of children's literature in the 1980s, that it would be impossible to do them all justice without writing an extensive study. Therefore, I want to consider some of the more innovative endeavours that have focused on the socio-historical and political aspects of children's literature. In my opinion, this focus can be attributed to the fact that the anti-Vietnam War movement and student protests of the late 1960s, along with the feminist movement and struggle for equal rights by various minority groups in the States and England during the 1970s, generated a fundamental change in attitudes toward childhood, children, and children's culture.

No longer is the child considered the repository of innocence, truth, and untarnished nature, symbolical of an idyllic past that we are nostalgically urged to recover. Rather, on social, economic, and psychological levels, the child has become a multi-investment for the future, transferable as evil or good currency that can be exchanged to benefit or destroy society. There is a general consensus that the quality of socialization of the child will determine: the moral and ethical fibre of society; the manner in which the child will consume and be consumed as commodity; and the structural nature of society and psychic well-being of future generations. Moreover, the social investment in children's socialization, that is, the energy, money, priorities, and time that is to be expended, has clearly become a crucial part of the power struggle among social classes and political parties. The secret agenda (which is really not so secret) of all official and basically conservative endeavours to reform schools and improve literacy concerns the child only insofar as he or she is to be controlled and computerized in forming an identity that will not cause trouble to the conservative forces that want to maintain a capitalist market system in which children are primarily commodities. Consequently, the struggle in children's culture that we are witnessing today concerns various political questions of power and manipulation. Essentially, the forces on the Left want to 'decommodify' the child and enable the young girl or boy to gain a sense of autonomy and take a critical stance *vis-à-vis* the social forces that are exploiting and reifying children; the forces on the Right want greater moral and social control over children and feel that they should be more compliant and not question certain eternal truths such as God, fatherland, and the state. This dichotomy that I have drawn is perhaps too black and white since there are various shades of grey in the debate about the future of our children, how to make them literate, how to make the world safe for them, etc. Nevertheless, the polarization in this intense debate has not lessened since two significant studies by Neil Postman and Marie Winn at the beginning of the 1980s announced the disappearance and disintegration of childhood.[3] Pointing their fingers at the mass media, drugs, sexual permissiveness, governmental indifference, and poor educational systems, Postman and Winn have argued that there is no longer a safe and carefree phase in a child's development that would allow children to make important discoveries about themselves and become truly autonomous thinkers. Instead, they must mould themselves to images provided by the mass media and adults, who want them to begin sharing burdens at an early life and become part of a socialization process that no longer stresses the differences between adults and children. In fact, play and study are oriented toward the capitalist market system, and schools themselves are becoming increasingly commercialized so that they do not serve the community but rather the interests of the economy. Even the debate about literacy is connected to corporate and governmental endeavours to provide proper literary canons and curriculae that have little to do with the real degrading experiences of children today.

In sum, the changes in the criticism of children's literature can only be understood if they are analysed against the broad background of the struggle over the future of our children that has assumed new contours in the US and England. And my broad black and white strokes are meant to be reminders of the debates and conditions that have led to the new political criticism dealing with children's literature.

One of the key books on children's literature that reveals the influence of this struggle is Fred Inglis' *The Promise of Happiness: Value and Meaning in Children's Fiction* (1981). Inglis is above all concerned with how to make value judgements about children's literature, or put bluntly: what makes for a good children's book? For Inglis, 'The structure of a novel and the structure of a person are the same, and both are moral.' Therefore, each author's style is an indication of his or her integrity in terms of coping with the world, and the plotting of the fiction is representative of the author's teleological action that calls for appreciation and emulation. Inglis is quick to point out that 'moral behaviour takes both form and content from social structures, it *expresses* social structures, and it is at the same time one of those structures itself.' As a result, every work of fiction is stamped by its socio-historical structural context and must be judged by the manner in which it contributes to the moral growth of readers in its own time. Whether it becomes a classic and continues to play a role in the great tradition of children's books will depend on the mode in which the author seeks to make sense out of his/her life and times. 'The best writers seek to create an ideal social order out of the values there are to hand . . . a novelist ought to create fictions which criticize the life he finds about him from the standpoint of the finest life he can imagine. His work enables his readers to find the best and fullest, the freest and most admirably self-aware versions of life which is possible to lead in the circumstances of the time.' Wary about the general abstractness of his superlatives like 'best', 'fullest', and 'freest', Inglis insists that he does not argue for fixed absolute standards, but for the inescapability of judgement, and since authors write with a purpose and values, readers must be able to judge 'in the name of the best you can convincingly imagine'. From this point on in his book, Inglis studies texts within their contexts and endeavours to put his moral theory into practice by demonstrating what books should or should not be read by children.

Somewhat in the tradition of F.R. Leavis,[4] but much more political, Inglis wants to establish the great moral tradition of children's literature, and he asserts with Stendhal in mind that 'all great art holds out "the promise of happiness".' Therefore, the crucial question in determining whether a work for children is significant is: 'How shall the promise be kept?' From this point on, Inglis examines various authors such as Arthur Ransome, Rudyard Kipling, E. Nesbit, Laura Ingalls Wilder, E.B. White, J.R.R. Tolkien, Richard Adams, Gillian Avery, Joan Aiken, Alan Garner, Philippa Pearce, William Mayne, and others to demonstrate how they deal with questions of gender, social class, friendship, and culture in keeping with the categorical principle of 'the promise of happiness'. Though Inglis does not cite Ernst Bloch, his basic criterion concerning the value of a work of art has a great deal to do with Bloch's utopia notion of *Vor-Schein*,[5] that is, the anticipatory illumination in a work of art that points a way to a better future. The aesthetic quality of a work of art is determined by the manner in which it critically reflects the conditions in society to anticipate a better one, and it is the 'duty' of this art to provide hope. As Inglis concludes,

> Children's novels are proposed to children by adults as the imaginative forms of life which they work with and turn into their future lives. To take such an argument seriously is to place the study of fiction at the very heart of education, both official and informal. It is to cut back the dominance of social calculus and computational science in public thought and its schemes of reason. Literature is then no longer for consolation of your private life. Fiction-making cannot guarantee virtue, but it can freedom. And it is much better able to work for the common good than any of the alternatives which ensure the death of public thought and feeling in and out of school.

Though Inglis' study is insightful and forthright in its moral vigour, his argument is dangerously reminiscent of some of the enlightened critics of the late eighteenth and early nineteenth centuries who wanted to have a decent, morally responsible, and realistic literature for children. The major difference between Inglis and these critics is that he accepts all modes of fantasy literature and is against censorship. Otherwise, the categories that he establishes to judge 'good' children's literature could be twisted around by the so-called moral majority and conservative liberal forces to preach what type of literature should or should not be read in schools. There has been no consensus reached on the definition of such terms as happiness, the future of society, integrity, etc., and while Inglis is clear about his own notions, they do not provide a systematic framework informed by complex and evocative theoretical approaches that might enable a critic or reader to astutely assess children's literature. What saves his analysis of the books he discovers is his own sensitivity, social awareness and historical consciousness of the function of children's literature. His book does not really introduce new ideological or aesthetic criteria or present a new methodology for interpreting children's literature. Rather it is more an urgent plea for greater social responsibility among adults and writers to produce and use literature in a way that will help young people see through the mystified conditions of social relations.

The same thing could be said about Ariel Dorfman's *The Empire's Old Clothes* (1983), except that the author's background has led him to focus more polemically on the imperialist nature of children's literature that is also examined more systematically from a Marxist viewpoint. Forced to flee Chile in 1973, after Salvador Allende had been assassinated, Dorfman had worked with young people in his country to try to bring about an autonomous popular culture that was not determined by the profit motive to make mass market consumers out of the Chilean people. One of the fruits of his labours was the book that he had written with the Belgian sociologist, Armand Mattelart, *How to Read Donald Duck: Imperialist Ideology in the Disney Comic* (1975). The collection of essays in *The Empire's Old Clothes* stems in part from his writings and experiences in Chile and his reflections on the subject of mass culture after his arrival in the United States. In much the same manner that Roland Barthes[6] endeavoured to expose the myths by which we govern our lives as socially constructed fictions that have strong ideological ramifications, Dorfman scrutinizes such heroes as Babar, Donald Duck, and the Lone Ranger and examines *The Reader's Digest* to show that they all have a common purpose: to infantilize readers so that they do not have to think for themselves and will accept the world as it is presented to them as fundamentally unalterable and good. In his superb analysis of the Babar books, Dorfman explains historically how Babar became king of the jungle after being civilized by an old, cultured lady (obviously representative of France), and how he imported western values to educate the elephants of his kingdom (clearly Africa) and maintain his superiority and consequently that of the West. It is, however, not just colonization and imperialism that are celebrated in the Babar books, but a particular way of thinking, reading, and acting that one can find in the Donald Duck cartoons, the Lone Ranger, and the *Reader's Digest*. As Dorfman argues,

> just as Babar created a kingdom where nature and development were allies, in which civilization and barbarism could be reconciled, so the little ducks present to their readers—children of all ages—the possibility of realizing the most dogged, undying dream of the twentieth century, the dream which led to the founding of the USA, the dream of working and being your own boss at the same time. Once again they bear witness, in their individual bodies and in the body of the comic strip, episode after episode, to the same mythic, instantaneous evolution that Babar's country suffered. Such a movement, from inferior to superior, from primitive to urban, from poverty to progress, coincides with the aesthetic experience of reading that the reader has of the world, the way that he vicariously consumes the life of its characters. The reader begins these cartoons as if he were in an underdeveloped territory, with no control over events, and ends up having acquiesced to illumination, revelation, and success—thereby resolving his tensions and ignorance.

Whether the 'authors' of such popular works consciously intend to indoctrinate their readers in this way does not matter. The fact is, according to Dorfman, 'mass media, as opposed to art, leaves hardly any space for interpretation by the audience.'

Here Dorfman is in perfect accord with Inglis, but both critics, despite their good intentions, do not provide evidence that readers consume the ideologically nefarious works produced for mass consumption the way they argue, nor do they really distinguish great art from mass media and popular art. If one is to level charges against the manipulative and mystifying aspects of popular culture and regressive children's literature, then a more sophisticated analysis of reception is necessary. However, from a production point of view, the production of ideas and forms, Dorfman's argument is convincing: manipulation of child readers of all ages that reinforces dependency of thinking and acting is central to the production of children's books and popular works for the masses.

The manipulation of the child in and through children's literature is a central thesis to two studies that deal with children's literature in England from its beginnings to the mid-nineteenth century: Geoffrey Summerfield's *Fantasy and Reason* (1984) and Mary V. Jackson's *Engines of Instruction, Mischief, and Magic* (1989). Summerfield's work is a selective study of the more important books on eighteenth-century children that centre on the debate between the imagination and reason and how children were to be socialized through literature. He demonstrates that the ideas of Locke, Addison, and Rousseau were gradually twisted throughout the eighteenth century to serve the interests of religion and science. Though fantasy literature survived the attack in chapbooks, collections of fairy tales, and romances, it suffered enough disparagement in the hands of religious pundits and rational scientists that Summerfield feels obliged to claim,

> many rationally disposed adults came to hold the view that the sooner the children could be educated out of poetic 'fairy' foolishness, the better for all concerned. In essence, we have inherited such views, and mostly subscribe to the view that intellectual and moral growth involves an increase in the capacity to construe the world in terms of the empirical sciences, and a complementary willingness to abandon the metaphors, the multi-valances, the poetic resonances of the cosmic fictions that we call fantasy. Empiricism and the protestant work-ethic have bitten deep into our collective psyche. Even when we agree to allow children to have a childhood, we still tend to assume that the sooner they abandon the modalities of fantasy, the sooner they will begin effectually to exercise and prove their intelligence in useful ways.

Summerfield is at his best in analysing the works of Thomas Day, Maria Edgeworth, Sarah Trimmer, Charles Lamb, and William Godwin as they all sought in various ways, under the influence of the misunderstood Locke and Rousseau, to establish moral and rational criteria in children's books for the explicit purpose of making reasonable, virtuous human beings out of young people. His book concludes by claiming that, even though the rationalists prevailed, they were contested by the romantic movement and have continued to be opposed up to the present by imaginative writers who offer the possibility of alternative realities and options in life.

Although the broad contours of Summerfield's historical survey of the debate between reason and fantasy are correct, he neglects the imaginative appeal of some of the works produced by the so-called rationalists and does not realize that the differences between the defenders of reason and fantasy often became mixed in their works and arguments. Therefore, Mary Jackson's book is a good counterbalance, for she focuses on many of the inadvertently positive aspects of literature for children produced by the rationalists. She begins with the premise that

> children's literature was rooted in the conditions and imperatives of the adult world and was regarded first and foremost as a tool to shape the young to the needs of that world . . . children were resources to be molded or engineered to needs and specifications determined by a prevailing social standard.

Though this statement is in agreement with Summerfield's general thesis, her socio-historical survey of English children's literature is much more comprehensive and deals with the practices and policies of publishers, the relationship of different kinds of publications such as the trade novel, miscellanies, chapbooks, poetry, the juvenile magazine, educational theory and practice, religious attitudes, the interaction between polite adult and children's literature, and political events. By paying careful attention to the manifold socio-political factors involved in the evolution of children's literature, Jackson is able to revise some of Summerfield's one-dimensional notions regarding the puritanical and rationalist nature of early children's literature and its reception. For instance, she points out that the early publishers were men who had worked hard to become successful and had found greater opportunities for themselves by becoming literate. Therefore, the emphasis on social advancement through literature (alphabet books, miscellanies, chapbooks) was a leitmotif in their productions, and whatever might encourage children to learn to read and write, whether it was fantastic or religious, was given priority over dull books. Moreover, the publishers were interested in attracting buyers and making money.

> In addition to the amusement and instruction that post-Newbery books of polite conduct and courtesy provided, they also purveyed both the idea and to an extent the wherewithal for lower-middle class readers to shed habits deemed vulgar and to emulate or at least mimic the genteel manners of their social superiors, the middle and upper-middle classes. Clearly, such books aided—and later critics

charged they abetted—what many considered the improper social pretensions of the 'lower orders'. In varying degrees, most children's books published between 1740 and 1790 inadvertently undercut faith in the inviolability of class distinctions by encouraging aspirations and by heightening economic or social expectations. Indeed, during this period Britain's class system was somewhat more fluid than after the outbreak of the French Revolution and the Napoleonic Wars (1789–1815), when fears of Jacobin (French revolutionary) influences on the poor and even the artisans of the lower-middle class both widened and intensified class conservatism. Simultaneously, however, economic and religious forces were steadily enlarging England's middle classes and stimulating the spread of bourgeois social values.

Given this situation, Jackson points out that books, which contemporary readers and critics might find overly didactic, rational, and ghastly, were probably received in a more hopeful and tolerant manner in their own time.[7] In fact, there was a certain utopian verve to the early children's books that encouraged the young to become independent. Later, by the end of the eighteenth century and beginning of the nineteenth, children's books began to encourage more servility than autonomy.

> The 'new child' lingered in a fondly sentimentalized state of childishness rooted in material and emotional dependency on adults. This child lapped up lessons hungrily, was eagerly obedient or lavishly repentant, but most important, the new good child seldom made important, real decisions without parental approval. Bad children struck out on their own on some project, erroneously assuming themselves capable of judging what was proper and having the right to act independently. In short, the new good child was a paragon of dutiful submissiveness, refined virtue, and appropriate sensibility.

This does not mean that, by 1830, children's literature was used exclusively to socialize children in instrumental ways according to the needs and interests of the ruling forces in society. On the contrary, Jackson convincingly points out throughout her book that there was always

> a precarious but long-lasting balance between the moral utilitarians and the apostles of fancy. The pattern that emerges continued to hold throughout the century. Each type had its fanatical adherents; each

tried to dominate the field from time to time. But in fact they both held their own, for the moralists and the artists ministered to divergent, possibly inimical, but apparently ineradicable human needs.

Perhaps because Jackson (like Summerfield) is in the camp of the apostles of fancy, she overlooks the manner in which writers of fairy tales, romances, and fanciful works for children in the first half of the nineteenth century actually succumbed to moral and conservative ideological pressures and revised the content and style of the fairy tale to reinforce patriarchal notions of gender and the protestant ethic. That is, there was no real balance between reason and fantasy in the production of children's literature, both fiction and nonfiction, because most narratives and poetry endorsed the conservative norms and subscribed to the imperialist views of the British nation. The hegemony of conservatism in its rational and fantastic form was only challenged after 1848, and the major innovative work here was Lewis Carroll's *Alice in Wonderland* (1865).

In Juliet Dusinberre's fine study *Alice to the Lighthouse* (1987), she explains how Carroll's work introduced both a new aesthetics and attitude with regard to the representation of the child in a children's book and an innovative manner of addressing children with more respect for their autonomy as creative readers.

> The irreverence which Carroll authorised in the *Alice* books was towards the pretensions of the pious author and of the entire adult world in its attitude to children, whom Carroll understood on their own terms as no writer had done before. . . . *Alice in Wonderland* is both symptom and catalyst to a new sceptical generation, not because Carroll mocks God, but because his book refuses to convey a religious message. . . . Carroll laughs at the hierarchies of the adult world in which God and the author dance a lobster quadrille. He was irreverent not as a Christian but as an artist, which is why Roger Fry wanted to rescue the *Alice* books from the deluge in which he would gladly have submerged most of Victorian culture.

Dusinberre is quick to acknowledge that Carroll was not alone in his radicalization of children's fiction. She deals with such other writers as Robert Louis Stevenson, Edith Nesbit, Rudyard Kipling, Kenneth Grahame, Mary Molesworth, Mark Twain, Louisa M. Alcott, Joel Chandler Harris, Susan Coolidge, and Frances Hodgson Burnett, who 'anticipated in different ways' the radical experiments of Virginia Woolf's novels. It is this relationship—between the innovative children's fiction of the late nineteenth century and Virginia Woolf's work—that is the central focus of Dusinberre's study, for she wants to demonstrate that literary critics have neglected the importance of children's literature for understanding the development of literature for adults, and she convincingly reveals how new attitudes toward children and aesthetic innovations in children's literature did in fact find their way into Woolf's novels and set the stage for further experiments in literature for adults.

Ever since the 1970s, the political emphasis of the literary criticism has finally become more concerned with the ideological impact and socialization of young readers. What is needed now, it seems to me, are studies that treat the reception and distribution of children's literature with regard to the impact it has. Moreover, more attention must be given to the mass media and its relationship to literary works for children. Finally, very few studies have been conducted about how children's literature is used inside and outside of schools. What books and comics are read? What films are watched? What canon is preached in the schools and why? These questions are still concerned with the manipulation of children—but in the new theoretical and critical approaches, instead of accepting the literary canons and sanctioning the traditional socialization processes, those who are trying to *regulate* children and images of childhood are the ones who are fortunately being questioned.

Notes

[1] There are a few exceptions such as Gillian Avery, *Nineteenth Century Children: Heroes and Heroines in English Children's Stories* (London: Hodder and Stoughton, 1965) and F.J. Harvey Darton, *Children's Books in England*, 3rd ed., revised by Brian Alderson (Cambridge: Cambridge UP, 1982 [1932]).

[2] For an interesting collection of essays representative of different political viewpoints, largely from the period 1972–88, see Betty Bacon, ed., *How Much Truth Do We Tell the Children? The Politics of Children's Literature* (Minneapolis: MEP Publications, 1988).

[3] Cf. Neil Postman, *The Disappearance of Childhood* (New York: Delacorte, 1982) and Marie Winn, *Children without Childhood* (New York: Pantheon, 1983). See also Barry Richards, ed., *Capitalism and Infancy* (Atlantic Highlands, NJ: Humanities Press, 1984) and Robert Coles, *The Political Life of Children* (Boston: Houghton Mifflin, 1986).

[4] Cf. F.R. Leavis, *The Great Tradition* (London: Chatto & Windus, 1955).

[5] See Ernst Bloch, *The Utopian Function of Art and Literature*, trs Jack Zipes and Frank Mecklenburg (Cambridge, MA: MIT Press, 1988).

[6]Cf. *Mythologies* (New York: Hill and Wang, 1972).

[7]Cf. Robert Leeson, *Reading and Righting: The Past, Present and Future of Fiction for the Young* (London: Collins, 1985).

Epilogue: Some Thoughts on Connecting

Sheila Egoff and Wendy Sutton

In the summer of 1995, the University of British Columbia was making plans for its annual Open House. The Special Collections Division of the University Library began preparing for a display of items from its large and valuable collection of early children's books. It was to feature four of the best known and best loved children's books of the nineteenth and twentieth centuries, here described in shorthand as Alice, Oz, Anne, and Pooh. Their dates of publication are, respectively, 1865, 1900, 1908, and 1926. The idea of the exhibit was to make a reading or a literary link ('only connect') between adults (chiefly parents) and children who would be thronging the campus.

Undoubtedly, there have been more and better books written and published for the young in the last three decades than in the whole previous development of children's literature which spans almost four hundred years. The reference here, of course, is to those books *deliberately* written for the young and so excludes folklore, myth and legend, and much poetry that children have appropriated unto themselves. While books for the young have always been based on the public manners and mores of the times in which they were written, they tended to remain static over a long period. Modern children's literature, however, particularly that written since the middle of the 1960s, and chiefly in its realistic genre, has been quick to reflect all manner of social changes: divorce, dysfunctional families, missing parents (chiefly fathers), the effect of drug use, alcoholism, child abuse, and such concerns as feminism, the destruction of the environment, and the treatment of minorities, to name but a few. In the past, except for an often drastic look at poverty, an emphasis on manners, and a large dose of religiosity, social themes did not loom large. Stylistically, they were as uniformly dull as their storylines. Today's books with their rather adult themes are often very well written. Many of their authors show a poignant empathy with their young protagonists and bring them through their shocks, rages, and disappointments to a new maturity.

The shift in themes may be of less significance than the quantity of titles published. Back in the mid-1950s, the great American teacher of children's literature, Frances Clarke Sayers was bemoaning the increased commercialism of children's books and the greater numbers being churned out. She entitled her 1956 speech 'Of Memory and Muchness'[1]—a phrase she neatly borrowed from the tea party scene in Lewis Carroll's *Alice's Adventures in Wonderland*.

'Muchness'—the sheer numbers of books published annually in the English language—poses even more of a problem today, forty years later. Although precise figures even for English-language publications are not easily available, anyone dealing with children's books senses overproduction. It is certainly safe to say that in the last fifteen years output has risen by at least a third, probably giving us five thousand new titles a year, besides all the reprints and the retellings of old tales. In the United States alone, the children's book publishing industry by 1994 had become a 1.2 billion dollar business,[2] a fact which makes it a significant part of the current world of communication with its mergers, its focus on entertainment, tie-ins, and its aggressive competition. It is worth while noting that many children's authors write a great many books (Enid Blyton could turn out one every two weeks). Such 'writing machines' evidently support the publishers in their belief that making a quick return is what matters, not quality. Quantity has also had a hitherto unforeseen impact on another aspect of books for the young. It has made criticism virtually impossible unless it is examining a very narrow segment of the output. Who can now connect with hundreds of books in any given genre, even ignoring books in translation or those in a language other than English? With today's output, a critical review covering a single genre alone would be out of date in about two years.

How does all this newness and muchness stand up both to literary criticism and the interests of children? Anyone who professes to deal seriously with children's literature must face these issues. The first and chief point to be acknowledged is that children and young adults need books of their own time and place. This is a time for realism in literature. Most child readers of a former generation tended to see literature as an exciting adventure, escaping perhaps from rather ordinary lives into Scott, Dickens, and Dumas at about age eleven and then moving quickly into strictly adult, more sophisticated literature. This is no longer the case. The young today are much more likely to want a book 'about a kid just like me', surely a sign of the egomania of the times. Publishers know and exploit this: with the exception of picturebooks, realistic fiction makes up the largest group of modern publications for the young. In one sense this is surprising since in the past, fantasy has been the great survivor in terms of delight as well as longevity (three of the great Alice/Oz/Anne/Pooh quartet are fantasies). Today, television, the movies, and computer games are capitalizing upon the world of fantasy and escapism.

There are, of course, many types of realistic fiction. The light and humorous stories of child and family life on the order of Beverly Cleary's *Henry Huggins* and *Ramona* series, popular in the 1950s, still form a substantial group, and oddly enough do not seem to have been replaced in children's affections by more modern series such as Betty Waterton's *Quincy Rumpole* series of the 1980s. Then there are the hundreds of recent series books of romance and/or mystery either so sickly sentimental or so violent or so feebly constructed that Nancy Drew and the Hardy Boys are welcome by comparison.

A smaller group is composed of quality writing that tends to win prizes and/or critical acclaim. Often these are based on the 'in' topics mentioned above but, unlike a classic which a child will reread and enjoy even more at an older age, they do not offer themselves to a wide variety of readers and age spans.

Modern authors of serious realistic fiction appear to be somewhat obsessed with two major topics: death and missing parents. In Victorian times, death was also rampant in children's books but it was generally the death of the child (a highly realistic event), described in comforting religious terms. Nowadays it is the living child who is bereft. In Cynthia Ryland's *Missing May* (the 1992 Newbery Award Winner), an elderly man and a child sorrow at the death of the man's wife and the child's aunt; in Patricia MacLachlan's *Baby* (1992) a young girl is violently upset because her new-born brother had been buried without being named and the parent do not talk about him. In Sarah Ellis's *The Baby Project* (1986) there is a crib death, with a resulting impact on the whole family. The feelings in such books are presented strongly and there is a healing process with the young sometimes initiating it, as in the three books mentioned here. Still, sorrow and grief are the motivating forces while reconciliation, a major process for the Victorians, is given short notice. Many modern writers of realistic fiction are minimalists—they pack a great deal of emotion into quite short books. Those by Patricia MacLachlan, for example, do not exceed a hundred pages. Is the reading time involved sufficient to work the emotion through the psyche? Is there enough to support the emotional impact?

Some writers work hard to cushion the shock of a death. Constance Greene in *Nora Maybe a Ghost* (1993) provides a thirteen-year-old with her mother's gentle ghost as the girl struggles to come to terms not only with her mother's death, but with her father's remarriage. It is palpably a device which fails to convince. In Mary Louise Cuneo's *Anne is Elegant* (1993) there are two deaths, those of an infant and an elderly woman, and the emotions that derive from them are filtered through the mind of a Grade Six child, sensitive and precocious. Here the cushioning comes plausibly in glimpses of school life, sledding, Christmas festivities, and family gatherings.

For emotional impact, no rendering of a child's death (in recent times) has matched Katherine Paterson's *A Bridge To Terabithia* (1977) which has become a modern classic. The reason for such an accolade is obvious: it is a rich story, contrasting the lives of two children, with a strong component of their friendship and imaginative play. It has both a power and a depth of sorrow that haunts the reader as well as the protagonist. It is a book that proves the point that it is *how* a theme is handled, not the theme itself, that can make a memorable story. In her much shorter *The Baby Project*, Sarah Ellis is also an effective storyteller as she builds up a humorous picture of two children preparing to entertain and educate a baby before the unexpected disaster.

On the whole, death is now treated more realistically in terms of children's reactions than in the past. In Robert Cormier's *The Chocolate War* (1974), and Peggy Mann's *There Are Two Kinds of Terrible* (1977), the mothers die after a long illness and the young are shown in terms of raging helplessness. Earlier writers either tended to treat death or illness or hardship through fantasy, or they gave the children something to do while mourning, as in Edith Nesbit's *The Story of the Treasure Seekers* (1899). Here Oswald, the young narrator, briefly shows his feelings: 'Our Mother is dead, and if you think we don't care because I don't tell you much about her you only show that you do not understand people at all.' With this statement Oswald and his siblings spend their energies in trying to earn much needed money for their father. In an even earlier book, Johanna Spyri's *Heidi* (1881), Heidi who is both an orphan and a displaced child is given opportunities for power and choice.

The missing parent (generally the father) is another prevalent theme of the day, the cause usually divorce as exemplified in Alice Mead's *Crossing the Starlight Bridge* (1994), in which a child of the Penobscot people faces the trauma of a suddenly vanished father and the resulting forced transition into the white world. Fortunately she has a wise grandmother and an artistic talent to support her. But mothers can also do a disappearing act. In Patricia MacLachlan's *Journey* (1992), an eleven-year-old boy is grieving for his mother who has abandoned him and his younger sister. In Cynthia

Voigt's *Dicey's Song* (1983), a grandmother and the oldest child have to take on family responsibilities.

However ubiquitous this theme, there are still writers who can be innovative with it. In *Pick-Up Sticks* (1991), Sarah Ellis describes the feelings of a fourteen-year-old girl whose mother tells her that she had wanted a child but not the father. In Virginia Hamilton's *Plain City* (1993) a twelve-year-old yearns for the father she thinks is dead. It is a book rich in plot, characters, and setting. In an equally rich and unusual book, *Adam and Eve and Pinch-Me* (1994) by Julie Johnston, a young teenager decides to stay with her foster family rather than with her birth mother who has been searching for her.

Another constant factor in contemporary realistic fiction is the presence of adults. Today's children are deemed (and portrayed in books) as more mature, more sophisticated, more self-reliant and better educated than those of the past. Writers routinely use adults (parents, and to a far lesser degree, grandparents and teachers) as foils; they are the ones who cause the problems around which the plot revolves. In contrast, from the early 1900s to the 1960s writers tended to get rid of the parents by one means or another, leaving the children to operate on their own. This is the world of the Nesbit children, and those of Johanna Spyri, Frances Hodgson Burnett, Arthur Ransome, Astrid Lindgren, Louise Fitzhugh, E.L. Konigsburg, Jill Paton Walsh, and many others. The high point of this approach to childhood came in 1930 with Arthur Ransome's *Swallows and Amazons*. Four children, having asked their father to go sailing and camping alone on an island, receive a telegram that says: 'Better drowned than duffers. If not duffers, won't drown.' Of course, Ransome gave the children a father who is a sea captain and so experienced in sailing. Ransome had no opportunity to read Johann Huizinga's theories on the value of play: *Homo Ludens* was not published in English until 1949. Huizinga propounded the sensible theory that through play children rehearse in a safe environment for the unsafe things to come in adult life. Today's authors seem not to have read him: few children in recent realistic novels engage in play. A significant title, although not a significant book, is Budge Wilson's *Oliver's War* (1992) which cumulates all the burdens modern writers feel appropriate for the young to handle. Because of a move from a Canadian prairie city to Halifax, Nova Scotia, Oliver is at war with his grandfather, his schoolmates, his teachers, his brother, the Gulf War—and himself. All in a hundred and one pages—with a happy ending in about two! Modern writers with their emphasis on adults (people often not that well characterized) have a greater connection with the seventeenth and eighteenth centuries, when adults were *never* out of children's lives, than they do with writers earlier this century. As the Bible says: 'There is no new thing under the sun.'

The increase in the number of picturebooks is nothing short of phenomenal, but it is explainable. The modern young parent is almost fanatical about giving the children (generally just one or two) a good start in life. The importance not only of *how* to read but of reading with ease and with pleasure is more and more widely recognized. For such parents, a bedtime reading (at first generally with a picturebook) is now almost as mandatory as the goodnight kiss. A related theory in childhood education is the value of very young children playing and learning in groups. Daycare centres, nursery schools, kindergarten and public library programs for babies and children aged two to five are a great market for picturebooks, but they also have to compete with glitzy TV and computer graphics. No wonder they have never been more varied or more numerous. They treat of almost every topic that adults want to bring to the attention of the young, from accepting a new Daddy to saving the whales. They are now also designed to attract every age level (including that growing proportion of adults who are illiterate). At the same time, many picturebook artists and/or illustrators aim for the sophisticated. Nancy Willard's *Pish Posh Said Hieronymous Bosch* (1991) is one of hundreds of picturebooks with an adult theme. Here, in rollicking rhyme, the great painter is tricked into marrying his housekeeper. Michael Bender's superbly paper-engineered pop-up life of the Renaissance architect, Filippo Brunelleschi (1995), is clearly not designed for a five-year-old. It can now be said that the profusely illustrated book has transcended its traditional market, the preschooler, and now connects with every age.

What a publisher will now designate as for the 'young adult' also warrants examination. It is true that children mature earlier, both physically and emotionally, than they did some decades ago. Still, it is somewhat surprising to find publishers designating a title on the 'blurb' as 'young adult' when the protagonist is no more than eleven years of age. Of course, advertising a book this way gives the publisher a chance at two audiences. It is also true that most pre-adolescents yearn to be a 'teenager', a stage in life they associate with freedom. They find books so designated attractive and are flattered to have their ages advanced. There is some evidence to support the thesis that *children* (ages nine to twelve) read young adult novels more than do teenagers.

One important and distressing result of this is a shortage of recent outstanding novels for the pre-teenager for whom a wide variety of realistic fiction was formerly written, ranging from Arthur Ransome's *Swallows and Amazons* series and Laura Ingalls Wilder's *Little House on the Prairie* series to Scott O'Dell's *Island of the Blue Dolphin* (1960). Louise Fitzhugh's *Harriet the Spy* (1964) may be the last significant and popular novel to deal with a child and an aspect of childhood. It would appear that writers and children do *not* connect well these days. The former concentrate on writing about people in the fourteen-to-sixteen age group in order to give themselves greater scope to indulge in emotional traumas of one sort or another, issues and situations previously faced by older protagonists.

It should be remembered that in the mid-1960s and early 1970s, it was the teenage novel that changed the face of literature for the young with revelations of homosexuality, lesbianism, alcoholism, child abuse, and other topics previously deemed taboo in books for young people. However, with the spread of real-life news on such topics, the shock element has worn off and writers of the young adult novel are more and more dependent upon their talents of writing than on content. Although there is much evidence that the young adult novel has come of age, have any attained the cult status of J.D. Salinger's *The Catcher in the Rye* and William Golding's *Lord of the Flies*—books *not* deliberately written for them?

It is perhaps too early in the 1990s to comment on the numbing sameness of realistic fiction whether for children or for young adults, but one reason may be the effects of Political Correctness (PC). Perhaps the phrase should be Social Correctness; few children's books deal with politics per se. Some recent exceptions are William Bell's *Forbidden City* (1990), which describes the events and the aftermath of Tienanmen Square as seen through the participation of a Canadian teenager, the same author's recent environmental novel, *Speak to the Earth* (1994), and Jim Heneghan's *Torn Away* (1994) set on British Columbia's Vancouver Island but backtracking to a teenager's violent experiences in the recent 'Irish troubles'. Books about World War II may be considered 'political' but the majority of those set in North America concentrate on the emotional and disruptive effects of the war on the lives of the young at home, not on its effects on the lives of children caught in the theatres of war. Generally speaking, authors make no attempt to *inform* children in a political sense. Judging only by what is written for them, American and Canadian youth appear to be viewed as the most a-political in the world with only one strong interest—themselves: themselves as they relate to parents, or the lack thereof, to their friends or those not so friendly to them, to peer pressures and to the rather mild domestic trials that beset them. The circumstances may vary but the large ego element remains constant.

Girls are very much in evidence in the literary world of PC. As protagonists, they now outnumber boys. This may simply be a result of the number of women writers who naturally describe what they know best. The girls are consistently shown as self-reliant, responsible, and forceful but in the firmament of modern children's literature which of the new breed has become a star of the calibre of Jo in Louisa May Alcott's *Little Women*, Mary Lennox in Frances Hodgson Burnett's *The Secret Garden*, Johanna Spyri's Heidi, or L.M. Montgomery's Anne? Stardom like that calls for some eccentricity. The new girls all seem to be cut out of the same cloth.

It may well be necessary to look at other types of literature to recapture a sense of story and some feeling of excitement and adventure. Fantasy for the young in print form has not totally disappeared, but it has changed perhaps even more dramatically than realistic fiction. Indeed there has almost been a reversal from the fantasy of the past.

From Victorian times until the recent past, fantasy worlds were chiefly seen as places *to go to* and the prospective heroes and heroines were transported thither from their home environment by magic. Carroll's Wonderland and Looking-glass realms, Barrie's Never-land, Baum's Oz, Lewis's Narnia are wholly and perfectly created. Other fantasies held worlds within worlds—that of North Wind in George MacDonald's *At the Back of the North Wind* (1871) and the miniature home of the dolls in Rumer Godden's *The Doll's House* (1947). In some, the natural world was only lightly (but believably) touched with fantasy as is the forest in Beverley Nichols' *The Tree That Sat Down* (1945) or the seascape of Eric Linklater's *The Pirates in the Deep Green Sea* (1949). Then there were the stories that took the reader into a magical world from the first sentence on the first page—Tolkien's Middle Earth in *The Hobbit* (1939) and *The Lord of the Rings* (1954–5).

In all these earlier works the events are played out in a Secondary World, an Other World, a retreat from everyday surroundings. In most modern fantasy, this process is reversed. The supernatural comes to the real world as we know it, breaking into it and shattering the division between the real and the unreal. It would appear that the change began in the 1960s. In William Mayne's *Earthfasts* (1966) a drummer boy of the eighteenth century suddenly comes drumming out of a cave into a sleepy English county town; Stonehenge-like boulders move, wild boars run amok in the marketplace, and electrical forces cause a teen-age boy to disappear. In Alan Garner's *The Owl Service* (1967), a Welsh valley is invaded by the forces of a myth, and three modern young people are forced to replay an old tragedy. Another depiction of the invasion of the real world by supernatural forces came with Susan Cooper's *The Dark Is*

Rising quintet (1965–77) in which a modern seventh son of a seventh son (aged eleven) becomes the youngest of the 'Old Ones' to lead the battle against the forces of the Dark who are bent on taking over the world. These books are set in England, a land steeped in legend, and make much use of the Matter of Britain—the Arthurian legends and the tales from the Mabinogion. Thus the aura of an Other World is sustained.

The most powerful and popular exponent of witches, magicians, and ghosts flourishing in the clear light of day is the New Zealand author, Margaret Mahy. In her *The Haunting* (1983), eight-year-old Barney senses that his mind is being intruded upon by a dead boy—Barney's uncle as a youth. The sympathy evoked for Barney is strong indeed; he is such a quiet, sensitive, loving child. Barney is also under an additional stress. His stepmother, whom he loves dearly, is expecting a baby and Barney fears that she will die in childbirth as did his own mother. Barney's uncle turns out to be alive; he is a magician and he wants Barney as his apprentice. The reader eventually discovers (that is, eventually in a very short book) that there have always been men in the family who have had 'powers and peculiarities most people just don't have. . . '. The real surprise comes at the end when it is discovered that the new magician in the family is Barney's hitherto self-effacing older sister.

Except for Barney's view of the dangers of having a baby, the family life as portrayed in *The Haunting* is a happy one. By contrast, most fantasies of the past decade, including Mahy's *The Changeover* (1984) have an unhappy protagonist or at least one that is unhappy or under stress long enough to make the plot work. In *The Changeover*, fourteen-year-old Laura is upset and angered at her father's desertion of his family and she has already had a mental warning that something else dreadful is about to happen. True enough: her three-year-old brother Jacko falls ill, and the mother turns to a lover for support rather than to Laura. Because of her special powers, Laura realizes that Jacko's life is being sucked dry by an 'incubus' or a 'lemure' who preys on the life force of others to ensure his own immortality. Laura is helped by a witch family who train her to develop her own latent witch powers. In one of the most bizarre scenes in fantasy since the demise of the Wicked Witch of the West in Frank Baum's *The Wizard of Oz*, she defeats the incubus. But Oz is a fantasy land; Mahy's witches flourish in modern New England.

Most modern Canadian and American fantasists now co-mingle fantasy and reality without the buffer of an Other World. Some use is made of legend. Werewolves play a legendary role in modern Ireland in Michael Scott's *October Moon* (1994) when a wealthy visiting American family is plagued by werewolves in a plot which rises to a fever pitch of terror. The family is saved through the heroic efforts of the teenage daughter, but back in California she begins to turn into a werewolf. Indian masks and the legends that accompany them provide the inspiration for Joan Clark's *Wild Man of the Woods* (1985), set in the foothills of the Canadian Rockies, and Welwyn Wilton Katz's *False Face* (1987), which concerns Iroquois masks. The protagonists in both these works are troubled young teenagers. So is Virginia Hamilton's Tree in *Sweet Whispers, Brother Rush* (1982), in which a fourteen-year-old girl, under the pressure of too much responsibility, escapes into the past until her mother and her new stepfather take over their parental duties. 'Pressure' is the key word in these novels by Clark, Katz, and Hamilton and in Monica Hughes's *Castle Tourmandyne* (1995), in which two cousins at odds with one another play out their resentments through dreams concerning an antique paper doll's house. In such novels, the reader has a choice of what to believe: are the events real or do they happen only in the minds of the protagonists? The term psychological fantasy may perhaps best describe these often dramatic and inventive works. However the Mahy tradition is also strong, as evidenced in the writings of Michael Bedard. In his first book, *A Darker Magic* (1987), with its psychic implications, he proves that there are really no boundaries and rules to the creation of fantasy.

However subtle the differences in recent fantasy, the fact remains that the emphasis on reality has infiltrated fantasy. In these newer books we learn a great deal about the protagonists in their everyday life: their home situation, their problems, their schooling and so on. In this respect, the fantasies differ little from contemporary realistic novels. In earlier fantasies it was the experience in the Other World that had meaning (as in the Narnia books) or the returning home from a quest as in *The Hobbit* or Lloyd Alexander's Prydain series. The characters in these stories, and so their readers, came back to their ordinary world refreshed, renewed, and with the sense of looking at their world with new eyes. The new fantasy changes this old purpose: it tries to illuminate the supernatural. In times when there were protests against fantasy as a pack of lies, it was easy to assure worried adults that writers made a clear distinction between the real and the unreal and that children grasp the distinction. This cannot be said generally of the new fantasy, although there is no evidence to show that young readers are bothered by the lack of a clear-cut demarcation. On the whole, the new fantasy is more violent than that of the past, if still less so than most video games. Although there are still many light and humorous fantasies being published, the writers of serious fantasy appear to be engaged in (to paraphrase a title from the English author, William Mayne) games of dark.

Because the new fantasy is so firmly rooted in reality, other differences arise between the present and the past. The new writers, while often excellent at plot and everyday conversation, are neither image-makers nor wordsmiths. Who can forget Carroll's White Rabbit taking a watch out of its waistcoat pocket, or Tolkien's well-described hobbit, or Arrietty of Mary Norton's *The Borrowers* fixing her candle on an upturned drawing pin which served as a holder, or the celluloid doll, Birdie, of Rumer Godden's *The Doll's House* throwing herself on a candle to save her doll son? For memorable phrases, it is hardly fair to quote *Alice's Adventures in Wonderland* since almost every line is quotable, but there are many memorable phrases in other early fantasies: 'There is *nothing*—absolutely nothing—half so much worth doing as simply messing about in boats' (Kenneth Grahame, *The Wind in the Willows*, 1908) or, 'To die will be an awfully big adventure' (J.M. Barrie, *Peter Pan*, 1911).

A sudden upsurge in readership, even to cult status, is not uncommon in fantasy—one remembers the rage for Tolkien's *The Lord of the Rings* and Richard Adams's *Watership Down*. In both these cases adults as well as children became staunch fans. The newest example, Brian Jacques's *Redwall* series, appears at the moment to be limited to child readers, but their fame may spread. The animals are as completely anthropomorphized as those in Kenneth Grahame's *The Wind in the Willows*—they live in the English countryside but they wear clothes, use weapons, tend the sick, and engage in most other human activities. Indeed the chief clue that the characters are animals comes simply in the use of the word 'paws' for hands; in the first two pages of *Salamandastrom* we find 'chin in paw', 'heavy-pawed authority', and 'hooked out a left paw'. Another clue is the kind of food they find in the fields and forest around them, as well as in the Redwall Abbey garden—the ingredients of a Redwall cake make the mouth water. The plot in each book is as old as literature itself—the struggle between good and evil. The good is represented by Redwall Abbey and its mouse inhabitants supported by animals such as moles and voles and badgers; as in *The Wind in the Willows* the bad ones are weasels, ferrets, and stoats. There is a contrast between the peaceful life of the Abbey, which is frequently under attack, and the wars that rage outside its walls. The books (seven of them to date) do not have the depth of either *The Wind in the Willows* or *Watership Down* but they have a page-turning, storytelling quality that is rare in modern children's literature, even in fantasy. And Jacques can sustain these qualities through close to 400 pages in each paperback and with a fair amount of English dialect.

Since the past cannot be changed, it might be reasonable to expect that historical fiction, as a genre, might remain relatively unchanged. Not so. In the past stories of swashbuckling adventure, flamboyant heroes and spirited heroines were the staple fare of generations of children who probably, because of their own confinement to home and hearth, succumbed to the enchantment of distant times and places and high adventure.

For a time it appeared that historical fiction was declining in numbers and readership. There are two probable reasons: the children of the 1960s wanted books about themselves, and the designers of school curricula mixed up history and geography and lumped them together under the unappealing term of 'socials' or 'social studies'. However, stories of past times had already taken too firm a hold on children's literature to be ignored. Between the 1950s and the middle of the 1970s, historical fiction was given new life by four very different English writers: Rosemary Sutcliff, Leon Garfield, Hester Burton, and Barbara Willard. The numbers of their publications over a twenty-year period gave the genre a well-earned feeling of substance. Rosemary Sutcliff still keeps a substantial following with her sweeps of early British history combined with very flesh-and-blood heroes. She had the ability to give all her characters universally human problems while making them vital and recognizable in their own time settings. Sutcliff used language powerfully and memorably. At the end of *The Lantern Bearers* (1959), the Romans have left Britain forever but a beacon is ashine in the great lighthouse of Rutupiae. It is seen as a symbol of continuity for two young Romans who have decided to make Britain their home. The ending symbolizes Sutcliff's philosophy of history:

'I sometimes think that we stand at sunset', Eugenus said after a pause. 'It may be that the night will close over us in the end, but I believe that morning will come again. Morning always grows again out of the darkness, though maybe not for the people who saw the sun go down. We are the Lantern Bearers, my friend; for us to keep something burning, to carry what we can forward into the darkness and the wind.'

While Barbara Willard skilfully combined history and family history, Hester Burton and Leon Garfield began the trend towards the present emphasis on social history with a concentration on the lives of young people either caught in the web of great events or, more commonly now, in ordinary circumstances of times past.

The American Civil War provides the springboard for Betty Cummings's *Hew Against the Grain* (1977), but the emphasis is on a family in Virginia as split by the war as was the state itself. The same war rages in

Paul Fleischman's *The Borning Room* (1991), but the war with its death is outside; inside is the continuity of life as represented by 'the borning room'. The past is filled with large social and political issues. These have made their way into North American children's books from the oppression of the Blacks as expressed in Mildred Taylor's *Roll of Thunder, Hear My Cry* (1976) to the 1946 strike action in Valleyfield, Quebec, told by Marsha Hewitt and Claire Mackay in *One Proud Summer* (1981). The most recent historical fiction eschews any mention of large issues. Modern writers prefer to deal in small detail as does Patricia MacLachlan with *Sarah Plain and Tall* (winner of the Newbery Medal for 1985), in which a young woman travels from New England west to the prairies to be a housekeeper for a widower with three children. The children (and the father) come to adore her and she stays on as a much-beloved stepmother and wife. It is a vivid and charming picture of an American prairie family in the 19th century. Celia Barke Lottridge's *Ticket To Curlew* (1992), winner of the Canadian Library Association Book of the Year for Children, is also a quiet story of a family moving from Iowa to Alberta. One senses its authenticity as one does in most of these short books of social history: the weather, the hardships, the neighbours, the helping hands, the celebrations, the mother's careful management, and the children's acceptance of their new life. There is no whining here about moving to a whole new way of life as the young often whine and groan in modern realistic fiction if they have to move to another city or even to a new house or school in the same city.

However, even writers of historical fiction try to seek new ways of revealing the past. Karen Cushman has found a fresh and authentic voice in her fourteen-year-old narrator of *Catherine, Called Birdie* (1994). Birdie, the sister of a monk, has been taught to read and has been urged by her brother to keep a journal. This she does with honesty, wit, and a shrewd appraisal of the adult world. Birdie belongs to the knightly class (a very minor one) and this particular aspect of medieval life is here revealed in all its domesticity: its food, its cleanliness (or lack thereof), its privies, its festivities, and its feudalism. All this and much more is contained within a hard-edged and convincing plot as Birdie's father determines to marry her off to the first prosperous bidder. Birdie conducts her own, somewhat more subtle war to defeat him. The journal is interspersed with her longing for freedom (she would like to be a boy, or at least a villager). She frequently expresses her frustrations at her position in life as she is trained to be a lady with such epithets as 'Corpus Bones' or 'God's Thumbs', both of which deserve to join the list of English mild swear words. While Birdie's style of writing and tone of voice keep her journal on an almost comic level (she is irrepressible even in adversity), Cushman's second foray into the Middle Ages, *The Midwife's Apprentice* (1995), has a more serious outlook. There is nothing amusing about being a homeless child in medieval times. There is an element of 'Goody Two-Shoes' about the plot since the child learns by listening to and spying upon adults to gain the knowledge upon which her existence depends. The writing has the same crispness as Birdie's journal with just enough selected details and expressions to give a flavour of the times. In both books, you are there—completely engrossed in times past.

A return to the past is frequently combined with fantasy, a tradition that goes back to Edith Nesbit's *The House of Arden* (1908). A touch of fantasy still continues to work its magic on the events of history. The historical component of Janet Lunn's *Shadow in Hawthorn Bay* (1986) lies in a group of United Empire Loyalists who have fled to southern Ontario in the wake of the American Revolution. Their hardships, life style and community standards (they are hard-headed, practical Yankees) are contrasted with the character of a fifteen-year-old Scottish girl who has made her way across an ocean and half a continent in answer to a mental cry for help from her childhood sweetheart, a cousin who has emigrated to Ontario with his parents. It may well be that Scottish second sight should not be equated with fantasy, but still the combination of the two demonstrates the range and flexibility of historical fiction. Such writers as Janet Lunn are as historically accurate as a Leon Garfield or a Hester Burton.

The strict definition of a historical novel is one that deals with a period 'beyond the memory of those living'.[3] This brings in an age element; what is *not* historical to an adult may be very much so to children. World War II is the chief example here. Kit Pearson, the author of a popular war-time trilogy, was not born until 1947, so it may be said that the events of 1939 to 1945 are historical to her. The events portrayed in the first book, *The Sky Is Falling* (1989), set the stage for the sequels: *Looking at the Moon* (1991) and *The Lights Go On Again* (1993). Two children from a lower middle-class English family are sent to Canada in the evacuation program that began in 1939 and lasted until the *The City of Benares* was torpedoed by the Germans. By this time Norah and her young brother, Gavin, are safely ensconced with a wealthy Rosedale family in Toronto. What will happen when the war ends? Pearson tells an engaging story with the war information introduced naturally. Lillian Boraks-Nemetz's *The Old Brown Suitcase* (1994) is partially based on its author's own experiences in Poland as a child, ending with the family's escape to Canada. It is told in the first person and expresses a child's bewilderment at the terrifying events that changed her life.

Historical fiction has always been and still is the best way to make history come alive. If the young can be persuaded to read it, they will find that writers of the new wave can be as modern as their favourite authors of realistic fiction without destroying authenticity and historicity. Karen Cushman's Birdie, for example, is a slave to her father regarding her marriage; she escapes it only by good fortune, not by a change in medieval manners and mores. But it makes sense to acknowledge that there were girls and women in the past who chafed against their servile position, otherwise society would not have changed. In language there are no 'prithees' and 'forsooths' as exemplified in Robert Louis Stevenson's historical novel of the Wars of the Roses, *The Black Arrow* (1888). All in all, the safest generalization to make about historical fiction is that it is alive and well and this may be its Golden Age.

Back in 1975, the writer and critic of science fiction, Brian Aldiss, described it as 'a wacky sort of fiction that grabs and engulfs anything new or old for its subject matter, turning it into a shining and often unsubstantial wonder'.[4] It certainly does grab and engulf, taking in fantasy, realistic fiction, historical fiction, social fiction and science, melding them frequently into a *substantial* wonder. With such wide parameters, the wonder is that it does at times succeed. However, in its narrowest definition, that is, as a fiction that extrapolates from scientific fact, it has seemingly disappeared. The term science fiction now appears to be a misnomer. Jules Verne, considered the father of scientific science fiction with *Twenty Thousand Leagues Under the Sea* (1870), has basically given way to H.G. Wells, considered the father of social science and imaginative science fiction. In his *The War of the Worlds* (1898), he invented and described Martians! Since science now appears to have outstripped fiction, the term science fiction has yielded to the more accurate term, science fiction fantasy.

For many years the model for science fiction fantasy was Madeline L'Engle's *A Wrinkle In Time* (1962), a highly eclectic and sentimental work that has kept its popularity over the years. A better candidate for the honour is Monica Hughes's *The Keeper of the Isis Light* (1980). Here, on the planet of Isis, a guardian robot has changed the physical make-up of his charge (after her parents have been killed), to make her body adaptable to the thin mountain air of the planet. But when Earth colonists arrive, they are shocked and terrified by her appearance, no matter how kind and supportive the girl had been towards them. Unfortunately there is a human tendency to fear anyone different from oneself. It is a warning message at which science fiction in all its forms excels. Hughes has written a great deal of science fiction varying from the early computer story, *The Tomorrow City* (1982), to her latest science fiction environmental fantasy, *The Golden Aquarians* (1994). She has the ability to tell a compelling story while obeying the first law of science fiction: to make readers aware of a present that can affect the future.

Lois Lowrey's *The Giver* (1993) has most of the aspects of science fiction fantasy that should not work yet do so very well. Its picture of a future society is richly delineated showing its history, its social customs, and its educational system with a strong dose of a science-fiction staple, mind touch and ESP. Lowrey's special gift here is her simulation of real time; it takes a while for the reader to discover that the society portrayed is not the utopia it purports to be but a dystopia. In a highly original plot a young adolescent, having been especially trained because of his special mental talents, makes his escape. Lowrey adds to the drama by leaving the ending open: are the boy and the young child he has taken with him on a journey to freedom or to a similar society or to death?

In general, science fiction for children is both optimistic and humanitarian. It has a special place in children's literature in that it can give the young an intellectual awareness of the present and the future. Considering the highly personal, almost narcissistic role of much of modern realism, it is of considerable value to have a literature that still looks at a society in general and its social structure. Whether called science fiction or science fiction fantasy, its unique role is still to present alternative future societies and possibilities.

It has always been possible to see the patterns that characterize the literature of a previous generation and synthesize them into an aesthetic and societal logic. The literature of the last twenty-five or thirty years is no exception but it is simply more difficult to see a pattern in it. The unprecedented number of publications hampers the emergence of a clear image of the literature of the 1980s and 1990s in particular. A tug at any one of the loose ends of its fabric will release any number of mediocre books that may mirror the time but provide no insight into it. Equally, the very scale and swiftness of social change and its immediate absorption into books for the young have made the characteristics of the literature distinct from those of the past. Contemplating each book in its own right may support Saint Exupery's thesis in *The Little Prince* that each rose is unique; still only a single step backwards reveals that the garden is filled with flowers of the same species.

In the past, educators and librarians who worked with children and their books were inclined to leave most editorial, production, and advertising decisions to publishers and book editors. It was recognized that along with the jewels of children's books came a certain proportion of trash and even more of mediocrity, but there was also a tacit assurance that the jewels in the long run would survive. Today the trash and the mediocre are more threatening. The sheer economic need of publishers to push things into, through, and out the other end of the pipeline means that the best is less visible and consequently is often remaindered and disappears. Because of these publishing conditions it is more necessary than ever for professionals dealing with children and their books to take responsibility for seeking and purchasing the best books with children, reviewing them, and enjoying them with young readers and so helping keep them in print. Only in this way will the commonality of children's reading be preserved. Otherwise we are like the great Canadian humorist Stephen Leacock's Lord Ronald, who jumped on a horse and rode off in all directions at once.

Children's literature continues today to fulfil its ancient and most important role, that of reflecting society's view of the young and the young person's view of society. In spite of a variety of individual situations, there is a fairly consistent theme that the process of growing up is something difficult, if not fearful. The best of modern writers are not concerned, as were their predecessors, with a state called childhood, either distinct from or in tandem with adulthood, but rather with an investigation of those conundrums of life most evident in the psychological transition from childhood to adulthood.

Revelation and revolution hover in the air. If the young are not always at the barricades, they are chiefly depicted in an adversary position toward either an individual or a situation that represents the world at large—a world that is disillusioning, ominous or, worse still, conforming. Yet, as writers of the early religious and moral books brought their young charges to an understanding of the goodness of God, contemporary writers hope to bring their young protagonists to an understanding of and belief in themselves.

The 1990s have so far produced a wealth of books for children. Fortunately, the classics of the past are still in print, due in large part to their illustrators. It would appear that every illustrator wants to give an individual interpretation of *The Secret Garden* or *Little Women* just as every serious actress yearns to play Lady Macbeth and every actor, the Prince of Denmark. The old classics are still needed: Alice, Oz, Anne, and Pooh, as are the more modern ones such as C.S. Lewis's *The Lion, the Witch and the Wardrobe* (1950), E.B. White's *Charlotte's Web* (1952), Philippa Pearce's *Tom's Midnight Garden* (1958), and Natalie Babbitt's *Tuck Everlasting* (1975). These are the glue that hold children's literature together.

Contemporary writers have changed the face of children's literature and there is little doubt that another generation will change it again. It will be up to future generations to sift out what it wants from the books of the last twenty-five years. Judging from the past, one can expect that what is truly literature will keep its place—those books that are central to a cultural heritage, those that present the coherent and unifying power of human sympathy in vivid images.

The task is not impossible, it is simply more difficult than ever before. It will take more effort on the part of teachers, librarians, critics, publishers, and booksellers to 'connect' with the best that is being written and to give it a chance to make its way into the hearts of children who, after all, are the final arbiters of what is to last and what is not. As Lewis Carroll's Red Queen said to Alice in *Through the Looking-Glass*, '. . . it takes all the running *you* can do, to keep in the same place. If you want to get somewhere else, you must run at least twice as fast as that.' The magic of fine children's literature only works when it connects with the young. To ensure this connection, *we* may have to run twice as fast.

Notes

[1]Frances Clarke Sayers, *Summoned by Books* (Viking, 1965).

[2]Bowker Annual, 40th edition (New Providence, NJ: Bowker, 1995): 518.

[3]Alfred T. Sheppard, *The Art & Practice of Historical Fiction* (London: H. Toulim, 1930): 3.

[4]Brian W. Aldiss, *Billion Year Spree* (London: Weidenfeld & Nicholson, 1975): 2.

NOTES ON CONTRIBUTORS

AIKEN, JOAN
Daughter of the poet Conrad Aiken, Joan Aiken is author of over fifty novels, short stories and plays, and many children's books, including *The Wolves of Willoughby Chase* (1962; made into a film 1988), *Black Hearts in Battersea* (1964), *Night Birds in Nantucket* (1966), and *The Cuckoo Tree* (1971). Her works cover a wide range of theme, from horror and suspense stories to historical fiction.

APSELOFF, MARILYN FAIN
Marilyn Fain Apseloff is a Professor of English at Kent State University. Her books include *They Wrote for Children Too* (1989), *Elizabeth George Speare* (in Twayne's English Author Series, 1992), and, as co-author with Celia Catlett Anderson, *Nonsense Literature for Children*.

ATWOOD, MARGARET
Margaret Atwood is a Canadian novelist and poet of international prominence. While her works generally have a serious theme (frequently connected with women), her contribution here shows her dry, infectious sense of humour.

ATTEBERY, BRIAN
Brian Attebery teaches in the Department of English and Philosophy at Idaho State University. He is the author of *The Fantasy Tradition in American Literature* and co-editor with Ursula Le Guin of *The Norton Book of Science Fiction: North American Science Fiction 1960–90*.

BABBITT, NATALIE
Natalie Babbitt is a well-known American writer and illustrator whose children's novel, *Tuck Everlasting* (1975), has been described as a 'modern classic'. While studying illustration, she was inspired by Tenniel's drawings in *Alice in Wonderland*, which may account for her favourite medium being pen and ink.

BRIGGS, JULIA
Author of *Night Visitors, The Rise and Fall of the English Short Story*, and *A Woman of Passion: the Life of E. Nesbit* (1987), Julia Briggs is a Fellow and Tutor at Hertford College, Oxford. With Gillian Avery she edited a collection of essays to celebrate the work of Iona and Peter Opie, entitled *Children and their Books* (1989).

CAMERON, ELEANOR

Eleanor Cameron is an American author and critic of children's books. She first became popular with young children through her science fiction series, 'The Mushroom Planet'. She has also written sensitive and well-plotted books for young teenagers such as *The Court of the Stone Children* (1973).

CHESTER, TESSA ROSE

Curator of Children's Books of the Renier Collection of children's books at the Bethnal Green Museum of Childhood, London, Tessa Rose Chester is a co-author with Joyce Irene Whalley of *A History of Children's Book Illustration* (1988). She also compiled a valuable reference work, *Children's Books Research: a Practical Guide to Techniques and Sources* (1989).

COWARD, ROSALIND

A regular contributor to the Manchester *Guardian*, Rosalind Coward is a post-structuralist feminist writer and lecturer. Her works include *Patriarchal Precedents: Sexuality and Social Relations* (1983) and *Our Treacherous Hearts: Why Women Let Men Get Their Way* (1992). She has taught Visual Communications and Media Studies at Reading University.

EGOFF, SHEILA

Educated at the University of Toronto and the University of London, Sheila Egoff became actively engaged in library work, first in Eastern Canada, then since 1962 at the University of British Columbia, specializing in Children's Literature in the School of Librarianship. Since retiring she has continued to write reviews and other articles and do editorial work. The third edition of her guide to Canadian children's books, *The New Republic of Childhood* appeared in 1990. In 1994, Sheila Egoff was named an Officer of the Order of Canada for her contribution to Canadian children's literature.

ELLIS, SARAH

Sarah Ellis is a well-known Canadian writer of realistic fiction for children. Her first publication, *The Baby Project*, was named winner of the Sheila Egoff Book Prize in British Columbia (1987). Other awards have followed: the Governor-General's Award for *Pick-up Sticks* (1991) and more recently the Mr Christie Book Award for the best English language book for children age 12 and over, *Out of the Blue* (1995).

GIBLIN, JAMES CROSS

Born in Cleveland, Ohio, Giblin is a regular contributor to magazines, and the recipient of many awards and honours for his books, which include *The Truth about Santa Claus* (1985) and *The Riddle of the Rosetta Stone* (1990). He served as editor and publisher of Clarion Books from 1979 to 1989. He has also been associated with the Society of Children's Book Writers, the Children's Book Council, and the Author's Guild.

HOLLINDALE, PETER

Peter Hollindale first developed critical interests in children's literature during postgraduate teacher training at the University of Bristol, where he was taught by Margaret Meek. He is at present senior lecturer in English and Educational Studies at the University of York. His book *Choosing Books for Children*, a guide for parents, was published in 1974. More recently he has edited works by J.M. Barrie, and he is currently completing *Signs of Childness: a Short Philosophy of Children's Literature*.

HUGHES, MONICA

Born in Liverpool, England in 1925, Monica Hughes now lives in Edmonton, Alberta. She is widely known for her science fiction novels, which include *The Keeper of the Isis Light* (1980) and *Crystal Drop* (1992). Hughes has been much praised for her adolescent novel, *The Hunter in the Dark* (1982), set in Alberta; its theme is that of a teenager facing inescapable death.

HUNT, PETER

Peter Hunt is Director of Communication Studies and Senior Lecturer in English at the University of Wales in Cardiff. He has visited many universities and colleges as a lecturer on the subject of children's literature. His articles have appeared in *Signal, Children's Literature in Education*, and other periodicals. His books for younger children include *Sue and the Honey Machine*; and for older ones *Maps of Time* (1983) and *A Step off the Path* (1985). He has also written a study of the life and work of Arthur Ransome.

KENNEDY, X.J. (Also known as Joseph Charles Kennedy)

Kennedy was born in 1929, in Dover, New York. He is a writer of diverse interests who has published a number of volumes of poetry for both children and adults, and a critical work—*An Introduction to Poetry* (1978). Among his more recent books are *Ghastlies, Goops and Pincushion Verse* (1989), *Fresh Brats* (1990) and *The Beasts of Bethlehem* (1992).

LEWIS, DAVID

A teacher and psychologist, David Lewis's books include *The Secret Language of Your Child, How to be a Gifted Parent*, and *Thinking Better*. He is a member of the Faculty at Goldsmith's College, London, and has been researching picture books and reading for several years.

LIVINGSTON, MYRA COHN
An American writer, Myra Cohn Livingston received the National Council of Teachers of English Award for Excellence in Poetry for Children in 1980. The titles of some of her works are *Earth Sings* (1986), *A Lollygag of Limericks* (1987), *Dilly Dilly Piccalilli* (1989), *If You Ever Meet a Whale* (1992), and *Flights of Fancy* (1994). She has also been the editor of a number of anthologies.

LYNN, JOANNE L.
Joanne L. Lynn is a Professor of English and Comparative Literature at California State University, Fullerton. She has a special interest in children's literature and was for some years a professional story-teller for both adult and children's groups.

MAHY, MARGARET
Born at Whakatane in 1936, New Zealander Margaret Mahy is well-known throughout the world as a novelist and creator of picture books. Her forte for the young is the ghost story set in realistic surroundings, such as *The Haunting* (1983) and *The Changeover* (1984).

NODELMAN, PERRY
Dr Perry Nodelman teaches in the English Department of The University of Winnipeg. He is the author of books, articles and papers on all aspects of children's literature, as well as works of fiction. Among his monographs are *Words About Pictures* (1988) and *Pleasures of Children's Literature* (1992). Between 1986 and 1989 he was editor of a three-volume publication of the Children's Literature Association entitled *Touchstones: Reflections on the Best in Children's Literature*.

PATERSON, KATHERINE
Katherine Paterson has been the recipient of two Newbery Awards: the first for *A Bridge to Terabithia* (1978) and the second (for a slightly older audience) *Jacob Have I Loved* (1981). Both of these probe sensitively into the feelings of children, as do all her works.

PIERCE, TAMORA
Tamora Pierce has worked in a number of different fields including investment banking, social work, publishing, and radio. A resident of New York City, she is the author of several fantasy novels for young adults: *Alanna, the First Adventure* (1983), *The Woman who Rides like a Man* (1989), *In the Hand of the Goddess* (1990), *Wild Magic* (1992).

PRATCHETT, TERRY
Terry Pratchett lives in the west country of England and as a hobby grows carnivorous plants. Born in 1948, he is a journalist, press officer, and novelist. His first fantasy, *The Carpet People*, was published in 1972. Other titles that

have achieved popularity are *Pyramids; a Fantasy Novel* (1989) and *Moving Pictures* (1990). He has said, 'Civilization depends on getting children to read.'

RAYMO, CHET
A professor of physics and astronomy at Stonehill College in Massachusetts, Chet Raymo is also a teacher, writer, illustrator, and naturalist, exploring the relationships between science, nature, and the humanities. Among his books are a novel, *In the Falcon's Claw*, and a number of non-fiction works including *Honey from Stone* (1990) and *The Virgin and the Mouse Trap: Essays in Search of the Soul of Science* (1991).

ROSENTHAL, M.L.
M.L. Rosenthal, Professor Emeritus of New York University, is the author of many publications in poetry and other fields, including *The View from the Peacock's Tail* (1972), *Poetry and the Common Life* 1974), and *Running to Paradise: Yeats' Poetic Art* (1994). He also translated Collodi's *The Adventures of Pinocchio* (1983).

SHULEVITZ, URI
Uri Shulevitz was born in Warsaw, Poland, in 1935, and has lived in Paris and Israel. Since publishing his first book in 1963, he has written and illustrated more than twenty-five children's books. In 1969 he was awarded the Caldecott Medal for his illustrations in Arthur Ransome's retelling of *The Fool of the World and the Flying Ship*. He teaches the writing and illustration of children's books at the New School for Social Research in New York City.

SLEATOR, WILLIAM
Born in Maryland in 1945, William Sleator graduated from Harvard, then went to England to study music. For a while he combined a career as rehearsal pianist for the Boston Ballet Company with writing books for young people. Among his recent publications are *The Duplicate* (1988), *Strange Attractions* (1990), and *Others See Us* (1993). Regarding science fiction, he likes 'psychological stories and time-travel stories, but especially stories about people'.

SMITH, SUSAN
Susan Smith teaches English at a private girls' school in Toronto. She also contributes articles and reviews to *The Globe and Mail* and to the *Irish Times* and the *Irish Independent*.

STAHL, JOHN DANIEL
John Daniel Stahl is a member of the Department of English at Virginia Polytechnic and State University, at Blacksburg, Virginia. His most recent book is *Mark Twain, Culture and Gender: Envisioning America through Europe* (1994).

STOKES, ROY

Roy Stokes was the founder of the Loughborough School of Librarianship in the United Kingdom. He settled in Canada in 1970, following his appointment as Director of the School of Librarianship at the University of British Columbia, where he taught his favourite subject, bibliography. His second great love was children's literature and he was always ready to write or lecture upon the subject. He died in 1995.

SUTTON, WENDY

Wendy Sutton is a professor of children's and young adult literature at the University of British Columbia and has taken a leadership role nationally and internationally in organizations dedicated to promoting quality literature for young people. She is a well-respected presenter at English/language arts and children's literature conferences in Canada, the United States, and Great Britain and in 1994 at the IBBY Conference in Spain.

THOMAS, JOYCE

Joyce Thomas has held academic positions at the University of Tennessee and other institutions, where she has specialized in children's and women's literature. In 1983 she received the Association of American Publishers' Award for her novel *Marked by Fire*. Besides fiction she has written reviews and articles in various periodicals. One of her most recent publications is a volume of poetry, *Brown Honey and Broomwheat Tea* (1993).

TOWNSEND, JOHN ROWE

After a successful career in journalism, mainly on the staff of the *Guardian*, Townsend began writing books for children. An active interest in the social conditions of poorer children prompted him to write his first novel, *Gumble's Yard*. It was much praised and led to other books for children, and to invitations to lecture at universities in the United Kingdom and in North America. He has recently completed a revised edition of his well-known critical study of children's literature, *Written for Children*.

TRAVERS, PAMELA

A native of Australia, Pamela Travers has spend most of her life in England. Her literary career started with the writing of poetry, then she contributed articles to English magazines and to *The Irish Statesman*. For her own entertainment while recovering from an illness she began to write the Mary Poppins stories, which have brought her international fame.

VALPY, MICHAEL

Michael Valpy was born in Toronto in 1942. He is a columnist and deputy managing editor of *The Globe and Mail*, and a winner of national newspaper awards for foreign reporting. He collaborated with Robert Sheppard in writing *The National Deal: the Fight for a Canadian Constitution* (1982).

WARNER, MARINA
The article in this publication by Marina Warner ('The Absent Mother') is adapted from her inaugural lecture as Tinbergen Professor of Cultural Studies at Erasmus University, Rotterdam. Her books have included *Monuments and Maidens: the Allegory of the Female*; also a biography of Joan of Arc and (more recently) a work of fiction, *Indigo; or Mapping the Waters*.

WRIGHTSON, PATRICIA
One of Australia's most noted writers for children, Patricia Wrightson is particularly adept at melding aboriginal and white culture in her stories of indigenous spirits and folktales. This aspect of her work came into prominence with *The Nargun and the Stars* (1973) and her 'Wirrun' trilogy for older readers.

WYNNE-JONES, TIM
Tim Wynne-Jones is the author of many popular books for children, including *Some of the Kinder Planets* (1993), which won the Governor-General's Award and the Canadian Library Association Children's Book of the Year. He has also written radio plays and three novels for adults and is an active editor of children's books.

YOLEN, JANE
Born in New York City in 1939, Jane Yolen was twenty-three when her first book was published. Her many published works, mainly for children, have achieved great success, and in some cases gained honours and awards. Among her most popular books are *The Girl Who Loved the Wind* (1972), *Owl Moon* (1987), and the series books featuring Piggins and Commander Toad.

ZIPES, JACK
Jack Zipes is a professor of German at the University of Minnesota. A specialist in folklore and fairy tales, he has served on the International Board on Books for Young People and the International Association of Theatre for Children and Young People. He is well-known as a writer and translator, and among his many publications are *Breaking the Magic Spell: Radical Theories of Folk and Fairy Tales* (1984), *The Complete Fairy Tales of the Brothers Grimm* (1987), and *The Trails and Tribulations of Little Red Riding Hood: Versions of the Tale in Sociocultural Context* (1993).

SELECTED
BIBLIOGRAPHY

BACON, BETTY, ed. *How Much Truth Do We Tell the Children? The Politics of Children's Literature.* Minneapolis, MEP Pub., 1988.

BATOR, ROBERT, comp. *Signposts to Criticism of Children's Literature.* Chicago, American Library Association, 1983.

BOOTH, DAVID. *Poems Please! Sharing Poetry with Children*, by David Booth and Bill Moore. Markham, Ontario, Pembroke, 1988.

CARPENTER, HUMPHREY. *Secret Garden: the Golden Age of Children's Literature.* Boston, Houghton Mifflin, 1985.

CHAMBERS, AIDEN. *Booktalk: Occasional Writing on Literature and Children.* London, The Bodley Head, 1985.

CHAMBERS, NANCY, ed. *The Signal Approach to Children's Books.* Metuchen, NJ, Scarecrow Press, 1981.

DARTON, F.J. HARVEY. *Children's Books in England.* 3rd ed., rev. by Brian Alderson. Cambridge, Cambridge University Press, 1982.

DUSINBERRE, JULIET. *Alice to the Lighthouse: Children's Books and Radical Experiments in Art.* New York, St Martin's Press, 1987.

EGOFF, SHEILA A. *The New Republic of Childhood*, by Sheila A. Egoff and Judith Saltman. Toronto, Oxford University Press, 1990.

EGOFF, SHEILA A. *Worlds Within: Children's Fantasy from the Middle Ages to Today.* Chicago, American Library Association, 1988.

GORE, ELLIOTT. *Mere Creatures: a Study of Modern Fantasy Tales for Children.* Toronto, University of Toronto Press, 1988.

HARRISON, BARBARA. *Innocence and Experience: Essays and Conversations on Children's Literature*, by Barbara Harrison and Gregory Maguire. New York, Lothrop, Lee & Shepard Books, 1987.

HEARNE, BETSY. *Beauty and the Beast: Visions and Revisions of an Old Tale.* Chicago, University of Chicago Press, 1989.

HILLMAN, JUDITH. *Discovering Children's Literature.* Englewood Cliffs, NJ, Prentice-Hall, 1995.

HUNT, PETER, ed. *Children's Literature: the Development of Criticism.* London, Routledge, 1990.

HUNT, PETER. *An Introduction to Children's Literature.* Oxford, Oxford University Press, 1994.

INGLIS, FRED. *The Promise of Happiness: Value and Meaning in Children's Fiction.* Cambridge, Cambridge University Press, 1981.

KIEFER, BARBARA Z. *The Potential of Picturebooks: from Visual Literacy to Aesthetic Understanding.* Englewood Cliffs, NJ, Prentice-Hall, 1995.

LEESON, ROBERT. *Reading and Righting: the Past, Present and Future of Fiction for the Young.* London, Collins, 1985.

LUKENS, REBECCA J. *A Critical Handbook of Children's Literature.* 5th ed. New York, HarperCollins Coll. Pub., 1995.

LURIE, ALISON. *Don't Tell the Grown-ups: Subversive Children's Literature.* Boston, MA, Little, Brown, 1989.

MEEK, MARGARET and others. *The Cool Web: the Pattern of Children's Reading.* London, The Bodley Head, 1977.

NODELMAN, PERRY. *The Pleasures of Children's Literature.* New York, Longman, 1992.

POSTMAN, NEIL. *The Disappearance of Childhood.* New York, Delacorte, 1982.

POTTER, BEATRIX, *Letters to Children from Beatrix Potter,* coll. & intro. by Judy Taylor. London, Warne, 1992.

REYNOLDS, KIMBERLEY. *Children's Literature in the 1890's and 1990's.* Plymouth, UK, Northcote House in association with The British Council, 1994.

ROSE, JACQUELINE. *The Case of Peter Pan: or The Impossibility of Children's Fiction.* London, Macmillan, 1984.

RUBIO, MARY HENLEY, ed. *Harvesting Thistles: the Textual Garden of L.M. Montgomery: Essays on her Novels and Journals.* Guelph, Ontario, Canadian Children's Press, 1994.

RUSTIN, MARGARET AND MICHAEL. *Narratives of Love and Loss: Studies in Modern Children's Fiction.* London, Verso, 1988.

SAXBY, MAURICE, ed. *Give Them Wings: the Experience of Children's Literature,* eds Maurice Saxby and Gordon Winch. Melbourne, Macmillan Company of Australia, 1987.

SHAVIT, ZOHAR. *Poetics of Children's Literature*. Athens, University of Georgia Press, 1986.

SWINFEN, ANN. *In Defence of Fantasy: a Study of the Genre in English and American Literature since 1945*. London, Routledge, 1984.

TARTAR, MARIA M. *Off with their Heads! Fairy Tales and the Culture of Childhood*. Princeton, NJ, Princeton University Press, 1992.

TOWNSEND, JOHN ROWE. *Written for Children: an Outline of English-Language Children's Literature*. 4th ed. New York, Harper Trophy, 1992.

INDEX